EYEWITNESS **COMPANIONS**

World History

PHILIP PARKER

"THOSE WHO CANNOT
REMEMBER THE PAST
ARE CONDEMNED TO
REPEAT IT."

George Santayana, 20th-century philosopher

"THINK OF TOMORROW, THE PAST CAN'T BE MENDED."

Confucius, *Analects*, 6th century BCE

LONDON, NEW YORK,
MUNICH, MELBOURNE, DELHI

Managing Editor Camilla Hallinan
Managing Art Editor Karen Self
Project Editor Sam Atkinson
Project Art Editor Anna Hall
Cartographers Simon Mumford,
Paul Eames
Production Controller Imogen Boase
Production Editor Luca Frassinetti
Art Director Bryn Walls
Publisher Jonathan Metcalf
Associate Publisher Liz Wheeler

Produced for Dorling Kindersley by

cobaltid

The Stables, Wood Farm, Deopham Road,
Attleborough, Norfolk NR17 1AJ
www.cobaltid.co.uk

Editors
Marek Walisiewicz, Kati Dye,
Louise Abbott, Judy Barrett, Robin Sampson

Art Editors
Paul Reid, Darren Bland,
Claire Dale, Lloyd Tilbury, Annika Skoog

First published in 2010 by
Dorling Kindersley Limited
80 Strand, London WC2R 0RL
A Penguin Company

2 4 6 8 10 9 7 5 3

Copyright © 2010 Dorling Kindersley Limited.

A CIP catalogue record for this book is available from
the British Library.

ISBN 978-1-4053-4124-0

Colour reproduction by Media Development
Printing Limited.
Printed and bound in China by
Leo Paper Products Limited.

See our complete catalogue at

www.dk.com

KEY TO SYMBOLS USED IN THIS BOOK
🏴 Country of origin ⚔ Date of origin

Foreword 10

CONTENTS

HISTORY IS AN INESCAPABLE PART OF OUR LIVES. EACH ELEMENT OF PRESENT-DAY SOCIETY HAS BEEN SHAPED BY THE ACTIONS OF OUR ANCESTORS, AND THOSE IN TURN BY CHAINS OF EVENTS STRETCHING BACK INTO AN ALMOST UNIMAGINABLY REMOTE PAST. THE GOAL OF HISTORY IS TO TRY TO BRING SENSE AND ORDER TO OUR VIEW OF THAT PAST.

The past is frustratingly hard to pin down. It seems that the more we examine a historical event, the more any pleasing neatness of it simply having taken place falls away, and a chaos of complex and competing causes begins to cry out for our attention.

Scores of reasons, for example, have been put forward for the fall of the Roman Empire, from an excess of other-worldliness caused by the rise of Christianity, to an excess of worldliness promoted by luxury imports into the empire from the east. More recently, historians have begun to question whether the word "fall", with its resonance of sudden, violent change, is the right one to use at all, arguing that we should think in terms of a "transition" and look for continuity between Rome and the Germanic successor states which replaced it in western Europe.

All of these theories seem to have at least some merit, yet not one of them, in truth, is the sole explanation for the collapse of Rome. There are many books on this single subject alone, and the life of just one person in the Roman world – Julius Caesar – has been the focus of dozens of works.

TELLING THE STORY
It might seem, therefore, a daunting task to attempt a "world" history. To select which of the myriad tales should be told, and which of the countless people described in the historical records should be included

The battles of the past command our attention; historians investigate their causes and consequences.

in the pages of a single volume might seem almost impossible. Yet by condensing the whole of history down to its essentials – the personalities and events (as well as the causes) that shaped our world – the whole scope of the human story becomes more comprehensible.

CONTRASTS AND COMPARISONS
In this book, the reader can trace the history of nations, such as China – from the first villages along the banks of the Yangtze to a sophisticated 21st-century society that has sent men into space – yet also find out what was occurring in Central America, for example, while the Romans were conquering Britain. The final, reference section of the book brings together a wealth of information that supplements and expands on the main text. Inevitably there has been a process of selection as to what can be included, but I hope nevertheless that this book will introduce readers to the key elements of world history and give them a glimpse of a subject which, for me, contains an almost infinite (and growing) store of fascinating stories.

The tombs of the Egyptian pharaohs give us an unparalleled insight into the history and customs of one of humankind's most ancient civilizations.

WHAT IS HISTORY?

H ISTORY IS NOT THE SAME AS THE PAST. We can never directly experience the past – we can never know how it felt to be a gladiator fighting in the Colosseum of ancient Rome, or exactly what Napoleon had in mind when he decided to invade Russia in 1812. What actually happened in the past is gone – history is our attempt to reconstruct the past from the evidence that remains.

The word "history", while commonly taken to mean "everything that has happened up until now", has its root in the Greek word *historein*, meaning "to find out by enquiry". The same root gives us the word "story". We could say, then, that history is our enquiry into the story of the human race.

HISTORY AND FACT

History is something very distinct from facts. Historians ask not only "What happened?", but also "Why did it happen?", "How did it happen?", and "What were the consequences?", and use the answers to forge the links in chains of events, creating a continuous narrative. These are the kinds of "enquiries" that historians make, and from their conclusions, the past, for most of us, becomes a much more comprehensible place.

Even today, however, there are cultures that do not concern themselves with recording history in the conventional sense – that is, as a chronological narrative that aims to represent what actually happened in the past. Many indigenous peoples, especially those with a strong oral tradition, instead weave together events of the distant and recent past, and both mythological and actual happenings. The result is a body of knowledge that is relevant to that culture, which is passed down through the generations via storytelling and ritual.

Passing on stories is a vital part of the oral culture of peoples such as the San of Namibia.

Whether oral or written, history is always an incomplete puzzle, made up of fragments, hints, and selections from the evidence that is available.

HISTORICAL SOURCES

The ingredients from which historians construct history are their "sources". These may range from the types of pollen found in an ancient Near Eastern site (revealing which crops once grew there), to a charter recording a land sale in medieval France, the writings of a historian living in ancient Rome, or the oral testimony of a World War II soldier.

Sources are themselves subdivided into those that are primary and those that are secondary. A primary source is something produced or written at the time – the writings of the Latin author Tacitus about 1st-century CE Rome, say – while a secondary source is something written after the event itself, making use of primary sources. The distinction between the two may not always be clear, of course. For example, Niccoló Machiavelli's 16th-century study of Roman history is a secondary source about Rome, but the obvious influence on his writing of his own view of the world gives us a primary source into life and attitudes in Renaissance Italy.

In some eras, particularly the very ancient past before writing existed, there are no primary sources at all in the conventional sense. Here, archaeology – the study of bones, buildings, and artefacts recovered from past societies – must help out.

VARYING PERSPECTIVES

History can be written from many different viewpoints. A 19th-century European writing shortly after the French Revolution is likely to have very different interests from a Chinese bureaucrat living in the 2nd century BCE, or a 10th-century Muslim traveller. Moreover, the interpretation of facts is always open to dispute, and historians often disagree about how one fact is linked with another. Throughout history itself, we see evidence of different ideas about the same events. The perspective of

chroniclers such as the French scholar Geoffrey Villehardouin, who travelled with the Christian forces on the Fourth Crusade, is very different from that of his contemporary on the opposing side, the Arab historian Ibn al-Athir.

Inevitably, we are all prone to adjusting history according to our own prejudices and beliefs, but for most, at its simplest, history answers a very human desire for order. Names for eras and ages (the Classical world, the Medieval world, and so on), and for movements and cultures, may not necessarily have been used at the time, but today they serve to break down the past and its interpretation into convenient and digestible blocks, making history accessible for all.

"THE PAST IS A FOREIGN COUNTRY, THEY DO THINGS DIFFERENTLY THERE."

L.P. Hartley, *The Go-Between* (1955)

Monumental remnants of long-dead civilizations inspire a host of questions about the peoples that built them.

THE ANCIENT PAST

The era before humankind invented writing is called "prehistory", and our knowledge of this time relies largely upon the skill of archaeologists. Once early societies developed scripts, they left not only artefacts but also written evidence from which their history could be deciphered.

Fascination with the far-distant past is not a new phenomenon. In 81 BCE, the Roman general Sertorius had his men dig up a skeleton in North Africa, doubtless that of a dinosaur, but which he decided were the bones of the giant Tingi, the traditional founder of the local town. However, it was not until the 19th century, when a fierce debate erupted over Charles Darwin's *Descent of Man* (1871) – which argued that humanity had descended from apes – that the greatest advances in the study of the ancient world were made.

Inspired by Darwin's theories, the Dutch scholar Eugene Dubois set out to find an early ancestor of humankind and in 1891 unearthed the remains of *Pithecanthropus erectus* or "Solo Man" (later called *Homo erectus*) in Java in Indonesia. Dubois' 20th-century successors, such as Richard and Louis Leakey working in East Africa's Rift Valley, have since discovered remains that shed valuable light on humanity's physical evolution into its modern form.

THE FIRST CIVILIZATIONS

European scholars and archaeologists of the 19th and early 20th centuries became fascinated by the remote past, and in particular, the rise and fall of ancient empires. This was, after all, an age of empire for Europe, and the wealthy travelled abroad as part of their education. On the "Grand Tour", as it was called, they inspected the ruins of Classical cities such as Athens and Rome, but soon the older civilizations of the Near East drew attention.

Scholars began to uncover evidence that revealed previously little-known cultures, or shed dramatic new light on more familiar ones. For example, in a single decade – the 1920s – Leonard Woolley excavated the early Sumerian city at Ur; Howard Carter discovered the tomb of Tutankhamun in Egypt's Valley of the Kings; Sir John Marshall began the first consistent study of the Indus Valley civilization with his digs at Mohenjo-Daro; and Sir Arthur Evans' work at Knossos revealed the Minoan civilization.

WRITTEN CLUES

The first steps to decipher Sumerian cuneiform script were also taken in the 1920s. While paintings, carvings, and other early

The Sumerians made records of, for example, livestock tallies, in a wedge-shaped script we call cuneiform.

Howard Carter's discovery of Tutankhamun's tomb is perhaps even more famous, as a historical event, than any of the details of the boy-pharaoh's reign.

artforms all reveal something of the ancient world, the most illuminating records were left once writing had been invented, in around the mid-4th millennium BCE. The earliest pieces of written evidence – dating to before *c.*500 BCE – were not narratives about life at the time, but lists and rosters on practical matters: cuneiform records of merchants' stocks from Sumeria, and royal archives from Assyria. Hieroglyphic tomb inscriptions that identify the Egyptian dead may not provide us with stories, but give us a lot of information about how ancient peoples lived.

MYTH AND TRADITION

Perhaps the most colourful insights into the ancient world are preserved in myth and tradition. Some of the earliest stories to be told by early societies relate to the origins of their race, or its legendary heroes: Aztec tales of their wanderings before settling at Tenochtitlán, for example, or the Sumerian *Epic of Gilgamesh.* Few have survived so intact as the traditions in the Old Testament of the Bible. Stories such as the exodus of the Jews from persecution in Egypt, and their subsequent conquest of Palestine, doubtless reflect the chaotic migrations and political instability of the Near East in the late 2nd millennium BCE. But the purpose of these accounts was primarily cultural or religious, and the task of relating the stories within them to precise historical events is not easy.

The ancient *Epic of Gilgamesh* contains an account of a great flood, a mythic legend that has many parallels with the story of Noah's ark in the Bible.

THE FIRST HISTORIANS

It was in ancient Greece that historical "enquiry" first arose, perhaps inspired by the questioning spirit of the age that also produced the world's first philosophers. In the new empires of Rome and China, scholars were prompted to investigate their people's rise to greatness.

The Classical era has left us some of the finest literature and most majestic architecture ever produced – the latter embellished with statues and inscriptions that provide crucial evidence for the power and extent of empires, their social structures, and rituals of the time. But even seemingly trivial finds give us clues about the minutiae of daily life – for example, the discovery at a watchtower in southwest Germany of a shoehorn showed that the Romans wore sandals closed at the back, whereas previously they were believed to have been open.

However, it is not only through art and artefacts that we can understand the Classical world. From around the 5th century BCE appear the first writers whom we can call "historians".

THE GREEKS

Known as the "Father of History", the Greek scholar Herodotus (*c*.485–*c*.430 BCE) travelled widely throughout the Aegean and Near East in search of the raw material for his *Histories*. What makes Herodotus exceptional is that he was the first chronicler of the past to state openly that he intended to discover the reasons behind events, rather than simply recording the events themselves. A generation later, Thucydides (*c*.460–*c*.411 BCE), in his *History of the Peloponnesian War*, recounts the conflict between Athens and Sparta. He gives incredibly lengthy accounts of the political and military manoeuvres of each side, and his attention to detail and careful narrative were to become a model for many histories in the centuries to come.

Greek art provides a window on Classical life – for example, what a hoplite soldier wore into battle.

THE ROMANS

By the early centuries BCE, Rome, the Mediterranean's new imperial power, was inspiring histories of its own. Scholars such as Livy (59 BCE–17 CE) and Tacitus (55–120 CE) analysed the reasons for their city's power – and the start of its perceived decline. In the view of Tacitus, the effect of imperial rule had been to undermine the moral fabric of the state. Roman historians were also not averse to purveying gossip about their emperors, such as the salacious details of imperial habits that appear in Suetonius's *Lives of the Twelve Caesars*. More akin to the military histories of today is Julius Caesar's *Gallic Wars*, an account of the conquest of Gaul in which Caesar was the commanding general – a history that also served to glorify Caesar's reputation and promote his political career. From Pliny the Younger (61–*c*.112 CE), we have a graphic description of the eruption of Mount Vesuvius in southern Italy in 79 CE which destroyed the city of Pompeii and killed his uncle, the naturalist Pliny the Elder. Although Pliny's description

Herodotus. From China, in particular, much has survived from this period. There are accounts as early as 753 BCE of official scribes at the court of Ch'in tasked with compiling records of significant events, and a set of such annals covering the period 722–481 BCE in the state of Lu has survived.

Perhaps the most famous Chinese historian, Sima Qian (*c.*135–86 BCE) – son of the official astrologer at the court of the Han emperors – composed the *Shih Chi* ("Records of the Historians"), the first attempt to compile a complete history of China from ancient times. Falling out of favour with the emperor, he was sentenced to castration. But rather than committing suicide (the expected outcome of such a sentence), Sima Qian accepted his punishment so that he might finish his history.

is almost scientific in its precision, giving no role to supernatural forces, other Romans believed that such events were caused by the anger of the gods. This was not merely common superstition: as late as the 4th century CE, even educated Roman senators sacrificed at the Altar of Victory in the Senate House, believing that abandoning the old ways might cause their city's ruin.

THE CHINESE

Other Classical cultures also produced histories, entirely separate from the Greco-Roman tradition that began with

In 79 CE, the volcano Vesuvius, in southern Italy, erupted, burying the city of Pompeii – a catastrophic event graphically documented by Pliny the Younger.

> "MANY BESOUGHT THE AID OF THE GODS, BUT STILL MORE IMAGINED THERE WERE NO GODS LEFT."

Pliny the Younger, on the eruption of Vesuvius, 1st century CE

AN ERA OF SCHOLARSHIP

The western Roman empire became Christian in the early 4th century CE, but collapsed around 150 years later, leaving the Christian church in possession of the most widespread network of power throughout Europe. Its scholarship was soon matched by that of a rising eastern faith – Islam.

After the fall of the western Roman empire, a series of national histories written in Europe sought to discover, rediscover, or even invent the origins of the Germanic kingdoms that had inherited formerly Roman-occupied territory. The writers were ecclesiastical figures such as bishop Gregory of Tours and the English monk Bede. Between the 8th and 10th centuries, the European record becomes rich with chronicles. At first simply monks' scribbled notes on ecclesiastical calendars, these became more elaborate accounts of whatever interested the author, from the Creation onwards – often a litany of fables, plagues, and disasters that cannot be relied upon as historical evidence. Almost all chronicles had their origins in the

Ecclesiastical chronicles owed much to royal patronage; here the monk Guillaume de Nangis presents his *Chroniques* to Philip IV of France.

Christian church, which, as virtually the sole fount of literacy at the time, had tight control on what books were written, copied, and circulated. Later in the Middle Ages, however, some chronicles escaped their ecclesiastical origins and religious bias to give a more rounded view of events – for example, Geoffrey Villehardouin's account of the Fourth Crusade.

THE RISE OF ISLAM

The Islamic world of the 6th to 10th centuries experienced an era of expansion, political strength, and cultural creativity. Islamic scholars were keenly interested in establishing accurate biographical information from the past, prompted by the need to determine which of the traditions about the life of the prophet Muhammad and the first caliphs were accurate. It was Muslim scholars, too – chiefly in the Abbasid capital of Baghdad – that preserved the works of many ancient Greek and Roman authors lost to Europe. The Islamic historical tradition culminated in such great writers as Ibn Khaldun (1332–1406), a North African scholar whose monumental work, the *Muqqadimah*, covered the whole of Islamic history, and included aspects of social history and economics that

European historians would investigate only some centuries later.

THE EUROPEAN RENAISSANCE

From the 12th century, key Classical texts such as those by the philosopher Aristotle and the medical writer Galen started to return to Europe through Muslim-controlled Sicily and Spain. Soon yet more Classical works became available, some from the dwindling Greek-speaking territories of the Byzantine empire. The pace of scholarly change in Europe quickened into a cultural flowering known as the Renaissance. A central preoccupation of Renaissance writers, artists, and scholars was the rediscovery of the past. The Roman era in particular was perceived as a time of scientific, literary, and artistic achievement. The study of Roman history and historians became extremely popular, and writers such as Niccolò

Islamic manuscripts feature scenes and accounts of events at court and diplomatic encounters.

Macchiavelli produced works such as *The History of Florence* in imitation of their Roman ancestors. Renaissance authors wrote not only in Latin, but also in the vernacular, or everyday language, making their works much more accessible.

NEW MEDIA

The spread of printing at this time dispersed new works more widely, and also resulted in a wealth of printed "primary sources" for historians. Pamphlets, posters, and news-sheets were used to disseminate news and also to spread new ideas to a wider audience: for example, the distribution of printed material greatly assisted the success of the radical religious changes of the Reformation as it swept through Europe in the 16th and 17th centuries.

Printed sheets brought news to a wide audience, detailing in words and pictures events such as the Gunpowder Plot of 1605 against the British king.

A NEW AGE OF EMPIRE

The 18th and 19th centuries were a time of expansionism and empire, and much of our information about this era displays the bias of the empire-builders. But it was also a time of revolution, with established power structures being questioned, challenged, and often overthrown.

During the 18th century in Europe, religion gave ground to the human-centred ideology of the Enlightenment, and it is evident from the works of thinkers and writers how the scope of history and commentary widened. The Scottish economist Adam Smith (1723–90) included in his *Wealth of Nations* a new, historical approach to the study of capitalism. The French philosopher Voltaire (1694–1778) argued not only that social and economic history was just as important as the prevailing focus on political and diplomatic matters, but also that much could be learnt by studying the histories of civilizations such as China and India. The philosophy of Romanticism found its way into history, as Johann von Herder

Newspapers brought eagerly awaited news and colourful images of events and practices in far-flung lands.

(1744–1803) encouraged his fellow historians to "feel" their way inside historical cultures and, through empathizing, to really come to understand how they worked.

GREAT POWERS

As European empires gathered power, other writers viewed national and imperial greatness as the pinnacle of human achievement. In Germany, historians began to concentrate on tracing the history of their nation (which was unified, politically, in 1871), while the *History of England* written by Baron Macaulay (1800–59) detailed what he saw as the steady, virtually uninterrupted English ascendancy to greatness.

Images of slavery cast a shadow over imperialism, even though support for the sale of slaves was widespread at the time.

Outside Europe, views of empire were at times similarly positive. In the view of the Indian writer Ghulam Hussain Tabatabai (in his *Siyyar al-Muta' 'akhkhirinin* of 1781), the gradual British takeover of India was valuable in filling a power vacuum created by the decline of Mughal power. In Japan, the *Nihon Gaishi* ("Unofficial History of Japan") by Rai Sanyo (1780–1832) argued that domination by powerful military clans had been Japan's undoing, and that power rightfully belonged to the emperor alone. This proposal influenced many of the leaders of the movement that restored imperial power to Japan in 1868.

NEW SOURCES

The spread of literacy in this era compared to previous centuries has left historians a wider range of sources than just the views of the educated classes. There are revealing accounts, for example, made by common soldiers during the Peninsular War campaign (1808–14) of the Napoleonic Wars. Alex de Tocqueville (1805–59) wrote his history of the French Revolution making use of first-hand accounts of events and a huge range of administrative documents, such as the *cahiers de doléances* (lists of grievances) that the French communes sent to the legislature in 1789.

In the 19th century, the vastly increased availability of primary sources was complemented by new methods of recording events as they happened. The spread of photography from the 1830s made it possible for future historians to see what the past actually looked like. By the end of the 20th century, the first moving pictures and the first voice recordings had given us the possibility of an even more thrillingly direct insight into the past. History had come alive.

The Neo-Classical style in architecture allied itself to the noble ideals of the past, both in imperial Europe and, in buildings such as Washington's Capitol, the burgeoning new nation of the USA.

PAST, PRESENT, AND FUTURE

The revolutions and terrible wars of the 20th century profoundly affected people's views of their times and the histories that they wrote. The 21st century has continued to confront us with deeply shocking events, on which we have yet to gain a full perspective.

The Revolution of 1917 that toppled the Russian tsars had at its base a brand-new ideology – Marxism. Karl Marx (1818–83) argued that history should be seen as a process by which societies develop through a series of stages, from ancient to feudal, then bourgeois, which would in turn be superseded by a "communist" society. Marx argued that there is an uncontrollable development from one stage to another, fuelled by struggles between social classes over the ownership of wealth. In Marx's view, violent social revolution was necessary to move from one phase to another. This is exactly what occurred in Russia in 1917, but it was not, as Marx predicted, repeated in the more industrialized countries of Europe, such as Germany.

Marxism may have challenged modern historians to take a different view of history, but the advent of two world wars led to other major preoccupations. World Wars I and II devastated large parts of Europe and Asia, and profoundly affected the political systems of large parts of the world. The sheer quantity of evidence available from a conflict such as World War II – from first-hand accounts to photographs and films – appears to make the job of the historian disarmingly simple, but it has also become dauntingly complex, in that there is so much information from every side of the conflict to be sifted through and compared.

INSTANT ACCESS

At the beginning of the 21st century, technology has become so advanced that it gives us multiple records of major events. These are records that can all be accessed in an instant, through our television sets, personal computers, and now even our mobile phones. The development of the Internet since the 1990s means that we can now capture, store,

The Russian Revolution of 1917 promised a new world order, yet Communism itself was overthrown in 1989.

and transmit information at a speed that would have seemed supernatural only 200 years ago.

Art gives us a very different perspective on the past; Picasso's visual interpretation of the bombing of Guernica during the Spanish Civil War provokes a more visceral response than any documentation.

FUTURE PERSPECTIVES

Access to information, as well as the first-hand accounts we can hear for ourselves from people who have made history (such as the veterans of World War II), can lull us into feeling as though somehow we "know" our recent history. However, just as the "enquiries" of the ancient Greeks were only the first step in producing a history, so our recordings and

with hindsight that we can focus fully on the causes and consequences of events. In years to come, our own ideas and biases may well be held up for scrutiny (and perhaps disapproval) by the historians of the future. And when these individuals ask not only "What happened"?" but "Why did it happen?", they may arrive at answers that are very different to those we may think we are so certain of today.

"REVOLUTIONS ARE THE LOCOMOTIVES OF HISTORY."

Karl Marx (1818–83)

transcriptions of events in the modern world are simply contributions to an abundance of sources that we leave for the historians who will look back on the 20th and 21st centuries. Then, as ever, it will be how historians interpret their sources that makes history, not the sources themselves.

Historians perpetually revisit the past, reassessing it in the light of updated social attitudes – for example, toward women or ethnic groups – as they do so. In many cases, it is only

Television has become an important medium for propaganda, used ably by al-Qaeda leader Osama bin Laden to disseminate his messages worldwide.

TIMELINES OF
WORLD HISTORY

THE PREHISTORIC WORLD
4.5 MYA–3000 BCE

Measured against the estimated 4.5-billion-year age of the Earth itself, modern man – *Homo sapiens* – evolved astonishingly recently, becoming the sole survivor of several "hominin" species around 25,000 years ago. By 5,000 years ago, several sophisticated civilizations had evolved.

c.4 MYA
Australopithecines ("southern ape-humans") in East Africa; walk upright: brain one-third the size of modern humans.

c.3.75 MYA
Australopithecus afarensis inhabits East Africa.

c.2.75–1 MYA
Earliest-known stone tools found, Ethiopia. Meat now apparently a central part of energy-rich diet of hominids.

c.2.3 MYA
Evidence of early species of human, *Homo habilis*, Olduvai Gorge, East Africa.

c.1.8 MYA–500,000 YA
Earliest evidence for deliberate use of fire.

c.1 MYA
Homo erectus well established in North Africa and Middle East.

c.400,000 YA
Homo heidelbergensis flourishes in Central Europe; uses stone tools carefully flaked on both surfaces.

c.350,000 YA
Homo neanderthalensis emerges in Europe.

c.150,000 YA
Emergence of *Homo sapiens*, Africa; subsequently coexists with *Homo erectus* in Asia and *Homo neanderthalensis* in Europe and Middle East.

c.70,000 YA
Population spread halted, possibly owing to catastrophic volcanic eruption of Toba, Sumatra; global temperatures lowered for a millennium.

c.40,000 YA
Cro-Magnon cave art and decorated artefacts in Europe.

c.25,000 YA
Disappearance of *Homo neanderthalensis*.

c.20,000 YA
Ice Age populations live by hunting and gathering, building shelters from scarce resources.

c.11,000 YA
Rising temperatures, retreating ice sheets, rising sea levels. Siberia becomes separated from North America.

c.10,000 BCE
Earliest pottery from Jomon, Japan, heralds gradual revolution in transportation and storage of food.

c.8500–6000 BCE
First settled agriculture in Anatolia (Turkey), Middle East, and Mesopotamia. Evidence of sheep and goat domestication in northern Mesopotamia.

c.8000 BCE
Jericho, Palestine, is the world's oldest inhabited town.

c.7000 BCE
First Chinese agricultural communities, Yangtze Valley. Agriculture spreads into the southeast of Europe from modern Turkey.

c.6000 BCE
Copper smelting and trade in obsidian at Çatalhöyük, modern Turkey.

c.6500 BCE
Cattle are successfully domesticated in North Africa, the Indus Valley, and Asia.

c.6000 BCE
Early town cultures, such as the Halafian in Mesopotamia.

c.5500 BCE
World's earliest irrigation system, Mesopotamia.

c.5500–4500 BCE
Linearbandkeramik farming culture, with distinctive pottery, flourishes in Europe.

c.5000 BCE
Copper first used, Mesopotamia; gold and copper artefacts produced in southeast Europe.

c.5000 BCE
Corn (maize) cultivated in Ecuador, parts of North America, and in the Tehuacán Valley, Central America.

c.4800–3750 BCE
Emergence of world's first city-states in Mesopotamia; Uruk possibly the first city.

c.4500 BCE
Introduction of irrigation techniques in Indus Valley. Horse domesticated in Asia.

c.4000 BCE
First use of the plough in Mesopotamia.

c.3200 BCE
First hieroglyphic script in Egypt. Evidence of use of wheeled transport in Sumer. Stone circles and rows of standing stones built in north and west Europe.

c.3100 BCE
King Narmer completes unification of Upper and Lower Egypt and becomes first pharaoh. Nekhen, Egypt, an important trading town.

THE ANCIENT WORLD
3000–700 BCE

Trade, increasing prosperity, and technological advances produced increasingly powerful centralized states and, in time, empires. The same factors also brought many of these new societies into conflict with each other, particularly in the relatively highly populated Middle East.

*c.*3000 BCE
Beginning of Early Dynastic period of Mesopotamian city-states, including Sumerian-speaking Uruk and Ur.

*c.*3000–2750 BCE
First cities develop in South America; several settlements featuring temple complexes, such as Caral, emerge in coastal Peru.

*c.*2900 BCE
Early marble figurines made by the Cycladic culture of Greece.

*c.*2800 BCE
End of Early Harappan phase of Indus Valley civilization, which began *c.*3300 BCE.

*c.*2750 BCE
First Chinese bronze artefacts. Start of Bronze Age in Europe – in Crete and the Cyclades islands of Greece.

*c.*2700 BCE
Mythical king Gilgamesh may have ruled Uruk in Mesopotamia. Silk weaving practised in China.

2649 BCE
3rd dynasty of Egypt heralds the beginning of the Egyptian Old Kingdom.

*c.*2610 BCE
Step Pyramid of Djoser built at Saqqara; start of great period of pyramid-building in Egypt.

*c.*2600 BCE
Evidence for use of plough, Indus Valley.

*c.*2600 BCE
Rich array of grave goods buried at Royal Graves at Ur, Mesopotamia, indicates trade links extending as far as the Indus.

2575 BCE
Beginning of 4th dynasty in Egypt – the age of the first true pyramids.

*c.*2550 BCE
Outer stone circle erected at Stonehenge, Britain.

*c.*2528 BCE
Great Pyramid of Khufu built in Giza, near Memphis, Egypt.

*c.*2500 BCE
Indus Valley civilization reaches its peak. Metalworking, in the form of copper, spreads across Europe to British Isles.

*c.*2500–2350 BCE
Border conflict between Umma and Lagash in Mesopotamia is the earliest international dispute to be recorded.

*c.*2334 BCE
Sargon founds and rules the city of Akkad, uniting city-states of Mesopotamia into the first empire.

The Great Ziggurat of Ur, in modern Iraq, was a Sumerian temple dedicated to the moon-god Nanna.

c.2300 BCE
Destruction of city of Ebla in Syria; palace archives are conserved.

c.2300 BCE
Beginning of Bronze Age in rest of Europe.

c.2200 BCE
First pottery in South America.

2134 BCE
Egyptian 6th dynasty ends with collapse of Old Kingdom; First Intermediate Period of Egyptian history begins.

c.2100 BCE
3rd dynasty of Ur revives Sumerian civilization in southern Mesopotamia; King Ur-Nammu of Ur builds a ziggurat (stepped tower), the typical structure of grand Mesopotamian architecture, while renovating Ur's temple.

c.2083 BCE
In Mesopotamia, decline of Akkadian empire founded by Sargon; rise of regional rulers of city-states, notably Gudea of Lagash.

2040 BCE
Mentuhotep II, ruler of Thebes, unites Upper and Lower Egypt and initiates Egypt's Middle Kingdom.

c.2000 BCE
Trading city of Ashur rises to become predominant in north Mesopotamia. Inscrptions indicate Middle Kingdom Egypt run by powerful officials, such as viziers.

c.2000–1800 BCE
Lapita people move out from Indonesia to settle Melanesia in the Pacific. On Crete, Minoan civilization at height; palace of Knossos built; Linear A script.

1943 BCE
Sesostris I of Egypt conquers Nubia and extends southern frontier of Egypt to the second cataract of the Nile.

c.1900 BCE
Old Kingdom of Babylon established in Mesopotamia.

c.1900 BCE
City of Erlitou develops on the Yellow River, China.

c.1900–1700 BCE
Indus Valley civilization in decline.

c.1890 BCE
The short-lived empire of Shamshi-Adad unites north Mesopotamia as a precursor to the Assyrian empire.

c.1800 BCE
Beginnings of Shang state, China. Possible sun worship in Scandinavia, indicated by bronze artefacts. Long-distance trade networks are established in North America. In Peru, the ceremonial centre of La Florida is built.

c.1763 BCE
Hammurabi, king of Babylon, defeats neighbouring Elam –and conquers and integrates kingdom of Larsa.

c.1761 BCE
Babylon controls all of Mesopotamia.

c.1755 BCE
Law code of Hammurabi, king of Babylon, is displayed on monumental stelae (memorial stones) in temples throughout Mesopotamia.

c.1750 BCE
Massive ceremonial architecture arises at Sechin Alto, Peru.

c.1730 BCE
Disintegration of Middle Kingdom Egypt; start of Second Intermediate Period.

c.1700 BCE
Most cities of the Indus Valley civilization deserted.

c.1680s BCE
Development of leavened bread in Egypt.

c.1650 BCE
Anatolian city-states unite as Hittite Old Kingdom, with capital at Hattusa. Arrival of Aryan people in India.

c.1650–1550 BCE
During Second Intermediate Period, Lower Egypt is ruled by the Hyksos, a warrior élite of Asiatic origins; Upper Egypt remains ruled from Thebes by native kings.

c.1627 BCE
Beginning of several years' global cooling, documented by tree rings, possibly indicates massive volcanic eruption, perhaps of Vesuvius (Italy) or on the island of Thera (modern Santorini).

c.1600 BCE
Mycenae, Greece, emerges as centre of civilization in Aegean; development of Linear B script by Mycenaeans.

1595 BCE
Hittite king Mursili I sacks Babylon: end of Hammurabi's dynasty and the Old Kingdom of Babylon.

16TH CENTURY BCE
The Kassites, the warrior elite of the fallen Old Babylonian state, gain control over south Mesopotamia.

c.1570–1070 BCE
Egyptian rulers are buried in rock-cut tombs in the Valley of the Kings (near modern Luxor).

c.1550 BCE
Aryans settle northern India. Rise of Egypt's New Kingdom, with new capital, Thebes, facing the Valley of the Kings.

c.1500 BCE
Hittite Old Kingdom of Anatolia declines; kingdom of Mittani emerges nearby in north Mesopotamia. Volcanic eruption on island of Thera buries Minoan town of Akrotiri.

c.1500–900 BCE
Vedic-period Aryans expand over north India; hymns of the *Rig Veda*, sacred text of Hinduism, composed.

EARLY 15TH CENTURY BCE
Bronze-working evident in Thailand and Vietnam. Copper worked in Sahara. Evidence of first metalworking in Peru. First pottery in Central America.

c.1450 BCE
Island of Crete falls under Mycenaean control.

MID-15TH CENTURY BCE
Lapita people of Melanesia begin colonizing rest of Pacific. Mycenaean Greece at summit of power, with trading links stretching from the eastern Mediterranean to Sicily.

LATE 15TH CENTURY BCE
Warfare between New Kingdom Egypt, Hittite New Kingdom, and Mittani for control of the eastern Mediterranean region.

c.1400 BCE
Anyang becomes capital of Shang dynasty China; first Chinese inscriptions on oracle bones. Nomadic cattle-herding develops on the steppes.

1391 BCE
Egypt's New Kingdom reaches peak under Amenophis III.

This small coffin from the tomb of Tutankhamun (1333–1323 BCE) held the king's viscera, removed from the body during mummification.

14TH CENTURY BCE

First alphabets evident on Sinai peninsula (now in Egypt) and in city of Ugarit (Syria). Kassite Babylonia, the Hittites, Mittani, and Egypt linked diplomatically and by intermarriage.

c.1353 BCE

Amarna Period of Egypt; Amenophis IV styles himself "Akhenaten", founds short-lived capital El-Amarna, advocates monotheistic worship of Aten, the sun, and instigates an artistic revolution.

MID-14TH CENTURY BCE

City of Ashur breaks free from Mittani; its rulers proclaim themselves kings of Assyria.

c.1335 BCE

Priests of Amun restore religious and artistic orthodoxy in Egypt during young Tutankhamun's reign.

13TH CENTURY BCE

Middle Assyrian period: kings such as Tukulti-Ninurta I build an Assyrian empire in northern Mesopotamia, Syria, and Anatolia. Cult of Osiris, involving the "Book of the Dead", popular in Egypt.

c.1274 BCE

Egyptians under Rameses II fight Hittites at Battle of Kadesh.

c.1258 BCE

Hittite king Hattusili III agrees Treaty of Kadesh with Rameses II of Egypt.

c.1250 BCE

Stronger defences around Mycenaean palaces indicate increasing threats.

c.1250 BCE

Chavín civilization emerges in coastal Peru.

1223 BCE

Death of Rameses II.

c.1207 BCE

Hittite capital Hattusha destroyed by unknown invaders; Hittite state collapses.

c.1200 BCE

Urnfield Culture emerges in Danube area of Europe. Olmec civilization develops in Mexico. Jewish exodus from Egypt to the eastern Mediterranean.

12TH CENTURY BCE

Mycenaean cities destroyed. Ugarit letters give account of maritime raids on eastern Mediterranean. Egypt battles with the "Sea Peoples" – some linked with the Philistines. Chariots spread to China from Central Asia.

1158 BCE

Death of Rameses III, Egypt's last great pharaoh.

1154 BCE

Kassite dynasty of Babylon ends when the city is sacked by neighbouring Elam.

c.1100 BCE

First fortified hilltop sites in western Europe. Settlement established in Poverty Point, present-day Louisiana.

11TH CENTURY BCE

Migrants, including the Philistines, settle in Syria and the eastern Mediterranean. Phoenicians expand across Mediterranean.

c.1070 BCE

Mycenaean Greece collapses; start of Greek Dark Age.

1069 BCE

New Kingdom Egypt fragments into smaller kingdoms.

Swirling dragons feature on bronze ritual vessels from China's Western Zhou dynasty.

c.1050 BCE
Assyria loses territories to Aramaeans migrating into Middle East, but survives as a state. Dark Age throughout Middle East.

c.1030 BCE
Aryans expand along Ganges valley in India.

1027 BCE
Western Zhou dynasty supplants the Shang in China.

1006 BCE
According to Biblical tradition, Israelite kingdom united under King David.

c.1000 BCE
Western Zhou record geography of China. Wet rice and bronze technology exported to Korea. Ironworking reaches central Europe. Greeks migrate to Asia Minor. Etruscans arrive in Italy.

c.1000 BCE
Assyria reintegrates lost territories by conquest.

10TH CENTURY BCE
Phoenicians major maritime power in Mediterranean; their alphabetic script widely used. Settled Aryan agricultural states in India. Adena culture develops in Ohio River valley. Polynesian culture evolves in Pacific.

c.965 BCE
Solomon king of Israel.

c.950S BCE
Megiddo important royal fortress in Israel.

945 BCE
Civil war in fragmented Egypt.

c.926 BCE
Death of Solomon; Kingdom of Judah splits from Israel.

c.900 BCE
Kingdom of Urartu established in eastern Anatolia. Later *Vedas* composed in India. Nubian state of Kush established south of Egypt. Olmec site of San Lorenzo destroyed; Olmec site of La Venta assumes leading role.

c.900–700 BCE
Scythians adopt pastoral nomadism, and build *kurgans* (burial mounds).

883 BCE
Assurnasirpal II inherits Assyrian throne and moves capital from Ashur to Nimrud.

c.850 BCE
Village established on Palatine Hill, Rome. Chavín politically and culturally dominant in Peru.

817 BCE
Traditional birth date of Parshvanatha, first teacher of India's Jain religion.

814 BCE
Traditional date for founding of Carthage, a Phoenician colony in North Africa.

The splendours of the Palace of Nimrud, built by Assurnasirpal II, king of Assyria, are imagined in this 19th-century print.

c.800 BCE
Rise of urban culture in India's Ganges valley. Evidence of first ironworking south of Sahara. First phase of Celtic Iron Age. City-states develop in central Italy. Greeks adopt the Phoenician script. Evidence of writing in Central America.

776 BCE
Pan-Hellenic athletics festival in Olympia.

771 BCE
Collapse of Western Zhou in China; Eastern Zhou establish new capital at Luoyang.

753 BCE
Traditional date for the founding of Rome by brothers Romulus and Remus.

c.750 BCE
Amos first great prophet of Israel. Works of Homer and Hesiod first written down. Kush conquers Egypt to its north.

727–722 BCE
Shalmaneser V makes Israel an Assyrian province and deports the peoples of Israel; they become the "Lost Tribes" of the Biblical Old Testament.

701 BCE
Assyria besieges Jerusalem.

THE CLASSICAL WORLD
700 BCE–600 CE

It has been estimated that by 1 CE, the great Classical civilizations of
Eurasia – Greece, Rome, Persia, India, and China – contained half
the world's population of 250 million. But elsewhere, in Central and
South America, Africa, and Japan, new civilizations were emerging.

c.700 BCE
Scythians from Central Asia
settle in eastern Europe. Rise
of Greek city-states. Early
Celtic Hallstatt culture in
Europe. Agricultural villages
in southeast North America.

689 BCE
Babylon destroyed by
Sennacherib of Assyria.

663 BCE
Assyrians sack Thebes in Egypt;
their empire reaches its
greatest extent.

660 BCE
Beginning of the reign of
Jimmu, the legendary first
emperor of Japan.

c.650 BCE
First coins minted, Lydia,
Asia Minor. Rise of "tyrants"
in many Greek cities. Start of
ironworking in China.

616 BCE
Accession of Tarquinius Priscus,
Etruscan king of Rome.

610 BCE
Assyrian empire ended with
sacking of Nineveh and Nimrud
by Medes and Babylonians.

c.600 BCE
Birth of Lao Tzu, founder of the
Chinese religion Taoism.

c.600 BCE
Ironworking in Nok, Nigeria.
Greece continues colonization
of Mediterranean with colony of
Massalia founded in southern
France. First Greek coins.
Paracas culture begins in Peru.

EARLY 6TH CENTURY BCE
Much of Middle East falls under
the control of the short-lived
empire of the Medes;
Mesopotamia dominated by
Neo-Babylonian empire.

587 BCE
Neo-Babylonian empire under
Nebuchadnezzar II destroys
Jerusalem's temple and sends
the Israelites into exile.

c.563 BCE
Possible birth date of the
Buddha, Siddhartha Gautama.

c.551 BCE
Zoroastrianism dominant
religion of Persia. Birth of
Confucius.

c.550 BCE
Cyrus the Great of Persia
defeats Medes and founds
Persian (Achaemenid) empire.
Cast iron produced in China.

539 BCE
The Babylonian empire is
absorbed by Persia.

530 BCE
Etruscans at their height in Italy.

525 BCE
Persian king Cambyses II annexes Egypt.

521 BCE
Persian empire reaches greatest extent under Darius I.

c.520–460 BCE
Indian scholar Panini assembles Sanskrit grammar.

c.515 BCE
Darius builds royal residence at Susa, former capital of Elam.

509 BCE
Romans expel Etruscan royal family and establish Republic.

507 BCE
Cleisthenes establishes democratic government in the Greek city-state of Athens.

c.500 BCE
Rice farming reaches Japan from China. Ironworking spreads to Southeast Asia and East Africa. Bronze coins used in China. Zapotecs develop hieroglyphic writing in Central America. Indian caste system in place.

496 BCE
Rome defeats Latins, led by the former Etruscan king, at Lake Regillus.

490 BCE
Athenian Greeks defeat Persians at Battle of Marathon.

481 BCE
End of "Spring and Autumn" annals, first chronological history of China.

480 BCE
End of Archaic Period of Greek art; start of Classical Period.

480–479 BCE
Xerxes's Persian invasion of Greece is defeated at Salamis, Plataea, and Mycale.

478 BCE
Confederacy of Delos, later the Athenian empire, founded.

c.460 BCE
Persian administration adopts parchment for written records.

c.450 BCE
Athenian power at its peak. Celtic La Tène culture emerges in Central Europe; Celts expand east and south and into British Isles. Steppe nomads buried at Pazyryk and Noin-Ula in Siberia.

448–429 BCE
Athens flourishes during "Golden Age" under Pericles.

447 BCE
In Athens, construction of second Parthenon begins, to replace the one destroyed by the Persians.

431 BCE
Start of Peloponnesian War between rival Greek states of Athens and Sparta.

c.410 BCE
Xenophon, an exiled Greek, accompanies an army of 10,000 Greek mercenaries supporting a Persian rebellion, from Babylon to the Black Sea.

c.400 BCE
Ironworking in Korea. Carthage dominates west Mediterranean. Celts settle northern Italy. Moche culture in Peru. In Central America, final phase of Olmec civilization; Zapotecs flourish in Monte Albán.

c.390 BCE
Celts sack Rome.

c.384 BCE
Greek philosopher Plato completes *The Symposium*.

370 BCE
Eudoxus of Cnidus's theory of planetary movement determines the length of a year.

c.360 BCE
Crossbow known to have been in use in Chinese warfare.

359–338 BCE
Macedonian king Philip II extends his power.

336 BCE
Alexander succeeds Philip II of Macedonia.

331 BCE
Battle of Gaugamela: Persian empire falls to Alexander; Alexandria founded, Egypt.

323 BCE
Death of Alexander.

321 BCE
Chandragupta Maurya founds Mauryan empire, India.

c.300 BCE
Hopewell culture develops in northeast North America. First Celtic states in Europe. Alexander's empire partitioned and ruled by Seleucid, Antigonid, and Ptolemaic dynasties.

c.290 BCE
Euclid's *Elements* sets out principles of geometry.

The Greek Temple of Poseidon at Cape Sounion in Attica was destroyed by the Persians during their invasion of Greece in 480 BCE.

c.286 BCE
Qin expansion begins in China.

272 BCE
Tarentum, leading Greek city in Italy, falls to Rome.

c.268 BCE
Ashoka ascends Indian throne; embarks on imperial conquests.

264–241 BCE
Rome and Carthage fight the First Punic War.

262 BCE
Emperor Ashoka allegedly converts to Buddhism.

250 BCE
Rome controls the entire Italian peninsula.

c.247 BCE
King Devanampiya Tissa of Sri Lanka converts to Buddhism.

236 BCE
Carthaginians conquer parts of the Iberian peninsula (Spain).

221 BCE
China united by first Qin emperor, Qin Shi Huang.

218–201 BCE
Second Punic War between Rome and Carthage.

c.212 BCE
Building of "Great Wall" of China begins.

206 BCE
Qin empire succeeded by Han dynasty under Liu Bang.

c.200 BCE
Peak of Alexandrian learning. Liu Bang founds Han Chinese capital at Chang'an. Maya culture emerges in Central America. Nazca lines carved in Peru. Lapita people reach the Marquesas Islands.

c.185 BCE
End of Mauryan dynasty, India.

171–138 BCE
Mithridates lays foundation of Parthian empire.

168 BCE
Rome expands in eastern Mediterranean.

165 BCE
First official exams held for Chinese civil servants.

c.150 BCE
Great Serpent Mound constructed in Ohio.

149–146 BCE
Rome crushes Carthage in Third Punic War; creates province of Africa in its place; absorbs Greece. Nomads related to the Scythians invade Bactria.

142 BCE
The Jews free Jerusalem and make it their capital.

123 BCE
Parthian empire reaches its greatest size.

101 BCE
Han China control Central Asia, Korea, and North Vietnam.

The god Krishna (right) is the narrator of the *Bhagavad Gita*, one of Hinduism's sacred scriptures.

c.100 BCE
Maritime trade spreads Indian influence to Southeast Asia. In India, *Bhagavad Gita* begun. Rise of Axum (Ethiopia). Celtic fortified settlements in Europe. Height of Ohio's Adena culture.

c.90 BCE
Gandhara (northwest India) falls to steppe nomads.

89 BCE
Roman citizenship extended to all Italians.

63 BCE
Pompey captures Jerusalem and annexes Judaea; allies with Antiochus I of Commagene.

58–52 BCE
Julius Caesar conquers Gaul.

46 BCE
Julius Caesar proclaimed dictator of Rome.

44 BCE
Julius Caesar assassinated.

30 BCE
Suicide of Mark Anthony and the Egyptian queen Cleopatra.

27 BCE
Octavian assumes title of Augustus, and begins rule as first Roman emperor.

4 BCE
Probable birth date of Christ.

c.1 CE
Kushans invade northwest India. Buddhism spreads in coastal Southeast Asia. Moche culture flourishes in Peru. Nabataeans, allied with Rome, control Red Sea trade.

2 CE
First census taken of the population of China.

9 CE
Occupying Roman forces driven back to the Rhine in Germany.

14 CE
Augustus dies; stepson Tiberius succeeds him.

c.25 CE
First representation of Buddha at Gandhara, northwest India.

c.30 CE
Crucifixion of Christ.

c.40 CE
Arawak people migrate down Orinoco and settle Caribbean.

43 CE
Roman invasion of Britain.

47–57 CE
Journeys of St Paul.

c.50 CE
Axum now major trading centre.

60 CE
Kushan empire established in India and Central Asia.

65 CE
Evidence of Buddhism in China.

66–70 CE
First Jewish revolt against Roman rule.

73 CE
Peak of China's Han dynasty military success.

79 CE
Eruption of Vesuvius (near Naples, southern Italy) buries the Roman towns of Pompeii and Herculaneum.

87 CE
Embassy from the Kushans of India to the new Eastern Han capital of Luoyang.

99 CE
Kushan empire dispatches embassy to Rome.

c.100 CE
Teotihuacán, Mexico, expands; Building of Temples of the Sun and Moon begin. Alexandria is centre of Christian learning. Kushan emperor Kanishka propagates Buddhism.

117 CE
The Roman empire is at its greatest extent.

122–28 CE
Hadrian's Wall built at Roman frontier in northern Britain.

132–35 CE
Second Jewish revolt against Rome is crushed; the Jews are expelled from Jerusalem.

Hadrian (117–138 CE) was unusual among the Roman emperors in wearing a beard, in a tribute to the Greek culture he admired.

c.150 CE
Han China regains dominance of Central Asia. Christianity spreads west across Roman North Africa. Ptolemy of Alexandria's *Geographia*, first world atlas, completed. Peak of Nok Iron Age culture in Nigeria.

166 CE
Embassy of Syrian merchants to China; German tribes invade northern Italy.

180 CE
Goths (Germanic Scandinavians) settle on Black Sea coast.

c.200 CE
Peak of trade between India, China, and Rome. Korea free of Han – Koguryo, Silla, and Paekche states appear. Teotihuacán largest city in Americas; rise of Maya city of Tikal. Hopewell mound-building culture flourishing in North America.

c.219 CE
Hebrew edition of *Mishna* – sayings and teachings from the Torah, sacred text of Judaism.

c.220 CE
Han dynasty collapses; replaced by three kingdoms: Shu, Wu, and Wei.

226 CE
Parthian empire falls to Ardashir I, who founds the Sassanid Persian dynasty.

235 CE
Raids by Germanic Alamanni on Roman empire's Black Forest and Rhine frontiers.

c.250 CE
Lodestone compass invented in China. Start of Classic period of Maya civilization.

269–72 CE
Queen Zenobia of Palmyra takes Egypt and Syria from Rome, but is in turn defeated and taken prisoner by the Roman emperor Aurelian.

280 CE
China is reunited under the Chin dynasty.

293 CE
Emperor Diocletian sets up system of four co-emperors (The Tetrarchy). Maya calendar in use, Tikal.

c.300 CE
Armenia adopts Christianity.
Axum (Ethiopia) issues coins.

304 CE
Xiongnu invade China. Christians
persecuted in Rome by the
emperor Diocletian.

312–13 CE
Constantine wins Battle of
Milvian Bridge and confirms
religious freedom for Christians
with Edict of Milan.

320 CE
Gupta dynasty of India heralds
"Golden Age".

330 CE
Constantine makes Byzantium
(Constantinople) the capital of
the eastern Roman empire.

c.350 CE
Yamato state emerges in Japan.

370 CE
White Huns move west from
Central Asia; defeat the
Ostrogoths in Ukraine.

376–415 CE
Chandragupta's rule represents
peak of Gupta dynasty.

378 CE
Goths defeat Romans at the
Battle of Adrianople.

c.400 CE
Population of Teotihuacán,
Mexico, reaches 250,000.
Polynesian people settle remote
Easter Island in Pacific.

404 CE
Translation of the Bible into
Latin completed.

410 CE
Goths under Alaric sack Rome.

439 CE
Vandals take Carthage from
Rome; establish a North
African kingdom.

452 CE
Huns invade Italy under Attila.

475 CE
Visigoths rule Spain and
southwest Gaul.

477 CE
Buddhism is state religion of
China; Liu Song dynasty falls.

478 CE
First shrine of Shinto religion
built, Japan.

479 CE
Short-lived Southern Qi dynasty
begins in China.

480 CE
White Huns overthrow Gupta
empire of India.

481 CE
Accession of the first Frankish
king, Clovis I.

493 CE
Ostrogoths under Theodoric
conquer Italy.

c.496–506 CE
Clovis converts to Christianity.

c.500 CE
Angles, Saxons, and Jutes
migrate to Britain; Celts survive
in Wales and Ireland. Camel
trains cross Sahara from Ghana
to North Africa.

6TH CENTURY CE
Early Classic Maya civilization
at its height.

527 CE
Justinian becomes Byzantine
(Eastern Roman) Emperor.

529–34 CE
Codex Justinianus codifies
Roman law.

552 CE
Buddhism arrives in Japan.

568 CE
Byzantium concedes much of
Italy to the Lombards.

c.570 CE
Birth of Muhammad, prophet of
Islam, Mecca.

c.581–88 CE
Sui dynasty reunites China.

590 CE
Papal power extended by
Gregory the Great. Avar
state established on
Hungarian plains.

595 CE
Decimal system devised, India.

597 CE
Papal mission to England under
St Augustine.

The Pyramid of the Sun was the
most imposing structure of the city
of Teotihuacán, Mexico.

THE MEDIEVAL WORLD
600–1450

In the chaos following Rome's fall, Europe's progress faltered while Tang China and new Islamic nations surged ahead. Other societies – in the Americas, India, and Southeast Asia – promised much. Yet by the 1400s, Europe was poised once again to dominate the globe.

615
Persian conquests of Syria, Mesopotamia, and Palestine are complete.

618
Tang dynasty established in China; Xi'an becomes capital.

622
Hegira (Muhammad's flight to Medina) marks start of Islamic era.

624
Muhammad's army defeats Meccans at Battle of Badr.

632
Death of Muhammad.

641
Islamic conquest of Egypt.

642
Islamic conquest of Persia.

661
Umayyad caliphate established.

668
Silla kingdom unifies Korea.

692
Dome of the Rock mosque completed in Jerusalem.

698
Islamic conquest of Carthage, North Africa.

c.700
Lindisfarne Gospels written in England. Rise of Kingdom of Ghana, West Africa. Teotihuacán, Mexico, abandoned. North Peru dominated by Chimú state.

711
Muslim invasion of Spain; Arab invasion of Sind in India.

725
Anglo-Saxon scholar Bede disseminates the Christian AD – Anno Domini – dating system throughout Europe.

726–9
Byzantine emperor Leo III bans worship of religious icons.

c.732
Muslims defeated by Franks at Poitiers, France, halting Muslim expansion into Western Europe.

739
Byzantine army defeats Umayyad caliphate at Akronion and expels Umayyads from Asia Minor.

c.740
High point of Later Classic period of the Maya civilization, Central America.

750
Revolt against Umayyad caliphs leads to foundation of Abbasid caliphate.

753
Italy invaded by Franks under Pépin, father of Charlemagne.

756
Breakaway Umayyad emirate established in Cordoba, Spain.

760
Indian system of numerals adopted by Abbasid dynasty.

774
Lombards in northern Italy defeated by Franks under the emperor Charlemagne.

c.782
Scholars attracted to Charlemagne's court stimulate Carolingian renaissance.

786
Haroun al-Rashid, immortalized in *The One Thousand and One Nights*, becomes the fifth Abbasid caliph.

c.790
Viking raids against Western Europe begin.

794
Emperor Kammu moves Japanese capital from Nara to Kyoto.

800
Charlemagne crowned emperor of the Romans by Pope Leo III.

802
Angkorian dynasty founded by King Jayavarman II in modern Cambodia, Southeast Asia.

809
Death of Haroun al-Rashid.

814
Death of Charlemagne.

832
Caliph Al-Ma'mun establishes "House of Wisdom" in Baghdad: translates ancient Greek learning into Arabic.

843
Treaty of Verdun divides Charlemagne's empire: west and east portions roughly correspond to modern France and Germany.

c.850
Arab navigators perfect astrolabe. Cholas under King Vijayalaya gain power in south India.

858–1180
Fujiwara clan in power in Japan.

860
Cyrillic alphabet created in eastern Europe.

866
Vikings take city of York and establish a kingdom in northern England.

868
Diamond Sutra, the world's oldest surviving printed book, produced in China.

874
Muslim Samanid dynasty established in Turkestan.

878
Alfred, king of Wessex, defeats Danes at Battle of Edington to halt Danish advance in England.

c.900
Beginning of golden age of Hindu temple-building in India.

906
Collapse of Tang dynasty, China. Magyars destroy Moravia (eastern Czech Republic) and begin to raid western Europe.

910
Foundation of reformed Benedictine abbey at Cluny in Burgundy, France.

911
Vikings found duchy of Normandy, northern France.

916
Foundation of Siberian Khitan empire, Mongolia.

935
Foundation of the state of Koryo in Korea.

936
Abbasid caliphs in Baghdad lose effective power to their Turkish troops, the Mamluks.

938
Kingdom of Dai Viet in Vietnam throws off Chinese rule.

947
Nomadic Qidan people invade northern China and establish Liao dynasty.

955
King Otto I of Germany defeats Magyars at Lechfeld, halting their westward expansion.

960
Song dynasty is established in China.

962
Election of Otto I ("the Great") as German emperor.

966
Polish state is founded by Mieszko I.

969
Fatimids of Tunisia assume control of North Africa from Tunisia to Egypt and relocate to new capital, Cairo.

972
King Edgar crowned at Bath, uniting English kingdoms. Formation of unified Hungarian state under Duke Geza.

986
Erik the Red begins Viking settlement of Greenland.

987
French Capetian dynasty of kings founded.

c.990
Toltecs take over Maya city of Chichén Itzá.

1000
Stephen, Grand Prince of Hungary, becomes its first king.

1008
First Muslim raids into northern India, led by Muhammad of Ghazni (modern Afghanistan).

1013
Renewed Danish invasion leads to conquest of England.

1016
England, Denmark, and Norway united under King Canute.

1031
Fall of Umayyad caliphate of Cordoba during Christian reconquest of Spain.

1040
Formula for gunpowder published, China.

1045
First printing with moveable type, China.

1047
Beginning of Norman conquest of southern Italy and Sicily.

1048
Fatimids lose control of Libya.

1054
Final schism (split) between Catholic and Orthodox Christian Churches.

1055
Seljuk Turks capture Baghdad.

1066
Battle of Hastings leads to the Norman conquest of England.

1070
Almoravid capital founded at Marrakesh, North Africa.

1071
Battle of Manzikert: Seljuk Turks defeat Byzantines. Normans capture last Byzantine possessions in Italy.

1076
Empire of Ghana in West Africa falls to the Almoravids.

1076
Investiture controversy: Pope Gregory VII excommunicates the German emperor Henry IV.

1099
Capture of Jerusalem during First Crusade.

c.1100
Rise to prominence of Great Zimbabwe, southeast Africa. Beginning of Inca state, South America. Emergence of Pueblo culture, southwest North America.

c.1115
Renaissance of Byzantine art under Alexius Comnenus.

c.1118
Crusading order of the Knights Templar founded.

1122
Concordat of Worms ends the investiture controversy.

1125
Chinese Liao dynasty defeated by Jin from Manchuria.

1130
Chinese Song dynasty move capital to Hangzhou after Jin take control of northern China.

1144
Crusader state of Edessa falls to Muslims.

1145
Start of Second Crusade.

1147
Almohads seize city of Marrakesh from Almoravids and take control of North Africa.

1147
Almohads established in southern Spain.

c.1162
Birth of Genghis Khan, founder of Mongol empire.

1169
English conquest of Ireland launched under Henry II.

1171
Ayyubid sultan Saladin overthrows Fatimid caliphate in Egypt.

c.1180
Angkor empire of Cambodia reaches greatest extent under Jayavarman VII.

1185
Foundation of the Kamakura shogunate, Japan.

1187
Crusader armies destroyed by Saladin at Battle of Hattin.

1189
Start of Third Crusade.

1192
Minamoto Yoritomo becomes shogun, Japan.

c.1194
Mayapán becomes Maya capital.

c.1200
Incas under Manco Capac settle in Andes near Cuzco; Aztecs enter Valley of Mexico.

Battles between Crusaders and Muslims occupied almost two centuries of religious warfare.

1204
Constantinople taken during Fourth Crusade.

1206
First Muslim empire in India, the Delhi Sultanate, founded.

1206
Genghis Khan proclaimed leader of the Mongol tribes.

1209
Albigensian Crusade is launched against heretics in southern France.

1215
Mongols under Genghis Khan capture Zhongdu (Beijing).

c.1216
Dominican and Franciscan monastic orders founded.

1217
Start of Fifth Crusade.

1218
Mongols conquer Persia.

1227
Genghis Khan dies.

1235
Foundation of Mali kingdom, West Africa.

1258
Abbasid caliphate falls as Mongols sack city of Baghdad.

1260
Mamluks defeat Mongols at Ain Jalut, Palestine.

1261
Byzantines retake city of Constantinople from Crusaders.

1266
Kublai Khan founds new Mongol capital at Khanbaliq (Beijing); Marco Polo visits his court.

1274
Mongols try to invade Japan; a second unsuccessful attempt is made in 1281.

1276
First European paper mill, Italy.

1279
Last Song resistance crushed by Mongols: Yuan dynasty founded by Kublai Khan.

1291
Crusader port of Acre falls to Mamluk Turks.

c.1300
Osman I founds Ottoman state: first phase of Ottoman expansion begins.

1302
Last Christian outpost in Holy Lands falls to Mamluk Turks.

1324
Mansa Musa, emperor of Mali, performs Pilgrimage of Gold to Egypt and Mecca.

c.1325
Aztecs found capital at Tenochtitlán, Mexico.

1333
End of the Kamakura shogunate in Japan.

1336
Ashikaga shogunate is founded, Japan.

1337
Start of Hundred Years' War between England and France.

1347
Black Death reaches Europe after ravaging western Asia.

1349
Chinese settlement of Singapore; start of Chinese settlement of Southeast Asia.

c.1350
Conflict between Inca and Chimú states, South America.

c.1354
Ottomans occupy Gallipoli, gaining first foothold in Europe.

The Mongol warrior Tamerlane, also known as Timur, conquered much of western and central Asia to form the Timurid empire.

1360
Treaty of Brétigny ends first phase of Hundred Years' War.

c.1360
Vijayanagara empire reaches greatest extent, south India.

1368
Ming dynasty founded, China.

1375
Catalan Atlas, the first atlas of known trade routes, produced.

1378
Great schism between rival popes in Rome and Avignon.

1389
Battle of Kosovo: Ottomans gain control of Balkans.

1392
Start of Choson dynasty, Korea.

1398
Mongol warrior Tamerlane destroys Delhi, India.

c.1400
Emergence of empire of Benin, Nigeria.

1415
England defeats French army at Agincourt. Portuguese capture Ceuta, first permanent European possession in North Africa.

1429
Expansion of Aztec empire begins, Central America.

c.1430
Bruges emerges as commercial focus of northwest Europe.

1436
Portuguese explorers start charting West African coast.

1438
Inca conquests in South America begin under Pachacuti.

1445
Johannes Gutenberg introduces printing press to Europe.

c.1450
Eclipse of Great Zimbabwe by Mutapa empire, Africa.

THE EARLY MODERN WORLD
1450–1750

Voyages of exploration established Europe as the world's first global power, in the face of formidable opposition. At least until 1700, Ming – and later Qing – China, Mughal India, and Safavid Persia were Europe's equals, while Ottoman Turkey presented a persistent threat.

1453
Constantinople is captured by the Ottomans: the Byzantine empire falls.

1455
The Gutenberg Bible is printed in Germany.

1455–85
Wars of the Roses, a dynastic struggle for the English throne.

1467
Onin War in Japan begins, marking start of century-long "Era of Warring States".

1468
Songhay recapture Timbuktu from the Tuaregs and become leading power in West Africa.

***c.*1470**
Chimú is conquered by the Incas; greatest Incan imperial expansion begins.

1471
Annamites expand south, invading Hindu state of Champa (South Vietnam). Final decline of Khmer civilization begins. Portuguese take Tangiers from Moors.

1472
Marriage of Ivan III of Russia to Zoë, niece of Byzantine emperor; Ivan takes title of Tsar.

1477
Battle of Nancy: Charles the Bold is killed; Habsburgs acquire the majority of the Burgundian territories.

1479
Union of Castile and Aragon (together forming modern-day Spain) through marriage of Isabella I and Ferdinand.

1480
Muscovy under Ivan III escapes Tatar Mongol domination.

1485
Battle of Bosworth: Henry VII of England defeats Richard III and establishes Tudor dynasty.

1492
Christian reconquest of Spain completed as Muslim Granada falls to Spain. Columbus makes first Atlantic crossing and lands on Caribbean islands.

1494
Treaty of Tordesillas: the New World is divided between Spain and Portugal. Italian wars begin with Charles VIII's invasion of Italy to lay claim to Naples.

1497
Italian navigator John Cabot reaches Newfoundland.

1498
First European voyage to India around Cape of Good Hope made by Vasco da Gama. Columbus first European to reach South America.

1499
France invades Lombardy, seizes Milan. Amerigo Vespucci lands on northern coast of South America at mouth of Amazon.

1500
Louis XII of France invades Italy to claim Milan. Cabral reaches Brazil, claiming it for Portugal.

1502
First shipment of African slaves sent to Cuba to work in Spanish settlements, beginning triangular slave trade between Europe, West Africa, and the Americas.

***c.*1510**
Height of Italian Renaissance.

1513
Ponce de León, explorer and Spanish governor of Puerto Rico, reaches Florida and claims it for Spain.

1514
Battle of Chaldiran: Ottomans defeat Safavid Persians.

1517
Ottomans under Selim II conquer Syria, Egypt, Hejaz, and Yemen. Martin Luther writes the *95 Theses*, triggering the Reformation.

1520
First Portuguese trading mission to China. Ferdinand Magellan discovers navigable route south, around tip of South America.

1529
Vienna besieged by Ottomans. Peace of Cambrai relinquishes France's rights in Italy, Flanders, and Artois. Charles V renounces claims to Burgundy.

1531
Spanish conquistador Francisco Pizarro lands in Peru.

1533
Pizarro encounters, captures, and kills Inca emperor Atahuallpa, and conquers Inca capital, Cuzco.

1534
Henry VIII of England, denied a divorce, breaks with Rome. Ottoman–Safavid war results in the Ottoman capture of Baghdad. Jacques Cartier explores Strait of Belle Isle and St Lawrence.

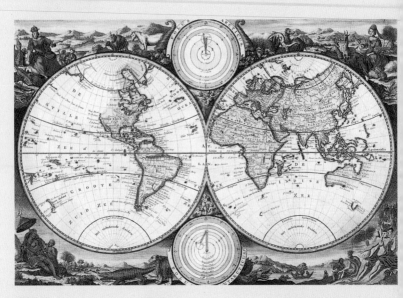

1536
Wales and England formally united under Act of Union. Henry VIII begins dissolution of the monasteries in England; crushes Catholic rebellion.

1545
Council of Trent called to counter growing threat of Protestantism. Silver is discovered at Potosí, Bolivia.

1547
Battle of Mühlberg: Protestant League of Schmalkalden defeated by Emperor Charles V.

1550
Building of Suleyman mosque begins in Istanbul.

1552
Henri II of France assists the German Protestants in overturning the authority of Charles V in Germany.

1555
Charles V concedes "Accord of Augsburg" giving German princes freedom to select Protestant or Catholic religion.

1555–56
Humayan restores Mughal rule, but shortly dies; his 12-year-old son Akbar becomes emperor.

1558
Elizabeth I becomes Queen of England. Akbar conquers region of Gwalior in central India. England loses Calais, its last French possession.

1565
Beginning of Ivan IV's "reign of terror" in Russia. Spain claims Philippines. South American Indian population decimated by European diseases.

1570
Portugal founds colony in Angola; starts slave trading.

c.1570
Flemish cartographer Mercator presents new map projection.

1571
Battle of Lepanto: Ottoman expansion in Mediterranean is halted.

1576
Mughal forces capture Bengal in north India.

1582
Japan begins reunification.

1585
Spain establishes Cebu, first major European colony in Philippines. England aids Dutch rebels in struggle against Spain.

New cartographic methods pioneered by Mercator presented the continents of the world in the shapes we recognize today.

1587
Accession of Shah Abbas to the throne of Safavid Persia; some Ottoman territorial gains are reversed.

1588
Spanish Armada fails to conquer England.

1590
Peace treaty negotiated between Safavid Persia and Ottomans. Toyotomi Hideyoshi achieves unification of Japan: capital moved from Kyoto to Edo (modern Tokyo).

c.1590
Maori population increase causes strain on resources; warfare intensifies.

1592
Japan invades Korea but is repulsed by Chinese troops and Korean navy.

1593
Beginning of "Long Turkish War" between Habsburgs and Ottomans.

1595
Henri IV seeks to unite religious divisions in France by declaring war on Spain.

1600
Battle of Sekigahara gives Tokugawa Ieyasu control of Japan. British East India Company established.

1602
Founding date of Dutch East India Company.

1618
Bohemian Protestant revolt against Habsburg rule breaks out. Protestant and Catholic intervention sparks off the Thirty Years' War across Europe.

1620
Mayflower sets sail from England with the Pilgrim Fathers; arrives in Plymouth, North America later that year; one year later they celebrate the first Thanksgiving with American Indians.

1624
Shah Abbas retakes Baghdad and extends Safavid empire deep into Anatolia. Cardinal Richelieu becomes French first minister.

17th-century spice traders brought coffee, long popular in Africa and the Muslim world, to western Europe.

1625
Dutch found a colony in North America named New Amsterdam (modern New York).

1631
Battle of Breitenfeld: Gustavus Adolphus consolidates position of the Swedes in Germany.

1635
French intervention in the Thirty Years' War prevents a pro-Habsburg settlement at the Peace of Prague.

1638
Murad IV retakes Baghdad from the Safavids.

1642
First English Civil War begins. Dutch explorer Abel Tasman discovers Tasmania.

1644
Manchu conquest of China and establishment of Qing dynasty.

1648
Peace of Westphalia agreed: ends Thirty Years' War. France collapses into civil war.

1652
Dutch establish colony at Cape of Good Hope.

1653
Oliver Cromwell appointed Lord Protector, England.

1654
Construction of the Taj Mahal completed in Agra, India.

1660
Royal Society founded in London under Charles II for the advancement of science.

1661
First Jesuit mission to Tibet. Louis XIV, crowned in 1643 when five years old, assumes personal rule of France.

1664
Second Anglo–Dutch War begins; English seize New Amsterdam from Dutch.

1666
French Royal Academy of Sciences founded, Paris.

1668
Portuguese independence conceded by Spain. Treaty of Aix-la-Chapelle concedes French territorial gains in the Spanish Netherlands.

1669
Coffee is introduced to Italy, then rest of western Europe.

1672
Louis XIV launches his armies against the Dutch: sparks off first great European coalition war against France.

1682
La Salle navigates Mississippi, USA; claims Louisiana for France. Louis XIV establishes Versailles as base for his court and government. Peter I becomes Tsar of Russia.

1683
Ottoman siege of Vienna fails; followed by collapse of Ottoman power in the Balkans.

1687
Principia Mathematica published by Isaac Newton: principle of gravity established.

1689
Treaty of Nerchinsk settles territorial dispute between Russia and China. William and Mary joint Protestant monarchs of England. Protestant Grand Alliance formed to counter Louis XIV.

1690
English trading post Fort William established in Calcutta, India.

1694
Bank of England established.

***c.*1700**
In the USA, Boston emerges as the principal New World port of the Atlantic slave trade.

1701
War of Spanish Succession begins. Swedish invasion of Poland begins first phase of Great Northern War. Ashanti begin rise to prominence, West Africa.

1704
Opticks written by Isaac Newton, exploring theories on light.

1707
Death of Aurangzeb heralds decline of Mughal India.

1713
Treaty of Utrecht: ends War of Spanish Succession, confirms separation of French and Spanish crowns and British control of Newfoundland and Nova Scotia.

1717
Blackbeard begins plundering ships in the Caribbean.

1720
Qing oust Mongols from Tibet. Spanish acquire Texas, USA.

1722
Afghans overthrow the last Safavid *shah*.

1724
Kingdom of Dahomey becomes principal supplier of slaves to European traders.

1727
First coffee plantation in Brazil.

1728
Hindu Marathas defeat the Nizam of Hyderabad, India. Danish-born Vitus Bering begins Russian exploration of Alaska.

1734
Lloyd's List begins publishing shipping news from a London coffee house. In Africa, the Sultan of Bornu becomes ruler of neighbouring Kanem and forms a major sub-Saharan trading state.

1735
John Harrison of Britain unveils his marine chronometer.

1736
Nadir Shah becomes ruler of Persia and begins a period of Persian expansion. Marathas extend control of north India. French occupy Madras in southern India.

1739
Persians defeat Mughals at Karnal, occupying Delhi; Persia now controls all territory to north and west of the Indus River. Treaty of Belgrade stabilizes position of Ottoman empire in Balkans.

1745
Jacobite rebellion of the Stuarts aims to overthrow the Hanoverians in Britain.

1747
Afghanistan kingdom established by Ahmad Khan Abdali. Yoruba tribe begins conquest of Dahomey (Benin).

1748
Punjab invaded by Afghans. Peace of Aix-la-Chapelle: War of Austrian Succession ended.

1749
Mysore Kingdom rises to prominence, south India.

***c.*1750**
Wahhabi movement to purify Islam begins, Arabia. Lancashire cotton mills supplant South Asian textile trade in western Europe.

A Yoruba shrine figure, thought to depict a hunter collecting medicines in the bush. The Yoruba remain one of West Africa's largest ethnic groups.

THE WORLD OF EMPIRES
1750–1914

The American and French revolutions transformed Western political expectations. Demands for political liberation echoed through the 19th century, against a background of unprecedented European global supremacy and imperial expansion on every continent.

1750
Treaty of Madrid agrees boundary between Spanish South American colonies and Brazil.

1751
Diderot publishes first volume of his *Encyclopédie*.

1755
The Lisbon earthquake, one of the deadliest in history, kills between 60,000 and 100,000.

1756
The Seven Years' War begins; of the major European powers, Hanover, Britain, and Prussia (led by Frederick the Great) clash with France, Austria, and Russia.

1757
Victory at Battle of Plassey secures Bengal for the British East India Company; Prussia defeats Austria at Battle of Leuthen to control Silesia.

1758
Britain defeats France at Fort Duquesne, USA; Britain takes Senegal from the French. Battle of Zorndorf between Prussia and Russia; result favours Prussia.

1759
Anglo–Prussian force defeats French at Minden, north Germany; Britain takes Quebec from France.

1760
Boer settlement of South African interior. Work begins on Britain's first "modern" canal, the Bridgewater Canal.

c.1760
Height of the Enlightenment, led by thinkers such as Adam Smith and Voltaire.

1762
Catherine the Great comes to the Russian throne. France cedes upper Louisiana to Spain.

1763
Treaty of Paris; British supremacy in North America confirmed.

1768
Russian–Ottoman War. James Cook begins his first Pacific voyage (to 1771).

1769
Egypt declares independence from Ottomans.

1772
Partition of Poland by Austria, Prussia, and Russia.

1773
The Boston Tea Party, a protest against British taxes on American colonies.

1775–83
American Revolutionary War.

1776
American Declaration of Independence is signed.

1777
Treaty of San Idelfonso: Spanish possession of Uruguay and Portuguese possession of Amazon basin confirmed.

1778
France joins America in Revolutionary War. Cook's third Pacific voyage.

1781
Battle of Yorktown: George Washington and French allies defeat British; Articles of Confederation ratified. Massacre of Xhosa by Boers, South Africa.

1782
Britain sues for peace with American rebels. Native revolt in Peru quashed by Spanish.

1783
Treaty of Paris: American independence is recognized by the British.

1784
India Act: British take direct control of Indian territories.

1789
French Revolution begins. George Washington is elected as first president of the USA (to 1797).

1792
Louis XVI overthrown; French republic declared; France declares war on Austria, Prussia, and Piedmont.

1793
Louis XVI and Marie-Antoinette executed; beginning of "Terror" led by Maximilien Robespierre.

1798
Napoleon Bonaparte invades Egypt; French fleet is destroyed by the British at the Battle of the Nile. Ceylon (modern Sri Lanka) becomes British colony.

1799
The *Coup de Brumaire* brings Napoleon to power as First Consul. Britain assumes control of south India.

1803
Britain declares war on France (to 1815). Cape Colony, South Africa, restored to Dutch. Louisiana Purchase: France sells territory between the Mississippi river and the Rockies to USA.

Napoleon crossed the Alps (although allegedly on a mule) in order to surprise Austrian troops and win the Battle of Marengo.

1823–26
First Anglo–Burmese War.

1824
Ottomans joined by Egyptians against Greek nationalists. Peru becomes independent from Spain, aided by Simón Bolívar.

1826–28
Russo–Persian War.

1828
Russia acquires Armenia, declares war on Ottomans, takes Varna, Bulgaria. Egypt agrees withdrawal from Greece.

1829
Ottomans agree Greek and Serbian independence. First passenger railway in USA.

1830
Revolution in Paris topples Charles X; Louis-Philippe crowned king of France. Belgian War of Independence (to 1831). First wagon train to California.

1831
Belgium attains independence. Mass immigration to USA from Ireland begins.

1832
Russia annexes Duchy of Warsaw.

1834
Slavery abolished in British empire; Boers move north.

1838
Battle of Blood River: Boers massacre Zulus.

1839
Mahmud II introduces reforms to Ottoman empire. Charles Darwin publishes diary of voyage on *HMS Beagle*. Opium War, China, between British and Chinese; Chinese forced to negotiate.

1840
Maoris obliged to accept British rule in New Zealand.

1803–6
Meriweather Lewis and William Clark explore territories of Louisiana Purchase and reach the Pacific coast.

1804
Napoleon assumes title of Emperor of France. Napoleonic Code introduced.

1805
The Battle of Trafalgar; Britain defeats the Franco–Spanish fleet. Battle of Austerlitz: France defeats Austrians and Russians.

1806
France defeats Prussia; serfdom abolished in Prussia.

1809
Anti-Spanish uprising in Mexico starts revolts across Latin America. Sweden cedes Finland to Russia.

1812
Napoleon invades Russia; occupies Moscow, but forced to retreat. Egypt reclaims Mecca and Medina from Ottomans.

1813
Battle of the Nations; allies including Britain, Prussia, and Russia defeat France; British cross into France.

1814
Anti-French allies occupy Paris; Napoleon exiled to Elba. Congress of Vienna to agree future of Europe.

1815
Napoleon escapes Elba; defeated at Waterloo; exiled to St Helena; French monarchy restored. Serbia throws off Ottoman rule. Britain takes control of India.

1818
Chilean independence from Spain confirmed by victory in Battle of Maipu. Shaka unites Zulus, South Africa.

1819
USA buys Florida from Spain. Colombia gains independence.

1821
Greek War of Independence (to 1829) against Ottomans. Mexico achieves independence.

1842
Treaty of Nanjing: China cedes Hong Kong to Britain, opens ports to foreign trade. Webster–Ashburton Treaty: US–Canadian border agreed.

1846
Japan refuses US demands to open trading links. Mexican–American War begins (to 1848): Mexico defeated. USA claims California from Mexico.

1848
Gold discovered in California, prompting the California Gold Rush. Karl Marx and Friedrich Engels publish *The Communist Manifesto*.

1851
Pseudo-Christian Taiping rebels march north through China: immense devastation. Great Exhibition opens, London.

1852
Britain accepts independence of Transvaal Boers.

1853
Crimean War (to 1856): Britain and France ally with Ottomans, declare war on Russia.

1854
Britain recognizes independence of Orange Free State, South Africa.

1857
Indian Mutiny; revolt attempts to end British rule. Last Mughal emperor exiled by Britain. France and Britain declare war on China: take Guangzhou.

1859
Second Italian War of Independence; Garibaldi serves as major-general. Suez Canal begun. Darwin's *On the Origin of Species* published.

1860
Taiping rebels attack Shanghai.

1861
Abraham Lincoln takes office as president of the USA; the slave states cede from the Union; American Civil War begins (to 1865). Serfdom abolished in Russia. Italy unifies.

1862
Otto von Bismarck becomes prime minister of Prussia. Foreigners expelled from Japan.

1863
Slavery is outlawed in the Confederacy, but not abolished until end of Civil War.

1865
Union victory in American Civil War; the South is devastated; Lincoln assassinated. French colony established in Senegal, West Africa.

1867
Austro–Hungarian dual monarchy. Bismarck chancellor of North German Confederation. Meiji restored, Japan. USA purchases Alaska from Russia.

1870
Franco–Prussian (or 1870) War: France capitulates.

1871
German unification: France cedes Alsace-Lorraine to Germany. Paris Commune revolt suppressed. Modernizing reforms, Japan.

1875
Anti-Ottoman rebellion in the Balkans.

Abraham Lincoln became the 16th president of the USA in 1860. Within a year, he was leading the country through civil war.

1876
Serbia and Montenegro declare war on Ottomans: Serbia defeated. Alexander Graham Bell patents telephone in USA.

1877
Britain annexes Transvaal, South Africa.

1878
Serbia, Montenegro, and Romania gain independence from Ottoman empire.

1880
Boers drive Britain from Transvaal; declare new republic.

1881
Britain recognizes self-government in Transvaal. Anti-Jewish pogrom in Russia; mass Jewish immigration to USA.

1882
Germany, Austria, and Italy form anti-French alliance. Nationalist revolt in Egypt prompts British occupation.

1884
Berlin Conference agrees European partition of Africa.

1885
King Leopold of Belgium acquires Congo. Madagascar becomes a French protectorate, Tanganyika becomes a German protectorate. First automobile, Daimler and Benz, Germany.

1889
First Italian colony in Eritrea, Africa. Rhodesia colonized. Brazil declared a republic.

1894
Ottomans massacre nationalist Armenians. Britain occupies Buganda and Uganda. French conquer Dahomey. First Sino–Japanese war begins (to 1895).

1895
Battle of Weihaiwei: crushing Japanese victory over China; Japan annexes Taiwan. Anti-Spanish uprising in Cuba.

1897
Greek–Ottoman war: Ottomans force concessions from Greeks. Cuba granted autonomy. Anti-British uprisings on the northwest frontier of India. Germany occupies Rwanda.

1899
South African (Boer) War (to 1902). Britain and Egypt agree to share power in Sudan.

1900
Boxer Rebellion, China; European forces occupy Beijing.

1901
Commonwealth of Australia proclaimed. British monarch Queen Victoria dies.

1905
Revolution in Russia: Tsar Nicholas II grants limited concessions. Norway gains independence. Special Theory of Relativity proposed by Albert Einstein.

1909
"Young Turks" oust Ottoman sultan; Ottomans recognize independent Bulgaria.

1910
Monarchy overthrown in Portugal: republic proclaimed. China invades Tibet. Japan annexes Korea. Mexican Revolution begins.

Gottlieb Daimler is driven by his son in his first "horseless carriage" in 1885.

THE MODERN WORLD
1914 ONWARD

Two world wars dominated the 20th century, leaving Europe prostrate, and directly contributing to decolonization across Africa, the Middle East, and Southeast Asia. Ideological conflict between East and West has been overtaken by shifts in the economic balance of global power.

1914
Great Powers vie for influence in the Balkans; assassination of Austrian Archduke Franz Ferdinand in Sarajevo. Austria declares war on Russia and sets World War I in motion; Germany invades France and the Ottomans ally with the Central Powers.

1915
Italy enters World War I on the Allied side; US invades Haiti and Dominican Republic. Nationalist risings in Dutch East Indies. Ottomans massacre or deport around one million Armenians.

1916
On the Western Front, battles of Verdun and the Somme. Sykes–Picot agreement between Britain and France on division of the Ottoman empire.

1917
Russian Revolution: tsar abdicates, liberal government under Kerensky; Bolshevik revolution under Lenin; armistice agreed with Germany. USA enters World War I on Allied side.

1918
Treaty of Brest-Litovsk: Russia surrenders Ukraine to Germany. World War I ends: Ottomans surrender; armistice agreed with Germany and Austria. Spanish influenza epidemic: six million die in Europe.

1919
Paris peace treaties: break up of German and Austrian empires. League of Nations founded. Rutherford splits the atom. First powered transatlantic flight by Alcock and Brown.

1920
Ottoman Middle East territories mandated to Britain and France; German African territories to Britain, France, and South Africa. US senate rejects Versailles settlement.

1921
Bolshevik victory in Russian Civil War; six million die in famine. Nationalist uprising in Turkey. Washington disarmament conference.

1922
Irish Free State created.

1923
Turkish republic under Atatürk; secular reforms launched. Nationalist Kuomintang government in China. Hyperinflation in Germany. Military coup in Spain.

1924
Death of Lenin leads to power struggle in USSR. Military coups in Chile and Brazil. Hitler imprisoned following attempted coup. Exchange of Turkish and Greek populations ends Turkish–Greek conflict.

1925
Civil war in China. Nationalist uprisings in Syria. First television picture created.

1926
Chinese heartland united under Chiang Kai-shek. Anti-Dutch communist revolt in Indonesia. Italy becomes a one-party state under Mussolini.

1927
Oil is discovered in Iraq. Chinese nationalists purge communists. Talking pictures introduced to cinema.

1929
Wall Street Crash leads to global economic depression. First Five Year Plan in USSR: massive industrialization and collectivization of farms. Communists establish Jiangxi Soviet, south China.

1930
Communists establish Pu'an Soviet in China. Military revolution in Brazil: Getúlio Vargas in power. More than 3,000 banks fail in USA. Frank Whittle invents jet engine.

1932
Famines in USSR leave millions dead. Iraq gains independence. Kingdom of Saudi Arabia proclaimed. Chaco War: Bolivian claims to northern Paraguay. Disarmament conference in Geneva.

1933
Hitler chancellor in Germany. Dollfuss begins authoritarian rule in Austria. Communist Party purged in USSR. Roosevelt president of USA: launches "New Deal". World Economic Conference in London.

1934
Death of Hindenburg: Hitler becomes Führer of Germany; one-party rule established; "Night of the Long Knives"; rearmament begins. USSR joins League of Nations. Communist "Long March" in China.

1936
"Great Terror" in USSR: start of show trials and purges. Spanish Civil War begins. Germany remilitarizes Rhineland. Anti-Comintern Pact between Germany and Japan. Military dictatorship in Mexico.

1937

Italy resigns from League of Nations; joins Anti-Comintern Pact. US Neutrality Act passes into law. Sino-Japanese war: Japan sacks Nanking. Anti-French uprising in Tunisia. Authoritarian "New State" government, Brazil.

1938

Germany annexes Austria and, with British and French agreement, Sudetenland. Royal dictatorship in Romania. Japanese "New Order" proclaimed in Asia.

1939

Germany advances into Czechoslovakia. Franco imposes right-wing dictatorship in Spain. German–Soviet Non-Aggression Pact. Germany invades Poland: Britain and France declare war.

1940

German forces conquer Denmark, Norway, the Netherlands, Luxembourg, Belgium, and France; Italy declares war on Britain and France; Battle of Britain; Japan allied with Germany and Italy.

1941

German invasion of USSR; "Final Solution" ordered; Japan attacks Pearl Harbor: US enters war on Allied side; Japan invades Malaya, Burma, Philippines, and Dutch East Indies.

1942

Battle of Midway: USA repulses Japanese carrier fleet; German invasion of USSR stalls at Stalingrad; Axis forces defeated at El Alamein; USA invades North Africa; killings begin at Auschwitz concentration camp.

1944

900-day siege of Leningrad lifted. D-Day landings: second front in France; Paris and Brussels liberated; Battle of the Bulge: German offensive checked; Germans fire V2 rockets at London.

1945

Russians storm Berlin; Hitler commits suicide; German surrender; USA drops atomic bombs on Hiroshima and Nagasaki: Japanese surrender. United Nations formed.

1947

India and Pakistan independent: widespread violence. USA sponsors Marshall Plan. UN agrees partition of Palestine. GATT agreed, USA. Sound barrier broken in USA.

1948

State of Israel proclaimed: first Arab–Israeli war. Berlin blockade. Communist regimes in Poland, Czechoslovakia, and Hungary. Burma and Ceylon become independent. Korea partitioned. Gandhi is assassinated.

1949

Mao's Communists victorious in Chinese Civil War. East and West Germany established, the former as part of the Communist Bloc. NATO formed. USSR acquires atomic bomb.

1950

Korean War: first major Cold War armed confrontation. US military support for French in Indochina. China invades the province of Tibet. Unitary state of Indonesia declared.

1952

Military coup in Egypt. Mau Mau uprising in Kenya. Founding of the European Coal and Steel Community. First hydrogen bomb built.

1953

Anti-Soviet uprisings suppressed in Poland and East Berlin. Death of Stalin. Double helix structure of DNA discovered by Crick and Watson. Polio vaccine is developed. Hillary and Tensing conquer Mount Everest.

1954

France defeated in Southeast Asia: Laos, Cambodia, and (partitioned) Vietnam independent. *USS Nautilus* is the first nuclear-powered submarine built.

1955
Creation of Warsaw Pact. Soviet military support for Egypt. Widespread nationalist riots in Algeria and Morocco. Perón ousted in Argentina. US military intervention in Iran.

1956
Hungarian uprising suppressed by USSR. Suez Crisis: failed Anglo–French invasion of the canal. Morocco and Tunisia gain independence from France and Sudan from Britain.

1957
Treaty of Rome leads to the founding of the European Economic Community.

1958
China's "Great Leap Forward": forced industrialization, around 20 million die. Fifth Republic in France: de Gaulle president. Boeing 707 the first long-haul commercial jet airliner.

1959
Communist revolution in Cuba: Fidel Castro imposes Soviet-style regime. Tibetan uprising crushed by China.

1960
Decolonization of Africa: 12 French colonies gain independence, plus Congo (from Belgium), Nigeria, and Somalia (from Britain). Hawaii becomes 50th state of the USA.

1961
John F. Kennedy president of USA. Berlin Wall built. Military coup in South Korea. South Africa leaves Commonwealth. Bay of Pigs: US-backed attempt to topple Castro. Yuri Gagarin is first man in space.

1962
Cuban missile crisis. France concedes Algerian independence. Uganda, Jamaica, Trinidad, and Tobago gain independence from Britain. First transatlantic television pictures.

1963
USA and USSR end atmospheric testing of nuclear weapons. Assassination of Kennedy. Civil war in Sudan. Federation of Malaysia: Singapore, Sarawak, Sabah, and Malaysia.

1965
US troops in Vietnam. Voting Rights Acts, USA: increases numbers of black voters. Indo-Pakistan War over Kashmir. Marcos takes power in the Philippines. Over five million women in the USA are using the contraceptive Pill.

1967
Six-Day War: Israel takes Sinai, Gaza Strip, West Bank, Golan Heights, and Jerusalem. Biafran War with Nigeria. Martial law imposed in Greece.

1968
"Prague Spring" crushed by USSR. Martin Luther King assassinated: race riots across USA. Ba'ath party seizes power in Iraq. Apollo 8 mission is first manned lunar flight.

The US Marine Corps played a central role in the Pacific War with Japan during World War II.

1969
SALT talks between USA and USSR. Gaddafi seizes power in Libya. Military rule in Somalia. Sectarian violence in Northern Ireland. First moon landing.

1970
USA, USSR, and Britain agree Nuclear Non-Proliferation Treaty. Allende president of Chile.

1971
Third Indo–Pakistan War: independent Bangladesh. Mogadishu Declaration denounces white rule in South Africa. Idi Amin seizes power in Uganda.

1972
Protestors clash with British army in Northern Ireland: Bloody Sunday.

1973
Yom Kippur War: raised oil prices spark global recession. US troops withdrawn, Vietnam. Pinochet's military coup ousts Allende in Chile. Britain, Ireland, and Denmark join EEC.

1974
Coup in Ethiopia: Haile Selassie ousted. Turkey invades Cyprus. Indonesia invades East Timor. President Nixon resigns in USA. Democracy in Portugal.

1975
Death of Franco: democracy and monarchy restored in Spain. Communist regimes in Laos and Cambodia. Civil war in Lebanon.

1976
Death of Mao in China; coup by "Gang of Four". Syria intervenes in Lebanon: imposes Arab peace force. First black homelands in South Africa; race riots, Soweto.

1977
Egypt–Israeli peace talks. Military coup in Pakistan. Gaddafi imposes "Islamic socialism" in Libya.

Apollo 11, launched on 6 July 1969 by NASA in Florida, was the first manned lunar mission, landing on the moon on July 20.

1978
Camp David Peace Treaty: Egypt–Israel rapprochement.

1979
USSR invades Afghanistan. Shah of Iran ousted: Ayatollah Khomeini imposes Islamic republic. Khmer Rouge overthrown in Cambodia.

1980
Saddam Hussein launches Iran–Iraq War. Anti-communist union, Solidarity, formed in Poland. Majority black rule in Zimbabwe.

1981
Ronald Reagan president of USA. Israel withdraws from Sinai. Militant campaign for Sikh state in Punjab. First flight of US space shuttle.

1982
Falklands War: Britain retakes islands from Argentina. USA initiates START talks with USSR. Martial law is imposed in Bangladesh, and in Poland.

1983
Democracy restored in Argentina. Martial law lifted in Poland. Islamic law introduced in Sudan: civil war. Foundation of militant Islamic terror group, Hezbollah, in Lebanon.

1985
Mikhail Gorbachev launches reform of USSR: *glasnost* and *perestroika*. State of emergency declared in South Africa. Israeli withdrawal from Lebanon.

1986
Superpower summit in Iceland: USA and USSR agree to disarm. Democracy restored in Brazil. Collapse of Marcos regime in the Philippines. USA bombs Libya. Nuclear reactor explodes at Chernobyl.

1987
Intifada uprising in Gaza Strip and West Bank: Arab–Israeli tensions heightened. INF Treaty: USA and USSR agree to cut nuclear stockpiles.

1989

Collapse of Iron Curtain: Solidarity elected in Poland; Berlin Wall breached. Partial elections in USSR.

1990

Iraqi invasion of Kuwait: UN coalition forces sent to Persian Gulf. Free elections in East Germany; Germany reunited.

1991

UN coalition expels Iraqi forces from Kuwait. Baltic republics assert independence from USSR. USSR dissolved, replaced by CIS. Slovenia and Croatia independent: at war with Serbia.

1992

Bosnia declares independence from Yugoslavia; civil war begins. Hindu extremists destroy mosque at Ayodha, India.

1993

Czech Republic and Slovakia formed from Czechoslovakia. Oslo Accords: PLO and Israel agree limited Palestinian autonomy. Democracy restored in Cambodia. HIV/AIDS epidemic in southern Africa.

1994

Civil war in Rwanda: 500,000 Tutsis massacred; two million Hutus flee. ANC wins multiracial elections in South Africa. Chechnya claims independence: Russian invasion. US invades Haiti: democracy restored.

1995

Austria, Finland, and Sweden enter European Union. World Trade Organization (WTO) supersedes GATT. Prime Minister Yitzhak Rabin of Israel assassinated. Dayton Agreement ends civil war in former Yugoslavia.

1996

Taliban capture Kabul: declare Afghanistan a fundamentalist Islamic state. Russian pull-out leaves Chechnya *de facto* independent. Yeltsin wins Russian elections: communists narrowly defeated.

Barack Obama was elected the first African-American president of the USA in 2008.

1997

Britain returns Hong Kong to China. Asian financial crisis. Coup in Zaire. Israeli pull-out from Hebron, West Bank.

1998

India and Pakistan test nuclear weapons. Serbs and ethnic Albanians clash in Kosovo. Economic crisis in Indonesia: overthrow of Suharto government. "Good Friday" peace deal, Northern Ireland.

1999

Russia re-starts Chechen war. Serbian "ethnic cleansing" of Kosovan Albanians. Renewed Indian–Pakistani clashes over Kashmir. Democracy restored in Indonesia. USA and UK begin air attacks on Iraq.

2000

Vladimir Putin becomes Russian president. First draft of human genome completed.

2001

Al-Qaeda terror attacks in USA: President Bush commits USA to "war on terror". USA–UK forces bomb Afghanistan: Taliban overthrown.

2002

Euro introduced in 11 of 15 EU countries. Renewed Palestinian attacks on Israel. Mugabe wins rigged election in Zimbabwe: attacks on opponents. UN weapons inspections in Iraq.

2003

Widespread ethnic conflict in Darfur, Sudan. US-led coalition invades Iraq: takes Baghdad; Saddam Hussein ousted; widespread violence and terror attacks; UN lifts sanctions. First manned Chinese space flight.

2004

Muslim fundamentalists bomb Madrid: 191 die. Indonesian earthquake sparks tsunami in Southeast Asia and Indian Ocean: more than 210,000 die. Ten new countries join EU.

2005

Muslim fundamentalist bombings in London: 52 die. Israel withdraws from Gaza; Syria withdraws from Lebanon. General election in Iraq: 98.8 per cent turnout. Kyoto Protocol on climate change comes into force.

2006

Genocide in Darfur. Renewed Israeli–Hezbollah conflict in Lebanon. North Korea tests nuclear weapon. Montenegro votes to split from Serbia.

2007

Iran develops nuclear programme despite UN sanctions. Devolved government returns to Northern Ireland. Sectarian conflict between Sunni and Shia militias escalates in occupied Iraq.

2008

Cyprus and Malta join the EU. Oil price reaches $150 per barrel. Dmitri Medvedev becomes Russian president. Nepal becomes a republic; Maoist rebels enter government. Global financial crisis. Political crisis in Thailand.

2009

Israeli army invades Gaza Strip. Barack Obama becomes US president. First trial of former Khmer Rouge leaders in Cambodia. Opposition leader Morgan Tsvangirai becomes Prime Minister of Zimbabwe in power-sharing agreement with Robert Mugabe.

THE PREHISTORIC WORLD

THE WORLD TO 3000 BCE

Set against the age of the Earth itself, which is some 4.5 billion years old, human history covers a comparatively short span. Human ancestors split genetically from their apelike ancestors around 5 to 6 million years ago, though anatomically modern humans – *Homo sapiens* – only appeared about 150,000 years ago.

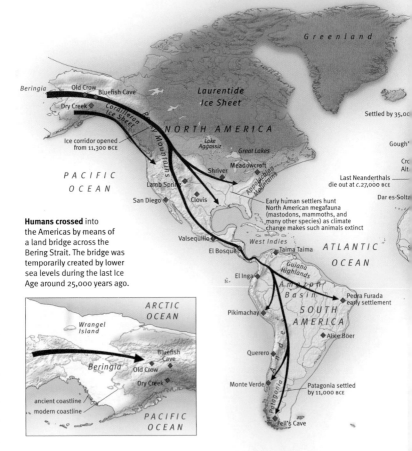

Humans crossed into the Americas by means of a land bridge across the Bering Strait. The bridge was temporarily created by lower sea levels during the last Ice Age around 25,000 years ago.

Early human settlers hunt North American megafauna (mastodons, mammoths, and many other species) as climate change makes such animals extinct

Last Neanderthals die out at c.27,000 BCE

Settled by 35,00

Ice corridor opened from 11,300 BCE

Patagonia settled by 11,000 BCE

Pedra Furada early settlement

ancient coastline
modern coastline

The spread of modern humans

➡ possible colonization route
◆ major site 100,000–12,000 BCE
▨ extent of ice sheet 18,000 BCE
▨ extent of ice sheet 10,000 BCE
⋯ coastline 18,000 BCE (main map)
◯ ancient lake

THE PREHISTORIC WORLD

Early humanity had reached Australia by 40,000 years ago, and the Americas by at least 12,000 years ago. The first towns and the earliest civilizations would emerge in Mesopotamia (in the Middle East), Egypt, northwest India, and around the Yangtze river in China, all between 5000 and 3000 BCE.

Humans rapidly migrated from their African homelands, and had spread to almost the entire world by about 12,000 years ago. Around 2,000 years later, the invention of agriculture in the Middle East led to the emergence of settled and increasingly complex societies – and eventually to the world's first cities.

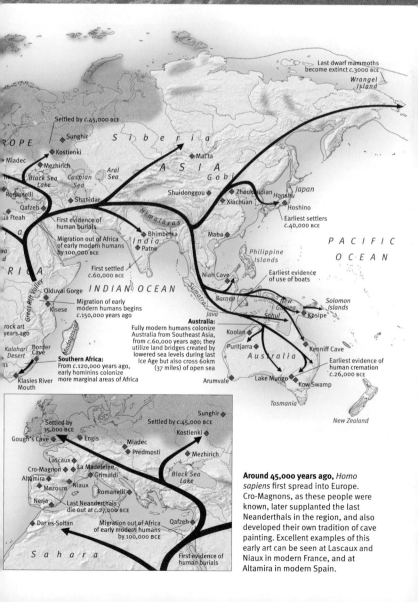

Last dwarf mammoths become extinct c.3000 BCE

Wrangel Island

Settled by c.45,000 BCE

Sunghir ◆

Siberia

ROPE

Kostienki ◆

Mladec ◆ ◆ Mezhirich

Black Sea Lake

Caspian Sea

Aral Sea

ASIA

Gobi

Mal'ta ◆

Romanelli ◆

Shanidar ◆

Shuidonggou ◆ ◆ Zhoukoudian
◆ Xiachuan

Honshu Japan

Qafzeh ◆

ua Fteah ◆

First evidence of human burials

Himalayas

Hoshino

Earliest settlers c.40,000 BCE

a

d

Migration out of Africa of early modern humans by 100,000 BCE

◆ Bhimbetka
India ◆ Patne

Maba ◆

Philippine Islands

PACIFIC OCEAN

RICA

First settled c.60,000 BCE

INDIAN OCEAN

Niah Cave ◆

Earliest evidence of use of boats

◆ Olduvai Gorge

Great Rift Valley

Migration of early modern humans begins c.150,000 years ago

◆ Kisese

Borneo

Sumatra

New Guinea

Sahul

Solomon Islands

◆ Kosipe

rock art years ago

Madagascar

Kalahari Desert

Border Cave

11

Southern Africa:
From c.120,000 years ago, early hominins colonize more marginal areas of Africa

Klasies River Mouth

Australia:
Fully modern humans colonize Australia from Southeast Asia, from c.60,000 years ago; they utilize land bridges created by lowered sea levels during last Ice Age but also cross 60km (37 miles) of open sea

Koolan ◆

Puritjarra ◆

Java

Arumvale ◆

Lake Mungo ◆

Australia

Kenniff Cave ◆

Earliest evidence of human cremation c.26,000 BCE

Kow Swamp ◆

Tasmania

New Zealand

Sunghir ◆

Settled by 35,000 BCE

Settled by c.45,000 BCE

Gough's Cave ◆ ◆ Engis

Mladec ◆
◆ Predmosti

Kostienki ◆

◆ Mezhirich

Lascaux ◆

Cro-Magnon ◆ ◆ La Madeleine

Altamira ◆ ◆ Grimaldi

◆ Niaux

Black Sea Lake

Mazouco ◆

Nerja ◆ ◆ Romanelli

Last Neanderthals die out at c.27,000 BCE

Qafzeh ◆

Dar es-Soltan ◆

Migration out of Africa of early modern humans by 100,000 BCE

Sahara

First evidence of human burials

Around 45,000 years ago, *Homo sapiens* first spread into Europe. Cro-Magnons, as these people were known, later supplanted the last Neanderthals in the region, and also developed their own tradition of cave painting. Excellent examples of this early art can be seen at Lascaux and Niaux in modern France, and at Altamira in modern Spain.

HUMAN ANCESTORS

The evolution of modern humans extends back millions of years, beginning with a genetic split between chimpanzees and humans 5 to 6 million years ago. The process is not easy to trace, as our evidence comes from scattered, unrelated finds. The emergence of *Homo sapiens*, modern humans, is a comparatively recent development, occurring around 150,000 years ago, and evidence of the first settled villages dates only as far back as about 10,000 BCE.

THE AUSTRALOPITHECINES

E Africa   4 million years ago

Among the earliest known human ancestors are the Australopithecines ("southern ape-men"), who evolved in the East African forests. By 3 million years ago, the Australopithecines had diversified into many forms that shared a vital characteristic – they were bipedal, standing on two feet.

THE LAETOLI FOOTPRINTS AND LUCY
Around 3.75 million years ago, a volcanic eruption deposited a layer of ash at Laetoli, Tanzania. This ash, made cement-like by rain, preserved the footprints of three Australopithecine individuals. The prints confirmed that they walked upright, with a rolling gait.

The most complete Australopithecine skeleton, discovered in Ethiopia in 1975, is of a young female, dubbed "Lucy". She stood around 1m (3ft) tall and weighed around 27kg (60lb), while her pelvis shows clear signs of adaptation for an erect posture.

Walking upright enabled the Australopithecines to operate away from the forests in the open terrain of the savannah, giving them a wider food-gathering range than their competitors. By 3 million years ago, they flourished throughout much of sub-Saharan Africa.

The African country of Tanzania, where archaeologists have discovered evidence of many of our earliest ancestors, has been called the "cradle of human life".

HOMO HABILIS

P E Africa   **⌛** 2.3 to 1.75 million years ago

The earliest "hominins" – human ancestors – to be placed in the same genus, *Homo*, as the modern human species *Homo sapiens*, evolved a little more than 2 million years ago. The first to be discovered, in Tanzania's Olduvai Gorge, was *Homo habilis* ("handyman"), so named for their use of stone tools.

Homo habilis resembled the Australopithecines (*see facing page*) but had a larger brain size, and teeth and hands that show a greater evolution towards those of modern humans, while still retaining a low, heavy-browed skull and long arms.

The *Homo habilis* camp site at Olduvai Gorge, where their fossil remains were first unearthed, included a scatter of simple stone tools such as shaped flints (*see p.62*) and broken animal bones, showing evidence of the deliberate breaking-up of carcasses. *Homo habilis* probably slept in trees, in relative safety from lions and other predators. There are some indications that *Homo habilis* was capable of primitive speech, permitting the development of more complicated social organization.

A skull of *Homo habilis*, one of the earliest human ancestors.

HOMO ERECTUS

P E Asia, Africa, Europe   **⌛** 2 to 0.5 million years ago

The very earliest examples of a new species of hominin, *Homo erectus* ("upright man") date from around 2 million years ago in East Africa. The tools that *Homo erectus* made were of significantly improved design from those of *Homo habilis* (*see above*), and included shaped hand axes and cleaving tools, which were used for specific functions, such as butchering animals. These early humans were skilled hunters and brilliant opportunists, quick to take advantage of different environments, which must have been a key factor in the success of the species. By 500,000 years ago, these early humans had adapted successfully to a wide variety of tropical and temperate environments, moving as far northeast as China. Numerous fragments of a species classified as

Homo erectus was powerfully built with massive brow ridges, a large face, and a long, low skull.

Homo erectus were found in Zhoukoudian Cave, near Beijing – the skeletons found there were dubbed "Peking Man". They are known to have used fire, making settlement possible in cold locations, and allowing them to cook food, which in turn led to the evolution of smaller jaws and less robust teeth.

TOOL-MAKING AND SPEECH

Although certain species of ape, including chimpanzees, have been observed to use tools such as sticks and stones for digging, opening shellfish, or menacing enemies, it was early human ancestors who were the first to deliberately shape tools around 2 million years ago. Around the same time, our ancestors began to evolve the necessary changes in the brain and voice box to permit language.

THE DEVELOPMENT OF TOOLS

The earliest tools were probably those made from bone and stone found at *Homo habilis* sites (*see p.61*) and dating from around 2 million years ago. Although crude, the stone artefacts include pebbles and rock fragments from which early human ancestors had deliberately removed flakes, and the flakes themselves. They used some tools as scrapers, others as choppers, and the basic forms did not change for thousands of years. The Neanderthals (*see facing page*) may have been the first to mount scrapers, spear points, and knives on wooden handles, around 300,000 years ago.

PHYSICAL EVOLUTION AND LANGUAGE

The development of articulate language was a key threshold in human evolution, because it allowed for an enhanced level of cooperation. Exactly when it emerged is difficult to define. *Homo habilis* had a slightly more human-like frontal lobe (the part of the brain that houses speech control) than the earlier Australopithecines. *Homo erectus*, around 1.8 million years ago, had a lower-positioned larynx, which would have allowed a wider variety of vocal sounds. A hominin dating to around 400,000 years ago, *Homo heidelbergensis*, was found to possess the hyoid bone at the root of the larynx that facilitates speech. It was only around 300,000 years ago that the base of the skull evolved to allow a full range of sounds.

Around 40,000 to 50,000 years ago, during what some anthropologists term the "Great Leap Forward", modern humans seem to have developed language of the kind we would recognize today. The first symbolic representations of the world, such as the cave art at Lascaux in France (*see p.69*), accompanied this leap. Language and art enabled our ancestors to pass on skills, traditions, and discoveries, an essential foundation for the complex societies that would emerge from around 10,000 BCE.

A flint blade shaped on both faces from a period when *Homo erectus* refined the tools of earlier ancestors.

THE NEANDERTHALS

Africa, Europe, W Eurasia 350,000 to 25,000 years ago

Around 350,000 years ago, a new species, *Homo neanderthalensis*, appeared in Africa. It would be the last major human-like species before the evolution of fully modern humans. The Neanderthals spread out from Africa, by 200,000 years ago reaching as far as Uzbekistan and Iran in the east and the Iberian peninsula in the west, then moving into northern Europe. They were named for the site in Germany where one of the first specimens was discovered, in 1856. They had a short, robust build, powerful limbs, a protruding face, and heavy brow ridges, but a body shape closer to that of modern humans than preceding species.

A Neanderthal skull shows a distinctive brow ridge. Neanderthals had large brains and more rounded heads than their predecessors.

NEANDERTHAL LIFESTYLE

The Neanderthals were expert hunters, who pursued animals such as bison with wooden and stone-tipped spears. They made sophisticated tools and dwelt in caves, rock shelters, and open camps. They may have been capable of speech, although their larynx is higher than in modern humans, which would have impeded the use of the broad spectrum

Gorham's Cave on Gibraltar is thought to have been one of the very last sites inhabited by the Neanderthals before their extinction.

of sounds necessary for full language. This was the first species to exhibit a sense of care for the dead. In one grave at Teshik-Tash in Uzbekistan, ibex horns had been placed in a circle around the skull, and a fire lit around the body.

DNA recovered from remains reveals that the Neanderthals were not our direct ancestors. They did, however, live alongside modern humans (*Homo sapiens*, or "wise humans"), who migrated northwards from Africa into Europe around 45,000 years ago. It may be that competition with (or possibly absorption by) the newcomers caused their extinction around 25,000 years ago.

THE EARLIEST HUMANS

Modern humans, *Homo sapiens*, evolved around 150,000 years ago in East Africa. Physically, they were not well adapted to cold conditions, and the Ice Age that began around the time they appeared confined them to a small area of tropical Africa and southwestern Asia. Despite this, their large brain size and capacity for language left them poised to expand out of this initial heartland.

THE ICE AGES

⚑ Worldwide, except tropical regions　　⧗ 2 million to 11,000 years ago

Over millions of years, Earth has experienced a series of Ice Ages. These periods of intense cold were punctuated by intervals of milder conditions, known as interglacials. The last Ice Age began around 2.5 million years ago, and we are currently in an interglacial period that began around 11,000 years ago. During the glacial periods of the last Ice Age, the Earth's natural environments experienced major changes. Huge ice sheets formed over Scandinavia and covered most of Canada and part of the USA as far south as the Great Lakes. There were ice sheets in the mountains of the Pyrenees and the Andes, and on Central Asian mountains. South of these areas, huge expanses of barren land extended from the Atlantic to Siberia. These environments suffered nine-month winters, making them uninhabitable for our ancestors, who instead moved south to more temperate and tropical regions. During interglacials, the ice sheets started to melt, sea levels rose, and humans returned north, following the animals they hunted and the plants they foraged.

Sea levels dropped as seawater froze during the last Ice Age. A land bridge at the Bering Strait allowed hominins to migrate from Siberia into North America.

HOMO SAPIENS IN AFRICA

Africa ☒ 195,000 to 50,000 years ago

Anatomically modern humans – *Homo sapiens* – appeared almost 200,000 years ago, probably in East Africa. They were taller than their immediate predecessors, males averaging about 1.75m (5½ft), and heavier. Their faces were less protruding than their Neanderthal contemporaries (*see p.63*) and their brow ridge was less prominent. Brain size was larger than in most previous species, though actually somewhat smaller than the average Neanderthal brain. The larynx was lower, so they could vocalize a wide enough range of sounds to form language as we know it.

Homo sapiens were long-limbed, giving them a greater skin surface area from which heat could be lost – an adaptation suited to warmer climates. The narrow pelvic girdle necessary for a fully upright stance meant that babies had to be born at an earlier stage in their development, with smaller skulls and brains – which is why human babies are dependent on their parents for so much longer, relatively, than any other species. The shorter gestation period allowed more frequent pregnancies, enabling greater population growth.

An early *Homo sapiens* skull discovered in South Africa shows very close affinities with the skull shapes of humans today.

Despite their advantages, *Homo sapiens* at this stage did not compete well with the Neanderthals in their territories in Europe and southwest Asia. The most important sites for early *Homo sapiens* lie within Africa, with a few in modern Israel. At the earliest known site, Omo in Ethiopia, bones have been dated to around 195,000 years ago. At Klasies Cave, South Africa, a population of *Homo sapiens* lived from about 120,000 years ago, hunting seal and antelope, and gathering roots and shellfish.

CULTURAL ADVANCES AND EXPANSION

The development of art is taken as an important indicator of when *Homo sapiens* developed fully modern cognitive abilities, because it requires reasoning, planning, and the expression of intangible feelings. The oldest definitively dated decorative items, beads made from ostrich eggshell, come from Kenya and Tanzania and are about 40,000 years old. They mark a shift into the Upper Palaeolithic period, in which *Homo sapiens*, whose population was probably only around a million, expanded both in numbers and, through a series of remarkable migrations (*see overleaf*), in their territories.

MITOCHONDRIAL EVE

Examination of a wide range of samples of mitochondrial DNA (matter outside the nucleus of the cell, which is passed down from every mother to her offspring) has revealed that all living humans have a common ancestor who lived in Africa around 200,000 years ago. This unknown matriarch has been dubbed "Mitochondrial Eve", and we all share at least some genetic information with her. By studying mitochondrial DNA, scientists have been able to track the movement of *Homo sapiens* across the globe.

SETTLING THE WORLD

 Worldwide   50,000 to 15,000 years ago

The most significant of all human migrations began around 50,000 years ago during the last Ice Age (*see p.64*). This period saw the spread of *Homo sapiens* out of Africa, until they settled the whole of mainland Eurasia and crossed land bridges into the Americas. *Homo sapiens* had also mastered tropical waters with canoes or rafts, which allowed them to drift to New Guinea and Australia. Colonizing the world was not a deliberate project, but a consequence of following game migrations and searching for new animals to hunt and new food plants to gather. The adaptability of *Homo sapiens* as a species made them capable of exploiting a vast range of new environments.

European cave paintings date from around 32,000 years ago. This scene, from Lascaux in France, shows a bison, a common theme in prehistoric cave art.

THE SETTLEMENT OF NORTH AMERICA

The ancestors of today's Native Americans crossed into North America via a land bridge that existed at the Bering Strait up until 10,000 years ago. The earliest human sites in the Americas have long been thought to be in Alaska, at Broken Mammoth and Healy Lake; they date from around 11,000 to 12,000 years ago. However, finds at Bluefish Caves in Canada dating to 25,000 years ago, and at Monte Verde in Chile to around 14,000 years ago, suggest much earlier settlement.

The settlers in Alaska established what is known as the Clovis culture, and this eventually extended as far south as

Human footprints found at the Willandra Lakes, New South Wales, Australia, reveal that this area was inhabited around 40,000 years ago.

Panama. The Clovis people may have been responsible for the widespread extinction of gigantic mammals that took place at about this time. That extinction could in turn have contributed to the end of their culture around 11,000 years ago.

EXPANSION INTO AUSTRALIA

Some 50,000 years ago, Java, Sumatra, and Borneo were joined by land, but to reach Australia and New Guinea required a series of sea crossings and must have involved the use of boats. *Homo sapiens* had certainly reached the Australian mainland by 35,000 years ago, but rock shelters in the Northern Territory indicate that settlement may have begun as early as 50,000 to 60,000 years ago. Dating back some 40,000 years, Lake Mungo in New South Wales is the most important early site. The *Homo sapiens* remains found there were partially covered in red ochre, indicating a ritual element to the burials.

The arrival of humans in Australia coincided with the extinction of massive vertebrates that had previously inhabited the continent, although it is not clear whether the newcomers hunted them to extinction, or whether

brushfires set by early humans destroyed their habitat. The early settlers, ancestors of today's Aboriginal peoples, developed an isolated and unique culture, many elements of which still survive; the earliest boomerang found – at Wyrie Swamp, Tasmania – dates from around 8000 BCE.

EXPANSION ELSEWHERE

Homo sapiens gradually infiltrated almost every other habitable part of the globe, reaching southwestern Europe by around 45,000 years ago. The group of *Homo sapiens* that settled here are referred to as Cro-Magnon, and they entirely displaced the Neanderthal population in this region. By around 40,000 years ago *Homo sapiens* had migrated to eastern Europe and southwestern Siberia, colonizing Japan by around 30,000 to 35,000 years ago.

Although the Clovis people, who had colonized North America from Alaska to Panama, did not penetrate South America themselves, later groups reached the very tip of the continent by around 9000 BCE. After this, with the exception of certain Pacific islands and particularly remote regions of the globe, the long migration of *Homo sapiens* out of Africa was complete.

Clovis spear points have a bifacial, concave, and fluted shape, which was replicated throughout the entire area occupied by the culture.

HUNTER-GATHERERS

Hunting and foraging for food was the only way of life for humans until around 12,000 years ago. It was a successful lifestyle that, in its flexibility, had significant advantages over the settled agricultural societies that would supplant it. Today, only a handful of hunter-gatherer societies survive, in the Amazon Basin and in Africa, which provide vital evidence for their prehistoric forebears' way of life.

EARLY EVIDENCE

Hunter-gatherers have to range across a wide area for food, and so carry few possessions with them. As a result, prehistoric hunter-gatherers have left few material remains. Rare finds of digging sticks, such as at Gwisho in Central Africa, and flint sickle blades show that people dug for tubers and harvested wild grasses. Broken animal and fish bones and plant pollens reveal details of the hunter-gatherer diet, as do deep middens (waste sites) crammed with discarded mollusc shells.

Spear-fishing with barbed poles, such as this 10,000-year-old harpoon made from an antler, was widespread in later prehistoric times.

Sites such as Star Carr in northeast England, from around 9000 BCE, show that hunter-gatherers might return again and again to the same places, establishing seasonal settlements close to where game was plentiful. Small figurines and carvings of bears and mammoths discovered at Dolní Věstonice in the Czech Republic, and remarkable fish sculptures from Lepenski Vir in Serbia, show the level of cultural sophistication that such early societies could reach. Eventually, however, hunter-gathering was replaced by farming. Probably, as agriculturalists encroached on their territory, some hunter-gatherers adopted the new way of life, while others were forced into the margins. In marginal environments, farming always carries the risk of starvation if crops fail, and today there are still isolated groups, such as the San of the Kalahari desert in Africa, that maintain the ancient hunter-gatherer traditions.

A hunter is depicted in a cave painting from Faraway Bay, Western Australia, dating to around 20,000 years ago.

ART AND RITUAL

🏴 Worldwide   ⌛ 40,000 to 4,000 years ago

Around 40,000 to 50,000 years ago early humans began to create the first examples of art – graphic representations of reality or an imagined symbolic life – incised on animal bones, painted on cave walls, and sculpted from bone or ivory. This artistic activity coincides with the first evidence of religious belief, and both of these developments indicate an ability to think about ideas or concepts that lie outside immediate, everyday existence.

In later rock art, symbols such as this circular sign filled with dots start to feature alongside depictions of animal and human figures.

CAVE ART

About 40,000 years ago, the Cro-Magnon people of western Europe developed a flamboyant artistic tradition that survives mainly on cave walls, where it has been sheltered from the elements. The cave paintings depict a wide range of animals, some of them, such as mammoth and woolly rhinoceros, long extinct; others, like wild horses, European bison, and reindeer, still familiar today. In a society dependent on hunting, animal paintings may have been the focus of rituals intended to ensure success and a rich supply of meat.

By contrast, human figures in cave paintings are rare, and when they do survive are highly stylized or masked. However, impressions of human hands and indecipherable signs do appear on the walls of caves, including Altamira in Spain, and Chauvet, Niaux, and Lascaux in France.

The "Venus of Willendorf", carved around 20–25,000 years ago, may have been a fertility talisman.

One theory is that the art was created by shamans who acted as mediums with the spiritual world, communicating with ancestors and spirit totems. Other artistic creations, including carved female statuettes known as "Venus figurines", may have been related to hunter-gatherer fertility cults, while the burial of possessions alongside bodies indicates belief in an afterlife.

FROM RITUAL TO RELIGION

As societies grew more complex, they began to devote particular areas and spaces to cult practices. At Çatalhöyük in Turkey, murals identify places used for ritual around 7000 BCE. In time, lavish temples would be built for the worship of complex pantheons of gods, who demanded elaborate rituals performed only by a priestly elite. A glimpse of hunter-gatherer beliefs can now only be seen in societies such as that of the Australian Aborigines, who continue to commemorate their ancestral spirits with spectacular rock art.

The cave paintings at Lascaux, France, date from around 16,000 years ago. They include a wealth of animal representations, such as this bison, as well as symbolic and human forms. Many figures are in inaccessible corners that may have required the use of scaffolding.

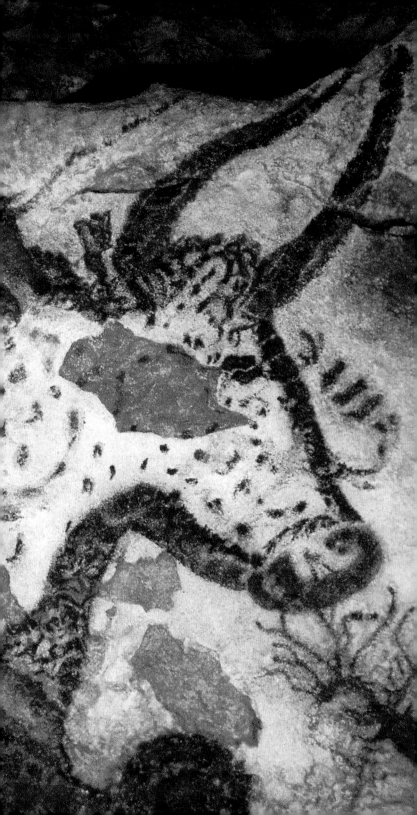

EARLY SOCIETIES

The transition to an agricultural existence, which began around 11,000 years ago and was virtually complete by about 2000 BCE, gave rise to new ways of life, including the first settled communities. From this period of early farming, known as the Neolithic, also emerge the earliest monumental remains, including striking megalithic structures that appear across northern and western Europe.

THE CRADLE OF AGRICULTURE

Turkey, Syria, Iraq, Pakistan, China, Mesoamerica   8500–6000 BCE

The end of the last Ice Age around 11,000 years ago, and the accompanying rise in temperatures, was the trigger for the switch from the hunter-gatherer lifestyle to one of agricultural and animal domestication. This first took place in around 8500 BCE, in an area known as the "Fertile Crescent" that includes Turkey, Syria, and Iraq. The hot, dry summers and cool, wet winters, together with a wide variety of altitudes and a large number of wild cereals and

legumes, provided ideal conditions for agriculture to succeed. Agriculture arose independently in other regions with favourable climatic conditions – in China's Yangtze Valley in around 7000 BCE and, a thousand years later, in Mesoamerica and possibly at Mehrgarh in Pakistan.

EARLY AGRICULTURE

The first plants to be adapted from their wild forms for cultivation were cereals – emmer and einkorn, barley and rye. These are found at sites such as Abu Hureyra in Syria, where a small foraging settlement became a compact farming community of mudbrick dwellings.

At around the same time, animals were domesticated – goats first, then sheep, pigs and cattle – providing a reliable source of meat, milk, and other animal products. The settled nature of agriculture compared with hunter-gathering, and the ready availability of food, led to large increases in population – the site of Ain 'Ghazal in Jordan more than doubled in size between 7250 BCE and 6750 BCE.

Ears of emmer, originally a wild grass that early agriculturalists selectively bred to enhance its crop yield.

THE SPREAD OF FARMING

⚑ Worldwide ⌛ 7000–2000 BCE

Around 7000 BCE, agricultural societies of the Near East began to show signs of stress caused by growing populations. Some sites shrank in size; others were abandoned. This may have led to a dispersal of the agricultural population, and increased pastoralism (animal herding).

Agricultural living increased the need for food storage vessels and pottery.

FARMING IN EUROPE AND ASIA

Farming seems to have reached the Balkans in southeast Europe by around 6500 BCE, and by around 5500 BCE had penetrated as far west as the Iberian Peninsula. Its range extended by 3500 BCE to northern Germany, Scandinavia, and the British Isles.

Agriculture moved east from the Zagros mountains of the Iran–Iraq borderlands to reach the Caucasus, Turkmenistan, and Pakistan (although farming in Pakistan may have developed independently). By 3000 BCE farming had reached India's Ganges Valley, and by 2500 BCE it extended as far as the Altai in Central Asia. In eastern Asia, an agricultural economy based on rice and millet spread from its origins in the Yangtze Valley to reach southern China by 3000 BCE and Southeast Asia by at least 2300 BCE.

FARMING IN AFRICA AND THE AMERICAS

Agriculture first arrived in Egypt around 5500 BCE, and spread southwards (it may also have arisen independently in sub-Saharan Africa around 2000 BCE).

In the Americas, sunflowers were grown for food in 4000 BCE. The staple crops of native American agriculture, maize and beans, were domesticated in Central America by 3500 BCE. In the high altitudes of the Andes in South America, potatoes were cultivated as early as 5000 BCE, and llamas were domesticated around 1,000 years later.

In Mesoamerica, with few animals available for domestication, the llama was used as a pack animal, for meat, and for the materials woven from its hair.

THE FIRST VILLAGES

 Jordan, Syria, Turkey   ⌛ 9600–7000 BCE

Once prehistoric peoples had begun to cultivate domestic crops and keep livestock, they established permanent settlements. The earliest farming villages were compact huddles of mudbrick houses. At Abu Hureyra, Syria, several hundred farmers lived in close proximity to their fields and to one another. By 8000 BCE, Jericho, in the Jordan Valley, had become a small walled town, whose inhabitants lived in beehive-shaped houses with stone foundations and plastered floors (under which they were eventually buried).

Skara Brae, a well-preserved Neolithic settlement of stone houses on Orkney, Scotland.

more than 1,000 years. Its population lived in rectangular houses, built very close together, which were entered through the roof. The houses were whitewashed and painted with geometric patterns.

Çatalhöyük probably prospered because of its trade in obsidian, a highly prized black volcanic glass found in Turkey that was used for cutting tools. Trading networks are another sign of society's increasing sophistication. They allowed village settlements to acquire resources from elsewhere, "paying" for their goods by exchanging their agricultural surpluses.

TRADE, SOCIETY, AND RELIGION

Another highly successful settlement was Çatalhöyük in Turkey, which thrived from 7000 BCE and was inhabited for

Village life arose in South America's Andean region around 2500 BCE, and by 800 BCE had spread to the fringes of the Atacama Desert at Tulor.

With less time needed to find food, people had more time to specialize in other aspects of life. Some became skilled workers, such as potters and masons, while others became shamans or priests and guided the growing ancestor and fertility cults.

DISCOVERY OF METALS

📍 Eurasia, Mesoamerica   ⏳ 8000–2000 BCE

Humans had made tools out of stone, bone, and wood for thousands of years. The advent of copper-working around 7000 BCE was a significant watershed in human history and the beginning of a long association with metals.

Copper ores are relatively common around the Mediterranean, found in surface outcrops easily identifiable by their distinctive green colour. The earliest copper items were hammered crude axes and beads, but it was the discovery of copper smelting – heating ore with charcoal to extract the metal – that opened the way to the development of a range of practical and decorative items. At first, smelting was done in open fires, until it was found that crucibles – heat-resistant vessels of fired clay – produced metal more efficiently.

The discovery of copper allowed prehistoric humans to manufacture much more effective tools and weapons, such as these copper axe heads.

THE SPREAD OF METALLURGY

This discovery of smelting seems to have occurred independently in western Asia around 6000 BCE and in east Asia before 2000 BCE. The earliest use of gold and silver dates to around 6000–5000 BCE, both metals being used for decorative and ritual purposes, as their malleability makes them unsuitable for everyday use.

Between 4000 and 2000 BCE, knowledge of metalworking reached most of Eurasia and North Africa. The demand for metals promoted the growth of trade networks; lowland Mesopotamia, for example – the focus of the earliest civilizations – has no native metal or ore and societies there needed to import metal from Anatolia or the Iranian plateau. In Europe, copper mines existed from around 5100 BCE at Varna in Bulgaria.

FROM COPPER TO BRONZE

Some time after 3500 BCE, people discovered that mixing copper and tin together to create an alloy, named bronze, produced a much more durable metal, suitable for weaponry, armour, and tools. By 3300 BCE, the Mesopotamians had adopted the technique, as had the Egyptians around 3100 BCE, beginning the Bronze Age. Bronze-working was discovered in China around 2000 BCE and from there spread throughout eastern and Southeast Asia.

A grave from Varna in Bulgaria, where rich metal deposits allowed a culture to develop in which costly goods accompanied the dead.

MEGALITHS

As agriculture spread across Europe, new and more centralized communities – mainly in the north and west of the continent, but also as far afield as Malta – created monuments with vast pieces of stone, called megaliths. We may never know their exact purpose, but they are clearly an expression of a belief system, marking out the seasons and the cyclical movements of the sun, moon, and stars.

BARROWS AND HENGES

In the 4th millennium BCE, European farming communities created long earthen burial mounds ("barrows") and stone-chambered tombs, such as that at West Kennet in Wiltshire, southern Britain, where a passageway in a barrow leads to side chambers in which as many as 46 corpses were interred. At Newgrange in Ireland a similar chambered tomb features patterns of spirals and circles, typical of a new artistic technique that characterized the art of the megalith builders.

"Henge" monuments appeared around 3200 BCE. Henges consist of a circular or oval area enclosed by a bank, containing a circle of wooden posts or huge stones. Wooden circles have largely perished – although at Woodhenge in Wiltshire, the post-holes have survived; the deepest measure about 2m (6ft), indicating posts that stood some 5.5m (17ft) high. The stone circles, however, are the most remarkable monuments of the megalithic age. These are spread throughout northern and western Europe, with the British Isles alone containing perhaps 1,000 stone circles. The circle at Avebury, Wiltshire, 420m (1,381ft) in diameter, is among the largest that survive, and probably acted as the ritual focus for a large area of southwestern Britain. At Carnac in France, elaborate long rows of standing stones form a similarly striking ensemble.

The dramatic stone circle at Stonehenge is thought by some to have been built to mark the summer and winter solstices – critical events in farming societies.

The Mnajdra temple complex on Malta, built around 3500 BCE, is the crowning achievement of a flourishing megalithic culture on the island.

STONEHENGE

Stonehenge, in southern England, is perhaps the most famous megalithic site of all. First begun around 3000 BCE as a simple earthwork enclosure, the site was developed over the next 1,000 years in several stages. A circle of bluestones – transported all the way from Preseli in south Wales, a distance of some 250km (155 miles) – was erected in around 2500 BCE. Then, about 2300 BCE, an outer circle of giant sandstones (or sarsen stones) was set up, each weighing around 26 tons. Each was shaped into the correct size by hammering with great stone balls or "mauls". How exactly the sarsens were erected is unknown, but the complex must have demanded a huge investment in time and labour, implying a highly centralized society.

THE END OF THE MEGALITH AGE

By around 1500 BCE, the megalithic age in Europe was on the wane. Construction of stone circles ceased in Britain and northern France. The focus of religion in northern Europe turned to the ritual deposit of weaponry in lakes and bogs and the last evidence of additions at Stonehenge dates to around 1100 BCE. At some time in around 1000 BCE, some of the stones were deliberately overturned. Although the monuments were not forgotten, their makers and their meaning became utterly obscure.

This stone-built passageway leads to a burial chamber at the 5,000-year-old megalithic passage-tomb at Newgrange, Ireland.

THE FIRST TOWNS

Near East   5000–3000 BCE

The world's earliest known large towns and cities developed in Mesopotamia in the 4th millennium BCE, perhaps through the need to organize the construction of irrigation channels fed by the Tigris and Euphrates rivers. At first the towns were little more than agglomerations of villages and related families, but soon they became major centres of trade and vast irrigation works that watered the countryside and produced several crops a year. The irrigated fields' increased productivity could now support larger populations; in Egypt the Nile (*see facing page, below*) fulfilled a similar role.

Jericho, in Jordan, after 6000 BCE, developed from a permanent village into one of the first towns.

CITIES AND HIERARCHIES

The change was not simply a matter of size, but was accompanied by radical changes in the region's society, economy, and politics. Society became increasingly hierarchical, with rulers (often kings) at the top, who were frequently seen as living gods, and below them a small privileged class of high officials and priests. Lower down the social scale came craftsmen, lesser officials, soldiers, and the commoners. The authority of the rulers came not just from a threat of force, but from religious ideas about authority. These beliefs are commemorated by art and by writing on temple walls and were reinforced by elaborate ceremonies. Each city clustered around temple precincts, those in Mesopotamia built on top of mudbrick pyramids, called ziggurats.

From its original heartland in southern Mesopotamia, urbanism spread northwards to sites such as Nineveh on the Tigris, Mari on the Euphrates, and Susa in western Iran. Each town or city tended to remain an independent entity (or city-state). In Egypt, however, a process of consolidation into a single state was complete as early as 3000 BCE.

Çatalhöyük in modern Turkey, founded *c.*7500 BCE, had a population of some 8,000 at its peak, yet it did not survive into the Bronze Age to become a city.

EARLY MESOPOTAMIA

⚑ Iraq, W Iran, SE Syria ⚒ 6000–3000 BCE

By around 6000 BCE, a culture known as the Halafian had become established in northern Mesopotamia. Communities lived in villages of domed houses built of clay, relied on long-distance trade, and buried their dead in distinctive shaft graves. They were replaced by the 'Ubaid culture, a pre-eminent Mesopotamian culture that was the first to use irrigation to increase crop yields. It was also at this time that the first urban centres appeared, at Eridu and Uruk.

A small statuette from 3rd millennium BCE Uruk shows a worshipper bearing offerings to the gods.

THE FIRST CITIES

As with many other Mesopotamian cities, Eridu was originally a shrine. It honoured the god Enki, ruler of the Abyss, who had created order from chaos. The shrine went through six or more incarnations before finally becoming an imposing step pyramid.

Uruk arose between 4800 and 3750 BCE. By 2800 BCE, it occupied around 250 hectares (615 acres) and may have housed 5,000 people. It depended on trade networks for goods in exchange for its grain, and may have had satellite colonies as far as the Zagros Mountains, several hundred kilometres to the north, to ensure control of key trade routes.

PREDYNASTIC EGYPT

⚑ Egypt ⚒ 4000–3100 BCE

In 4000 BCE, Egypt consisted of a valley of farmers living in small communities along the Nile; the river's annual flooding, or inundation, deposited rich, fertile silt on a broad strip along its banks. There were many small kingdoms, the largest of which were based in growing towns such as Abydos and Nekhen. The first walled towns in Egypt were erected at Naqada and Hierakonpolis around 3300 BCE. Alongside them were constructed rich tombs for their rulers.

By this time there were only two main kingdoms, Upper and Lower Egypt. It was the rulers of Upper Egypt who unified the country in around 3100 BCE. Exactly which of them achieved this is unclear. Narmer, traditionally the first ruler (pharaoh) of the 1st dynasty, is often given the credit, but his successor Aha (also called Menes), who may in fact be the same person as Narmer, may have been responsible. He also seems to have strengthened the ruler's position as a divine king, and possibly founded the new royal capital at Memphis.

The Palette of Narmer depicts a pharaoh, wearing a crown and bearing a mace and a flail, in a victory procession that may celebrate Egypt's unification.

THE ANCIENT
WORLD

THE WORLD IN 3000–700 BCE

By 3000 BCE, complex civilizations had arisen in the Tigris and
Euphrates valleys of Mesopotamia and along the banks of the Nile
in Egypt. China's first civilization flourished along the Yangtze
river; somewhat later, the advanced cultures of the Chavín and
Olmecs developed in Peru and Mexico respectively. Eventually,

The world in 750 BCE

.... undefined border

● Greek cities and territories

● Phoenician cities and territories

small Chinese states under
the Eastern Zhou dynasty

NOTE: Settlements in italics were
not in existence in 750 BCE but were
significant during this chapter's era.

THE ANCIENT WORLD IN 750 BCE

By 750 BCE, Egypt's New Kingdom empire had
waned, and much of the Middle East was under
Assyrian control. While the Greeks had begun
to colonize the Mediterranean, Rome was but
a tiny village. In China, central authority had
collapsed with the Zhou dynasty, while India's
Indus Valley civilization had long since dissolved

rade and technological innovation led to increased prosperity. In the lensely populated Middle East, competition between neighbouring tates led to warfare, and to conquest by the Egyptians, Hittites, Assyrians, and Babylonians. Europe's first sophisticated culture, he Minoans, flourished on the island of Crete around 2000 BCE.

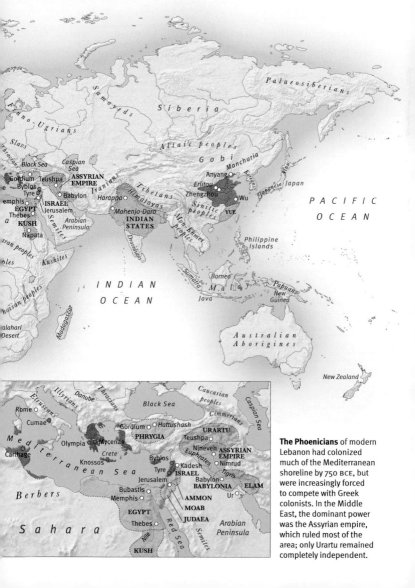

The Phoenicians of modern Lebanon had colonized much of the Mediterranean shoreline by 750 BCE, but were increasingly forced to compete with Greek colonists. In the Middle East, the dominant power was the Assyrian empire, which ruled most of the area; only Urartu remained completely independent.

THE NEAR EAST

The world's first complex societies arose in the Near East within the fertile area, known as Mesopotamia, between the Tigris and Euphrates rivers. By 3000 BCE, competing city-states of great wealth flourished here, with advanced irrigation schemes, established trade, and grand palaces and temples. The earliest civilization, that of Sumeria, was followed by the Babylonian and Assyrian empires, which established their dominance over almost the entire region.

THE SUMERIANS

▶ Modern Iraq   ☒ c.3000–c.2340 BCE

The first civilization in Mesopotamia arose in the south, where a number of growing city-states forged trading and diplomatic ties. This Sumerian culture, as it is known, was characterized by centralized hierarchies headed by rulers who often had priestly roles but, unlike Egypt's pharaohs, were rarely thought to be divine. Each of the cities was seen as the home of one of the major Sumerian gods (Nanna at Ur, Ishtar at Uruk) and in the period known as the Early Dynastic (c.3000–c.2340 BCE), the

Sumerians began to build stepped temple towers, or ziggurats, in honour of their deities. The sophisticated palace cultures were supported by specialist administrators, merchants, and scribes, whose need to keep records led to the development of the first full writing system, in a script known as cuneiform.

CONQUEST AND DECLINE

The separate city-states of Sumeria were briefly united in around 2400 BCE, when King Lugalzagesi of the city-state of Umma conquered Ur and Uruk and reduced the eastern city of Lagash to dependent status. But within half a century, the whole area had been absorbed into the empire of Sargon, king of Akkad (*see box, facing page*).

The city of Uruk was the earliest the Sumerian cities to flourish, and incorporated the sacred precinct of Eanna, the "house of the sky."

UR

📍 South of modern Iraq   ⧗ *c.*3000–*c.*2000 BCE

One of the city-states of Sumeria (*see facing page*), Ur began to thrive around 2800 BCE, becoming extremely wealthy; the tombs of rulers such as Queen Pu-abi and Meskalamdug have yielded artefacts of great value.

Ur was eclipsed politically during the occupation of Sumeria by Sargon (*see below*), but in around 2100 BCE, Ur-Nammu founded the Third Dynasty of Ur. For 70 years Ur dominated a huge area divided into 20 provinces, stretching from Susa in southwest Iran to Ashur, far to the northwest of the Sumerian heartland. During this time the population increased and cities flourished, supported by a system of forced labour. The city of Ur itself was enhanced with the construction of a great ziggurat. Ur-Nammu's heirs extended the empire, especially under Shulgi (ruled 2094–2047 BCE), but under Ibbi-Sin (ruled 2028–2004 BCE) outlying regions broke away, and invaders from nearby Elam finally ended the Third Dynasty's power.

A Sumerian gaming board, inlaid with shell and lapis lazuli, was among the treasures excavated from the Royal Cemetery at Ur.

THE AKKADIAN EMPIRE

📍 Modern Iraq, SW Iran, Syria, Lebanon, SE Turkey   ⧗ *c.*2300–*c.*2083 BCE

The northern part of Sumeria, known as Babylonia, gave rise to the earliest successful attempt to unite the Near East when Sargon smashed the power of Lugalzagesi of Umma, securing control over the whole region. His capital at Akkad dominated an empire that became ever more centralized. A calendar was introduced for the whole of Babylonia, new systems of taxation and standardized weights and measures were imposed, and Akkadian became the language of government. Sargon's armies reached as far as the Mediterranean coast, but it was difficult to control the outlying regions. Rebellion broke out in the reign of Sargon's grandson,

SARGON OF AKKAD

Born a commoner, Sargon (ruled 2334–2279 BCE) rose to power in the city of Kish and took the name Sharru-kin (Sargon), "the king is legitimate". From his new base at Akkad, he sent his armies to establish the world's first empire.

Naram-sin (ruled 2254–2218 BCE), who took on the title "king of the world" and was worshipped as a god while alive. Naram-sin was victorious, but thereafter the Akkadians were on the defensive; their empire eventually fell during the reign of King Sharkalisharri, the son of Naram-Sin.

THE RISE OF BABYLON

📍 Modern Iraq, SE Syria ⌛ c.1900–1595 BCE

From around 1900 BCE, the Babylonian kings began annexing states to the north, such as Sippar and Kish, marking the start of the "Old Babylonian" period. They were prevented from further advances by Shamshi-Adad, who held a strong state in upper Mesopotamia.

BABYLON UNDER HAMMURABI

After Shamsi-Adad's death, Hammurabi of Babylon extended his city-state's reach even further, conquering the whole of southern Mesopotamia between 1766 and 1761 BCE. Only further west, in modern Syria, did kings such as Zimri-Lim (ruled c.1775–1762 BCE) of Mari seek to maintain independence. Late in his reign, Hammurabi attacked even Mari and reduced Zimri-Lim to vassalage. Having achieved his

HAMMURABI AND HIS LAW CODE

A warrior, statesman, and lawgiver, Hammurabi (ruled 1792–1750 BCE) raised Babylon from the status of a minor city-state to the principal Mesopotamian power. He described himself as "the king who has made the four quarters of the earth subservient" and his "law code", containing some 282 legal decrees, was probably more an attempt to portray himself as a supporter of justice than a practical legal document. Its penalties are often harsh and retributive, such as the loss of an eye for blinding a free man.

> "AT THE COMMAND OF THE SUN GOD... MAY MY JUSTICE BECOME VISIBLE IN THE LAND."
>
> The law code of Hammurabi, c.1750 BCE

territorial ambitions, Hammurabi issued his famous code of law. By the time of Hammurabi's death, Babylon had become the regional superpower.

THE DECLINE OF BABYLON

Under Samsuiluna (ruled 1749–1712 BCE), Hammurabi's son, Babylon faced a serious rebellion during which cities such as Nippur and Ur broke away from its control. The south of Mesopotamia went into decline, but the Old Babylonian dynasty continued to rule the north until 1595 BCE, when a new group, the Kassites, sacked the city.

Hammurabi receives his code of law from the justice god Shamash, in a highly evocative image of a just ruler.

THE HITTITES

📍 Central and SE Turkey   ⌛ c.1700–c.1200 BCE

he kingdom of the Hittites, alled Hatti, was based in central natolia around their capital city Iattusa, but constantly shifted its orders, extending at times as far s western Syria in the south and ne coasts of the Black Sea and ne Aegean in the north and west.

Comparatively little is known of ne Hittite Old Kingdom, the first der of which, Hattusili, founded Iattusa in about 1650 BCE. Under Iattusili's successor Mursili I (ruled 1620–c.1590 BCE), Hittite armies ampaigned in Syria, but by the eign of Telipinu (c.1525–c.1500 BCE), Iatti was once again reduced to its ore territory around the capital.

Under Tudhaliya III (ruled c.1360–1344 BCE), the first ruler of the New Lingdom, the Hittites expanded again, efeating the rulers of Aleppo and the Iitanni. Hatti reached its height under uppiluliuma I, who conquered northern

A statue of a Hittite goddess, one of a pantheon of deities headed by the storm god Teshub and his female counterpart, the sun goddess Hebat.

Syria and threatened Egyptian control over Palestine. Mursili III (ruled 1295–1272 BCE) fought the Egyptians in a bitterly contested battle at Kadesh in 1274 BCE, which both sides claimed as a victory. However, the aftermath of the battle firmly cemented Hittite control in Syria. The growing threat from Assyria to the east, and the rebellion of vassal states in the west, rapidly undermined the Hittite kingdom and in 1207 unknown raiders sacked Hatti again, after which the Hittite state collapsed completely.

SUPPILULIUMA I

One of the most militarily successful Hittite kings, Suppiluliuma I (ruled 1344–1322 BCE) conquered Mitanni to the north and parts of Syria. So great was his prestige that Tutankhamun's widow invited one of his sons to come to Egypt as her husband.

ne Gate of the Lions at Hattusa (now Bogazköy Turkey) provided an impressive ceremonial ntrance to the Hittite royal capital.

THE LATE BRONZE AGE COLLAPSE

The Near East   *c.*1200–*c.*1050 BCE

In the late Bronze Age of the Near East, a diplomatic community of empires had maintained a thriving international system based on bronze. Between 1200 and 1050 BCE, records hint at upheaval, as raids and migrations overwhelmed the established powers. The collapse appears to have begun a little before 1200 BCE, when the citadels of Mycenaean Greece (*see p.101*) were destroyed.

THE FALL OF EMPIRES

In 1207 BCE, the Hittite capital of Hattusa was sacked and the empire fell. The Egyptians had to fight off invasions by groups they called the "Sea Peoples",

A group of Philistine captives taken by the Egyptian pharaoh Rameses III in *c.*1182 BCE; the Philistines, or "Peleset", were one of the "Sea Peoples".

which eventually led to the demise of the New Kingdom in 1069 BCE. Elsewhere, the Kassite dynasty of Babylon collapsed around 1154 BCE while, in Assyria, the archives speak of constant skirmishes. The ensuing "Dark Age", with almost no written sources, would last for 150 years.

THE PHOENICIANS

Lebanon, the Mediterranean coastline   *c.*1200–146 BCE

From around 1200 BCE, the coastal cities of Tyre, Byblos, and Sidon, in an area the Greeks called Phoenicia, formed the core of a sea-based trading network. The Phoenicians used maritime power to control a dense web of routes crossing the Mediterranean, with trading links as far afield as Mesopotamia and the Red Sea, supplying a range of goods from rich, exotic fabrics and glass to cedar wood.

They also established colonies that included Lixus in Morocco, Gades (Cadiz) in Spain, Motya in Sicily, and, most importantly, Carthage (in modern Tunisia), founded around 814 BCE. After Phoenicia itself fell to Assyria in the 9th century BCE (and then to Egypt, Babylon and Persia), Carthage became the principal centre of Phoenician politics, conquering its own empire in the western Mediterranean. Carthage ultimately lost the battle for dominance of this region to the Romans, who defeated the Carthaginians in three Punic Wars in the 3rd and 2nd centuries BCE.

The Phoenicians were skilled navigators and built many forms of boat, from smaller vessels to multi-oared galleys.

THE ASSYRIAN EMPIRE

📷 Modern Iraq, W Iran, Syria, Lebanon, SW Turkey   ⏳ c.2000–c.610 BCE

Assyria came to prominence around 2000 BCE, prospering from the copper trade with Anatolia. During the reign of Assur-Ubalit (1363–1328 BCE), the Assyrians carved out an empire, culminating in the conquest of Babylon in the reign of Tukulti-Ninurta I (ruled 1243–1207 BCE). Assyria then fell victim to invasion by the "Sea Peoples" and it was not until around 1000 BCE that the Neo-Assyrian empire emerged. The Neo-Assyrians won fame as fierce warriors, utilizing armies of chariots, infantry, and horseback riders that made ample use of the new iron weaponry.

They used terror tactics to suppress their enemies, with mass executions, impalements, and deportations. Assurnasirpal II (ruled 883–859 BCE) and Shalmaneser III (ruled 858–824 BCE) expanded the Assyrians' territory as far west as the Mediterranean. After a brief decline, the Neo-Assyrian empire revived under Tiglath-Pileser III and his heir Sargon II (ruled 721–705 BCE).

VICTORY, THEN COLLAPSE

In 689 BCE, in the reign of Sennacherib (704–681 BCE), the Neo-Assyrians sacked Babylon, then, under Assurbanipal (ruled 668–627 BCE), they occupied parts of Egypt. However, the Neo-Assyrians became overstretched, and in 612 BCE a coalition of Medes and Babylonians captured the Assyrian capital Nineveh. By 610 BCE the empire had vanished.

TIGLATH-PILESER III

The administrative reforms of Tiglath-Pileser III (ruled 744–727 BCE) strengthened Neo-Assyria. He extended Assyrian control along the Mediterranean coast, becoming king of Babylon and leading an army to the gates of Teushpa, the Urartian capital.

The reconstructed Nergal gate of Nineveh, which was one of the chief cities of the Assyrian empire, and its last capital under Sennacherib and his successors.

THE INVENTION OF WRITING

Writing represented a leap forward in the intellectual evolution of humans. Its development occurred independently in five different areas: Mesopotamia, Egypt, India, China, and Mesoamerica. Much of the earliest extant writing is on stone, but many inscriptions survive on papyrus from Egypt and clay tablets from Mesopotamia, and these documents shed precious light on ancient cultures.

FROM SYMBOLS TO SCRIPT

The development of writing – as the symbolic representation of spoken language – was a gradual process that probably began in the Middle East in the middle of the 4th millennium BCE. Early writing was made up of pictures, which helped create visual records of trading transactions. Over time, these pictures were simplified into symbols. In Mesopotamia, this process resulted in wedge-shaped cuneiform writing, and, in Egypt, pictorial hieroglyphs were used – from around 3200 BCE – for a period of more than 3,000 years.

Cuneiform script, imprinted on clay tablets, is one of the earliest forms of written expression.

Many of these early scripts were logographic, meaning that each symbol represented an entire word or idea. Egyptian hieroglyphic and Mesopotamian cuneiform writing mixed logograms with symbols that represented sounds. As writing advanced, this combined approach enabled people to reproduce spoken language accurately in written form.

Archives such as those at Mari and Ugarit in Syria yield a wealth of information about the dealings of rulers, who used writing to manage information about their estates. From the Mayan kings of Mesoamerica to the Egyptian pharaohs and Chinese

Egyptian hieroglyphs remained unchanged over centuries, in part because of their religious use, such as in this 20th-century BCE coffin panel.

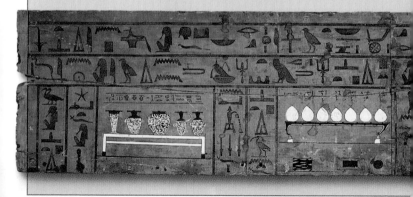

The Rosetta Stone enabled François Champollion, in 1822–24, to decipher hieroglyphs, because it has parallel texts in hieroglyphic and in Ancient Greek, which was already understood.

emperors, rulers also set up monumental inscriptions as a means to record their achievements and inspire awe in their subjects.

SCRIBES AND LITERACY

The establishment of written archives and governments created a need for a literate class able to produce and read them. In Egypt, the education of scribes – who

> ## "TO THE PHOENICIAN PEOPLE IS DUE GREAT HONOUR, FOR THEY INVENTED THE LETTERS OF THE ALPHABET."
>
> Pliny the Elder (Roman author), *Natural History*, 1st century CE

were elevated to a position of great prestige in society – began in youth, and included mathematics and accountancy. Although literary and devotional texts were produced in Egypt and Mesopotamia, reading them remained the province of the elite members of society.

THE ALPHABET

The concept of an alphabet in which every symbol denotes a particular sound only arose in the late 2nd millennium BCE. The people of Ugarit in Syria developed a cuneiform alphabet around 2000 BCE. Turquoise miners in Sinai used another early alphabet system shortly afterwards, and it may have been this script, with 30 signs, that spread northwards through Palestine into Phoenicia, where it evolved into the 22-sign Phoenician alphabet around 1000 BCE. The Phoenicians' trading network, in turn, exported their script throughout the Mediterranean, where it cast its influence in the developing scripts of Greece and Rome.

EGYPT

Around 3100 BCE, a unified kingdom of Egypt emerged – ruled by a single king, or pharaoh – which occupied the banks of the Nile as far south as Aswan. Under the Early Dynastic period (*c.*3100–2469 BCE), the Old Kingdom (2649–2134 BCE), the Middle Kingdom (2040–1640 BCE), and the New Kingdom (1550–1070 BCE), Egypt experienced nearly 3,000 years of prosperity and cultural continuity, before foreign invaders occupied it from the 8th century BCE

THE OLD KINGDOM

⚑ Egypt   ⚔ 2649–2134 BCE

Around 3100 BCE, the two kingdoms of Upper Egypt (the south) and Lower Egypt (the north) merged into a single state at the hands of a pharaoh named Menes. Then, from 2649 BCE, under the rulers of the 3rd dynasty, the Old Kingdom was inaugurated. Its most striking remains are the great funerary monuments known as the pyramids, but there is also evidence of a centralized state based around the capital at Memphis. A vast political and administrative bureaucracy grew up that included local governors, who oversaw regions called *nomes*. The pharaoh himself came to occupy a central religious role, because he upheld a system that ensured the Nile brought silt-rich annual floods each year and kept the valley fertile. Vast irrigation schemes directed the waters to wide areas of agricultural land and devices called "nilometers" predicted the rise of the river and the bounty (or dearth) of the subsequent harvest.

Under the Old Kingdom, Egypt first began to project its power abroad, with expeditions during the reign of Snefru (2575–2551 BCE) to Nubia to collect raw materials, and campaigns into Libya by the 6th-dynasty pharaohs (2323–2150 BCE).

During the long reign of Pepi II (2246–2152 BCE), central authority began to dissolve and, within 20 years, the Old Kingdom collapsed, as famine wracked the land and officials in the provinces established their own rule. A century of uncertainty ensued, known as the First Intermediate Period (2134–2040 BCE).

Tomb treasures, such as this effigy of an Old Kingdom official and his family, teach us much about ancient Egypt.

THE PYRAMIDS

📍 Egypt ⚔ c.2600–c.1525 BCE

Early Dynastic pharaohs were buried in mud-brick box-shaped tombs known as mastabas. During the reign of the 3rd-dynasty pharaoh Djoser (2630–2611 BCE) a new, grander structure appeared. His step pyramid at Saqqara was essentially a series of mastabas set one on top of the other, and prefigured a series of massive true pyramids constructed during the 4th dynasty (2575–2465 BCE). Snefru probably built pyramids at Dahshur and Meidum, but under his successor Khufu, the Great Pyramid at Giza, near Memphis, was erected. Containing over two million blocks of stone, each weighing around 2,300kg (2½ tons), its construction involved a truly prodigious expenditure of precious resources.

The courtly elite were also buried at Saqqara. This Egyptian bas-relief is from the tomb of Hezyre, physician and scribe to the pharaoh Djoser.

Each pyramid was both a tomb and a temple dedicated to the cult of the dead pharaoh. The pyramids were constructed in limestone, with the royal burial concealed in a granite chamber deep in the interior. They were accompanied by funerary temples, smaller pyramids for queens, mastabas for officials, pits in which to bury sacred boats, and a causeway leading to a valley temple, which was the ceremonial entrance to the complex.

THE DECLINE OF THE PYRAMIDS

The pyramids of the 5th and succeeding dynasties were sited in places other than Giza, including at Abusir near Saqqara, and were smaller than Khufu's Great Pyramid. The last true royal pyramid built in Egypt was that of Ahmose I (ruled 1550–1525 BCE). The New Kingdom pharaohs chose to be buried in less extravagant tombs located further south in the Valley of the Kings, near Thebes.

KHUFU

Surprisingly little is known of Khufu's reign (2551–2528 BCE), except through the existence of the Great Pyramid. The Greek historian Herodotus told of Khufu's cruelty, although this is probably no more than a reflection of the huge force of will that he must have needed to ensure the Great Pyramid's construction. The pyramid's burial chamber was robbed in antiquity, but the first recorded traveller to enter the tomb was British consul Nathaniel Davison, in 1765.

The largest and oldest of the three Giza pyramids, Khufu's Great Pyramid probably took around 20 years to build.

The funerary temple of Hatshepsut at Deir el Bahri, Thebes, is a spectacular monument to one of ancient Egypt's few female rulers. Hatshepsut (ruled 1473–1458 BCE) took on all the trappings of a male pharaoh. On one of the terraces are statues of her as the god Osiris.

THE MIDDLE KINGDOM

⚑ Egypt ⚔ 2040–1640 BCE

During the First Intermediate Period, the most powerful Egyptian rulers were at Heracleopolis, south of Memphis. From around 2150 BCE, there was civil war between the Heracleopolitan pharaohs and rivals further south at Edfu and Thebes. Finally, around 2040 BCE, the Theban king Nebhepetre Mentuhotep II (ruled 2061–2010 BCE) was victorious, reuniting Egypt and beginning the Middle Kingdom.

THE HEIGHT OF THE MIDDLE KINGDOM
Amenemhet I (ruled 1991–1962 BCE), the first pharaoh of the 12th dynasty, restored Egypt's vigour. He established a new capital at Itj-towy near Memphis, and sent expeditions to Nubia (modern Sudan), conquering territory as far south as the Second Cataract of the Nile. The 12th-dynasty pharaohs also mounted campaigns in Syria and Palestine.

The central authority's influence seems to have lessened during the 13th dynasty (1783–1640 BCE), which had a large number of short-lived rulers, but there is little evidence of decline. There

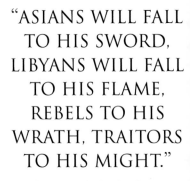

> ## "ASIANS WILL FALL TO HIS SWORD, LIBYANS WILL FALL TO HIS FLAME, REBELS TO HIS WRATH, TRAITORS TO HIS MIGHT."
>
> The Prophecy of Neferty from the time of Amenemhet I

are, however, indications of an increased number of immigrants from Palestine, foreshadowing the stresses that would, in time, bring down the Middle Kingdom.

THE END OF THE MIDDLE KINGDOM
Towards the end of the 13th dynasty, Egypt came under intensive pressure from Asiatic groups migrating westwards who began to occupy large areas of the Nile delta. Around 1650 BCE, one group, known as the Hyksos (a name derived from an Egyptian word meaning "foreign princes"), established their own kingdom in the north of Egypt. Native Egyptian rulers continued to rule in the south from Thebes, while the Hyksos could not be dislodged from their capital at Avaris. This century of political turmoil is referred to as the Second Intermediate Period.

Colourful wall paintings, such as this well-preserved example at the Tomb of Sirenpowet II, adorned the walls of Middle Kingdom tombs.

EGYPTIAN RELIGION

Egyptian religion was immensely complex, with a large number of gods, many of them localized and many appearing with different aspects. Earlier pharaohs associated themselves with the sky god Horus or the sun god Re, but gradually the cult of Osiris, king of the dead, became dominant. The need to ensure the immortality of the ruler's soul after death was the primary focus of Egyptian religious belief.

THE CULT OF THE DEAD

The unification of Egypt under the Old Kingdom rationalized the various local pantheons and, throughout the year, the pharaoh engaged in a series of ritual activities to ensure the fertility of the land and the crossing of the sky by the sun each day.

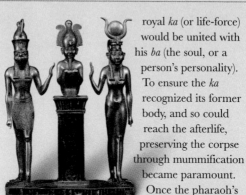

A "trinity" of Horus, Isis, and Osiris became the focus of religious belief by the time of the Old Kingdom.

Most important of all was the cult of the dead. Egyptians believed that, after death, the pharaohs were reborn as the king of the dead, Osiris. A complex mythology surrounded the rites that ensured this resurrection, when the

royal *ka* (or life-force) would be united with his *ba* (the soul, or a person's personality). To ensure the *ka* recognized its former body, and so could reach the afterlife, preserving the corpse through mummification became paramount.

Once the pharaoh's soul reached the underworld, a jury of 12 gods would weigh its misdeeds against a feather. If the two weighed the same, the pharaoh was ensured eternal life.

The official cults were only briefly challenged under Akhenaten (ruled 1353–1335 BCE), who tried to establish the worship of the sun disc (Aten) as the state religion – perhaps the first example of monotheism.

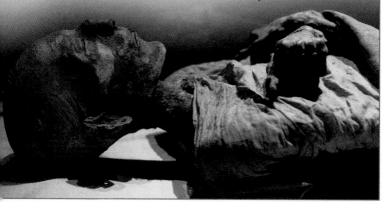

To preserve a pharaoh's body, vital organs were removed, then the corpse was stuffed with linen, soaked with preservatives, and wrapped.

THE NEW KINGDOM AND AFTER

⚐ Egypt   ⚔ 1550–1070 BCE

The Hyksos were finally expelled from Egypt by the Theban ruler Kamose (ruled 1555–1550 BCE) and his successor Ahmose I (ruled 1550–1525 BCE), the first pharaoh of the New Kingdom. This era is often seen as a time of glorious "empire" for Egypt, during which Egypt extended its trade links and refined its skill in diplomacy. It quashed threats to the throne making use of warfare techniques borrowed from the Hyksos.

IMPERIAL AND CULTURAL APOGEE

The early rulers of the 18th dynasty (1550–1307 BCE) sought to establish an Egyptian empire, first in Palestine and then in parts of Syria. Tuthmosis I (ruled 1504–1492 BCE) campaigned as far as the Euphrates river and there set up a stela – an inscribed standing stone – commemorating his army's achievement. Under the reigns of Tuthmosis II and his widow Hatshepsut, between 1493 and 1458 BCE, the pace of military expansion slowed. Hatshepsut's nephew, Tuthmosis III (ruled 1479–1425 BCE), however, led nearly 20 expeditions into Palestine and Syria, defeating peoples as far-flung as the Mitanni near the Euphrates and extending Egyptian control southwards down the Nile.

After a brief period of political weakness following the early death of the boy-pharaoh Tutankhamun (ruled 1333–1323 BCE), the 19th-dynasty rulers reasserted Egypt's control of its overseas empire, beginning with Seti I (ruled 1305–1290 BCE), whose aggressive campaigning brought him into conflict with the Hittites. His son, Rameses II (*see facing page*), continued the war, but in 1274 BCE his army was nearly destroyed near the Syrian town of Qadesh. Thereafter, Egypt's control over Palestine waned. Merneptah (ruled 1224–1214 BCE) fought a series of battles to keep Libyan tribesmen from the Nile Delta, but the respite was short-lived and Rameses III (ruled 1194–1163 BCE) faced a great army of "Sea Peoples", who had rampaged through Syria and Palestine. Rameses defeated them in 1182 BCE, but growing internal dissent, along with a series of weak successors, eventually brought the New Kingdom to an end.

The lavishness of the golden death mask of Tutankhamun belies the reality of a boy-pharaoh who had very little influence.

Throughout his reign, Rameses II dedicated himself to a programme of building, most spectacularly these huge statues of the pharaoh at Abu Simbel in Nubia.

the cult of Aten – worship of the sun disc alone – and renaming himself Akhenaten in honour of his beliefs.

THE THIRD INTERMEDIATE AND LATE PERIODS

For 150 years after the New Kingdom's end, the high priests of Amun and the rulers of Tanis in the Delta contested control of Egypt. Gradually, Egypt fell to foreign rulers, beginning with the 22nd dynasty, founded in 945 BCE by Shoshenq, a general from Libya. When Egypt was reunited in the 25th dynasty, it was by the Nubian king Shabaqa (ruled 712–698 BCE). Successive periods of Nubian, Assyrian, and Persian rule were punctuated by periods of native dominance, until Egypt had its last years of pharaonic rule under the Ptolemies (304–30 BCE), a dynasty that was Macedonian-Greek in origin.

The New Kingdom had been an age of spectacular architectural and artistic achievements, as well as religious ferment. The lavish tomb contents of Tutankhamun were interred and the monumental buildings and statues of Rameses II were erected. Royalty were now buried in underground tombs, centred on the Valley of the Kings, near Thebes. Amenophis IV (ruled 1353–1335 BCE) took sun worship to extremes, briefly imposing on his people

Opulent grave goods, such as this colourful jewelled scarab chest ornament, were a feature of New Kingdom burials.

EUROPE

Europe's first civilizations flourished in the southeast, the earliest on the island of Crete, where the Minoans established a highly sophisticated Bronze Age culture. After the collapse of their society by around 1450 BCE, the Minoans were supplanted by the Mycenaeans, incomers from mainland Greece, who adopted many aspects of Minoan culture and occupied its palaces, but who were in turn swept away around 1200 BCE in a period of political turmoil.

MINOAN CRETE

⚑ Crete ⚓ c.2000–c.1450 BCE

By around 2000 BCE, trading towns on the Cretan coast had expanded to give rise to an advanced civilization centred on a series of palaces, notably at Knossos, Phaistos, Mallia, and Zakros. The Minoans depended on long-distance trade and became skilled seafarers, building up a large fleet that carried their artefacts into the eastern Mediterranean. Minoan rulers seem to have played both a political and a religious role, and many government officials were probably also priests. They kept official archives, but we have yet to decipher their script, known as Linear A. Society was divided into classes, with the court supported by a large class of agricultural labourers. Craftspeople produced sophisticated goods, such as "Kamáres ware" pottery, with designs in black, white, and red.

THE END OF THE PALACES

The reasons for the decline of Minoan culture are unclear. Around 1500 BCE, a massive volcanic eruption on the neighbouring island of Thera may have disrupted or destroyed the Minoans' trading network, undermining the basis of their wealth. Around 1450 BCE, aided by an earthquake on Crete that destroyed some of the palaces, Mycenaean invaders delivered the fatal blow to the Minoan city-states, and the civilization collapsed.

The ruins of the palace at Mallia, an important Minoan administrative centre which, unlike Knossos and Phaistos, was defended by a town wall.

THE PALACE OF KNOSSOS

📍 Knossos, Crete ⬛ *c.*2000–*c.*1200 BCE

Knossos, near Heraklion, was the most elaborate of the Minoan palaces, so much so that it gave rise to the later legend of the labyrinth within which lurked a monstrous half-human bull. When British archaeologist Sir Arthur Evans excavated the site between 1900 and 1932, he uncovered frescoes that abound in images of bulls, as well as double-headed axes and snakes, and these must all have played an important role in Minoan religious symbolism. Damaged by an earthquake around 1700 BCE, the Knossos

palace was rebuilt on an even grander scale, measuring some 18 hectares (45 acres), with a large series of shrines. The palace flourished for a further 250 years, and seems to have survived the wholesale destruction of Minoan sites around 1450 BCE, after which it was occupied for a further two centuries, most probably by Mycenaean invaders.

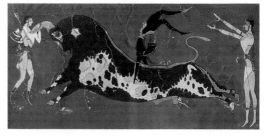

A fresco at Knossos depicts bull-leaping", which may have been a sport or a religious ritual.

THE MYCENAEANS

📍 Mainland Greece, Crete ⬛ *c.*1600–*c.*1070 BCE

Beginning around 1600 BCE, the Mycenaean culture grew from southern Greece, reaching as far north as Thessaly within 200 years. By around 1450 BCE, the Mycenaeans also expanded their rule southwards, toppling an already weakened Minoan civilization. Although not as adept at or dependent on trade as the Minoans, the Mycenaeans maintained commercial settlements on islands such as Rhodes.

The Mycenaean culture was based around fortified palace sites, such as Mycenae, Pylos, and Tiryns, with massive circuit walls and a central *megaron* – a square room that was the

A gold death mask, once believed to be that of legendary Greek king Agamemnon, found at Mycenae.

palace's focal point. Extensive archives, written in a script known as Linear B, have been found at the palace sites, providing a mass of information about Mycenaean social and economic life.

By around 1200 BCE, the Mycenaean culture was in decline, and most of its major centres had been destroyed by fire. Some centres limped on, exhibiting a lower and more provincial level of material culture, but by 1070 BCE the last Mycenaean palaces had been abandoned. Greece had entered its "Dark Age", a period in its history – lasting for centuries – for which no records exist.

SOUTH ASIA

A fertile cradle of river-fed land, crossing parts of modern India, Pakistan, and Afghanistan, gave birth to the Indus Valley civilization in the mid-4th millennium BCE. Its impressive, well-planned cities, most notably Harappa and Mohenjo-Daro, housed large populations and produced artefacts of great beauty. However, a deeper knowledge of this fascinating civilization is still tantalizingly out of reach, as the Indus Valley script remains undeciphered.

THE INDUS VALLEY CIVILIZATION

📍 Pakistan, NW India, SE Afghanistan ⚱ *c.*3300–*c.*1600 BCE

The Indus Valley civilization flourished across a large area of present-day Pakistan, northwest India, and Afghanistan, along the fertile Indus and Ghaggar-Hakra rivers. In common with the civilizations of Mesopotamia and Egypt, the Indus Valley depended heavily on land made fertile by regular floods and on the skilled use of of irrigation and water management techniques.

The "Early Harappan" phase of the civilization (*c.*3300–*c.*2800 BCE) saw the Indus Valley peoples grow crops, including peas, sesame seeds, and dates, and domesticate animals, such as the water buffalo. Sanitation systems and the earliest known examples of the Indus script also emerged in this phase.

Cities of the Indus Valley produced refined artefacts, including fine jewellery in gold and fired steatite (soapstone), gold and silver ornaments, and skilfully

The undeciphered Indus script is found on hundreds of clay seals, along with vivid animal images.

worked figurines in bronze, terracotta, and faience. Such treasures seem to indicate that this was a stratified society with an elite class that was able to commission precious works. The discovery of Indus Valley artefacts elsewhere in the world indicates that the civilization had widespread trading links, particularly with Mesopotamia, Afghanistan, and Iran.

From 2600–1900 BCE the civilization reached its peak, in what is known as the "Mature Harappan" period, when many large, well-planned cities thrived. The cities appear to have suffered from increased flooding from 1700 BCE onwards and from increased attacks by unknown outsiders. By 1600 BCE the quality of Indus Valley artefacts had declined and most of the main city sites had been abandoned.

MOHENJO-DARO

🏴 Pakistan   ⚱ *c.*2500–*c.*1600 BCE

Mohenjo-Daro was one of the world's first planned cities and, like Harappa some 500km (300 miles) to its northeast, was one of the Indus Valley civilization's principal settlements. Set out on a grid pattern, it had broad avenues and narrow side streets lined with spacious townhouses. Wells with high, sealed walls to prevent contamination were built to provide clean water for the inhabitants.

THE STRUCTURE OF THE CITY

A higher area set on an artificial mound some 12m (40ft) high has been dubbed Mohenjo-Daro's "Citadel", though it is thought to have been a place for public gatherings and an administrative centre rather than a fortified strongpoint. Within the citadel, the "Great Bath", an enclosed water tank or pool, may have had some ritual purpose. In the western quarter, large granaries indicate a central authority that was able to dictate the

The **"Lower Town"** of Mohenjo-Daro is in the foreground, with the city's "Citadel" dramatically rearing up on the mound in the background.

storing of surpluses. To the south, the "Lower Town" may have housed skilled craftsmen and the lower classes. What is certain is that the city stood at the centre of a network of trade and cultural exchange that reached as far as Tilmun (modern Bahrain) in the Persian Gulf.

Numerous religious artefacts have been found at the site of Mohenjo-Daro, notably images of a mother goddess often found in association with male symbols. These may indicate a fertility cult, although no temples or structures with an overt religious purpose have been identified.

DECLINE AND ABANDONMENT

Water was a constant threat to Mohenjo-Daro, which was flooded and rebuilt as many as nine times on the same site during its period of occupation. Around 1700 BCE, the city suffered a major flood from the Indus. A huge protective embankment was built to protect the city, but Mohenjo-Daro was abandoned once and for all within a century.

This striking statue has been frequently dubbed the **"Priest-King"**, although there is no evidence that such a figure existed in Mohenjo-Daro's society.

EAST ASIA

From around 4500 BCE, the Neolithic societies centred on the banks of China's Yellow River gave rise to a series of increasingly sophisticated cultures and then the first real towns. China's first centralized state emerged under the rule of the Shang dynasty (18th–11th centuries BCE). The Shang's rich culture of producing art and artefacts, particularly using bronze, is reflected in the artistic traditions of subsequent Chinese dynasties.

EARLY CHINESE CULTURES

China   c.4500–c.1800 BCE

Late Neolithic China gave rise to village cultures of some complexity. The Yangshao culture emerged along the banks of the Yellow River in central China, and more than one thousand sites have been excavated to date. Studies at one of the best-known sites, Banpo, show that Yangshao people cultivated millet, used polished stone tools, and wore hemp and possibly silk. They produced pots made of red clay, often decorated with spiral patterns, and some of the burials found at the village show evidence of belief in a connection with a spirit world.

At Longshan in Shandong province, at the lower reaches of the Yellow River, another culture created finer black pottery, some of it turned on a potter's wheel, and stone axes. This culture spread far along the banks of the middle and lower Yangtze to the south.

In 1959, archaeologists discovered the Erlitou culture in the Yellow River valley in Henan province, unearthing palace-like buildings, tombs, and bronze artefacts – the oldest yet found in China. More recent archaeological finds have revealed a variety of late Neolithic cultures outside the Yellow River valley, such as the Majiabang along the Yangtze in Jiangsu province, and the Dapenkeng culture in South China.

A Yangshao red vase from around 2000 BCE. Such pottery has been found in more than a thousand sites in the Yellow River area.

SHANG CHINA

📖 Eastern China   📖 *c.*1750–1027 BCE

The Shang, by tradition the second of China's dynasties, ruled over much of northern and central China from around 1750 BCE. They had several capitals, the last of which was discovered at Anyang on the banks of the Huan in the 1920s. Here, archaeologists have unearthed the remains of the large ceremonial and administrative centre of the late Shang state.

By around 1650 BCE, the Shang were established at the capital Zhengzhou, where a massive defensive wall, some 6.4km (4 miles) long, enclosed a large settlement with buildings constructed of stamped earth.

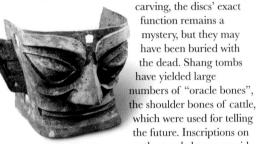

This mask is characteristic of the high level of bronze craftsmanship under the Shang dynasty.

SHANG CULTURE

The most prized archaeological finds from the Shang period are bronze objects, made primarily for ceremonial purposes. Many of the vessels found at Zhengzhou and Anyang had a ritual use, possibly for preparing sacrificial meats or heating wine. Highly stylized forms of bronze containers evolved, which would be produced for many centuries. The Shang also continued the production of jade discs, which had begun in Neolithic times. Often decorated with ornate carving, the discs' exact function remains a mystery, but they may have been buried with the dead. Shang tombs have yielded large numbers of "oracle bones", the shoulder bones of cattle, which were used for telling the future. Inscriptions on the oracle bones provide the earliest evidence of Chinese writing.

The Shang dynasty came to an end in around 1050 BCE when revolt, led by the Zhou, broke out in the west of the Shang territory. The Zhou, who had extended their influence throughout the present Shaanxi and Gansu provinces, finally overpowered the Shang emperor and became the dominant power.

In Shang tradition, when an important person died, his chariot, charioteers, and horses were buried with him, as in this example from a village near Anyang.

THE AMERICAS

From the mid-2nd millennium BCE, advanced societies began to develop in the Americas in two separate areas, Peru and Mesoamerica. The earliest civilizations in those regions were those of the Chavín and the Olmecs respectively. Both built large ceremonial centres and both followed a cult of the jaguar in their systems of religious beliefs, but they left little or nothing in the way of written records and their political history is almost impossible to reconstruct.

THE CHAVÍN OF PERU

🏴 Peru   ⚔ c.1250–c.200 BCE

By about 1250 BCE, village life based on the production of maize and pottery had spread throughout Peru's coastal and highland regions. However, it was not until around 900 BCE that the first identifiable culture spread across much of Peru. Centred on the great temple of Chavín de Huántar, at the confluence of the Wacheqsa and Mosna rivers, the Chavín culture touched all parts of Peru save the extreme south. As there is no evidence of fortresses, armies, or any of the other paraphernalia of empire, the culture's spread was probably not by force.

CHAVÍN SITE AND COLLAPSE

The site at Chavín de Huántar reveals its people's great engineering and architectural expertise. The Old Temple was built around 900 BCE on a massive terraced pyramid. From the central platform projected a series of fearsome fanged monsters, while at the temple's centre stood the Lanzón, a 4.5m- (15ft-) high granite stela – or stone slab – which may have been a devotional image. The site also includes a courtyard, perhaps an assembly place for ritual processions. Chavín wealth was used, at some time after 500 BCE, to build a New Temple twice the size of the old one. The power of the culture was waning, however, and outlying regions broke away. By 200 BCE the Chavín period was over.

Chavín art was characterized by images of snarling animals, such as these fierce jaguars from a staircase at Chavín de Huántar.

THE OLMECS

📍 Gulf coast of Mexico ⏳ c.1800–c.400 BCE

The Olmec culture established itself in the lowlands of southern Mexico shortly after 1800 BCE. By around 800 BCE, their influence had spread over an extensive area of Mesoamerica, underpinned by a simple agricultural economy that was based on maize.

An Olmec relief of a priest making an offering to a deity, in the form of a feathered, crested rattlesnake.

OLMEC CENTRES

The first important Olmec centre was San Lorenzo in southern Mexico, which was at its height between 1200 and 900 BCE. The city seems to have had an advanced drainage system and its buildings, erected on earthen mounds and arranged around open plazas, included a temple and houses made of poles and thatch. There were also many monuments, such as giant carved heads, altar-like structures, huge sculptures of seated people, and depictions of a variety of animals, notably the jaguar.

Near the San Lorenzo site, at Cascajal, archaeologists have found a stone dating from around 900 BCE. It bears symbols that may be Olmec writing, and thus might represent the first writing system in Mesoamerica.

There is evidence of widespread destruction of monuments around 900 BCE, when the centre of San Lorenzo seems to have come to an end. The other major Olmec centre was the city of La Venta, near the border of modern Tabasco and Veracruz states, which had a much larger population than San Lorenzo. Thriving between 900 and 400 BCE, La Venta effectively took over from San Lorenzo as the principal Olmec settlement. As at San Lorenzo, colossal stone heads and jaguar figures and imagery have been found, as well as ceremonial and temple complexes, including a giant pyramid. The major buildings at the site were all precisely aligned, perhaps linked with ideas about astronomy. By around 400 BCE, the Olmec culture was in decline, although its influence persisted in regional cultures, especially that of the Zapotecs of Monte Albán (see p.155).

An Olmec stone statue, from La Venta, known as the "Governor". His elaborate dress implies that he was a ruler.

THE CLASSICAL WORLD

THE WORLD IN 700 BCE–600 CE

The millennium that followed 750 BCE saw much of the world's population incorporated into the great Classical civilizations of Eurasia – Greece, Rome, Persia, India, and China. These empires went on to reach unparalleled levels of sophistication and military effectiveness, and set models for administration and scholarship

The world in 1 CE

——— international border

········· undefined border

Han empire

Roman empire and client states

Empire of Pontus under Mithridates Eupator, c.100 BCE

Numidia under Masinissa from 201 BCE

Burebista's Dacian kingdom, 45 BCE

NOTE: Settlements in italics were not in existence in 1 CE but were significant during this chapter's era.

THE CLASSICAL WORLD IN 1 CE

By 1 CE, the Greeks – who had earlier controlled an empire that stretched to India – had been conquered by the Roman empire, which jostled for power with the Parthian (Persian) empire. China, unified in 221 BCE, was now ruled by the Han dynasty, while India was fragmented after the fall of the Mauryan empire in 185 BCE.

hat would be followed for many centuries. In Central and South
America, Africa, and Japan, new civilizations also emerged, in
many ways equally as advanced, but with a much smaller reach
than those of Eurasia. The Classical era also saw the birth of some
influential religions – Buddhism, Judaism, and Christianity.

The Roman empire had conquered the
whole of the Mediterranean coastline by
1 CE, and had also extended into Asia
Minor (in modern Turkey), Gaul (modern
France), and parts of Germany. Over the
next century it would take Britain, Dacia
(Romania), and parts of Mesopotamia,
reaching its maximum area.

PERSIA

From provincial beginnings, a dynasty of Persian kings – the Achaemenids – emerged to exert power across Asia from the Mediterranean to northwest India. Two centuries after a failed attempt to subdue Greece in the 5th century BCE, the tables turned when Alexander the Great's Macedonians overthrew Achaemenid rule. Persian power re-emerged under the Parthians and Sassanids, who, from the 220s CE, struggled bitterly with the Romans until the 7th century CE.

THE ACHAEMENID EMPIRE

W Asia, Egypt   550–330 BCE

According to Persian tradition, Cyrus (ruled 559–530 BCE), founder of the Achaemenid empire, had been a vassal of Astyages, ruler of the Median kingdom to the north of the Persian homeland. Cyrus defeated Astyages in 550 BCE, securing dominance over eastern Iran, and then captured Babylon in 539 BCE. His heir, Cambyses (ruled 529–522 BCE), extended the empire to Egypt, before a revolt by his brother Bardiya led to his assassination. In the following years, the influential king Darius I (ruled 521–486 BCE) occupied parts of Libya and northwestern India, and also tried to invade Greece, but a coalition of Greek states defeated him in 490 BCE. A decade later, in 480–478 BCE Xerxes (ruled 485–465 BCE) failed in a similar enterprise, and the Achaemenid rulers' impulse for expansion waned.

VULNERABILITY AND FALL

The 4th century BCE was dogged by bitter dynastic struggles that undermine the power of later rulers. The empire was increasingly reliant on foreign mercenaries and, because of its vast size, vulnerable to revolt and invasion. I ended in the 330s BCE, when Alexander the Great (*see pp.124–5*) defeated the last Achaemenid emperor, Darius III.

The tomb of Cyrus was built at Pasargadae, where he had established the first Achaemenid royal capital some time before 550 BCE.

PERSEPOLIS

The royal capital of the Achaemenid empire was Persepolis, founded by Darius I around 518 BCE and connected to an efficient system of royal roads. While the administration of government usually took place at the palace at Susa to the west, Persepolis lay at the heart of the Achaemenids' regal power.

A CITY OF TREASURES

Darius founded his new capital on a high plain around 80km (50 miles) southwest of the old Persian centre at Pasargadae. Builders levelled an artificial terrace of 135,000 sq m (33 acres) on which to erect a series of palaces and audience chambers. Largest of these was the *apadana*, a reception hall that may have been able to hold up to 10,000 people. On the stairway to the *apadana*, a series of reliefs depicted tribute-bearers from the empire's 20 provinces bringing offerings to the Persian ruler, for Persepolis may also have acted as the Achaemenids' central

A golden griffin bracelet that forms part of the Oxus Treasure, a fabulous hoard from the Achaemenid era found in 19th-century Afghanistan.

treasury. A huge Throne Hall was built under Darius I, and additions to the complex were still being made in the reign of Artaxerxes III (ruled 358–338 BCE). In 331 BCE, Alexander the Great captured Persepolis, and the next year a fire razed it to the ground.

Dignitaries from Medea bearing tribute approach the Council Hall at Persepolis. The ruined city is now a UNESCO World Heritage site.

PERSIAN RELIGION

📖 Iran   ⏳ c.1000 BCE–7th century CE

At the heart of the Persian religious system lay a fusion between traditional Iranian religions and the teachings of the prophet Zoroaster, who lived either around 1000 BCE or in the 7th century BCE. He preached a dualist faith in which the supreme god Ahura Mazda, the personification of good, engaged in a constant struggle with the spirit of darkness, known as Angra Mainyu. The Achaemenids may not have been pure Zoroastrians and they revered other Persian deities, too. Their successors, th Parthians, set up Zoroastrian fire altars throughout the empire, on which a flam burned constantly as a symbol of purity

Under the Sassanids (*see facing page*), from the 3rd century CE, Zoroastrianism began to take on the characteristics of a state religion, and followers of other faiths, which had previously largely been tolerated, suffered persecution.

A bas-relief sculpture of two *fravashis*. In Zoroastrian belief, these winged guardian spirits guide and protect people throughout their life.

PARTHIAN PERSIA

📖 Iran, Iraq   ⏳ 247 BCE–226 CE

In the 3rd century BCE, the Greek successors of Alexander the Great, the Seleucids (*see p.126*), controlled Persia, but their hold slipped, and in 247 BCE the Parthians began to throw off Greek rule. They took control of the silk routes from China, and then under Mithridates I (ruled 171–138 BCE) pushed westwards to annex most of the Seleucid lands in Mesopotamia. Parthia, though, was politically divided and its princes often established near-independent fiefs, undermining further attempts at expansion.

A valiant Parthian king hunts a lion with bow and arrow on this decorated silver bowl.

Made up of expert cavalrymen, the Parthian army was almost invincible an at Carrhae in 53 BCE crushed a Roman army, starting a long period of tension with Rome, particularly over Armenia. Pretenders to th Armenian throne often sought Roman suppo against the Parthian and it was one such appeal that almost led to the Roman emperor Trajan's conquest of western Persia in 116–117 CE The Parthians survived only to succumb to an internal revolt in the southern province of Pars in the 3rd century CE.

SASSANID PERSIA

📍 Iran, Iraq ⚔ 226–651 CE

arthian Persia (*see facing page*) collapsed
1 226 CE as a result of internal revolt.
ersia's resurgence came under the
assanids, whose first king, Ardashir I,
uled from 226 to 241 CE. The Sassanid
ings, ruling from a capital at Ctesiphon
n the banks of the Tigris, established a
10re centralized state than the Parthians,
nd easily held their own against the
omans to their west. By 238 CE, they
ad taken the border cities of Nisibis and
1atra, and, under Shapur I (ruled
41–272 CE), dealt the Romans a double
low, first defeating the emperor Gordian
I in 244 CE, then Valerian in 260 CE.
hapur looked set to overrun the eastern
oman provinces, but the local Arab ruler
f Palmyra, in Syria, held him back.

Over the next three centuries the
endulum swang between Roman and
assanid advantage in a region thickly
efended by fortified frontier cities.
hen, in the early 7th century, Khusrau
Parviz (ruled 591–628 CE) finally broke

the deadlock, taking Roman Syria,
Palestine, and Egypt by 619 CE. Yet the
Byzantine (eastern Roman) empire
fought back, undoing all of Khusrau's
victories by 627 CE. The exhausted
Sassanids then fell prey to Arab-Muslim
armies invading from the south and west.
Defeated at Qadisiya in 637 CE and at
Nehavand in 642 CE, the last Sassanid
king, Yazdegird III (ruled 632–51 CE),
retreated eastwards and died a fugitive
at Merv in Central Asia.

> ### SHAPUR THE GREAT
>
> Having fought for his father Ardashir
> against the Parthians, Shapur I succeeded
> to the Sassanid throne in 241 CE while in
> his mid-20s. Almost immediately, he faced
> a Roman invasion, but this collapsed, and
> the emperor, Gordian, was murdered.
> This disaster forced the remnants of the
> Roman army, now under Philip, to sue for
> peace. Shapur's victory over the Romans
> near Carrhae in 260 CE was even more
> spectacular. Shapur captured the emperor
> Valerian, and later had his body flayed,
> stuffed, and mounted as a grisly trophy.

rock-cut relief at Naqsh-e Rustam, near Persepolis,
ows a mounted Shapur I lording it over the
efeated Roman emperors Philip and Valerian.

GREECE

From unpromising beginnings in a collection of small and quarrelsome city-states, the Greeks entered an era of unparalleled creativity and surprising military success, seein off the might of the Persian empire and establishing coloni throughout the Mediterranean and Black Sea. Under Alexander the Great, the Greeks held political sway over most of the Near East, and even after Alexander's death the cultural influence remained powerful there for centuries.

ARCHAIC GREECE

📍 Greece   ⌛ 700–500 BCE

We know little about the era following the collapse of Greece's Mycenaean civilization in 1070 BCE (*see p.101*), because no written records survive. But by around 750 BCE, scattered clusters of villages throughout the Greek mainland, islands, and Ionia (Greek-settled Asia Minor) had grown into city-states, or *poleis*. Rivalry between the *poleis* was fierce, and fighting frequent; by 600 BCE, Sparta, Thebes, Corinth, and Athens were dominant. Governing systems varied from *polis* to *polis*. At first monarchy was most common, but in the 7th century BCE some city-states overthrew their kings and instituted "tyrannies": rule by autocrats from new families, such as the Pisistratids at Athens. A basic form of democracy emerged

side-by-side with this in Athens (*see p.1* beginning with the reforms of the grea law-giver Solon in around 594 BCE.

Despite continuing rivalry, some cultural factors united the *poleis*: belief in common deities and participation in common cultural events, such as the pa Hellenic games at Olympia. Philosopher mainly in Ionia, began to speculate on th nature of the universe, while a rich legac of poetry includes probably the first writ versions of Homer's *Iliad* and *Odyssey*.

Rows of marble lions on the island of Naxos were dedicated to the god Apollo in the 7th century BCE.

THE GREEK–PERSIAN WARS

Greece, the Aegean, W Asia Minor ☀ 499–449 BCE

499 BCE, the Ionian cities of western Asia Minor, with some assistance from Athens, staged a revolt against Persia, which had conquered the region in 546 BCE. The Persians were victorious, suppressing the rebels in 493 BCE, after which the Persian king Darius I (*see p.112*) resolved to teach the Greeks a lesson. This was a mistake of epic proportions. Having easily occupied the Greek islands and found ready collaborators among certain of the northern Greek cities, Darius's army landed near Marathon (a small town on the coast of Attica, northeast of Athens) in late summer 490 BCE. There, a phalanx of Athenian citizen-soldiers – with shields locked together to form a united front – and their allies from the city of Plataea kept the Persians in check, despite being greatly outnumbered. Although Marathon was a minor setback, the damage to Persian prestige was profound and they withdrew.

THE SECOND PERSIAN INVASION

The Persians were not to give up and the fight was renewed under Darius's successor, Xerxes, in 480 BCE. A shaky coalition of Greek city-states formed to combat the invasion, but despite heroic resistance by the Spartan king Leonidas at Thermopylae (in which all the Spartans perished), the Persians soon won over the important state of Thebes to their side and had Athens at their mercy. The city was put to the torch, but Themistocles, a politician, had by then persuaded his fellow Athenians to finance a naval fleet. This policy bore fruit

in the naval defeat of the Persians at Salamis, with Themistocles at the helm, also in 480 BCE. A further victory on land at Plataea (in 479 BCE) stiffened Greek resolve and forced the retreat of the main Persian force, and this signalled the end of Persian ambition on the Greek mainland. Although the war spluttered on in Ionia and the Aegean until 449 BCE, the Greeks, by defending their independence, had in effect already emerged as the victors.

Leonidas, the Spartan king, led an army of only 300 Spartans against Persian forces at the the battle of Thermopylae.

ATHENS AND DEMOCRACY

📖 Athens   ⏱ 594–338 BCE

The oldest and most stable democracy in ancient Greece developed in Athens, invoking the right of all citizens – a category excluding women, children, slaves, and foreigners – to participate in political decision-making.

At the start of the 6th century BCE, the reforms of the Athenian statesman Solon had diluted the aristocrats' power in favour of the citizen assembly (*ekklesia*), but it was only under the magistrate Cleisthenes (*c.570–c.507 BCE*) that the Athenian constitution began to approach its final form. He divided Athens into about 140 voting districts (*demes*), which were grouped together into 10 tribes. Each of these supplied 50 members annually to a council of 500, and this group supplied the 50-member group of council leaders (*Prytaneis*) to administer the government's daily affairs.

THE ASSEMBLY

The composition of the *Prytaneis* changed regularly so that no one held power for too long. The full *ekklesia* – with a quorum of 6,000 people – convened around 40 times a year, meeting on the Pnyx, a hill near the Acropolis, to vote on important matters, including the election of the city's generals (*strategoi*). Pericles (495–429 BCE), the most brilliant

orator in 5th-century BCE Athens, consolidated the power of the masses by compensating the poor for the time they spent attending the assembly.

DEMOCRACY AND EMPIRE

As Athens' power waxed, the attractions of holding office grew. Ostracism – a vote by the *ekklesia* to exile over-mighty politicians – aimed to curb the abuse of power by a few. Athenian defeats in the Peloponnesian War (*see p.122*) twice suspended democracy, which, although later restored, became a shadow of its former glory by the time the Romans took over Greece in the mid-2nd century BC

The Porch of the Caryatids, on the Acropolis of Athens, had to be rebuilt after being burned down by the Persians in 480 BCE.

> "A MAN WHO TAKES NO INTEREST IN POLITICS HAS NO BUSINESS HERE AT ALL."
>
> Pericles, 495–429 BCE

GREEK COLONIZATION

From the late 9th century BCE, the Greeks dramatically expanded their world by despatching colonists from cities in Greece to all corners of the Mediterranean and the Black Sea. This process continued for more than three centuries. Exactly why colonization was so important is unclear, but it may have been both a catalyst for trade and a pressure valve for excess population or political difficulties in Greece itself.

THE ACQUISITION OF LANDS

Although the Greeks had set up foreign trading posts, such as at Al Mina in Syria, their new colonies were fully fledged citizen communities. Among the earliest were those in eastern Sicily, including Syracuse, founded around 733 BCE. Shortly after this, colonization began in southern Italy, with cities such as Rhegium, Sybaris, and Croton springing up in a network so dense that the area came to be known as Magna Graecia ("Greater Greece").

The movement spread far to the south and west, founding Cyrene in North Africa around 630 BCE, and Massilia (modern Marseilles, in France) around 600 BCE. The Greeks first reached the Iberian Peninsula –

A silver coin from Catana (modern Catania), a Greek settlement in Sicily that was colonized around 720 BCE.

at Tartessus in modern Spain – in around 640 BCE. In the east, colonies spread up the coast of the Black Sea, from Byzantium to the Crimea, and to Trapezus (modern Trabzon) on the northern coastline of the Anatolian peninsula. By the late 6th century BCE, the Greek impetus for colonization had faded, and as the system of city-states in Greece itself came under strain, future Greek expansion would come largely under the patronage of Alexander the Great's Macedonian empire and its successor states.

The city of Ephesus, a Greek colony located on Turkey's western coastline, was established in an 11th-century BCE wave of Greek expansion.

The Parthenon, the great temple to the goddess Athena, was built at Athens in the mid-5th century BCE. The project was initiated by the city's leading statesman Pericles, and the work was partly overseen by Phidias, one of Classical Greece's greatest artists. It was completed around 432 BCE.

THE PELOPONNESIAN WAR

⚑ Greece, W Turkey, Sicily ⚔ 431–404 BCE

The Peloponnesian War, a bitter 30-year struggle, arose from the rivalry between the two most prominent Greek city-states, Athens and Sparta. Unlike the democratic constitution of its rival (*see p.118*), Sparta was governed by kings and a small military élite, moderated by five annually elected magistrates (or *ephors*). The mass of the population were *helots*, effectively serfs, with no political rights. In the mid-5th century BCE, Athens established an empire based on its maritime strength, bringing it into conflict with Sparta's land-based power.

THUCYDIDES

One of the first true historians, Thucydides (*c.*460–*c.*404 BCE) wrote a *History of the Peloponnesian War*, recounting events he had lived through. The speeches he put in the mouths of the protagonists are some of the masterpieces of Greek literature.

THE STAGES OF WAR

The initial pretext for war was the attempt in 432–431 BCE by Potidaea, an Athenian client-city in northern Greece, to break away from the Athenian empire. Sparta and its allies came to Potidaea's aid, but the Athenians initially held the upper hand. Sparta fought back, winning a great victory at Amphipolis in 422 BCE, and both sides agreed to observe a 50-year truce.

A helmet typical of the protective gear of the hoplites, the heavy infantry of the Greek armies.

Hostilities broke out again in 415 BCE, when the Athenians, encouraged by the extremist anti-Spartan statesman Alcibiades, sent a great fleet to Sicily, intent on absorbing Syracuse into their empire. The Spartans reacted by supporting the Syracusans, and Athens was sucked into a debilitating and ultimately unsuccessful siege of the city.

In 413 BCE, the Spartans destroyed the Athenian armada in Sicily but still the war dragged on. Finally in 405 BCE, at Aegospotami on the Hellespont, the Spartans captured most of the Athenian fleet while it was beached on shore. Deprived of their naval support, the Athenians could not resist a Spartan blockade, and in 404 BCE they surrendered, agreeing to the destruction of their defensive walls. Athens would never again be such a dominant force among the Greek city-states.

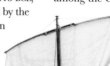

The Athenians' naval fleet included oared warships known as triremes. These vessels were fast and manoeuvrable, and were able to ram enemy ships.

CLASSICAL GREEK CULTURE

The Classical Greek city-states of the 6th to 4th centuries BCE gave birth to a civilization of extreme creativity, remarkable both for its uniformity of belief and culture, and its diversity of political systems. It has given us philosophers, artists, and playwrights whose works we still celebrate today.

Socrates (lived 469–399 BCE) revolutionized Greek thought, but his radicalism led to his execution.

RELIGION, ART, AND PHILOSOPHY

The possession of a common religion was a hallmark of "Greekness", and temples, shrines, and oracles to the principal gods – Zeus, their king; Hera, his wife; Apollo, the sun god – sprang up throughout Greece and the Greek colonies. Cult centres such as Olympia and Delphi became important pan-Greek gathering places and at some, in particular at Olympia, the Greeks held games in honour of the gods.

The temples the Greeks built to their gods are among the most breathtaking relics of the Classical age, and include the great marble temple of the Parthenon built on the Athenian acropolis between 447 and 432 BCE. Sculptors such as Phidias (born 490 BCE), who created the great cult statue of Athena for the Parthenon, are among the world's earliest named artists.

The Greeks excelled in the dramatic arts, too, with tragedies by Aeschylus, Sophocles, and Euripides, and comedies by Aristophanes, being performed at an annual religious festival, called the *Dionysia* in honour of the god Dionysus. Of equally profound and lasting influence was the work of Greek philosophers such as Socrates (*c.*469–399 BCE), Plato (*c.*427–347 BCE), and Aristotle (384–322 BCE), the first to apply rigorous logic in an attempt to understand the world, whose works were valued into the Middle Ages and beyond.

The art of vase painting reached new heights during the Classical period of Greece, often depicting scenes from myth.

THE CONQUESTS OF ALEXANDER THE GREAT

Greece, the Near East   336–323 BCE

In the 4th century BCE, Greece saw a struggle for power between several city-states, with first Sparta and then, from 371 BCE, Thebes emerging as the victor. From the early 350s BCE, the northern Greek state of Macedonia began to expand under an energetic and ruthless new king, Philip II. In 338 BCE, Philip, aided by his 18-year-old son Alexander, gained victory against the Thebans and their allies at Chaeronea. The other Greeks then rapidly submitted to Macedonian overlordship.

The young Alexander was not Philip's only son and his succession to the throne was by no means assured. Philip's assassination in 336 BCE has long been suspected to be at Alexander's prompting. Once his father was dead, Alexander moved with brutal speed to put down rivals and, in 335 BCE, suppress a Theban revolt.

THE INVASION OF PERSIA

Now secure on the Macedonian throne, Alexander embarked on an enterprise of staggering ambition: the invasion of the Achaemenid Persian empire. In 334 BCE, he led an army of some 50,000 across the Hellespont into Asia Minor – modern Turkey – with the initial intention of liberating the Greek cities there from Persian control. Disputed successions and rebellions had weakened the Achaemenid empire

The Temple of the Oracle, in the Siwa Oasis, Egypt, where Alexander came to consult the oracle of Zeus Ammon in 332 BCE.

In the 4th century BCE, but its ruler, Darius III, could still call upon resources vastly superior to those of Alexander. Nonetheless, Alexander, with tactical and strategic brilliance, and with more than an eye for his image as an all-powerful ruler, defeated a large Persian force at Granicus in 334 BCE, and then the next year bested Darius III himself at Issus in Syria. Utilizing the professionalism and manoeuvrability of his smaller forces against the vast, cumbersome Persian armies, he seemed unbeatable. Pausing to visit Egypt, he defeated Darius one final time at Gaugamela on the banks of the Tigris in 331 BCE. The fugitive Persian king was murdered the following year and Alexander took on the trappings of an oriental potentate, adopting Persian court dress and protocol and moving to secure all the former provinces of the Achaemenid empire.

FINAL CAMPAIGNS AND DEATH

Alexander spent 329 and 328 BCE suppressing revolts in the eastern provinces of Bactria and Sogdia, after which he pushed on into northwestern India, defeating the local ruler Porus at Hydaspes in 327 BCE. Finally, even his loyal Macedonians refused to go further. A long and gruelling return across desert terrain to reach central Persia, and the perceived influence of native Persians in Alexander's entourage, fuelled a series of mutinies. Then, in 323 BCE, aged only 32, the conqueror of the known world died of a fever at Babylon. His embalmed body was sent to Egypt, and his generals plotted to seize power for themselves, since, as he was still relatively young at the time of his death, Alexander had not chosen a successor.

A Roman-era mosaic showing Alexander riding his horse Bucephalus into battle, possibly at Issus in 333 BCE.

"HIS FRIENDS ASKED: 'TO WHOM DO YOU LEAVE THE KINGDOM?' AND HE REPLIED 'TO THE STRONGEST'."

Diodorus Siculus on the death of Alexander
(*Library of History*, XVII, 117)

THE SUCCESSORS OF ALEXANDER

 Egypt, Syria, Macedonia ⚔ 323–31 BCE

Alexander the Great's death in 323 BCE led to a long struggle for control of his empire. This began almost at once, for Alexander's wife Roxana was pregnant, and the army split between those wanting to see if she bore a son and those who supported the severely disabled half-brother of Alexander, Philip Arrhidaeus. In the end, the child was born male and as Alexander IV he ruled jointly with Arrhidaeus, who became Philip IV. However, this only masked the deep divisions between the generals, who then proceeded to carve out their own territories: Ptolemy in Egypt; Antigonus in Asia Minor; Lysimachus in Thrace; Eumenes in Cappadocia; and Seleucus in Persia. A series of wars between these *Diadochoi* (or "successors")

The Ptolemaic Greeks adapted Egypt's practice of mummification creating mummy portraits of the deceased in a western style.

erupted, which between 323 and 279 BCE gradually eliminated the weaker contenders.

DECLINE AND FALL

By 301 BCE, three main successor states survived – the Antigonids based in Macedonia, the Seleucids in Mesopotamia and Syria, and the Ptolemies in Egypt – together with a constellation of smaller statelets that fed off warfare between the big three. After Antigonus I of Macedonia was defeated by the others at Issus in 301 BCE and the other weaker states had been eliminated the tensions diminished and the three Greek kingdoms survived until they were successively swallowed up by the Romans: Macedonia in 168 BCE, a much-reduced Seleucid kingdom in 64 BCE, and finally, Egypt in 31 BCE.

The Greek city of Corinth in the Peloponnese was taken by the Romans in 146 BCE, marking the end of mainland Greece's independence.

HELLENISTIC CULTURE

Alexander's conquests left a large part of western Asia and North Africa in Greek hands. As part of his efforts to solidify his hold over this enormous territory, Alexander himself encouraged the foundation of Greek cities in the newly conquered lands, including most notably Alexandria in Egypt. These became the focus for the diffusion of Greek culture, known as Hellenism, throughout the East.

THE HELLENISTIC CITY

Greek-speakers were a definite minority in Alexander's empire and the successor states, but everywhere the cities bore the hallmarks of the mother country. These included temples built in the Greek fashion, a central marketplace and meeting space (or *agora*), and the gymnasium, which was not merely a place of exercise, but acted as a centre for Greek-style education where young men could study classic authors and obtain a sense of Greek culture.

DIVERGENCE AND DISSOLUTION

Although united by the Greek language, the Hellenistic cities and kingdoms did absorb eastern influences, notably in Egypt where the Greek-speaking kings ruled as pharaohs. Hellenistic art styles also travelled far to the east, influencing the Buddha figures of the Indian state of Gandhara in the 2nd century BCE. In science and literature, the Hellenistic Greeks continued the Classical tradition of creativity. The mathematicians Euclid (*c.*300 BCE) and Archimedes (287–212 BCE), the comic playwright Menander (342–293 BCE), and the historian Polybius (*c.*200–*c.*118 BCE) are a few of the influential figures whose work was absorbed by the Romans during their conquests of the Hellenistic lands, ensuring that Greece's cultural legacy lived on.

Antiochus I of Commagene (ruled 70–38 BCE) was ruler of a Hellenistic kingdom near Armenia and had this spectacular funerary monument built to himself in the Greek style.

ROME

From inauspicious beginnings as a small hill-top settlement in central Italy in the mid-8th century BCE, Rome survived turbulent early centuries to conquer the entire Italian peninsula – and then created an empire encompassing the whole of the Mediterranean world, parts of the Near East, and northwestern Europe. Rome's military and administrative strength allowed it to endure several crises until, finally, waves of barbarian invaders brought about its fall.

EARLY ROME

📕 Central Italy ⚔ 753–509 BCE

According to tradition, Rome was founded on 21 April 753 BCE by Romulus, said to have been the son of the god Mars. Like most of the traditions associated with Rome's earliest days, it is hard to disentangle truth from myth.

ROME UNDER THE MONARCHY

The first settlement, atop the Palatine Hill overlooking the Tiber river, was almost indistinguishable from the area's myriad small 8th-century BCE villages. Crucially, Rome seems to have been more receptive to outside influences than its rivals, and particularly to that of the more developed Etruscan civilization that flourished in central Italy. Some of Rome's early kings – there were seven by tradition – may have been Etruscan. The story goes that the second king, Numa Pompilius, established many of Rome's religious traditions, while Ancus Marcius in the 7th century BCE expanded the territory of the fledgling city-state through a series of localized struggles against the neighbouring Latin tribe.

In this Renaissance mosaic, Romulus, the legendary founder of Rome, and his twin brother Remus suckle from the she-wolf said to have raised them.

From the reign of Tullus Hostilius (673–642 BCE) comes the first evidence of a Roman senate, in the form of the Cura Hostilia building. The accession of his heir, Tarquinius Priscus – probably an Etruscan – in 616 BCE brought a new dynamism to Rome. However the next king, Tarquinius Superbus, was a tyrant, and his unpopular rule led to his deposition in 509 BCE by a group of aristocrats. From this point onwards Rome was a republic.

THE ROMAN REPUBLIC

Italian peninsula   509 BCE–c.250 BCE

When Rome became a republic in 509 BCE, it retained some of the elements of the old monarchical system, including the Senate – an amorphous group of elders with decision-making powers. Every year, a citizen assembly elected two consuls, whose dual authority was an attempt to prevent despotism.

A statue of a lictor, who carried the fasces, the bundle of rods and axes that symbolized the power of the Republic's magistrates.

THE STRUCTURE OF SOCIETY

The early Republic was dominated by the conflict between two groups of citizens, the patricians (elite landowners) and the underclass of plebeians. The patricians monopolized political power, and provided all the members for the Senate. Plebeian resentment of this hierarchy led to a series of violent conflicts, which in 494 BCE resulted in the creation of a plebeian assembly with

The Temple of Castor and Pollux (centre right), in the Forum at Rome, was where the patricians met to discuss the government of the early Republic.

two elected tribunes (who later came to have a veto over laws passed in the Senate). The codification of Roman laws in the "Twelve Tables" in 445 BCE eased other restrictions on the plebeians; and in 366 BCE the first plebeian consul was elected.

THE EXPANSION OF ROME

After a Roman victory against a league of Latin neighbours in 496 BCE, a series of "colonies" of Roman citizens set out from Rome, gradually forming a network of Roman-controlled or -inclined cities throughout central Italy. In 396 BCE, the Romans captured the leading Etruscan city of Veii, and by the early 3rd century BCE had also defeated the Samnites to begin the extension of their power into south-central Italy.

THE PUNIC WARS

📖 Italy, Spain, N Africa   ⚔ 264–148 BCE

Rome expanded its influence through the Italian peninsula during the first half of the 3rd century BCE, gradually creating conflict with other powers in the Mediterranean. Most notable among these adversaries were the Carthaginians, who, from their capital in modern Tunisia, North Africa, controlled an empire that included Sicily. War broke out with Rome in 264 BCE over a quarrel between Carthaginian-allied Syracuse and the Mamertines of Messana, also in Sicily, who appealed to the Romans for help. The fighting – known as the First Punic War – dragged on for 23 years, involving land battles and sieges that generally went the Romans' way, and more decisive naval battles ending in a Roman victory at the Aegates Islands in

"WE HAVE BEEN DEFEATED IN A GREAT BATTLE."

Marcus Pomponius announcing the disastrous Roman defeat at Lake Trasimene, 217 BCE

241 BCE. Carthage was stripped of its territories in Sicily, but compensated by going on to form a new empire in Spain.

A Second Punic War broke out in 218 BCE, when the Spanish city of Saguntum, fearing absorption by the Carthaginian general Hannibal,

appealed to the Roman Senate
for aid. The Romans demanded
Hannibal's surrender; the
latter responded with an
invasion. Crossing the
Alps – with an army
that included war
elephants – in the
winter of 218 BCE,
he soon defeated the
Romans at Ticinus
and Trebia, in the
north of Italy.

HANNIBAL'S
ITALIAN CAMPAIGNS

After this victory,
many Cisalpine Gauls
– Celts settled around Milan – flocked
to Hannibal's cause. A further Roman
defeat at Lake Trasimene, in central
Italy, in 217 BCE led to the deaths of
around 15,000 Romans. The next year
the Romans suffered an even greater

A Carthaginian stela from the tophet, or
graveyard, at Carthage. The horn-shaped
symbol is for Tanit, a moon goddess.

disaster farther south at
Cannae, where their
general Varro rashly
allowed his army to
be outflanked and
encircled by the
Carthaginian cavalry,
and then massacred.

Many cities then
defected from the
Roman cause, but
General Fabius
Maximus kept
Hannibal away from
Rome and halted
the momentum of his earlier victories.
In 207 BCE, Hasdrubal, the brother of
Hannibal, was defeated and killed at
Metaurus, northeast Italy, and five years
later a Roman counterstrike by Scipio
forced Hannibal to return to Africa.

romanticized view of the battle of Zama in
202 BCE, where Scipio finally defeated Hannibal and
destroyed his last army – 20,000 Carthaginians died.

THE END OF THE PUNIC WARS

In October 202 BCE, the Carthaginians
were defeated, and were stripped of
their Spanish territories and reduced
to a small territory around Carthage.
Yet Rome was not satisfied, and in 149 BCE
used a pretext to begin a Third Punic
War. With no land army to speak of,
Carthage was soon besieged, and was
stormed in 148 BCE. The Romans razed
the city, deported its people, and finally
annexed its remaining territory.

HANNIBAL

Born *c.*247 BCE, Hannibal became
Carthage's leading general during the
Second Punic War and commander-in-
chief in 221 BCE. His plan to lead an army
across southern Gaul (modern France)
into Italy was a bold one and he showed
tactical genius in a string of victories
against Rome. Yet he lacked strategic
vision and became bogged down once
Roman resistance stiffened. After the war,
he was chief magistrate of Carthage, but
Roman fears of a Carthaginian revival led
to his exile in 195 BCE. He died in *c.*183 BCE.

THE END OF THE REPUBLIC

📍 Italy, Gaul   ⚔ 137–44 BCE

During the 2nd century BCE the political situation in Rome became increasingly tense. Then, in the 80s BCE, the city was hit by a political and military struggle for power between Marius, the reformer of the Roman army, and Sulla, a politician who, after Marius's death, became Dictator, or sole ruler, in 82 BCE.

POMPEY AND CAESAR

That year, Sulla killed more than 500 of his opponents and packed the Senate with his supporters. After Sulla's death in 78 BCE, another popular general, Pompey, rose to power. For 15 years Pompey excelled at his political role, and bolstered his military reputation with several victories in the East. Yet, in 60 BCE, increasing factional violence led him to broker a three-way alliance, called the "First Triumvirate", with the rich financier

JULIUS CAESAR

Born in 100 BCE, Caesar became Roman consul in 59 BCE. He created a new province for Rome in Gaul from 58 to 52 BCE and this brought him great political power and popularity – which ultimately led to his murder in 44 BCE.

Crassus and a rising military star – Julius Caesar. This collapsed in 49 BCE and led to civil war between the factions of Caesar and Pompey.

THE FIRST CIVIL WAR

Caesar pushed Pompey out of Italy and in 48 BCE, defeated him at Pharsalus in Thessaly. Pompey was murdered in Egypt but his partisans fought on until, in 46 BCE, Caesar triumphed, becoming Dictator for life. Fearing Caesar would make himself king, a group of republicans, including Marcus Brutus, assassinated him. However, their murderous act failed to save the Republic from collapse.

The assassination of Julius Caesar was carried out by only a small group of senators; most fled or waited to see what actions the assassins would take next.

THE FIRST EMPEROR: AUGUSTUS

Italy, the Mediterranean   44 BCE–14 CE

After Julius Caesar died in 44 BCE, his chief lieutenant Mark Antony, attempting to manipulate public opinion, allied himself with Octavian – Caesar's 18-year-old adoptive son – in order to exploit his family connections and gain political support. Antony miscalculated, for Octavian, although young, was even shrewder than Caesar. He remained in alliance with Antony and Lepidus – who played the role of financier in this "Second Triumvirate" – for only as long as it took to defeat the armies that had been raised by Brutus and Cassius, Caesar's murderers.

In 32 BCE, war broke out among the Second Triumvirate. At Actium the following year, Antony was defeated, and both he and his mistress, the Egyptian pharaoh Cleopatra, committed suicide. Octavian did not seek immediate revenge against Antony's partisans. Nor did he have himself made dictator, as Caesar had done. Instead, he manipulated republican politics to acquire supreme power without seeming to usurp the Senate's authority.

FROM GENERAL TO EMPEROR

In 27 BCE, Octavian was granted a special form of authority, known as *proconsular imperium*, for 10 years, which in effect allowed him to act as he chose in all provinces where the army was currently based. In the same year, he took the title "Augustus". In 23 BCE, Augustus acquired the permanent power of a tribune of the plebeians, making him invulnerable to legal action. Although he did not refer to himself as an emperor, this was the position he now held.

MILITARY EXPANSION

Augustus secured the empire's borders along the Danube river and sent armies into Germany, which he was about to conquer when a disastrous defeat in 9 CE caused a retreat from the Elbe river back to the Rhine. His last years saw a defensive stance along existing frontiers.

> "WARS, BOTH CIVIL AND FOREIGN, I UNDERTOOK, BOTH ON SEA AND ON LAND!"
>
> Inscription of Augustus (the *Res Gestae Divi Augusti*) from Ankara, Turkey, *c.*14 CE

During Augustus's reign (27 BCE–14 CE), the production of images of the emperor, such as this statue from Prin, Italy, became a vital part of imperial propaganda.

THE GOVERNMENT AND ARMY

🏛 Roman empire ⏳ 27 BCE–*c.*200 CE

The empire over which Augustus assumed rule in 27 BCE was very different from the Rome of the early republic. Now ruling over territories that stretched from the Iberian peninsula in the west to Syria and Armenia in the east – as well as large parts of North Africa – the Roman government faced far greater challenges than the old, informal systems could manage.

GOVERNMENT AND THE PROVINCES

At the centre of Roman government, the role of the emperor remained ambivalent. Certain emperors, such as Claudius (ruled 41–54 CE), liked to flatter the old senatorial class with the fantasy that the emperor was just a superior sort of senator; others, such as Nero (ruled 54–68 CE), tended to much more direct, despotic, and capricious rule. The early empire had little in the way of a public service, and many important roles, such as running the

The legions' superior equipment and training made them more than a match for non-Roman enemies.

imperial treasury, were assumed by freedmen (former slaves). Provincial governors, however, who administered Rome's imperial territories, were almost all senators. The Roman government raised its revenue mainly through indirect taxes on sales or death duties. Some was spent on the upkeep or building of Roman roads, which linked the main cities of the empire but as much as 80 per cent was spent on the army.

THE ROMAN LEGIONS

Augustus had inherited 80 legions, which he cut to 28, each comprising around 5,000 men. Supporting them, and directly answerable to the emperor, were infantry and cavalry regiments of non-citizens (called "auxiliaries"). The total manpower may have been around 300,000. The legions formed a formidable strike force, almost irresistible in open combat. Their engineering expertise meant they could also conduct siege warfare expertly and take on large-scale construction projects, such as roads and fortifications. Over time the army formed its own power base, through the imperial guard (the Praetorians) based in Rome and the legionary frontier garrisons, and became as much a cause of internal instability as a guardian against outside threat.

The Roman road network, much of it paved, was vital for the rapid transit of Roman armies.

THE EARLY EMPIRE

 Roman empire 14–69 CE

Augustus died in 14 CE, having chosen Tiberius, the son of his wife Livia by her first marriage, as his heir. Tiberius was 55 when he came to the throne, having proved himself a capable general and administrator, yet he was never truly popular and, in the middle period of his reign, became dominated by Sejanus, the prefect of the Praetorian guard. In the last seven years of his life, Tiberius shut himself away in his palace on the island of Capri, leading to an atmosphere of frustration and stagnation in Rome.

A cameo showing Augustus's wife Livia and her son Tiberius, who became the second emperor of the Julio-Claudian dynasty (27 BCE–68 CE).

THE POST-TIBERIAN EMPERORS

Tiberius's rule gave way to a new, young emperor, Caligula (ruled 41–54 CE), whom the governing class welcomed with open arms. However, Caligula's latent instability and dangerous temper led to his assassination and replacement by a man the Praetorians thought would be a pliant weakling: Claudius (ruled 41–54 CE). Yet Claudius proved shrewd; he sponsored large-scale public works that included a new port at Ostia and, although not a military man, ordered the conquest of Britain from 43 CE. Claudius was succeeded by the mercurial Nero (ruled 54–68 CE), who, unsuited to power, became mired in corruption. When an army revolt broke out in Spain in 68 CE, civil war erupted, leading to four emperors in a single year, until finally Vespasian (ruled 69–79 CE), a tough-minded general, emerged triumphant.

The Colosseum, the empire's largest amphitheatre – begun under Vespasian and completed by his son Titus – housed spectacular gladiatorial shows.

THE EMPIRE AT ITS HEIGHT

🏛 Roman empire   ⌛ 69–180 CE

Vespasian's accession in 69 CE inaugurated a new dynasty, the Flavians, during which stability at first seemed to return to the empire. Vespasian's economic reforms filled the treasury, and new territory was occupied in northern Britain and parts of Germany and Asia Minor. But Vespasian's son Titus, succeeding him in 79 CE, was to die after just two years. Titus's younger brother Domitian (ruled 81–96 CE) made a promising start, but degenerated into tyranny and was assassinated, possibly on the orders of the Senate itself.

A marble frieze from Ephesus showing emperors Hadrian, Marcus Aurelius, and Lucius Verus. Hadrian has a beard, a Greek fashion he made popular at Rome.

THE "GOLDEN AGE"

The Senate then put forward one of their own as emperor, a 70-year-old, much-respected senator named Nerva. To ensure the succession, Nerva adopted

Hadrian's Wall is a monumental barrier stretching 80 Roman miles (117km) across northern Britain, built to defend the province against barbarian incursions.

the talented governor of Upper Germany, Trajan as his son, beginning a practice that would see the next emperors, Hadrian, Antoninus Pius and Marcus Aurelius, all adopted by their predecessor. This gave the empire a golden age – a century of stability.

TRAJAN AND HADRIAN

Nerva died after just two years, and Trajan soon began to enlarge the empire's frontiers, seizing Dacia (modern Romania) in two wars between 101 and 106 CE; the mercantile kingdom of Nabataea (largely in modern Jordan) in 106 CE; and much of Mesopotamia (now Iraq) from 115 to 117 CE. These victories brought massive booty that helped fill the treasury. Yet the eastern territories were not secure, and when Trajan died in 117 CE were already in revolt.

It was perhaps this that persuaded Trajan's successor, Hadrian, to be more cautious. He started no new wars of expansion and built defensive works in

TRAJAN

Trajan (ruled 98–117 CE) was from an Italian family that had moved to Spain, making him the first emperor with strong non-Italian roots. He made his name while fighting under Domitian along the Rhine in the 80s CE and as governor of Upper Germany. Popular with the army, he was an obvious choice to succeed Nerva. He showed astonishing energy in expanding the empire's frontiers, an achievement he celebrated in Trajan's Column, which was built beside the new Forum that Trajan commissioned in central Rome.

Germany and Britain. Hadrian travelled widely, seeing more of his domains than any emperor before him, and established a permanent imperial council that reduced the importance of the senate.

THE LATER ANTONINES

Hadrian adopted the elderly Antoninus Pius (ruled 138–161 CE), intending the latter's young protégé Marcus Aurelius to succeed him quickly. Yet Antoninus lived for another 23 years in a tranquil reign that saw few revolts. When Marcus Aurelius finally succeeded in 161 CE, ruling jointly with Lucius Verus – another of Hadrian's circle – he faced a series of crises. A plague between 168 and 169 CE killed thousands, including Lucius Verus, and the empire became entangled in the Marcomannic Wars against barbarians on the Danube, whom the emperor could never wholly subdue. Before his death in 180 CE, Marcus had chosen his own son Commodus to succeed him, the first son ever born to a ruling emperor. However, like Domitian's, Commodus's rule was unstable and would spell the end of Rome's golden age.

"HE WAS THE FIRST TO CONSTRUCT A WALL... WHICH WAS TO SEPARATE BARBARIANS AND ROMANS."

The *Historia Augusta* on Hadrian's building of the Wall

CRISIS AND REFORM

🏛 Roman empire   ⌛ 180–305 CE

The emperors of the late-1st and 2nd centuries BCE had handpicked their successors. Marcus Aurelius was the first emperor for a century to have an adult male son, Commodus – but he proved a lesson in the weakness of hereditary succession. Commodus was rash and fickle. His behaviour sparked a series of military revolts that led finally to the triumph of Septimius Severus (ruled 193–211 CE), the governor of Upper Pannonia (in modern Hungary). A firm and active ruler, Severus seemed set to restore confidence in the empire.

This Roman coin from c.218 CE bears a depiction of the controversial emperor Elagabalus.

He divided large provinces into two, to avoid any one governor having too much military power, and he conquered territories in Mesopotamia. Yet his successor Caracalla (ruled 211–217 CE) proved more capable of making enemies than ruling – he murdered his brother and co-emperor Geta. Caracalla himself was murdered in 217 CE near Carrhae (in modern Turkey) by an army faction fearful that he would execute them.

"THIS MAN... OVERTURNED THE WHOLE ORDER OF THINGS: FOR HE CHOSE THREE OTHER MEN TO SHARE THE IMPERIAL GOVERNMENT WITH HIM."

Lactantius, speaking of Diocletian, *De Mortibus Persecutorum*

THE BEGINNING OF THE END

For a while the empire teetered between hope and farce. Emperor Elagabalus (ruled 218–222), who was a Syrian high priest of dubious morality and Septimius Severus's great-nephew, scandalized and alienated Senatorial opinion. His cousin Severus Alexander, brought in to replace him, lost the support of the army and was murdered in Germany in 235 CE. This ushered in a half-century of chaos, when emperors, brought to power and then murdered by their own soldiers, barely lasted more than a few years.

For 20 years, Gaul broke away to be ruled by its own emperors. More dangerously, after the Persians captured the emperor Valerian (ruled 253–260 CE) in 260 CE, the city of Palmyra in Syria established its own eastern empire under Queen Zenobia and her son Vaballathus. To add to the official empire's woes, new groups of barbarians, including the Goths, pressed down from eastern and central Europe toward the Rhine and Danube frontiers. Aurelian (ruled 270–275 CE) finally defeated Zenobia and brought Gaul back into the empire, but he had to abandon Dacia and still barbarians such as the Franks and Alamanns raided Gaul, and the Goths pillaged across the Danube. It was all too much for a single emperor to deal with.

THE TETRARCHY

Nominated by the army as emperor in 284 CE, Diocletian chose an old military colleague, Maximian, to rule jointly with him. In 293 CE, he further subdivided the imperial office by selecting two junior emperors (or "Caesars") to reign with the two senior ones (or "Augusti"). Now that there were, in effect, four emperors – in a system known as the Tetrarchy – facing a challenge in one area of the empire no longer meant abandoning problems elsewhere. Diocletian also reformed the army, recruiting smaller legions better adapted to combat the barbarian incursions. In an unprecedented act, in 305 CE Diocletian abdicated voluntarily due to ill health, and retired to his palace at Spalatum (modern-day Split, Croatia).

The detailed carving on this imperial Roman marble sarcophagus shows Roman soldiers battling the Goths during the 3rd century CE.

CONSTANTINE AND THE NEW CHRISTIAN EMPIRE

▥ Roman empire ⚔ 306–337 CE

When Emperor Diocletian retired in 305 CE, his system of four rulers (the Tetrarchy; *see p.139*) fell apart. The new college of four emperors excluded Maxentius, the son of Diocletian's colleague Maximian, and Constantine, the son of a Caesar in the Tetrarchy. The result was chaos, and by 310 CE there were no fewer than seven competing emperors. In the civil war that followed, Constantine won out, first defeating Maxentius at the Battle of Milvian Bridge in 312 CE, and then finally, in 324 CE, becoming the unchallenged sole emperor.

CONSTANTINE'S REFORMS

Constantine divided the army between a mobile field force (the *comitatenses*) and the frontier garrisons (the *limitanei*). The bureaucracy became much more formal, hierarchical, and efficient, headed by a praetorian prefect. The new emperor also founded a new capital city at

CONSTANTINE

Born in the 280s BCE, Constantine took a long road to Christianity. He claimed to have received a vision before the Battle of Milvian Bridge in 312 BCE, and after this he honoured the Christian god. He was finally baptized on his deathbed in 337 CE.

Constantinople (now Istanbul), modelled on Rome with its seven hills, from which to administer the eastern empire.

CONSTANTINE AND CHRISTIANITY

Constantine is best known for his support of Christians, following their persecution under Diocletian. He decreed freedom of worship by the Edict of Milan in 313 CE, sponsored the first large churches in Rome, and allowed bishops to take an increasingly important role in politics.

Constantine (right) gives the symbols of imperial rule the Phrygian bonnet, canopy, and Lateran Palace – to Pope Sylvester I in this 12th-century fresco.

THE FALL OF THE ROMAN EMPIRE

Roman empire ⚔ 337–476 CE

Following the end of the reign of Constantine (*see facing page*), the Roman empire became overwhelmed, by an increasingly complex and inflexible political and bureaucratic system; by pressure from barbarians along the frontier; and by a series of ineffective rulers in the western empire. A division between eastern and western empires meant that after 395 CE, no one ruled both halves together as sole emperor. No longer able to absorb the outsiders pressing against its frontiers, by the mid-4th century the empire was on the defensive, and the catastrophic destruction of the eastern field army by the Goths at Adrianople in 378 CE almost led to a total collapse.

THE EMPIRE FRAGMENTS AND FALLS

The barbarians moved from raids to seizing land on which to settle, reducing the number of citizens the empire's central authorities could tax and put to work. Much of the eastern empire was shielded from this – it was the western half that lost much of Spain and Gaul to the Visigoths and the Franks in the first part of the 5th century CE, and the grain-rich provinces of North Africa to the Vandals between 429 and 439 CE. Britain broke away from the empire in 410–411 CE, and Rome itself was sacked – the first time it had fallen to a foreign enemy in almost 800 years – by the Goths in 410 CE. The westward movement of the Huns from the 430s meant that the empire was facing challenges on too many fronts, and the

A Roman legionary fights a Germanic warrior. Almost invincible at its height, the Roman army later suffered a decline in resources that left it vulnerable.

ineffective rules of Honorius (395–423 CE) and Valentinian III (424–455 CE) did nothing to stem the tide.

A series of short-lived western emperors became the puppets of the conquering German chieftains. In 476 CE, the Germanic general Odovacar demanded land in Italy for his soldiers. When the boy-emperor Romulus Augustulus defiantly refused, he was deposed. Odovacar did not bother to appoint a new emperor, ruling as a king himself, and as a result, the Roman Empire in the west was at an end.

The barbarians fought the Romans with primitive weapons, such as this francisca, a Frankish throwing axe.

> "THE IMPERIAL CITY... WAS DELIVERED TO THE LICENTIOUS FURY OF THE TRIBES OF GERMANY AND SCYTHIA."
>
> Edward Gibbon, *The Decline and Fall of the Roman Empire*, on the sack of Rome by the Goths, 410 CE

CELTIC AND GERMANIC EUROPE

Although it is through the Romans that we know much of the history of the peoples who bordered their empire, many of these groups had rich traditions of their own. The Celts thrived in central and western Europe until the Romans conquered Gaul and Britain, while the Germanic tribes migrated west and south, finally conquering much of the western Roman empire in the 4th and 5th centuries CE.

THE CELTS

Central and W Europe   500 BCE–83 CE

Fierce warriors and skilled ironworkers with a love of feasting, the Celts swept across large areas of Europe from around 500 BCE, dominating much of the centre and west of the continent by 200 BCE. Although they were not one cohesive people, they displayed a uniform culture (known in its later phase as the La Tène culture). It was typified by organization into tribes or clans, village or nomadic life, and a strong warrior tradition, with warfare common between tribes. Tribes or even individual families occupied hill forts – hilltops encircled by a ditch and bank – for protection.

BELIEFS AND DECLINE

The Celts relied on oral transmission of culture through bards and poets; their religion, governed by the priestly class (the Druids), had a complex pantheon. Metalworking was a speciality and was used to embellish objects from household utensils to battle-chariots.

From the 50s BCE, the Romans pushed the Celts to the margins of Europe: tribes in Gaul were conquered by Julius Caesar, and the British Celtic kingdoms were subdued between 43 and 83 CE. Only in Scotland and Ireland did Celtic culture survive.

A detail from the Gundestrup Cauldron, a silver vessel dating from around the 1st century BCE, perhaps used in ritual

SUCCESSOR STATES TO ROME

W and S Europe   418–774 CE

s the power of Rome waned,
arbarian groups began to
ut down permanent roots
n former Roman territory
nd establish more settled
orms of government.
he most successful of the
ew states to emerge was
e kingdom of the Franks.
t first a confederacy of
ermanic tribes in the area
' modern Belgium and Holland,
e Franks were united under the
adership of Clovis (ruled 481–511 CE),
ho conquered most of the old Roman
ovinces of Gaul. Clovis also converted
Catholicism, a sharp divergence from
e practice of many other Germanic
ngs, who had adopted a new form of
hristianity called Arianism (after the
h century priest Arius), which was
garded as heretical by other Christians.
lovis's descendants, the Merovingians,
led France until the 8th century CE.

Alaric, whose name means "king of all", was
the Goths' greatest war leader. He led his
tribe in a sack of Rome in 410 CE.

The Goths, who had
threatened the Roman
empire in the late 4th and
early 5th centuries CE, split
into two groups: Visigoths
and Ostrogoths. The
former settled in southwest
France under Theoderic I,
but in 507 CE were pushed out
by the Franks, finally settling in Spain.
The Ostrogoths, having stayed in the
Balkans, moved to Italy in 488 CE at the
urging of Zeno, the eastern Roman
emperor, who wanted revenge against
Odovacar – the deposer of the last
western emperor, in 476 CE. By 493 CE
Zeno was king of Italy, beginning
a dynasty that lasted until the
eastern Romans completed their
reconquest of Italy
in 554 CE.

e Battle of Tolbiac, recreated in this 19th-century
inting, saw the Frankish king Clovis emerge
torious against a group named the Alamanns.

PEOPLE OF THE STEPPES

The steppes – grasslands that stretch from Eastern Europe to China – have been home to nomadic and semi-nomadic groups for millennia. The history of the steppe people has been influenced by geography, while their migrations brought clashes with a range of powers, from the Romans in the west to the Parthians, Sassanids, and India's Mauryan empire in the east.

THE SCYTHIANS

Central Asia   6th century BCE–2nd century CE

First mentioned in historical sources in the 6th century BCE, the Scythians seem to have migrated from central Asia to southern Russia at about that time. Their warriors fought with bows, arrows, and axes, and most often on horseback. They sported felt caps, and, except for some members of the aristocracy, wore little or no armour.

CULTURE AND WEALTH

The Scythians possessed sizeable territories at different periods, although tracing them is made difficult by the tendency of Greek and Latin authors to refer indiscriminately to groups from the steppes as "Scythians". One group, the "Royal Scyths", controlled an area around southern Russia, where stunning grave finds of gold artefacts point to a well-developed culture.

By the 2nd century CE, the Scythians had been marginalized by Sarmatians – Iranian-speaking newcomers – who were in turn defeated by the Huns (*see facing page*) in the 4th century CE.

A gold comb from a grave at Socha *kurgan*, depictin Scythians in battle; the mounted warrior bears equipment far superior to that of the soldiers on foo

The Scythians have left a large number of pyramid-shaped burial mounds, known as *kurgans*, in the south Russian steppes, particularly at Pazyryk. In thes they buried the mummified bodies of rulers, together with their horses and lavish grave-offerings of gold.

THE HUNS

S Russia, central Europe, the Balkans   4th and 5th centuries BCE

rst mentioned in the 370s CE, the
uns, who became the most feared
d loathed of Rome's barbarian
emies, were most likely a composite
oup whose numbers were
elled by those they defeated.
   In 434 CE, the Hunnish
ng Rua died and his
n Attila initiated an
creasingly aggressive

policy, ravaging much of the Balkans and
sacking a string of cities in 441–442 CE
and again in 447 CE. In 451 CE, the Huns
turned west towards the rich lands of
Gaul, but were defeated by a
last-ditch alliance of Romans
under the general Aëtius
and his barbarian allies.
   Undaunted, Attila
moved into Italy the
following year, but was
deflected from an attack
on Rome, possibly by
an outbreak of plague.
After their father's death
the year after that, Attila's sons
failed to keep the empire together, and
within 10 years the Huns had almost
disappeared as an organized group.

ATTILA

Attila (ruled 434–453 CE) was
known as "The Scourge of
God" because he devastated
swathes of Christian Roman territory.
A ruthless warrior, he died as a result of
overindulgence at his wedding feast.

THE KUSHANS

Central Asia, N India   1st century BCE–c.350 CE

ssibly originating in a nomadic group
own to the Chinese as the Yuezhi,
e Kushans (or Kusanas) dominated
region of northern India around the
njab from the early 1st century CE.
   The Kushan empire reached its zenith
der Kanishka (c.78–100 CE), who ruled
tually all of northern India, including
e great cities of Ujjain and Pataliputra.
der great pressure from the Sassanid

Persians (*see p.115*) from the 220s CE, the
Kushan empire fragmented and the rise
of the Guptas to their south in the 320s
CE finally put an end to their rule.
Kushan art, influenced by Greece and
Buddhism (to which they converted),
is most notable for its elegant statues.

Although influenced by Zoroastrianism, the Kushans
converted to Buddhism and built temples such as this
4th-century CE example at Takht-i-Rustam, Afghanistan.

INDIA

From the 4th century BCE, northern and central India came to be dominated by a series of empires, beginning with the Mauryan, which reached its greatest cultural flowering under the rule of Ashoka, a great promoter of Buddhism. After an interlude of Kushan rule, the Guptas then emerge to dominate India for 150 years, before attacks by the barbarian White Huns led to the region reverting to a collection of smaller kingdoms.

CHANDRAGUPTA AND THE RISE OF THE MAURYANS

N and central India   c.321–185 BCE

Around 321 BCE, Chandragupta Maurya (ruled c.321–298 BCE) toppled the Nanda dynasty of Magadha, the most prosperous state in north India, to found the Mauryan empire.

MAURYAN RULE

By 303 BCE, Chandragupta had defeated the Seleucids, rulers of Persia, and had secured areas around modern Herat and in Baluchistan. He presided over a thriving agricultural state backed by a powerful army. His son Bindusara (ruled c.298–272 BCE) may have extended the Mauryan empire into south India, and his successor Ashoka (ruled c.268–232 BCE) conquered Kalinga (in modern Orissa) in 261–260 BCE. On Ashoka's death, the empire broke into western and eastern parts and, despite a brief reunification around 223 BCE, was gradually reduced to its heartland in Magadha. The assassination of the last emperor, Brihadratha, in 185 BCE brought the Mauryan era to an end.

The cave complex at Ajanta in Maharashtra contains paintings that span the period of time from the 2nd century BCE to the Guptas in the 6th century CE.

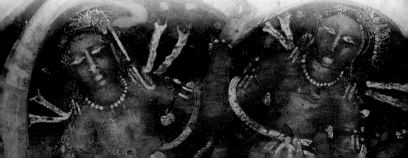

ASHOKA AND BUDDHISM

India ⌛ 268–232 BCE

fter a particularly bloody battle at
ayala in the state of Kalinga, where
e rivers ran red with the blood of the
ain, the Mauryan ruler Ashoka (*see
cing page*) is said to have been stricken
ith remorse and converted to Buddhism.
259 BCE, he toured his domains,
preading the Buddhist message of
amma, or moral principles, and ordered
e construction of stone pillars bearing
dicts that promoted the Buddhist creed.
e also sent missionaries abroad.
lthough Ashoka's reign was a period
peace and prosperity, subsequent
Iauryan rulers were more concerned
ith war than with religion.

metal relief of a symbol –a group of four lions –
at Ashoka chose to top many of the inscribed
lars he erected during the tour of his empire.

GUPTA INDIA

India ⌛ c.320–c.570 CE

fter the Mauryans (*see facing page*), the
ungas briefly ruled central India until
BCE. Thereafter, save for a century of
ushan dominance in the late 1st and
rly 2nd centuries CE, no one group
ominated as large an area as the

Mauryans, until Chandragupta I (ruled
c.320–330 CE) captured the old imperial
capital of Pataliputra, resulting in the
emergence of the Gupta empire
around 320 CE.

Under Chandragupta II (ruled
c.376–415 CE), the empire reached its
greatest extent, defeating the Saka
satraps (governors) who had ruled
western India, and expanding eastwards
into Bengal. Under Kumara Gupta
(ruled c.415–455 CE), incursions by
the Hephtalites (or "White Huns")
undermined the empire. By the mid-6th
century CE, it was reduced to a small
area around Maghada and then, around
570 CE, it disappeared entirely.

Carvings from the temple complex at Udayagiri in
Orissa, India. Possibly begun in the 2nd century CE,
the temples were in use into the Gupta period.

WORLD RELIGIONS

From the first millennium BCE, religions spread across huge areas. Hinduism and Buddhism made their way across Southeast Asia, while the Middle East saw the expanding influence of Judaism, followed by Christianity and Islam. By the 7th century CE, Hinduism and Buddhism were in retreat, and Christianity and Islam had taken root throughout the Roman and Sassanid Persian empires.

HINDUISM

By the 6th century BCE, the ancient religion of India focused on three main gods: a remote deity called Brahma; Vishnu the creator; and Shiva the destroyer. Around 500 BCE, the main form of worship was Brahmanism, and about this time great epics such as the *Mahabharata* and *Ramayana* were composed. Hindu beliefs spread as far as Java (where they gave rise to the lavish temple complex at Prambanan in the 9th century CE), Bali (where they survive still), Angkor in Cambodia, and Champa in modern Vietnam.

Reverence for Shiva the destroyer became one of the principal expressions of Hinduism, especially in southern Asia

BUDDHISM

A royal prince born in northeast India around 563 BCE, Siddhartha Gautama turned his back on his wealth to develop Buddhism. Promoting an ascetic way of life and a set of moral values rather than belief in a god, Gautama (the Buddha) taught that the only way to escape *samsara*, the cycle of death and rebirth, was to achieve moral perfection. Initially finding great success under the Mauryan ruler Ashoka in the 2nd century BCE, Buddhism became almost extinct in India, but spread into China and Japan, becoming established there from the 7th century CE.

MONOTHEISTIC FAITHS

Judaism, the first monotheistic religion to spread widely, evolved from an older, ritualistic form attributed to Moses. By the time of the Roman empire, Jewish communities had become dispersed throughout the Mediterranean. Despite intermittent persecution, Judaism has never lost its status as a world religion.

Christianity began as an offshoot of Judaism in the 1st century CE, but then became a distinct faith focused on the belief that Jesus Christ, the Son of God, died to atone for human sin. It endured waves of repression, notably under the Roman emperors Domitian in the late 1st century CE and Diocletian in the early 4th century CE. Yet once Emperor Constantine (ruled 306–337 CE) decreed its toleration in 313 CE, it became the empire's official religion and spread throughout the Roman world, reaching Germany, Russia, and Scandinavia by the 10th century.

The last principal monotheistic religion to emerge was Islam in Arabia in the 7th century CE, spread by the prophet Muhammad. His supporters proclaimed that he had received a divine revelation, encapsulated in the Qur'an. Arab armies inspired by Islam swept through the Near East and North Africa, reaching Spain by 711 CE.

This 4th-century Christian artefact is a bronze lamp in the form of a boat carrying St Peter and St Paul.

The stupas and Buddha images constructed around 800 CE at Borobudur in Java are among the world's most expressive images of Buddhism.

CHINA

By the 5th century BCE, China had disintegrated into a number of competing kingdoms known as the Warring States. The state of Qin conquered these one by one, and had defeated them all by 221 BCE under Qin Shi Huang, the first emperor of a united China. He brought a period of stability and prosperity to China, but the Qin dynasty did not survive for long. Around 200 BCE the Han seized power and would rule China for some four centuries.

THE WARRING STATES

China   481–221 BCE

The Zhou dynasty that followed the Shang (*see p.105*) was the last of the pre-imperial dynasties. The Zhou lasted longer than any other dynasty in Chinese history, but from around 722 BCE, it disintegrated into a number of independent states. From 481 BCE, China entered the Warring States period, when a series of conflicts between the minor territorial overlords led to a process of gradual consolidation. By the 3rd century BCE, there were just seven competing states, the most powerful of which was the state of Qin.

In 356 BCE, the chief minister of Qin, Shang Yang, established a new political philosophy – known as Legalism – based on rule of law, with a new legal code that diluted the power of the nobles and increased that of the ruler. The whole power of the state was directed towards warfare, with all adult males being registered for military service. By about 230 BCE, Qin was ready to begin the conquest of its remaining rivals.

A bronze lei, or wine vessel, from the Warring States period. Despite the political chaos that characterize this time, it also saw cultural achievements.

THE FIRST EMPEROR

📕 China ⬚ 246–206 BCE

In 246 BCE, Qin Shi Huang ascended to the throne of Qin. An energetic and ruthless ruler, from 230 BCE he set about the absorption of all the other Chinese states, completing the process with the conquest of Qi in 221 BCE. Having secured his position as the "First Emperor", Qin Shi Huang began a series of reforms to consolidate his rule.

THE FIRST EMPEROR'S REFORMS

Under the guidance of his chief minister Li Si, Qin Shi Huang put into place Legalist reforms, abolishing feudal fiefs and decreeing the adoption of a standardized written script and the establishment of official measurements for weights and lengths. In 213–212 BCE he ordered the burning of books that criticized his policies, and conducted a purge of scholars, executing some 450 of them.

An inscription celebrating the unification of China by Qin Shi Huang in 221 BCE, in the script he ordered the whole country to use.

Qin Shi Huang reinforced China's frontiers: his general Meng Tian constructed a defensive wall in the Ordos region of Inner Mongolia (the forerunner of the Great Wall of China); and he also had the Straight Road built, which ran 800km (500 miles) from the capital Xianyang to the Ordos region, to allow for the rapid transport of troops. He also sent troops to conquer new lands in Guangdong.

THE END OF QIN

Eventually, Qin Shi Huang's energies waned and he became obsessed with securing his own immortality. By the time the First Emperor died in 210 BCE, China was afflicted by popular uprisings and factional plotting at court. Although Qin Shi Huang had claimed his dynasty would last for endless generations, by 206 BCE Xianyang had been burned and Ziying, the last Qin emperor, had been deposed.

Near the burial chamber of Qin Shi Huang's mausoleum stood an army of terracotta warriors, intended to defend the First Emperor in death.

HAN CHINA

China   206 BCE–220 CE

The fall of Qin was accompanied by a complex civil war from which Liu Bang, who had captured the Qin capital of Xianyang in 206 BCE, finally emerged victorious after a decisive battle four years later at Gaixia (in modern Anhui province). He assumed the imperial title of Gaozu and began the Han dynasty, which went on to rule China for some 400 years.

A later Han glazed ceramic model of a watchtower, displaying precise architectural detail. Such pieces were often intended for the tombs of important personages.

THE RULE OF GAOZU

Gaozu established a new capital at Chang'an, simplified court ritual, and, as a counterpoint to the old regime's political philosophy of Legalism (*see p.150*), encouraged the rise of Confucianism, with the emperor becoming the centre of a state cult. He also strengthened central rule with the organization of commanderies (military districts) intended to avoid any return to the chaos of the Warring States. Gaozu did,

however, tolerate the existence of ten semi-independent kingdoms to the north and east Han China retained a strong bureaucracy, with a formal hierarchy established by the end of Gaozu's reign, in a decree of 196 BCE.

THE HEIGHT OF THE HAN

Under Wudi (ruled 141–87 BCE the Han reached the height of their dominance. Wudi cut down the remaining powers of the aristocrats, relying on a hand-picked civil service; in 124 BCE an academy was inaugurated for future office holders. In 115 BCE he also established state granaries to keep prices under government control.

Wudi expanded the borders of the Chinese empire, fighting a long series f wars against the nomadic Xiongnu the north from 114 to 91 BCE, but chieving greatest success in the ortheast, where he established four ommanderies in Korea after 128 BCE, nd in the south, where he occupied arts of Guangdong, Guangzi, and orth Vietnam from 111 BCE. Yet the tter part of the emperor's reign was arred by his increased introspection nd his search for immortality. His uccessors were generally feeble and the ourt became dominated by eunuchs. he economy was undermined by nancial mismanagement and the state eakened by widespread tax evasion.

WANG MANG AND THE LATER HAN

1 9 CE, Wang Mang, the regent for succession of child emperors, usurped e Han throne. He ordered large private states to be broken up and began a rogramme of reforms, including strictions on slavery. But a catastrophic mine that had begun when the Yellow iver changed its course in 11 CE led to idespread peasant uprisings, and in 5 CE the Han were restored under uang Wudi. A new capital was set up Luoyang, but it took 11 years to put own a series of pretenders who claimed e right to succeed Wang Mang. The Han never regained its former power.

LIU BANG

Born into poverty, Liu Bang was initially a supporter of Xian Yu, an aristocrat opposed to Qin rule. Yet he managed to build his own army and capture the Qin capital Xianyang in 206 BCE. He never learned to read, and distrusted court protocol, making him popular outside court circles.

A revolt by the Yellow Turban religious sect from 184 to 186 CE, and the brutal massacre of hundreds of court officials by a ruling eunuch clique in 189 CE, fuelled the chaos. In 196 CE, the general Cao Cao assumed power, ruling through a Han puppet, but after his death in 220 CE even this pretence was dropped and the dynasty ended.

China's first emperor had sought to protect a unified China within a protective wall, but internal conflicts became a greater threat in the centuries to follow.

THE AMERICAS

During the "Classic" period, from around 200 BCE, several cultures flourished in Central America. The Olmecs were superseded by a number of new groups, including the inhabitants of Teotihuacán, the Zapotecs of the Mexican Gulf coast, and, especially, the Maya civilization, which spread throughout southern Mexico, the Yucatán, and Guatemala. In South America, regional cultures, including Moche, Nazca, and Paracas, succeeded the Chavín of Peru

TEOTIHUACÁN

Central Mexico 2nd to 7th century CE

The greatest Classic period Mexican city was Teotihuacán. From the 2nd century CE, this enormous urban area was laid out on a grid pattern, its major axis (the "Avenue of the Dead") running 6km (3½ miles) roughly north–south. At the centre of the axis was a large palace complex, and at its northernmost reach the great Pyramid of the Moon. At its southern end was the Pyramid of the Sun, built with some 1.2 million cubic metres (42 million cubic feet) of sun-dried bricks and stone.

By the 4th century CE, Teotihuacán's population was as high as 200,000, and its influence spread throughout Mexico. Its wealth derived from its control of the resources of the fertile Valley of Mexico and domination of trade routes as far as the Gulf and Pacific coasts of Mexico. Teotihuacán ware has been found as far afield as the Maya city of Kaminaljuyu in Guatemala.

THE END OF TEOTIHUACÁN

At some time during the 7th century CE, Teotihuacán's palaces were burned and its temples defaced. What crisis precipitated the vandalism is unknown. The abandoned city was thereafter treated by successive Mexican cultures, including the Aztecs, with almost reverential awe.

A series of spectacular murals was found at Teotihuacán. This one shows a priest linked to the cult of a rain god or storm deity.

THE ZAPOTECS

 Valley of Oaxaca, Mexico   *c.*500 BCE–*c.*900 CE

round 500 BCE, a powerful ew regional culture, the apotecs, arose in the 'alley of Oaxaca near 1exico's Gulf coast, ased around the city f Monte Albán. Built n a levelled hilltop site, ne city flourished for 1ore than 1,000 years.

One of the city's most vocative monuments is ne Temple of the)anzantes, containing undreds of carvings of 1en in distorted postures, heir disarticulated limbs and closed eyes robably indicating that they represent ot dancers ("Danzantes") as was once nought, but the chiefs of rival cities illed by Monte Albán's rulers. Carved lyphs on the Danzantes stones reveal nat the Zapotecs used a sophisticated alendar and writing system.

A Zapotec deity is depicted on an urn dating from Monte Albán's Classic period, around 200 to 350 CE.

THE CLASSIC PERIOD AND DECLINE

By its Classic period, from 200 CE, Monte Albán had a population of about 25,000, with a series of satellite settlements on the lower ground surrounding the city. Around 170 subterranean tombs of nobles have been found from this period. Between 150 BCE and 150 CE, the city grew further with the building of a grand main plaza. A series of inscriptions here that feature upside-down disembodied heads are likely to refer to expansion by conquest. But by 900 CE, the urban centre of Monte Albán was mostly deserted. No one knows why the site was abandoned, but it was to remain empty until partial reuse by the Mixtec culture in the 12th and 13th centuries CE.

lost early Mesoamerican cultures played a very milar, ritualized "ball game" on spectacular sloping r terraced courts; this is the court at Monte Albán.

CLASSIC MAYA CULTURE

▣ Central America ⧖ *c.*300–*c.*900 CE

At its height (some 600 years referred to as the "Classic" period) the Maya culture flourished over a wide swathe of Central America, especially the Yucatán peninsula and Guatemala's jungle-clad lowlands. At its heart stood a number of important cities. Originally ritual centres, many grew into populous city-states. The Maya built huge, often pyramidal stone temples, such as those at Tikal in Guatemala, and showed a great talent for carved stone and stucco (plaster) reliefs, with some especially fine examples at Palenque in Mexico.

MAYA CULTURE

Maya cities featured palaces, open plazas, and terraces, as well as courts where the Maya people played their sacred ball game. Religious ritual played a major part in Maya life. The Maya practised a form of "auto-sacrifice", in which they pierced their own body parts to release blood as an offering to the gods, but more extreme reports of human sacrifice seem to be unfounded.

One of the pyramidal Maya temples at Palenque in Mexico, a city whose power reached its zenith under the rule of K'inich Janaab' Pakal from 615 to 683 CE.

The Maya developed a sophisticated writing system using some 800 characters, or glyphs. They also had a complex calendrical system, featuring a 260-day sacred year and a 365-day solar year.

MAYA HISTORY

Before Maya glyphs were deciphered in the 20th century, little was known of the history of the various city-states, such as Tikal and Palenque. But the glyphs have revealed an area riven by constant war, with unstable dynasties making rapid conquests and then vanishing into obscurity. The city of Yaxchilán, for example, produced one of the greatest Classic-period kings, Bird Jaguar IV (ruled 752–768 CE), who conquered a number of neighbouring lords and erected many new buildings, but within a generation of his death the city had stagnated.

EARLY SOUTH AMERICA

Peru *c.*500 BCE–*c.*600 CE

From around 500 BCE, a number of regional cultures began to supplant Peru's Chavín culture (*see p.106*). The Paracas people, who flourished in southern coastal Peru between 500 BCE and 200 CE, adopted many elements of Chavín iconography, including the feline representations that appear on their pots. The dry climate, which allowed bodies to be mummified, also preserved beautiful textiles, lavishly decorated with mythical creatures and more earthly animals. The largest cache of mummies, around 430, was found at Wari Kayan on the Paracas peninsula, all wrapped in textiles and accompanied by grave goods such as gold ornaments.

Perhaps the most famous of the Nazca desert images (or geogylphs), the spiral-tailed monkey is reminiscent of the spider monkeys found in Peru's jungles.

THE NAZCA

The Nazca culture flourished in the south of Peru from around 200 BCE to 500 CE. While largely a village-dwelling people, the Nazca did construct some imposing architectural complexes, such as the monumental religious centre at Cahuachi, which dates from around 100 CE. Although their textiles, metalwork, and pottery are of high quality, they are better known for the vast drawings that they made in the desert. They created a range of animal pictures and abstract representations by clearing stones from the desert surface and exposing the subsoil to create lines. The patterns, some of them many kilometres long, can be fully seen only from the air. Spectacular examples include a depiction of a

hummingbird sucking nectar, a plant, and a monkey with a coiled tail. Their precise purpose is unknown.

THE MOCHE

In Peru's northern valleys, the Moche came to dominate from around 100 CE. Talented craftsmen, they constructed large pyramids, known as *huacas*, and are particularly noted for their fine textiles, metalwork, and pottery. From great centres such as Huaca del Sol, with its flat-topped pyramids, the Moche rulers held sway over a predominantly agricultural society. Then, from around 300 CE, larger urban centres arose, the Moche expanded into southern regions, and indications of large-scale warfare appear (often depicted on the pottery). In the late 6th century CE, environmental disasters such as drought and flooding seem to have undermined the Moche's stability, and their culture collapsed.

Typical Moche cups, this one in the form of a fox-headed human, feature a "stirrup" handle/spout.

THE MEDIEVAL WORLD

THE WORLD IN 600–1450

Following the collapse of the western Roman empire in the 5th century CE, civilization in Europe fell behind the rest of the world for almost a thousand years. In this period China proved to be politically strong and technologically innovative under the Tang and Song dynasties, while much of the Middle East and

The world in 1300

—— international border

········ undefined border

▨ Byzantine empire

▨ England and possessions

▨ Aragon and possessions

▨ Venetian Republic and possessions

▨ Denmark and possessions

▨ France

▨ Castile

▨ Portugal

▨ Mongol empire on death of Genghis Khan 1227

▨ controlled by Khwarizm Shah 1219

—— Holy Roman empire

NOTE: Settlements in italics were not in existence in 1300 but were significant during this chapter's era.

THE MEDIEVAL WORLD IN 1300

By 1300, large parts of Eurasia were dominate by the Mongols. Areas of northern India, Nor Africa, and the Middle East were controlled b various Muslim rulers, such as the Mamluks i Egypt. In Mexico, the empire of the Aztecs was just beginning to expand, while the Incas had only just settled around Cuzco in Peru.

orth Africa was united under an Arab empire inspired by the
ew religion of Islam. The Americas, India, and Southeast
sia were also dominated by distinctive cultures. However, from the
te medieval period movements began to emerge in Europe that
ould ultimately lead to European domination of the globe.

The feudal monarchies of England and
France had consolidated into large
regional states by 1300, but conflict
between popes and emperors prevented
this process in the rest of Europe. In
Spain, the Christian states of Castile and
Aragon had reconquered much of the
peninsula from Muslim emirates, leaving
only Granada outside their control.

EAST AND SOUTHEAST ASIA

The early Middle Ages saw the rise of sophisticated new cultures and centralized states in east and southeast Asia: Japan, Korea, Angkor (Cambodia), Pagan (Burma), and Dai-Viet (Vietnam) all flourished under new kingdoms. China, after a period of disunity, reunited under the Tang dynasty in 618 (and their Song successors from 960), and reached astounding technological and artistic heights.

CHINA DISUNITED

🏳 China   ⚔ 221–618 CE

In 221 CE, the Han dynasty that had ruled China for 400 years (*see pp.152–3*) collapsed amid a welter of uprisings. China split into the Three Kingdoms: the Wei in the north, the Shu in the southwest, and the Wu in the southeast. Their rivalry is recounted in the great 14th-century Chinese novel *The Romance of the Three Kingdoms*, but in truth there was little romance about it, and the struggle left China debilitated by warfare.

A guardian deity at the Jinci temple, Shanxi province. The temple was restored and enlarged during Wei rule.

THE RISE OF THE SUI

The Wei conquered the Shu in 264 CE and, under a dynasty called the Western Chin, overcame the Wu in 280 CE, but the period of unity was brief. Under pressure from northern nomadic groups called the Xiongnu and Xiangbei, the Western Chin buckled, their capital Luoyang was sacked, and China fell apart, with the Sixteen Kingdoms ruling the north, and the Six Dynasties holding sway over the south. Finally, the north of China was united in 577 CE, and in 588 CE Yangdi – first emperor of the Sui dynasty – launched an invasion of south China. Only a matter of months later, the last Southern Chin emperor surrendered his capital at Jiankang (modern Nanjing), and China's three centuries of disunity was over.

TANG CHINA

China 618–907

In 617, Li Yuan, a frontier general, rose up against the Sui dynasty (see facing page), which was exhausted following an ill-fated invasion of Korea. Capturing the Sui capital Chang'an in 618, by 624 Li Yuan had secured all of China and ruled as Gaozu, the first emperor of the Tang. The dynasty is associated with prosperity, especially under Gaozu's successor Taizong (ruled 626–649).

TANG RULE

Taizong set up state schools and colleges and reintroduced the Han system of examinations for those wanting to work in official positions. Tang armies expanded into central Asia, defeating the Turks at Issyk Kul, in modern-day Kyrgyzstan, in 657 and advancing as far west as the borders of Persia.

The head of a colossal Buddha statue, some 71m (233 ft) tall, carved on a cliff near Leshan around 713 during the early Tang dynasty.

GAOZU (LI YUAN)

From a noble family, Li Yuan served as a general during the Sui attack on Korea in 613. When Emperor Yang was killed in a military coup in 618, Li Yuan took advantage of the chaos to push aside the last Sui emperor and seize power himself.

China attained a new level of cultural influence, with Chang'an, the terminus of the Silk Road, bringing in traders from across Asia, while painting and literature reached greater heights of sophistication. Late in the reign of Xuanzong (712–756), however, aristocratic factionalism led to a large-scale rebellion led by An Lushan in 755. Although this was finally put down in 763, the Tang never regained their authority, and in 907 the last Tang emperor, Ai, was killed by one of his generals. China split apart once more.

> "HAVE I NOT HEARD THAT PURE WINE MAKES A SAGE, AND EVEN MUDDY WINE CAN MAKE A MAN WISE?"
>
> from *Drinking Alone in the Moonlight*, by Tang "god of poetry" Li Bai, c. 710–762

SONG CHINA

◫ China ✇ 960–1279

The first half of the 10th century was a period of disunity for China. A succession of Five Dynasties ruled the north, while the south fragmented into Ten Kingdoms. Zhao Kuangyin, a general under the Later Zhou, the last of the Five Dynasties, usurped the throne in 960 to found the Song dynasty.

SONG PROSPERITY

Under the Song, China was reunited and entered a period of economic achievement, introducing the first paper currency in 1024 and developing new methods of rice farming that doubled output. A series of waterways improved China's infrastructure,

A Song Yaozhu-style vessel, delicately carved in a fashion typical of the dynasty.

and a fairer system for awarding the *jinshi* degree for officials overhauled the bureaucracy, so that a wider range of people could rise through the ranks.

Ladies of the Song court are shown ironing silk in this painting by the eighth Song emperor Huizong, a patron of the arts and an accomplished artist himself.

THE DECLINE OF THE SONG

In 1068, the emperor of the time, Shenzong, entrusted his minister Wang Anshi with the task of implementing radical reforms. Wang Anshi needed to raise money. He imposed a government monopoly on tea and challenged wealthy families who evaded taxes. To reduce the cost of the standing army, he ordered every household to supply men for a local militia. This measure was highly unpopular and Wang Anshi was dismissed, but the dynasty was weakened. Then in 1125, the Jurchen, semi-nomads from Manchuria, captured the capital Kaifeng and the Song court fled south. The southern Song emperors, based at Hangzhou, could never regain control over the north. The dynasty was culturally dynamic, developing Neo-Confucianism – which stressed self-cultivation and conformity to Confucian ideals – but it was enfeebled politically and militarily.

MONGOL AND MING CHINA

China ⚰ 1279–1644

1279, the southern Song were overrun
the Mongol armies of Kublai Khan
e pp.166–7). The Jin of northern China
d already been pushed aside by the
ongols in 1234, so China became
ited under the Mongol rule of the
an dynasty. The Mongols imported a
litary elite whose cultural differences
m the native Chinese hindered
egration. By the 1350s, dissatisfaction
th Yuan rule led to a series of revolts,
cluding, from 1351, that of the Red
rban Army. From the ranks of this
my rose Zhu Yuanzhang, who
tfoxed his rivals in a complex civil
r to seize power as the first Ming
peror, known as Hongwu, in 1368.

INA UNDER THE MING

e Ming ruled China for some
0 years, presiding over the growth
a vigorous urban culture. Emperor
ngwu reformed the army and the
xation regime, instituting a system of

The Pavilion of Myriad Springs in the Imperial
Garden of the Forbidden City, Beijing, which was
built in 1535 under the Ming dynasty.

secret agents to cement his rule. In 1403,
Emperor Yongle transferred the capital
from Nanjing to Beijing, and dispatched
a number of ambitious maritime
expeditions, led by the eunuch Zhen He,
that reached as far as east Africa. Later
emperors, however, were weaker and the
reforming instinct of the first rulers gave
way to inactivity and conservatism. By
the mid-17th century, the Ming's hold on
power had become brittle.

HE EMPEROR YONGLE

he third emperor of the Ming dynasty,
ongle ascended the throne after
verthrowing his older brother Jiangwen in
403. He oversaw an expansive phase in
Ming history, sending expeditions north to
mash the remnants of the Yuan, and in
406 dispatched an army south that
rushed the rulers of Vietnam and
bsorbed it as a Chinese province. At his
ew capital of Beijing, Yongle also
onstructed the vast
palace complex of the
orbidden City.

The Forbidden City, situated in Beijing, China, was constructed under Emperor Yongle of the Ming dynasty between 1406 and 1420. For almost five centuries, until the fall of the Qing dynasty in 1912, it served a dual role as the home of the emperor and the centre of Chinese government.

THE MONGOLS

Central Asia, E Europe, China, SE Asia   1206–1405

Before the early 13th century, a number of nomadic groups to the north and west of China periodically entered the settled regions. Some were defeated in battle, others contained, and others still assimilated into Chinese culture. The Mongols were one of these groups, but were hopelessly disunited until the leadership of Temüjin, who took the title Genghis Khan in 1206. Proclaiming his supreme rule, he welded together the Mongol clans, whose domination of the steppes and neighbouring lands would continue for more than a century.

A set of Mongol knives, part of the arsenal of weaponry with which Genghis Khan's army spread terror as it swept aside all opposition.

THE MONGOL CONQUESTS

By 1218, Genghis had overcome the Kara Khitan khanate of central Asia and he then unleashed a devastating six-year campaign against the Khwarezmid empire that controlled much of modern Iran and Afghanistan. It was during this time that the Mongols earned their reputation as merciless fighters, sacking the Silk Road cities of Samarkand and Bukhara and slaughtering the populations of any town that dared resist. The Mongols, excellent horsemen who were highly mobile and able to strike with speed, proved formidable enemies even for well-organized states.

Genghis died in 1227, and in 1229 Ogedei, who had inherited the title of "Great Khan", sent the Mongol armies into China, pushing the Jin (*see p.165*) out of the north of the country by 1234. Ogedei then despatched his horde westwards, overrunning almost the whole of Russia, including Kiev, its most important city, by 1240. Still the Mongol appetite for territorial aggrandizement seemed unabated and the following year their defeat of a Polish–German army at Legnica, Poland, struck terror in those further west, who thought their turn would come next.

GENGHIS KHAN

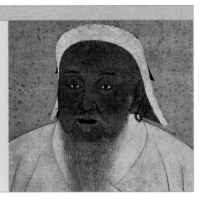

Born in 1162 as Temüjin to a family of minor chieftains, Genghis Khan spent much of his childhood as a precarious semi-outlaw. He earned a military reputation in minor skirmishes against the Chinese, eventually securing a leading position among the tribes. In 1206, he was proclaimed Genghis Khan, or "universal ruler", going on to command a feared army of more than 200,000 men. He is thought to have died following a riding accident in 1227, and was buried according to custom in an unmarked grave in Mongolia.

"IN MILITARY EXERCISES I AM ALWAYS IN FRONT AND IN TIME OF BATTLE I AM NEVER BEHIND."

Words attributed to Genghis Khan by a Chinese monk, c.1224

the death of Ogedei in 1241, however, caused the Mongol army to withdraw while the Mongols chose a successor.

LATER MONGOL RULERS

Mongke, who was selected as Great Khan in 1251, campaigned in northern China and against the Abbasid caliphate (see p.181) in the Middle East, sacking Baghdad in 1258. Shortly after his death in 1260, the Egyptian Mamluks (slave soldiers) defeated a small Mongol army at Ain Jalut, puncturing the Mongols'

reputation for invincibility. In the 1270s, Kublai Khan concentrated his attentions on the south of China (see p.165), and the Mongols ruled China until 1368. They dominated central Asia for a century after that, but the only real resurgence in their power came under Tamerlane, from 1370 to 1405, who united a large part of central Asia and very nearly destroyed the Ottoman Turkish empire (see p.183).

The citadel of Aleppo in Syria, which was captured by the Mongols in spring 1260, marking the high point of their success in the Near East.

EARLY JAPAN

📖 Japan   ⌛ 5th century BCE to 551 CE

The earliest recognized Japanese culture, the Jomon – who were predominantly hunters and fishermen – transformed under Chinese influence into the Yayoi culture around the 5th century BCE. Yayoi people lived in small farming communities in square or circular pit dwellings with thatched roofs. They were expert potters and stonemasons, and began a long tradition of Japanese metalworking, especially in bronze. From around the middle of the 3rd century CE, the Yayoi began to build large stone burial chambers and huge earthen tomb mounds (or *kofun*). Paintings found within these tombs, showing warriors wearing elaborate armour, indicate a powerful aristocracy.

Terracotta figures or *haniwa* were ritually placed around Yayoi burial mounds.

THE YAMATO

Japan's villages gradually coalesced into larger communities and, in the 4th century CE – possibl[y] under the influence of Korean refugees fleeing from a Chinese invasion in 369 – a larger kingdom emerged in southern Japan, on the Yamato plain. From then until the 6th century CE, the Yamato kings unified Japan.

THE ASUKA AND NARA PERIODS

📖 Japan   ⌛ 552–794

The arrival of Buddhism in Japan in 552 CE marks the beginning of the Asuka period. The regent Shotoku Taishi (ruled 572–622) founded the great monastery at Horyuji, and promoted Chinese models in politics, art, and religion. In 710, the Japanese capital was fixed at Nara, and Buddhism became more dominant in court life, especially during the reign of Shomu (724–749), who ordered the erection of the Great Buddha figure inaugurated at Nara's Todaiji temple in 752. Shomu was the first emperor to retire and become a Buddhist monk. Buddhism became so powerful that in 784 anti-Buddhist factions moved the imperial court north to Nagaoka to distance it from the old capital's monasteries. A decade later it moved again, this time to Kyoto.

The Gojunoto (five-storeyed) pagoda in the Horyuji temple complex, founded by Shotoku in the 6th century, is the oldest wooden pagoda in Japan.

THE HEIAN PERIOD

Japan   **794–1185**

In 794 the Japanese court moved to Kyoto, and the 400 years that followed is known as the Heian period. It was marred early on by a struggle to put down a rebellion in northern Japan. The rebellion was finally crushed around 801 by Tamura Maro, who was consequently honoured with the title *sei tai-shogun* ("barbarian-crushing general"), the first holder of the title in Japanese history. In 858, Fujiwara Yoshifusa became regent for the young emperor Seiwa, beginning a domination of the court by the Fujiwara family that would last for more than 300 years.

A painted scroll illustrating a scene from *The Tale of Genji*, a novel of Japanese courtly life.

JAPAN UNDER THE FUJIWARA

The most powerful of the Fujiwara regents was Michinago, who held sway from 995 to 1027, assisted by the marriage of four of his daughters to successive emperors. The Fujiwara period saw great cultural achievements, among them the *The Tale of Genji* – written, unusually, by a female author, the Lady Murasaki Shikibu – which encapsulates beautifully the refined aesthetic taste of the period.

After Michinago, the Fujiwara's power declined somewhat and an emperor named Go-Sanjo briefly managed to dispense with a Fujiwara regent. Under his successor, Shirakawa (ruled 1072–84), the curious practice of "cloistered emperors" (*insei*) emerged, whereby the emperor would abdicate in favour of a child successor and retire to a monastery but still, to some extent, direct affairs from there. This did nothing to temper the growing powers of warring clans, who were rivals to the Fujiwara. The tensions erupted into the Gempei Wars (1180–1185), a bitter struggle for dominance between the powerful Minamoto and Taira families.

This fine sculpture of a fierce guardian king, created during the Fujiwara period, is typical of the high level of craftsmanship of the time.

THE KAMAKURA AND MUROMACHI SHOGUNATES

Japan   1185–1573

In the early 1180s, the Gempei Wars racked Japan until Minamoto Yoritomo triumphed after a great naval victory at Dan-no-Ouro in 1185. However, peace did not come until the early 1190s, as Yoritomo, who in 1192 became "shogun" (or military dictator), subdued or killed any remaining lords who seemed to threaten his authority, including his long-time ally Yoshitsune, the victorious general at Dan-no-Ouro.

ASHIKAGA TAKAUJI

Among the most ruthless samurai, Ashikaga Takauji was employed by the Hojo regent to crush the revolt of Emperor Go-Daigo in 1333, but changed sides and restored imperial power. After 1335, he broke also with the imperial court and declared himself shogun.

THE SAMURAI AND SHOGUN POWER

From the factionalism of the Gempei Wars emerged the samurai, originally rough fighting men who evolved into a striking mix of the savage and the refined. The ideal warrior was as capable of dashing off a poem as he was of slicing off an enemy's head with his two-handed sword. He subscribed to an austere code of honour and, rather than face defeat, would commit ritual suicide (*seppuku*) by disembowelling himself.

The emperors of the time, although occasionally seeking to assert themselves, were largely powerless. Instead, the shoguns, based from 1185 to 1336 at the Minamoto centre of Kamakura, acted through a council and judicial board of enquiry that largely bypassed the imperial court at Kyoto. For much of

A scene from the *Tamamo-no-mae*, written during the Muromachi era, which tells of a beautiful courtesan who turns out to be the spirit of a malevolent fox.

e 13th century, the power of the
ogunate was itself subverted by
e regent, a position that was held
y ten successive generations of the
owerful Hojo clan.

HE END OF KAMAKURA POWER

ttempts by the Mongols to invade
1274 and 1281 were the only
al threat to Japan during this time.
he samurai pushed back the first
ttack, and a great storm, called the
mikaze ("divine wind"), ended the
cond. In 1333, Emperor Go-Daigo
ied to impose his direct rule,
tracting some support from the
obility. The Kamakura shogun sent
eneral Ashikaga Takauji to punish
is presumptuousness, but the
eneral defected and captured Kyoto
the name of the restored emperor.
amakura was burned and the last
lojo regent deposed.

Go-Daigo's rejoicing did not last
ng, as his two generals Takauji and
itta Yoshisada quarrelled. The
nperor supported Yoshisada, but
akauji won the power struggle.
Vhile Go-Daigo established an
ternative court in the Yoshino

The curved samurai sword or *katana*, the samurai's
badge of office, was made of hard layers of tempered
steel that gave it an extremely sharp cutting edge.

mountains south of Kyoto, Takauji
appointed a new emperor – Komyo
– and declared himself shogun, the
first of the Ashikaga period.

THE MUROMACHI SHOGUNATE

The Ashikaga shogunate (from 1392
referred to as the Muromachi) ruled
Japan for 240 years. It took nearly
60 years of intermittent war before
Yoshimitsu, the third Ashikaga
shogun, suppressed Go-Daigo's rival
court at Yoshino and restored the
imperial regalia to Kyoto. Then, for
five decades, Japan experienced
peace and a cultural renaissance.
However, peasant risings followed
famine and plague in the 1420s,
and when Shogun Yoshimasa
retired in 1467, civil war (the Onin
War) broke out over the succession.
A tense peace was restored in 1477,
but central authority was disrupted,
and real power rested with the
regional *daimyo* (warlords). This led to
a Japan that was unified in theory,
but wholly disunited in practice.

GUNPOWDER WEAPONRY

Europe adopted gunpowder in the 14th century, but it was not a European innovation – the Chinese had used it for centuries. It was, however, in Europe that its rapid spread and refinement led to a revolution in military tactics, and, ultimately, to the development of handheld weapons and field artillery of massive power with which European armies would come to dominate the battlefield.

EARLY GUNPOWDER

The earliest recipe for gunpowder was recorded in China around 1040, and the Chinese may have used gunpowder offensively in "fire-lances" as early as 1182. Yet, it was not until the Ming dynasty, in the 14th and 15th centuries, that the Chinese began to use gunpowder weapons on a wider scale, with innovations such as the deployment of dragoons, or mounted gunners.

This early Chinese gunpowder weapon fires a volley of arrows from a bamboo launching tube.

By then, the technology had been exported to Europe. The English first used cannons at Crécy in 1346, but these early firearms were liable to overheat or explode. More reliable mobile artillery came with the introduction of iron – rather than stone – cannon balls, which meant that the guns could be smaller, and the development of faster-burning gunpowder around 1420. The French defeat of the English at Castillon in 1453 was the first example of a battle won through the use of such artillery.

HANDGUNS

The 1450s saw the development of the first handguns. Called arquebuses, these muzzle-loaded weapons were fired by a matchlock mechanism, which allowed for reloading during combat. These firearms were able to pierce plate armour. However, reloading was slow, and the arquebusiers, as they were called, therefore needed to be protected by groups of pikemen (in a formation known as the Swiss phalanx).

The French army bombards a city's walls using new cannon weaponry during the Hundred Years War (1337–1453).

ARTILLERY

By the early 16th century, technological advances had boosted the capabilities of artillery. Trunnions – protrusions from the barrel of the gun – allowed it to be raised or lowered easily, vastly improving aim. Cities that had previously been protected by thick walls became vulnerable, and warfare returned to a pattern of field engagements.

THE SPREAD OF FIREARMS

During the Italian Wars (1494–1559), gunpowder weapons came of age. At the Battle of Ravenna in 1512, a two-hour artillery duel opened the fighting. Arquebusiers played a vital role in the decisive Imperial victory at the Battle of Pavia in 1525. New weapons appeared, notably the musket, which, although heavier than the arquebus and requiring a stand to allow the musketeer to fire it, had greater force and range. Although firearms were most advanced in Europe at this time, Asian powers, such as China, had also continued their development. The Chinese, for example, devised a primitive form of machine gun in the 16th century.

Firearms spread into Japan and India too, so that by the end of the 16th century, wherever there was conflict, it was almost bound to involve the use of gunpowder weaponry. Those cultures without firearms, such as the Aztecs and Incas in the Americas, and most sub-Saharan African peoples, became relatively easy prey once the gun-wielding Europeans arrived.

Matchlock muskets were a huge technological advance, and were effective at ranges of up to 100m (330 ft). Their simple design meant that they were used in Europe up until the 18th century.

MEDIEVAL KOREA

Korea ⌛ 108 BCE–1910 CE

The Korean peninsula was subject to Chinese influence from very early times. In 108 BCE, it was conquered by Han armies (*see p.153*), who established a series of commanderies there. With the decline of the Han from the 1st century BCE, three rival kingdoms vied for control of Korea: Silla in the southeast, Baekje in the southwest, and Koguryo in the north. A small group of city-states known as Kaya also flourished in the southeast from around 40 to 532 CE, escaping the grasp of their larger neighbours.

THE UNIFICATION OF KOREA

The protracted struggle for supremacy between Silla, Baekje, and Koguryo lasted until 668 and is known as the Three Kingdoms period. Silla, founded in 57 CE, emerged as the most powerful

The Bulguksa temple in South Korea. King Beophung founded the first temple on this site around 528.

WANG GEON

The founder of the Goryeo dynasty, Wang Geon (ruled 918–943) had been a general to the anti-Silla rebel Gung Ye, who created the state of Taebong with Wang Geon as prime minister. When Gung Ye's rule grew tyrannical, Wang Geon deposed him.

of the three. Under King Beophung (ruled 514–540 CE), who adopted Buddhism, the Silla encroached on Baekje's territory. Baekje had been a conduit for Buddhism into Korea in the 4th century, thanks to close ties to Japan and China. After the kingdom's eventual fall to Silla in 660, many Baekje nobles fled to Japan, becoming ancestors of several *daimyo* (warlord) clans.

Koguryo suffered frequent Chinese intervention, with its capital at Wandu destroyed several times. Yet the kingdom recovered, and under Gwanggaeto (rul

...ce guardian spirits of the north
...the south protect Korea's great
...dhist temple at Bulguksa.

...(—412) conquered most
...the Korean peninsula.
...wever, internal strife,
...ssure from Baekje and
...a, and conflict with Sui
...d Tang China (*see
...162 and 163*) in the
...ly 7th century led to
...guryo's decline and, in
...8, it too fell to Silla, completing the
...fication of Korea under the Silla
...g Munmo.

...Attempts under the unified Silla state
...mpose a Chinese-style bureaucracy
...d generally enhance royal authority
...ndered in the face of aristocratic
...istance, and in the late 9th century,
...rea broke up again. Civil war ensued,
...Korea was united once more in

this end, Sejong instituted a civil service
examination system along Chinese lines
and created a new phonetic alphabet
(called *hang'ul*) for the Korean language.
He also encouraged the advancement
of science, particularly in astronomy and
meteorology, and agricultural reforms to
increase the yields of the countryside.

Rivalries among scholar-officials
who vied for positions in the state

"BAEKJE IS AT FULL MOON, SILLA IS AT HALF MOON."

Prophecy of the decline of Silla and rise of Baekje, 659

...5 by Wang Geon, founder of the
...ryeo dynasty. Although generally
...osperous, the country suffered civil
...rs in the 12th century, and in the
...th century fell under the control of
...Mongol Yuan dynasty of China.
...ryeo finally collapsed in
...92 after a rebellion by the
...neral Yi Songgye.

OSON KOREA

...Songgye founded the
...10son dynasty, which
...uld rule Korea into
...dern times, only finally
...ng deposed in 1910. Yi's
...1 Sejong implemented a
...ies of Neo-Confucian
...orms, which aimed to
...rmonize all aspects of
...man behaviour with an
...derlying universal order. To

bureaucracy plagued Sejong's successors.
This sapped Korea's strength and the
country was unprepared when Japan
invaded in the 1590s. Two invasions in
six years devastated Korea, but the
Japanese were finally repelled.
Choson recovered in the
17th century, and the reigns
of Yeongjo (1724–76) and
his successors brought
peace until the end of the
19th century, when Korea
was drawn into rivalry
between Japan, Russia, and
China (*see pp.298–301*),
finally becoming a Japanese
protectorate. The Choson
were eventually removed from
the throne in 1910.

This *maebyong* wine vessel (from the
Chinese for "vase for plum blossom") is
characteristic of Korea's Goryeo period.

THE KHMER EMPIRE

Cambodia ☗ 889–1431

Around 800, King Jayavarman II (ruled 802–55) consolidated small central Cambodian kingdoms to establish a state called Kambujadesa, marking the start of the Khmer empire. Its culture was strongly influenced by India, and Jayavarman ordered the construction of Indian-style Hindu temples near Siem Reap. Under Indravarman, who became king in 889, a capital was established in at Angkor, which grew to become a vast ceremonial complex. Angkor reached its peak under Suryavarman, who from 1011 reunified Cambodia after a period of civil war.

EMPIRE AND DECLINE

In 1177, the Chams (*see facing page*) sack Angkor, but four years later were in turn defeated by Jayavarman VII, Angkor's greatest ruler, who then extended the empire to include parts of modern Thailand and Vietnam. Jayavarman V was a Buddhist and, after his death in 1215, a Hindu reaction set in during which all the images of Buddha at Angkor were defaced. The empire then went into decline and became a localiz power. It disappeared entirely after the sack of Angkor by the Thais in 1431.

The Angkor Wat temple was founded by the Khmer king Suryavarman II (ruled 1113–45).

PAGAN BURMA

Burma ☗ 849–1287

Burmese chronicles give 849 as the date when King Pyinbya founded the city of Pagan, which would become the centre of Burma's first powerful state. Later, under King Anawrahta (ruled 1044–77), Pagan emerged as a real power, conquering the Mon city of Thaton, a centre of Indian civilization, in 1057.

Anawrahta also annexed parts of Thailand, Arakan on the border of India, and Nan-chao in southern China, creating an empire that would last into the 13th century. The density of temples in Pagan itself was such that by the early

13th century, the empire established a new centre several kilometres to the ea

Under Kyaswa (ruled 1234–50), Pagan fell into decline, as the king confiscated the lands of Buddhist monasteries, an unpopular policy that undermined royal authority. The despotic ruler Narathihapate (ruled 1254–87) dared invade the Mongol vassal state of Kaungai in 1277, only f the Mongol armies to retaliate and sac Pagan in 1287. Narathihapate fled fro Burma and in the aftermath, Pagan's subjects rose up and its empire collaps

CHAMPA

S Vietnam
192–1471

e kingdom of Champa may have had origins in the state of Lin Yi, founded ound 192, but by the 7th century was lependent, with its own culture. ccessive capitals of Champa were stroyed by Javan attacks, fore king Indravarman II 54–93) founded a new ntre at Indrapura (in odern Quan-nam ovince). In 979, an vasion of Dai Viet (*see right*) l to a long struggle that ded only in 1471 with the ai Viet capture of Vijaya, e last Cham capital.

tized sculptures of fearsome ardians and mythical animals orned Champa temples.

DAI VIET

N Vietnam
938–1528

Dai Viet ("Great Viet") was established in 938 as an independent state in northern Vietnam 938 by Ngo Quen, after a revolt against Chinese overlordship. Under Dai Viet's Li dynasty (1009–1225), a series of wars broke out with Champa to the south (*see left*) over disputed border provinces. From 1225, during the Tran dynasty, Dai Viet fought off three Mongol invasions, and finally, under Le Thanh-Ton (ruled 1460–97), succeeded in conquering Champa. After 1528, Dai Viet broke up and was not reunited until the early 19th century.

SRIVIJAYA

Java   7th–14th centuries

om the 5th century, the island peoples Sumatra and Java set up prosperous ading communities rivalling the coastal ates of the Southeast Asian mainland. the 7th century the Srivijaya empire ntrolled most of Sumatra and the alay peninsula. The earliest account mes from a Chinese Buddhist pilgrim, 671, who remarked that there were a ousand Buddhist monks at the court, d Srivijaya clearly acted as a centre for e diffusion of Buddhism in the region. Srivijaya faced many rivals, including e Sailendra kingdom of central Java – ich constructed the vast temple at orobodur around 800 – and its hold gan to weaken in the 11th century. By -00, it had been replaced by newer aritime powers, especially the Malay ajapahit empire.

A gallery of Buddha statues from Wat Phra Borom in Chaiya in southern Thailand, which was a regional capital of the Srivijaya empire.

THE MIDDLE EAST AND NORTH AFRICA

In the early 7th century, the emergence of a new religion, Islam, changed the shape of the Middle East for ever. The new faith inspired unprecedented unity in the tribes of the Arabian peninsula, and Arab armies carried Islam through the Middle East and North Africa. Despite fragmentation in the Islamic world in the 8th century, Islamic empires, such as the Seljuk and Ottoman, still rose to prominence.

THE RISE OF ISLAM

▣ Arabia, the Near East   ⚔ 610–661

The prophet Muhammad was born around 570 in the prosperous central Arabian trading town of Mecca. Around 610, he received the divine revelation that would form the basis of the religion of Islam, and began to gather a group of followers.

THE SPREAD OF ISLAM IN ARABIA
Although some in Mecca accepted Muhammad's new creed, others were threatened by it and, in 622, Muhammad was forced into exile in Medina. The citizens of Medina were long-time rivals to Mecca and willingly accepted Muhammad and his teachings, providing him with many converts. This led to a bitter struggle with the Meccans, which finally ended with the capture of Mecca in 630. From there, Muhammad directed the conquest of much of the rest of the

Alam standards, carried in Shia religious processions, were intended to represent the sword of 'Ali. Holy names are carved along the blade.

Arabian peninsula before his death in 632. Abu Bakr was appointed caliph (or successor); under his rule (632–63) anti-Muslim uprisings in Arabia were put down and Arab armies began to penetrate Sassanid Persia (see p.115) and Byzantine-held Syria (see p.202). Under the next caliph, Umar (ruled 634–44), the Islamic empire expanded far beyond Arabia.

EARLY EXPANSION AND CIVIL UNREST
The Arabs smashed the Byzantine field army at Yarmuk in 636, leading to the capture of Jerusalem in 637 and the occupation of Egypt in 641. The Sassanid Persian empire also fell to the caliphate after the defeat of the Persian *shah* (king), Yazdegird III, in 642. Increasing disputes over the succession, especially after the murder of the third caliph, Uthman, in 656, finally led to a civil war and the assassination of 'Ali, the fourth caliph and Muhammad's cousin, in 661.

THE UMAYYAD AND ABBASID CALIPHATES

 Middle East   661–1258 CE

ter the assassination of the fourth
uslim caliph 'Ali, Mu'awiyah, the
vernor of Syria and a distant relative
 Muhammad, seized power, installing
nself in a new capital at Damascus.
u'awiyah founded the Umayyad
nasty, which borrowed heavily from
zantine and Persian institutions to build
strong central authority for the Islamic
te. The Umayyads extended their rule
North Africa, capturing the Byzantine
onghold of Carthage (in Tunisia) in
8, and swept into Spain in 711.

OM DAMASCUS TO BAGHDAD

spite these Ummayad successes, in
0 a number of anti-Umayyad factions
ned in a successful revolt against them
l by 'Abbas, who claimed the caliphate
d moved the seat of government to
ghdad. His descendants, the Abbasids,
uld be caliphs until 1258. Initially

osaic from the Umayyad mosque in Damascus,
eautiful Islamic–Byzantine building constructed
der the caliph al-Walid between 706 and 715.

HAROUN AL-RASHID

The greatest of the Abbasid caliphs,
Haroun (786–809) turned Baghdad into
the most prosperous city of its day. He
defeated the Byzantines in 806, and was
a fine diplomat, exchanging ambassadors
with the Frankish ruler Charlemagne.

'Abbas presided over a golden age, in
which art, science, architecture, and
Islamic jurisprudence flourished. In 756,
however, Spain broke away under a line
of the Umayyad family, and North
Africa followed with the foundation of a
rival Fatimid caliphate in Egypt in 969.
By the 11th century, the Abbasid caliphs
controlled little beyond the suburbs of
Baghdad and were firmly under the
thumb of the Seljuk Turkish emirs (*see
p.182*). In 1258, even this pitiful flame of
independence was snuffed out when the
Mongol Hulegu sacked Baghdad (*see
p.167*) and had Al-Mutasim, the last
caliph, trampled to death by horses.

THE SELJUK TURKS

⚑ Turkey, Syria   ☗ 1038–1306

Throughout the 9th century, groups of Turkish-speaking nomads migrated westwards from central Asia. In the 10th century they reached Persia, where many of them took service in Muslim armies and converted to Islam.

THE FIRST SELJUKS

One group, the Seljuks, led by Tugrul Beg, initially served the Kara-Khanid emirs of Bukhara in Persia, but became so powerful that in 1038, Tugrul declared himself sultan, in the city of Nishapur in northeastern Iran. From here his armies moved westwards. In 1055, Tugrul became involved in a

> ### ALP ARSLAN
>
> Initially a Seljuk governer, Alp Arslan succeeded to the sultanate in 1064. His first invasion of the Byzantine empire in 1068 failed, but after his victory against the Byzantines in 1071, Anatolia would always remain largely Turkish-occupied.

power struggle between the Abbasid (see p.181) caliph Al Qa'im and his Egyptian Fatimid rival, who had taken Baghdad. Tugrul took Baghdad for the Abbasid caliphs in 1060, but then reduced them to little more than figureheads. Tugrul's successor, Alp Arslan, conquered Georgia and Armenia in 1064, and in 1071 defeated the Byzantine emperor Romanus IV, leading to Turkish occupation of much of central Anatolia (in modern Turkey). The administrative reforms of Alp Arslan's Persian official Nizam al-Mulk supported the sultan's military victories and cemented Seljuk stability.

DECLINE OF THE SELJUKS

Alp Arslan's son Malik Shah I (ruled 1072–92) consolidated Seljuk rule in Anatolia, but a revolt by his cousin Suleyman in 1086 led to the rival Seljuk Sultanate of Rum, which controlled much of the west of Alp Arslan's former domain. By the 12th century, Malik Shah's Seljuks had disbanded; pressure from the Mongols in the early 13th century and competition with more vigorous Muslim emirates put the Rum Sultanate into decline, and after 1306 it disappeared entirely.

The main gateway of the Ince Menare *medrese* (school of theology) in Konya, Turkey, built by the Seljuks around 1267.

RISE OF THE OTTOMANS

⚑ Turkey ⌛ mid-13th century–1481

the 12th century, Turkish Seljuks minated Anatolia (*see facing page*), but eir influence weakened in the 13th ntury and rival Turkish groups vied for wer. Among them was a small band by Osman, after whom the Ottoman pire would be named.

man's group took vantage of a strategic sition on the eastern proach route to nstantinople (now anbul) to secure ssession of many zantine cities in stern Anatolia (*see* '03). This provided em with resources for rther expansion.

Blue tilework graces many Ottoman-era mosques at Iznik, an early Ottoman conquest.

E EARLY SULTANS

sman's son Orhan (ruled 1324–62) ok the major city of Prusa (Bursa) and ablished it as his capital, marking the ective establishment of the Ottoman pire. By the late 1330s, the Byzantines re confined to just a few settlements se to Constantinople. In 1352, aided the Byzantine emperor John VI antakouzenos, who was locked in civil r with his rival John V Palaiologos,

Orhan crossed into Europe to occupy Gallipoli. From this bridgehead, the Ottomans spread through eastern Thrace and across the Balkans. Murad I (ruled 1362–89), as well as expanding Ottoman land in eastern Anatolia, captured the great city of Adrianople (Edirne) in Thrace in 1369, which thereafter became the Ottoman capital.

RISE AND FALL

The Ottomans began to exert pressure on the other Christian regions of the Balkans, capturing Sofia (in Bulgaria) in 1385 and destroying the army of Prince Lazar of Serbia in 1389. It seemed only a matter of time before Constantinople would fall, but in 1402 the Mongol Tamerlane smashed the Ottoman army outside Ankara (*see p.167*). The Turkish emirates that the Ottomans had conquered over the previous century broke away, and it took 50 years under Mehmet I (ruled 1413–21) and Murad II (ruled 1421–51) to regain the Ottoman position in Anatolia and the Balkans.

MEHMET II

Known as "the Conqueror", Mehmet II (ruled 1451–81) was the Ottoman sultan who, in 1453, finally took the Byzantine capital Constantinople. Having constructed a series of fortresses to throttle the city's communication lines, he laid siege in early spring, using cannons to pound the city walls. In 1456, he failed to repeat his success at Belgrade, but he successively conquered Serbia (1458), Bosnia (1463), most of Albania (1478), and even, in the last year of his life, oversaw the capture of Otranto in the heel of Italy.

INDIA

Kingdoms and empires rose and fell in India in the Middle Ages. Following the demise of the Guptas, in 606 Emperor Harsha established a powerful state across much of northern India, but after his death the empire fragmented into small kingdoms, only really to be united under the Delhi Sultanate in the 13th century. Southern India saw similar struggles, with rival states fighting bitterly until the emergence of the Cholas in the 9th century.

CHOLA INDIA

South India   *c.*850–1279

Between the 7th and 9th centuries, the Pallava and the Chalukya kingdoms contested the right to rule southern India until the rise of the Cholas, around 850. They were to sweep away the two rivals to establish a new state that would dominate the area until around 1200.

RISE AND FALL

The Chola kingdom overthrew the Pallavas around 897 under Aditya, but then suffered a century of decline at the hands of the rival Rashtrakuta kingdom. Then, under Rajaraja I, who came to the throne in 985, Chola was on the ascendant once more, conquering all south India and even intervening as far north as Bengal. Rajaraja and his son Rajendra I built magnificent temples

A statue from the 11th-century Brihadishwara temple in the Chola capital of Thanjavur.

at Thanjavur and at Gangaikondacholapuram, a Hindu riposte to the growing power of Islam in northern India. Rajendra I also projected Chola power overseas, conquering Sri Lanka and exercising some influence, if not control, over the Srivijaya empire of Indonesia and the state of Kadaram (around Penang in modern Malaysia).

Back in south India, however, the Cholas fell into difficulties. Sri Lanka was lost in 1070 and around 1118 a resurgent Chalukya kingdom took much territory around Mysore. Beset by civil strife and faced with the threat of the Pandyan Empire on his borders, Rajendra III, the last recorded Chola ruler, struggled on until 1279, after which his kingdom disappeared.

THE DELHI SULTANATE

📍 North India   ⏳ 1206–1526

In 1193, the armies of Muhammad of Ghur (from modern Afghanistan) attacked Delhi, carving out an empire from a number of weak and fractious Rajput Hindu principalities. After Muhammad's death in 1206, his most trusted general, the former slave Qutb-ud-din Aibek (ruled 1206–11), gained control of his territories and established the Delhi Sultanate.

FRAGILE RULE

The rule of Aibek's successors was precarious. The nomadic tribes who made up the nobility did not have a strong tradition of hereditary kingship, and during the rule of the Slave Dynasty (1206–90) at least five of the 11 sultans were assassinated. Then, between 1299 and 1307, Sultan Alauddin Khilji launched a series of successful military strikes against the rich kingdoms south of Delhi. By 1321, much of the south was under the control of governors appointed by the sultan, and Sultan Muhammad ibn

> **MUHAMMAD OF GHUR**
>
> In 997, Muhammad of Ghur succeeded his father as the ruler of a minor state around Ghazni, in modern Afghanistan. From here, he created a vast empire encompassing large parts of Afghanistan, Iran, Pakistan, and northwest India before dying in 1030.

Tughluq even moved the capital and its whole population 1,100km (700 miles) south to Devagiri. Although Delhi was reinstated two years later, so many of its people had died in the two moves that travellers reported it to be a "ghost town". The sultanate's strength was now waning, and the establishment of the Hindu Vijayanagar empire in central India in the 1330s ended its rule there. The Delhi sultans, declining in policial force, limped on until 1526, when they were finally supplanted in Delhi by the Mughals.

The Qutb Minar mosque in Delhi has a minaret that is 73m (240 ft) tall. It celebrates Sultan Aibek's victories.

> "WHEN I ENTERED DELHI IT WAS ALMOST A DESERT... . ITS BUILDINGS WERE VERY FEW AND IN OTHER RESPECTS IT WAS QUITE EMPTY."
>
> Arab traveller Ibn Battutah, visiting Delhi in 1334 after Sultan Muhammad deported its population

SUB-SAHARAN AFRICA

Buoyed by trading links with Asia and Islamic North Africa
from the 8th century a number of prosperous empires and
commercial centres formed in Africa to the south of the
Sahara desert, including the Mali and Songhay empires in
West Africa and Great Zimbabwe in south-central Africa.
The spread of Islam across north and east Africa helped
create routes through the desert that became the first trading
networks to encompass the sub-Saharan regions.

THE MALI EMPIRE

West Africa   *c.*800–1545

In West Africa, between
the 8th and 11th
centuries, the Ghana
empire grew powerful on
the trans-Saharan gold
trade. Yet by the 12th
century it was in decline,
and was supplanted by the
Mali empire, founded in
1235 by Sundiata Keita.
Like Ghana, the Mali
empire was based in the
Sahel, the savanna region along the
Sahara's southern border. From here, it
too exploited the Saharan trade routes,
exchanging desert-mined salt for gold.

The walls of the Great Mosque at Djenné, a trading
city conquered by Sonni Ali, first great king of the
Songhay empire which rose to overcome Mali.

WEALTH AND COLLAPSE
Mali reached its peak in the 14th century
under Sundiata Keita's grand-nephew
Mansa Musa (ruled 1312–37). He is
most noted for his spectacular
"Pilgrimage of Gold" to Mecca in
1324–25, when he spent or gave away so
much gold that the inflation it caused
damaged the economy of North Africa

for a decade. Mansa Musa extended
Mali's territory and built up the city of
Timbuktu into a wealthy commercial
hub and a centre for scholarship.

   In the early 15th century, Mali's
subject states, notably Songhay, based at
Gao some 400km (250 miles) downriver
from Timbuktu, broke away. Having lost
control of the crucial trade routes after a
disastrous defeat by Songhay in 1545,
Mali's empire collapsed.

IFE AND BENIN

◆ Nigeria   ⌛ *c.*700–1500

The Ife kingdom developed among the Yoruba people of southwestern Nigeria around 700. At its height, between 900 and 1200, this kingdom had grown to dominate a large area of western Africa. The capital, Ife, was the centre of this sophisticated empire, most notable for its production of high-quality bronze heads. However, in around 1400 the Ife were supplanted by the empire of Benin, which grew up to their west. Under Ewuare – the first great *oba* (ruler) of Benin, from 1440 – the capital was fortified with a great moat and armies sent out that ultimately dominated an area of some 80,000 sq km (31,000 sq miles). Like their Ife predecessors, the people of Benin produced superb terracotta and bronze heads and they grew rich from a monopoly on contacts with European newcomers – initially the Portuguese – in the later 15th century, profiting from trade in ivory, palm oil, gold, pepper, and slaves.

A bronze Ife head, cast in a beautiful naturalistic style that has made the culture's artistic production justly famous.

GREAT ZIMBABWE

◆ Southern Africa   ⌛ 11th–15th centuries

One of the greatest urban centres of sub-Saharan Africa grew up from the 11th century at Great Zimbabwe (from which the modern state of Zimbabwe takes its name). The huge settlement sprawls over 7 sq km (3 sq miles), with a number of stone enclosures containing some 300 structures. Great Zimbabwe was in a strategic position to control trade – including in gold – from the interior to the east coast of Africa. It was also home to a thriving agricultural economy. With a population of around 15,000 people, Great Zimbabwe served as the centre of the Mwenemutapa empire. However, possibly as a result of over-cultivation of the surrounding land, in the mid-15th century, Great Zimbabwe was abandoned.

The 13th-century Great Enclosure is the most impressive of the stone structures at Great Zimbabwe. Its 25m (82ft) walls may have enclosed a royal palace.

EUROPE

Around the early 5th century CE, Germanic barbarian tribe
settled on the former territory of the Roman empire. But, b
around 600, the chaos had resolved itself and what had one
been the Roman empire was now a series of successor states
A Christian culture emerged in Europe, in part based on a
form of social and political structures known as feudalism
which would persist through wars and crises
into the mid-15th century.

OSTROGOTHS AND LOMBARDS IN ITALY

Italy　☗ 493–774

Between 488 and 493 CE, Theoderic I, ruler of the barbarian Ostrogoths (*see p.143*), conquered Italy. His kingdom drew deeply on Roman forms of administration, yet opposition to his rule drove him to execute Boethius, a leader of the old Roman Senate, in 525 CE.

After Theoderic's death in 526 CE, his daughter Amalasuintha acted as regent for his young grandson and designated heir, Athalaric. Dissent among the Ostrogoth nobles led to the whole state unravelling. Amalasuintha appealed to the Byzantine emperor Justinian (*see p.202*) for help, and after her murder (possibly on the orders of her cousin) in 535 CE, Justinian took the opportunity to intervene,

setting off the Gothic Wars. By 554 CE, after hard and bitter campaigning, Justinian's forces emerged the masters of a devastated Italy.

LOMBARD ITALY

In 568 CE, the barbarian Lombar
invaded Italy from the northeast
under Alboin (ruled *c*.565–72 CE
In 572 CE, they reached Pavia and
carved out a kingdom in northern
Italy. This soon split into 35 dukedoms, but was reunited und
Authari (ruled 584–90 c
and, from 589 CE, hel
off Byzantine advances. Under Agilulf (ruled 590–616 CE), the Lombards became
Catholic, controlling northern Italy until the Frankish Charlemagne (
p.190) deposed their last king, Desiderius, in 774.

An Ostrogothic brooch from around 500 CE, showing a vibrancy far removed from Roman art forms.

VISIGOTHS IN SPAIN

🏴 Spain ⚔ 469–711

he Visigoths, who settled in southwestern
aul in 418 CE as allies of the Romans,
gan from 469 CE to conquer territory
Spain. In 507 CE, when the Franks
feated them in a great battle at Vouillé,
ar Poitiers, the Visigoths fell back on
ese Spanish territories.

E VISIGOTHIC KINGDOM

nder Agila (ruled 549–54 CE) the
isigoths lost territory in southeast Spain
a resurgent Byzantine Empire. From
capital at Toledo, however, the
isigothic state recovered, reaching its
ogee under Leovigild (ruled 568–86 CE),
great organizer and legislator. Leovigild
as succeeded by his son Reccared, who
589 CE converted to Catholicism,
andoning the kingdom's previous

The church of San Pedro de la Nave at Zamora, built
under the Visigothic king Egica (ruled 687–701)
towards the end of Visigothic rule in Spain.

Arian form of Christianity. The
Visigothic kingdom finally came to an
end when, weakened by a civil war after
the accession of Roderick in 711, it easily
fell to invading Muslim armies (*see p.180*).

ANGLO-SAXON ENGLAND

🏴 England ⚔ 411–1066

itain was under Roman administration
til 411 CE, and in the little-understood
riod that followed, Germanic invaders
utes, Angles, and Saxons – began to
ttle on the island, displacing the
tive Romano-Celtic
pulation. By the 7th
ntury, these had coalesced
to a number of small
ates, conventionally
own as the "Heptarchy".

PANSION OF WESSEX

incipal among these states
re Wessex in the southwest,
ercia in the Midlands, and
orthumbria in the north. In the
ng struggle between them, it was
essex that would emerge victorious.
anish invasions in the 9th century

sapped the remaining power of
Northumbria and Mercia, whose last
great king, Offa, died in 796. Alfred the
Great fended off the Danish conquest of
Wessex with several victories in the
870s, but it was not until the
time of Edward the Elder
(ruled 899–924) that England
was united under a single
Anglo-Saxon monarchy.

ALFRED THE GREAT

As well as saving Wessex from
Danish invasion in 878, Alfred
(ruled 871–899) restored Wessex's
defences by building a series of *burhs*
(fortified towns), revising the legal system,
and overseeing the first major translations
of books into Anglo-Saxon.

MEROVINGIAN AND CAROLINGIAN FRANCE

France   511–987

After the fall of the Roman Empire, Europe fragmented into many states, the most successful of which was the Kingdom of the Franks. A confederacy of tribes originating from the area around modern Belgium and Holland, the Franks, under their leader Clovis (ruled *c*.481–511), conquered most of the old Roman province of Gaul.

THE MEROVINGIANS

Clovis overcame the Roman general Syagrius (who controlled large parts of Gaul) in 486, saw off rival Frankish kings, crucially converted to Catholicism in 496, and expelled the Visigoths from Gaul in 507. On his death the kingdom was divided between his four sons, establishing the Merovingian dynasty.

This dynasty continued to expand, taking the rest of Gaul (except Brittany and Septimania) by 536 and

dominating northern Italy in the 540s and 550s. However, in the 7th century, after Dagobert I (622–638), the power of the Frankish kings declined. Several died young and rival aristocratic factions started to vie for power. In the early 8th century, one of these factions, the Carolingians, emerged as dominant. Beginning with Pepin II (*d*.713), they developed their office as "mayor of the palace" to become the real power in the land.

THE CAROLINGIANS

In 768, Pepin III (ruled 747–768) obtained papal approval to depose the last Merovingian ruler and become the first king of the new Carolingian dynasty. Under his son, Charlemagne, the Frankish

The Baptistery of Saint-Jean, Poitiers, constructed around 360 and restored by the Merovingians in the early 6th century.

CHARLEMAGNE

Initially ruling with his brother Carloman (died 771), Charlemagne (ruled 768–814) faced few internal challenges to his authority, enabling him to embark on a bold programme of expansion abroad and reform at home. He built up a sumptuous new capital at Aachen, Germany, and his court was Europe's most important centre of learning in the 9th century. Charlemagne modelled aspects of his rule upon the Romans, crowning himself emperor and appearing on coins wearing the military cloak and laurel crown of a Roman ruler.

"A CHIEF IN WHOSE SHADOW THE CHRISTIAN PEOPLE REPOSE IN PEACE AND WHO STRIKES TERROR INTO THE PAGAN NATIONS."

Alcuin of York, in a letter describing Charlemagne c.796

ngdom reached the height of its power, itiating a series of aggressive overtures gainst its neighbours. Charlemagne's military campaigns resulted in conquests Saxony, the annexation the Lombard kingdom Italy in 774, and ctories as far afield as e lands of the Avar mpire in Pannonia, the Danube (modern ungary), in the 790s.

Charlemagne presided ver a glittering age of ltural achievements, which rned it the label "the arolingian Renaissance". order to reform the ankish church, he dered the importation works of liturgy and urch law from aly. The kingdom's lministration and legal

ornate water jug gifted to Charlemagne Haroun al-Rashid, Caliph of Baghdad, a gesture of diplomatic friendship.

system was thoroughly overhauled. These changes were overseen by the *missi dominici* – the personal envoys of the king.

CAROLINGIAN DECLINE

Charlemagne had himself crowned "Emperor of the Romans" in 800, but his successors struggled to equal his prowess. When Charlemagne's son, Louis the Pious, died in 840, the empire was divided between his three sons. Their quarrels, and the further subdivision of the empire among their heirs, sapped the dynasty's strength. The growing threats of Viking raiders (*see p.194*) from the north and of Magyar incursions from the east further helped to undermine the Carolingians' authority. Hugh Capet, a Frankish aristocrat, deposed the last Carolingian king, Louis V, in 987, to form a new dynasty, the Capetians.

FEUDALISM

The term feudalism describes the system of relationships between kings and nobles in northern and western Europe during much of the medieval period, and by extension to the wider society and economy in which these elites operated. At the heart of the feudal system lay the obligation that noblemen (and, in turn, their retainers) would provide military service in return for the holding of land.

FEUDAL EUROPE

The feudal system, although extremely complex, was never arranged into written law. Much of what is known about feudalism therefore comes with the benefit of historical hindsight. Feudalism contained elements of Germanic custom, mixed with the late-Roman practice of gifting land to barbarian groups in return for military service. It evolved during Carolingian times into the practice of a ruler assigning a parcel of land (known as a "fief") to a nobleman. In return for the land, the nobleman (who was known as a "vassal") swore his loyalty to the king – or another lord – and promised to perform various duties, particularly military service, for a set number of days each year. Many nobles further

A 14th-century French view of the investiture of a knight. The new knight kneels before his lord, pledging loyalty in exchange for privileges.

apportioned parts of their fiefs to sub-tenants, who in turn performed military duties and swore allegiance. It was not unusual for vassals to have allegiances to more than one lord.

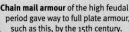

A hierarchy of obligations thus developed, helping to link together a country's web of lordships, but doing little to bolster the central authority of the king.

KNIGHTS AND CASTLES

The backbone of medieval European armies were the knights, heavy cavalry who by the 11th century represented an elite caste of warriors that fought on behalf of their feudal lord. Their status was confirmed through symbols and ceremonies, such as the

Chain mail armour of the high feudal period gave way to full plate armour, such as this, by the 15th century.

"accolade" – the king touching his vassal on the shoulders with a sword to confer knighthood.

A castle was a fortified base from which a feudal lord could dominate the countryside – as well as being his dwelling place and the seat of the local court of justice. Once ensconced inside, an uncooperative nobleman was extremely difficult for anyone, including the king, to dislodge.

CHANGES IN FEUDALISM

Toward the 14th century, a new variant, known as "bastard feudalism", arose in which vassals substituted their military obligations for monetary payments. This was a sign of a changing society. As feudal ties weakened and monarchs tried to assert direct control over their realms, the age of feudalism was coming to a close, finally ending in the 16th century.

> ## "THE FAITHFUL VASSAL SHOULD... COUNSEL AND AID HIS LORD."
>
> Fulbert of Chartres in a letter to Duke William of Aquitaine, 1020

The Rock of Cashel in County Tipperary, Ireland, is topped by a great castle, evidence of its feudal lord's power over the surrounding countryside.

THE VIKINGS

⚑ Scandinavia, NW Europe, Newfoundland   ⌛ 793–1069

In the late 8th century, possibly propelled by overpopulation in their Scandinavian homelands, a wave of shipborne raiders, the Vikings, began a reign of terror over northwestern Europe. Taking advantage of divisions in the Carolingian empire (*see pp.190–1*), Anglo-Saxon England, and Ireland, the Vikings first attacked soft targets, such as the island monastery of Lindisfarne in northeast England, in 793. But these fiercely effective warriors were capable of great mobility, even sailing up rivers, and moved on to dominate the territories they had previously pillaged. In England in the late 9th century, they colonized a large part of the Midlands and north, which became known as the Danelaw. They explored new lands in the Atlantic, too, settling Iceland from 870, Greenland in the late 10th century, and even North America in about 1000.

This replica Viking ship is modelled on a ship that was excavated in Oseberg, Norway. Dating from 815–820, it was built for ceremonial rather than practical purposes.

KIEVAN RUS

⚑ Ukraine, Russia   ⌛ *c.*800–1043

From the early 9th century, Viking Scandinavians, mainly Swedes, began to settle in trading towns in the north of modern Russia and Ukraine, principally at Staraya Ladoga on the Volkhov River.

THE CONQUEST OF KIEV
At first, the Vikings sought to control trade rather than plunder or conquer, establishing a trading network that extended as far as the Islamic world. In the mid-9th century, however, these merchants seem to have expanded their lands, setting up bases farther down the

Volga and Dniepr rivers. Then, around 850, trade turned to conquest, and tradition relates that in 862 the people of Novgorod invited a Viking group (the Rus) led by Riurik to defend them. In 879, Riurik's son Oleg travelled south to seize Kiev and established a Viking dynasty there, which would give rise to many medieval Russian principalities. Kievan Rus became Christian around 988, when its ruler Vladimir was baptised and, although it raided Constantinople in 1043, it became merely another eastern European principality.

THE NORMANS

Normandy, England, S Italy   911–1087

...ing raids affected Carolingian France (*pp.190–1*) badly, and in 911, the ...rolingians gave the leader of one ...d, Rollo, extensive territories in ...dern Normandy as a "pay-off" ...exchange for defending it ...m other marauders.

NORMAN CONQUESTS

...lo's descendants, the ...kes of Normandy, ...idly absorbed French ...ture to create a hybrid ...rman state. In 1066 ...ke William the Bastard ...er called "the Conqueror") ...k advantage of a disputed succession ...England to launch an audacious

WILLIAM THE CONQUEROR

With a distant claim to the English throne through a great-aunt, in 1066 William invaded to usurp Harold Godwinsson as king of England, defeating him at Hastings in October that year. William ruled England until 1087.

invasion and seize the English throne himself. The newly Norman kingdom of England imported French cultural and administrative practices and established the strongest centralized monarchy in Europe.

England was not the only place the Normans sought to satisfy their desire for expansion. From the 1040s, under Robert Guiscard, they conquered southern Italy and Sicily, founding a kingdom that lasted until the German emperor Henry VI suppressed it in 1194.

> "THEY ARE A RACE
> INURED TO WAR,
> ND CAN HARDLY
> IVE WITHOUT IT."

...liam of Malmesbury, from *Deeds of the Kings of ...e English*, describing the Normans, 12th century

This scene from the Bayeux tapestry, commissioned to celebrate the Norman victory at Hastings, shows the Norman army gaining the upper hand.

MONASTICISM

Egypt, Europe   *c.*350–1229

From the time of the early Christian church, men and women had chosen to devote themselves to a life of spiritual dedication as monks or nuns. Gradually communities arose with fixed codes of conduct, such as the "Rule" of St Benedict of Nursia (*c.*480–550) in Italy.

THE NEW MONASTIC ORDERS

Early monasticism became especially strong in the Celtic lands and above all in the Carolingian empire (*see pp.190–1*) of France, with wealthy monasteries such as that of Cluny (belonging to the Benedictine order) the frequent target of Viking raiders. Disenchantment with the materialistic approach these abbeys took, and a general desire for a more spiritual observance, led to the founding of new religious orders from the 11th century, beginning with the Carthusians, founded by Bruno of Cologne around 1082. The Cistercians followed in 1098, insisting on a rigorous life of manual work and prayer. Yet by the 13th century, the reformist zeal of even these communities had ebbed, and further new monastic orders sprang up, most notably the

The Benedictine monastery of Mont St Michel lies off the Norman coast of France and was occupied by monks from 966 until the late 18th century.

Franciscan and Dominican friars. The were known as mendicants, from the Latin word for "beggars", for they renounced personal property and were not attached to richly endowed abbeys To support themselves they depended on charity, bringing them closely in tou with ordinary people. In particular, the Franciscan friars, founded by St Franc

> ## "WHERE THERE IS CHARITY AND WISDOM, THERE I NEITHER FEAR NO IGNORANCE."
>
> St Francis of Assisi, *Admonitions*, c.1220

of Assisi in 1210, sought a return to th simplicity and poverty of the early church, while the Dominicans became committed to education and the fight against heresy. The popularity of the new orders was also at the root of their undoing, for they, too, receive bequests, grew wealthy, and becam complex organizations far remove from the ideals of their founders.

POPES AND EMPERORS

France, Germany, Italy   1049–1122

The collapse of the Roman empire
in the west in the 5th century did
not spell the end for Christianity,
as the Franks in Gaul soon became
Catholics, with the Visigoths
(see p.189) following in the late
6th century. Under the Frankish
emperor Charlemagne, church and
state enjoyed a close relationship,
and Charlemagne often used the
church's spiritual authority to
enhance his own.

PAPAL REFORMS AND THE INVESTITURE CONTROVERSY

In the 11th century, relations
between the secular rulers and
the church broke down. Pope
Leo IX (ruled 1049–54) tried to
limit practices such as clerical marriage
and simony (the purchase of positions
in the church hierarchy). His protégé
Pope Gregory VII sought to expand the
influence of the church, even if this
meant clashing with the authority of

On the imperial crown of Otto I (Holy Roman
Emperor 962–76) the biblical Solomon symbolizes
the wisdom of kings, illustrating how secular rulers
used Christian imagery to bolster their authority.

POPE GREGORY VII

Known as Hildebrand, Gregory served as
papal legate to France and Germany before
becoming pope. His papacy (1074–85) was
consumed by the struggle with the German
emperor Henry IV over investiture (*see right*).
In the end Henry won out, occupying Rome in
1084 and exiling Gregory to southern Italy.

kings and princes. In 1075, a dispute
broke out over investiture (the right
to appoint bishops), which the Pope
declared his own, but to which the
emperor had historically laid claim.
The German emperor Henry IV
persuaded his bishops to declare Gregory
deposed, and the Pope excommunicated
the emperor in response. His authority
undermined, and faced by a rebellion
of German princes, Henry was forced
into a humiliating climb-down, and at
Canossa in Italy in 1077 had to do four
days of public penance, after which he
received absolution.

CONTINUED CONFLICT

The conflict was only finally settled by the
Concordat of Worms in 1122. Disputes
over the borderline between papal and
secular authority never really dissipated,
and fed into the discontents that would
fuel the Reformation (see p.242).

THE CRUSADES

Lebanon, Syria, Palestine, Israel   1095–1291

The capture of Jerusalem by Muslim armies in 637 had long rankled in Europe, seeming to cut off Christianity from its well-springs in the Holy Land. Nevertheless, for a long time Christian pilgrims were in fact able to make the

November, in a field outside the cathedral at Claremont in France, the Pope called for a military expedition to liberate the Holy City of Jerusalem from Muslim rule. The crowd erupted with cries of "It is the will of God", and

"IT IS THE WILL OF GOD"

Response of the crowd to Pope Urban II's preaching of the First Crusade, at Claremont, November 1095

journey to Jerusalem, but in the 11th century the expansion of the Seljuk Turkish sultanate (see p.182) threatened to prevent access to non-Muslim travellers. In 1095, Byzantine emperor Alexius I sent envoys to the West to plead for assistance. They found a willing listener in Pope Urban II. That

thousands of crusaders, as these soldiers became known, "took the cross" to join the military pilgrimage to the Holy Land.

THE FIRST CRUSADES

The first of the armies to cross the Balkans into Anatolia was a rag-tag assortment of peasants, some knights, and religious zealots, all under the doubtful leadership of a charismatic preacher, Peter the Hermit. They were soon cut to pieces by the Turks. The force that followed them was far more professional: a largely Frankish army with a strong aristocratic component. Motivated by a mix of religious idealism, eagerness to acquire new lands, and the simple attraction of a sanctioned fight, the crusaders skirted Constantinople, then beat the Seljuk sultan Kilij Arslan at Dorylaeum in July, forcing the Turks to stand aside and let them march into the Holy Land. After besieging it eight months, they took Antioch in June 1098 and then marched on the ultima

The crusaders' sea voyage to the Holy Land was fraught with danger but avoided a trek across Anatolia with its threat of Turkish attack.

fort of Qalat al-Gundi was built by Saladin, …wned for being a devout Muslim, to guard …rimage routes to Mecca from the crusaders.

…ze of Jerusalem. After another …olonged siege, the city fell amid …rrific bloodshed, as the crusaders …ughtered Muslims and Jews alike.

…ANGING FORTUNES

…e crusaders established a series …small states along the coastline of …lestine and inland in Syria, chief …ong them the Kingdom of …usalem. They formed military …ders of knights – the Templars …d Hospitallers – who were …orn to monastic-type vows, but …ended the Holy Land with …ords, not prayers.

…However, the Muslim …ces regrouped, and they …gan to eat away at the …usader states, taking …essa in 1144. A …cond Crusade was …nched in 1145, but it …t with limited success. In the …80s, most of Syria and Palestine …ited under the Muslim sultan …ladin, who smashed the crusader …mies at Hattin in 1187, and a …v months later seized Jerusalem …elf. The Third Crusade, led by …e German emperor Frederick

SALADIN

Founder of the Ayyubid dynasty and unifier of the Muslim states in the Middle East, Saladin ruled as sultan of Egypt from 1138 to 1193. Despite his victory against the crusaders at Hattin, they considered him an honourable and chivalrous leader.

Barbarossa and the English and French kings Richard the Lionheart and Philip Augustus, checked Saladin's progress but did not regain Jerusalem. Thereafter the crusading movement declined: the Fourth Crusade in 1204 was unable to even reach the Holy Land, the participants content to sack the fellow-Christian city of Constantinople and dismember the Byzantine empire; while later the Fifth (1217–21) and subsequent crusades were sidetracked in Egypt. One by one the crusaders' fortresses fell, until in 1291 the Mamluk sultan al-Ashraf Kalil stormed Acre, their last stronghold. Although the crusaders launched more expeditions, they were hopelessly unsuccessful, and the age of the crusades was over.

This sumptuous cross is a sign both of the crusaders' wealth and the lavishness with which they adorned religious symbols.

THE BLACK DEATH

Europe, the Middle East ☒ 1346–1351

Although Europe had experienced many serious outbreaks of disease (the first recorded being the great pestilence that struck Athens in 430–429 BCE), the most devastating of all struck in the mid-14th century, killing between one-third and half the continent's population.

THE PLAGUE STRIKES

Known as the Black Death, the plague may have spread to Europe from central Asia. Theories abound on what caused the disease, although it is widely supposed to have been *Yersinis pestis*, a bacterium carried by fleas on rodents. The bacterial infection is transferred to humans when the fleas feed on human blood.

The infection has three variants: bubonic plague, which is characterized by buboes, or swellings, of the neck, groin, and armpits; pneumonic plague,

Physicians used leeches to try to cure patients. As leech drew blood, so "noxious vapours" causing th disease might be removed from his or her body.

Macabre outbreaks of religious fervou accompanied the progress of the disea and the *Danse Macabre*, or "dance of death", became a common artistic mo of the afflicted times. By 1350, the Bla Death had largely spent its course, but

"SO MANY DIED THAT ALL BELIEVED IT WAS THE END OF THE WORLD."

Italian chronicler Agnolo di Tura on the Black Death in Siena, *c.*1350

which infects the lungs; and septicaemic plague, or blood poisoning.

The plague was transmitted via Constantinople in 1347 and reached most parts of Europe during 1348 and 1349. It caused widespread terror and panic, and most attempts to fight its spread were useless.

with somewhere between 25 and 50 million Europeans dead, a sudden shortage of labour may have contribute to profound social changes. The peasan found their diminished numbers led to greater demand for their services, whic meant that their living conditions and legal rights greatly improved.

THE HUNDRED YEARS WAR

🏴 France ⌛ 1337–1453

the 12th century, the Plantagenet kings
England acquired territories in France.
his sparked hostility between the English
nd French, eventually leading to
e Hundred Years War.

AR BREAKS OUT

1328, Edward III of
ngland sought to assert his
aim to the French throne
y right of his grandfather,
hilip IV of France. Once
buffed, Edward prepared
r war. Open conflict broke
ut in 1337, culminating in an
nglish invasion of northern France in
346. Edward was victorious at Crécy
346) and Poitiers (1360), leading to the
reaty of Bretigny, by which England
as left in possession of much
f northern and western
rance. From 1369,
nder the French
ing Charles V, war

enry V led England
a decisive victory
Agincourt, northern
ance, in 1415.

broke out again when the
French pushed back the
English, who responded with
a series of devastating raids (or
chevauchées). However, the English
failed to recover the lost ground.

Henry V of England relaunched the
war in 1415, gaining victory at Agincourt
and securing almost all France north of
the Loire. Inspired by Joan of Arc, a
dejected France recovered to
take the last English outposts
in Gascony in the 1450s.
After a final defeat at
Castillon in 1453, the English
were left with almost no
territory in France,
save Calais.

BYZANTINE EMPIRE

After 395 CE, the Roman empire was divided into two halves, and its eastern portion, which survived the fall of Rome, is known as the Byzantine empire. With their capital at Constantinople, the Byzantine emperors experienced centuries of barbarian invasions, periods of resurgence and reconquest, and Muslim-Arab invasions that cut away half their territory. Then, finally, 1,000 years after Rome's fall, they succumbed to the Ottoman Turks in 1453.

THE EARLY BYZANTINE EMPIRE

Near East, Anatolia, Balkans, N Africa   395–717

In the 5th century CE, barbarian rulers invaded part of the eastern Roman empire, but the Byzantines weathered the storm, maintained their position, and, under Justinian (ruled 527–565 CE), even managed to reconquer many of the lost provinces in North Africa and Italy.

These were brittle victories, however, and many of the devastated territories produced little tax revenue, or loyalty. In 568 CE, the Byzantines lost much of Italy to the Lombards (*see p.188*), and exhausting wars with the

Persian empire, which ended in a Byzantine victory in 628, left both realms severely weakened. The invasions by Muslim-Arab armies from the 620s led to the fall of Jerusalem in 637, of Alexandria (and Egypt) in 640, and finally Carthage in 698, spelling the end of Byzantine North Africa. When Arab armies besieged Constantinople in 717, it looked as if the empire was finished.

A mosaic depicting Justinian from the Church of San Vitale, Ravenna, Italy. Justinian's legal reforms made him a hugely respected emperor.

BYZANTINE SURVIVAL AND FALL

Near East, Anatolia, Balkans   717–1453

The Byzantine emperor
Leo III (ruled 717–741)
beat off Arab invasion in
717 with the aid of the
Bulgarian *khan* (ruler).
In the mid-8th century
Leo III weakened the
empire by causing
uproar when he banned
religious icons, claiming
they were tantamount to
idol worship.

From the 9th century,
under the Macedonian
dynasty, the empire began
to recover. Nicephorus
Phocas (ruled 963–969)
won a string of victories in
Syria, and John Tzimiskes
(ruled 969–76) defeated the Bulgar tsar
Boris II, thereby securing the empire's
position in the Balkans, and reconquered
large parts of Syria.

A view of Constantinople, from a late 15th century
German history, shows the city as imagined a short
time after its fall to the Ottoman Turks in 1453.

THE REVIVAL PEAKS AND FALTERS

Under Basil II, "the Bulgar-Slayer"(ruled
963-1025), the revival of the empire
seemed to be complete. The Bulgars
were smashed at the Battle of Kleidion
(1014) and much of southern Italy was
retaken. But Basil neglected the empire's

BASIL THE BULGAR-SLAYER

The greatest of the Macedonian emperors,
Basil ascended the throne as an infant in
963, but did not rule in his own right until
976. In 995, he rampaged through the
Near East, sacking a string of Arab cities
and securing control of northern Syria.
From 1000, he won his greatest triumphs
against the Bulgars, culminating in the
victory at Kleidion in 1014, after which he
is said to have blinded all but one man in
every 100 of his prisoners, sending the
stumbling mass back to the Bulgarian Tsar
Samuel, who died of shock and shame.

eastern frontier and his successors
ignored the army, allowing the Seljuk
Turks (*see p.182*) to make incursions into
the empire, massacring the Byzantine
army at Manzikert in 1071. Much of
Asia Minor was lost by 1080 and only
the energy of Alexius I Comnenus
(ruled 1081–1118) staved off disaster.

Nevertheless, Byzantium's fatal decline
had now set in. Newly assertive enemies
such as the Normans chipped away at
Byzantine Italy and, in the Balkans,
the Slav kingdoms grew ever stronger.
Against the relentless pressure of the
Seljuk and Ottoman Turks, even the
most energetic emperors could do little
more than slow the pace of collapse.
By the early 15th century, Byzantium
controlled just a few territories and
Constantinople had become an isolated,
beleaguered outpost. On 29 May 1453,
the army of the Ottoman sultan
Mehmet II stormed the city walls and
the Byzantine empire came to an end.

THE AMERICAS

During the 9th century, the lowland Maya city-states were abandoned, leading to the end of the Classic era in Central America, but the Maya did continue to flourish in the northern Yucatán. In Mexico, the Toltecs built ceremonial centres and then, in the 14th century, the Aztecs established a great empire. In the 15th century in South America, the cultures of Tiwanaku and Wari gave rise to the greatest and most advanced empire Peru had yet known, that of the Inca

THE TOLTECS

Central Mexico　　　*c.*900–*c.*1180

Around the 9th century, Mexico gave birth to new, more militarized cultures, well placed to take advantage of the persistent warfare of the region. Among them were the Chichimecs, nomadic invaders from the north, and a more advanced culture known as the Toltecs, from whom the Aztecs claimed descent.

THE TOLTEC CAPITAL
The Toltecs first entered Mexico in the early 10th century and, under their ruler Topiltzin Quetzalcoatl, made a capital at Tollan (modern-day Tula). From here, between 950 and 1150, they held sway over a portion of the valleys of Mexico, Puebla, and Morelos. The racks at Tula that held the skulls of dead enemies, and the sacrificial motifs prevalent in its reliefs, speak of a warrior culture. Around 1180, outsiders invaded Tollan, burning the city and ending Toltec dominance in central Mexico.

One of the Atlantes – monumental columns carved in the form of Toltec warriors – that expressed the Toltecs' militaristic ideology in stone.

THE MAYA

📍 Mexico, Guatemala   ⏳ c.800–1697

istorians have proposed many explanations for e sudden collapse of the wland Maya city-states uring the 800s – from tural causes, such as sease or climate change, soil exhaustion, war, loss of control by the ling classes. However, theory has yet been oven absolutely.

After c.900, all the main aya centres were in the rthern part of the catán. One, Chichen zá, had been founded in e second half of the 8th century by a nfederation of various Maya lowland oups and the Itzá people.

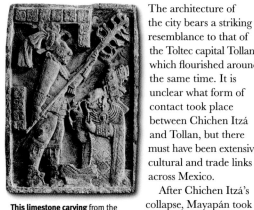

This limestone carving from the Mayan city of Yaxchilán depicts a bloodletting ritual.

HICHEN ITZÁ

he city, which experimented with new uals and forms of shared government, as a thriving community in the 9th to th centuries, but collapsed thereafter.

The architecture of the city bears a striking resemblance to that of the Toltec capital Tollan, which flourished around the same time. It is unclear what form of contact took place between Chichen Itzá and Tollan, but there must have been extensive cultural and trade links across Mexico.

After Chichen Itzá's collapse, Mayapán took over as the leading Maya city, ruling a confederacy of peoples that lasted until the arrival of the Spanish in the 16th century. Maya resistance to the Spanish was fierce, and independent Maya states lasted until the conquest of the final Itzá capital of Nojpeten (Tayasal) in 1697.

The vivid murals from Bonampak (near Yaxchilán) date from the late 8th century and are some of the finest surviving examples of Maya painting.

THE AZTECS

🏳 Mexico　　☠ *c.*1168–1520

The Aztecs, or the Mexica as they called themselves, began as an insignificant group in the Valley of Mexico, an area racked by constant warfare in the 13th century and ruled by petty kingdoms. They grew to be, by the 15th century, the most powerful people in Mesoamerica.

THE AZTEC EMPIRE

Aztec tradition relates that their peoples migrated from a land in the north named "Aztlán" in 1168, and in 1375 they appointed their first *tlatoani* (king), possibly from a family of Toltec origin. He ruled from Tenochtitlán (modern Mexico City), at the time the largest and most powerful city in Mesoamerica. In the vast marshes that surrounded Tenochtitlán, the Aztecs built dams to trap the fresh water from the rivers that flowed into the lake. They also grew crops on *chanampas*, artificial islands created in the shallow lake.

In 1429, the fourth Aztec ruler, Itzcoatl (ruled 1428–40), brokered a triple alliance that united his city with the cities of Texcoco and Tlacopan. In time, though, the Aztecs exploited

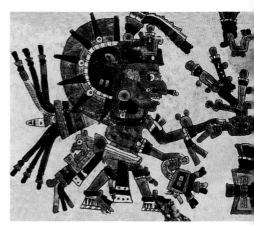

Detail from the *Codex Cospi*, an illustrated Aztec divinatory calendar, made from thin strips of plant fibres covered with whitewash.

their allies and went on to conquer all of Mexico. By 1500 even parts of Guatemala and El Salvador paid tribute to the Aztec empire. Yet soon after the Spanish arrived in Mexico in 1519 (*see p.233*), the Aztec civilization collapsed.

AZTEC RELIGION

The Aztecs had a large number of gods related to the creation of the cosmos, to the sun, and to fertility, death, and war. The two main temples of Tenochtitlán were dedicated to Huitzilopochtli, the god of war, and Tlaloc, the god of rain and water. Another important god, Quetzalcoatl, was the feathered-serpent god of wind, creativity, and fertility. The Aztecs believed that if they did not satisfy the gods with sacrifices of blood, the sun would not continue its journey across the sky

Sacrificial knives, such as this Aztec priest's knife with an ornately carved handle, were used to dispatch thousands of people at the temples each year.

EARLY NORTH AMERICAN CULTURES

SW and midwestern USA c.700–c.1450

southwest North America, small villages subsisting on corn gradually merged into three principal cultures – the Hohokam, the Mogollon, and the Anasazi – by 700.

By 900, the Hohokam, the earliest of the three traditions, had built canals up to 15km (9 miles) long and a sophisticated irrigation network that allowed them to grow two crops a year. Strongly influenced by Mexico, in their major settlements at Snaketown and Pueblo Grande they constructed ballcourts and platform temples in the Mesoamerican style. From the 10th century, the Mogollon, to the southeast of the Hohokam, lived in large adobe-built complexes (*pueblos*), and from earliest times were expert potters.

The most widespread culture of the three was the Anasazi, which reached its height between 900 and 1100. Around 1100, the Anasazi left their *pueblos* and began to take refuge in cliff-dwellings sheltered by canyon walls. By 1300, however, most of these were abandoned, possibly because of crop failure.

This ornamental gorget from the Mississippian culture was worn over the chest with a hide thong.

MOUND-DWELLERS

Further to the east, a separate group of cultures emerged in the Middle Mississippi Valley. Here, at the turn of the 8th century, sizeable towns appeared, most featuring large, rectangular mounds. The towns served as administrative and ceremonial centres for the Adena and Hopewell peoples. The greatest was Cahokia, at the confluence of the Mississippi and Missouri rivers. By the 13th century, Cahokia had a population of 30,000, with more than a hundred flat mounds containing high-status graves. By 1450, however, Cahokia was abandoned, possibly after an epidemic of disease.

The Cliff Palace" at Chapin Mesa is one of the largest Anasazi cliff-dwellings. It housed some people between about 1190 and 1280.

EARLY CULTURES OF SOUTH AMERICA

📍 Peru and Bolivia   ⏳ c.650–c.1470

From around 650, the highlands of the central Andes in South America came to be dominated by a series of empires.

TIWANAKU AND WARI

The earliest of these empires was Tiwanaku. Its capital was sited on the high altiplano of Bolivia. By 500 CE, its influence had spread into parts of the southern Andes and, at its peak, the city had around 50,000 inhabitants. The city was characterized by great monolithic portals, dedicated to a solar "gateway god".

The Tiwanaku rulers ordered large agricultural complexes of terraced fields to be built and controlled a thriving trade in textiles, pottery, and gold. In the end, it was probably a drought that saw Tiwanaku abandoned around 1000.

Around 700km (435 miles) northwest of Tiwanaku, the city of Wari emerged around 600. Its culture was characterized by large high-walled enclosures – scattered throughout Peru – where the Wari elite lived, dominating the local people by force. The empire seems to have been established rapidly, with most of the satellite colonies appearing around 650. Around 900, the Wari empire dissolved, possibly because of internal revolts that broke the bonds of a domain held together by military strength.

The great Gateway of the Sun, Tiwanaku's largest monumental portal, with its semi-subterranean temple in the foreground.

THE CHIMÚ

The collapse of the Moche culture around 800 (*see p.157*) left a political vacuum in coastal Peru. After the brief flourishing of a people known as the Sican, this void was eventually filled by the Chimú, who established their capital at Chan Chan near the Pacific coast around 900. Characterized by vast *ciudalelas* (palace compounds), at its height Chan Chan covered some 20 sq km (5,000 acres), and had a population as high as 35,000. The *ciudadelas* formed the enclosures of the Chimú lords, who from 1150 embarked on the conquest of the north coast of Peru. Ultimately, around 1370, this brought them into conflict with the growing power of the Incas (*see facing page*), who a century later finally conquered Chan Chan.

A feather hat from Peru's highland Wari culture, richly decorated with ferocious stylized animal heads.

THE INCA EMPIRE

 Peru and Bolivia c.1300–1532

e Incas first settled high in the
ruvian Andes around modern Cuzco
out 1300. However, in 1438, under
ir leader Pachacuti ("transformer of
 earth"), the Incas' expansion began
earnest, until the culture dominated
ch of modern Peru and Bolivia – an
a they called Tawantinsuyu, "the
nd of the Four Quarters". Around
70, the Inca empire absorbed its most
ngerous rival, conquering the Chimú
pital of Chan Chan, and by 1493 Inca
e reached north to Quito in Ecuador.

RARCHY, ADMINISTRATION,
D RELIGION

hacuti and his son Tupac Inca
ated a federal system consisting of
r provinces, each overseen by an Inca
vernor. At the top of the empire's
ial hierarchy was the Sapa Inca,
ose rule was absolute in political and
gious affairs. A complex bureaucracy
ninistered his empire but, being
olutely dependent on him, the whole
tem crumbled when the Sapa Inca
into the hands of Spanish
aders in the 1530s (*see p.233*).
The empire was linked by
etwork of roads, many of
m paved, which connected
outlying regions to the
pital Cuzco. The Incas
d no horses, nor had
y discovered the use of
wheel for transport, so
ays of runners carried
ssages, while llamas
ved as pack animals.
Lacking a developed
tem of writing, the Incas
t records on *quipus*,
lections of coloured

> ### PACHACUTI
>
> The ninth Sapa Inca, Pachacuti (ruled
> 1438–71) vastly extended the Inca empire,
> sending his armies north almost to Quito,
> and south nearly to Sucre in Bolivia. He
> rebuilt Cuzco in the shape of a puma and
> strengthened the cult of the sun god Inti.

threads that were knotted to calculate
taxation, keep records of livestock, and
pass on simple messages.

The Inca built large temples, many
of them to the sun-god Inti. The most
important of these was the Qorikancha,
which lay close to Cuzco's central plaza
and in which the Spanish conquistadors
would find an entire replica garden of
precious materials, including "maize" with
stems of silver and ears made from gold.

 gold disc representing the sun god
s one of the few Inca artefacts that the
nish conquerers failed to melt down.

The city of Machu Picchu was constructed in the mid-15th century, probably by the Inca ruler Pachacuti. Dramatically situated, it most likely served as a religious centre rather than a defensive one, and was abandoned a short time before the Spanish conquest of 1532–33.

POLYNESIA

Beginning around 200 BCE, the Polynesian people began
a major expansion and by approximately 1000 CE, settlers
had explored and settled all corners of the South Pacific,
achieving astonishing feats of long-distance navigation.
At their furthest extent, they reached New Zealand and
Easter Island, and established a diverse range of cultures,
making the Polynesians the most widely dispersed ethnic
group of the time.

POLYNESIAN EXPANSION AND NAVIGATION

Polynesia   c.200 BCE–c.1000 CE

The Polynesian people are likely to have
descended from a southeast Asian group,
possibly from modern Taiwan, and have
genetic affinities to a people indigenous
to Melanesia, a group of islands north of
Australia. This cultural mix gave rise to
the Lapita culture, whose fine red pottery
dates back to around 1600 BCE.

THE GREAT POLYNESIAN EXPANSION
The Lapita people used stone adzes
and cultivated yam and taro, as well as
coconut, breadfruit, and bananas, and
they domesticated pigs and chickens – all
elements that would form an important
part of later Polynesian culture.
Excellent navigators, they used
outrigger canoes to traverse great
distances. To guide them, they
used the stars, birds, winds,
currents, and tides, and

may also have used charts made of stick
They reached the Marquesas Islands
around 200 BCE; Easter Island, Tahiti,
and Hawaii in about 400 CE; and finally
New Zealand around 1000. At each the
established chiefdoms, which led to the
growth of sophisticated
and hierarchical
societies.

This model of a Polynesian canoe
shows the double hull that lent the
necessary stability for ocean voyages.

THE MAORI

New Zealand ☪ c.1000–1840

New Zealand was the last major area to be settled by the Polynesians, who reached it around 1000. Its climate is very different from tropical Polynesia, which led to changes in established Polynesian ways of life. Of the traditional Polynesian crops, only the sweet potato took hold. Much of South Island was not suitable for agriculture, promoting a culture based on fishing, hunting, and gathering. Around 1300, the Maori, as the descendants of the original settlers are known, did turn more to agriculture, probably because food for hunting became scarce.

Maori *tiki* talismans were traditionally worn for good luck, and by women to guard against infertility. This one is made in greenstone.

The population on North Island increased significantly, and the period after 1350, known as the Classic era, saw the building of massive earthwork forts, with rich burials. There appears to have been an upsurge in warfare between competing Maori groups, with the building of even larger forts (*pa*) with complexes of terraces and ditches. Despite their strikingly rich culture, the Maori never united politically, putting them at a disadvantage when European colonists arrived in the 19th century.

EASTER ISLAND

Easter Island ☪ c.400–1868

Easter Island (or to give it its Polynesian name, Rapa Nui) is one of the most isolated islands in Polynesia. It lies 2,000km (1,290 miles) from its closest neighbour and may have been settled by Polynesians around 400. Between 1000 and 1200 the trees on Easter Island began to disappear. This seems largely to have been triggered by the colonists' obsessive construction of giant stone heads, called *moai*. They were carved in one piece from compressed volcanic ash

and required enormous use of resources to move from the stone quarries and erect. Eventually, some time after 1600, when the last trees were cut, the islands' ecosystem collapsed as soil erosion leeched the land of its ability to bear crops, and there was no more wood to build boats for fishing. In the ensuing social turmoil, the *moai* were deliberately thrown down, beginning in the early 18th century, so that by 1868 none were left intact.

Re-erected *moai* statues on Easter Island are believed to embody revered ancestors.

THE EARLY
MODERN WORLD

THE WORLD IN 1450–1750

Europe underwent a cultural revolution – the Renaissance – in th[e]
15th and 16th centuries, in which much of the continent's ancie[nt]
learning was rediscovered. A spirit of scientific enquiry arose tha[t]
provided key technological advantages over the rest of the worl[d]
and voyages of exploration soon became tidal waves of colonizati[on]

The world in 1700

— international border

········ undefined border

▨ Ottoman empire

▨ Russian empire

▨ Safavid empire

▨ Mughal empire

▨ Qing empire

▨ ◆ England and possessions

▨ ◆ France and possessions

▨ ◆ Denmark and possessions

▨ ◆ Spain and possessions

▨ ◆ Portugal and possessions

▨ ◆ Netherlands and possessions

▨ Hohenzollern possessions

▨ Sweden and possessions

▨ Venetian Republic
and possessions

▨ Austrian Habsburg
territories

▨ Japan

— Holy Roman empire

THE EARLY MODERN WORLD IN 1700

By 1700, most of Central and South Americ[a]
(except Brazil) was controlled by Spain, with
large British and French colonies in North
America. Muslim empires were at their heig[ht]
in Persia, India, and modern Turkey. The
Russian empire had expanded eastwards to
Siberia, while the Qing held sway in China.

...aching most parts of the globe. By the mid-18th century, several ...uropean countries were global powers, though their rise was not ...nopposed. Ming and Qing China, Mughal India, Safavid Persia, ...nd the Ottomans resisted Europe's expansion, but their resources ...ere overwhelmed by superior technology and organization.

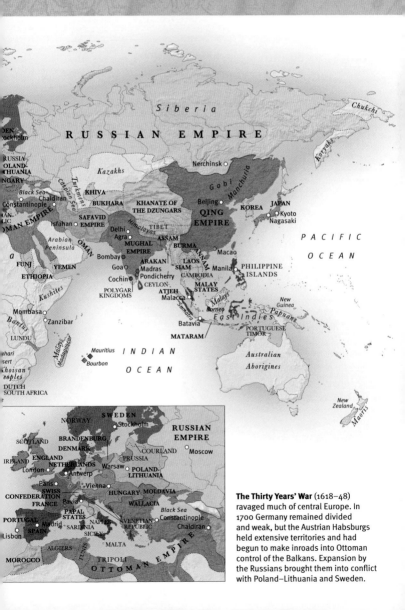

The Thirty Years' War (1618–48) ravaged much of central Europe. In 1700 Germany remained divided and weak, but the Austrian Habsburgs held extensive territories and had begun to make inroads into Ottoman control of the Balkans. Expansion by the Russians brought them into conflict with Poland–Lithuania and Sweden.

ASIA

The period from 1450 to 1650 was a time of great turmoil for Asia. China saw the collapse of the Ming dynasty and its replacement by the Qing, a dynasty that originated from Manchuria, in the northeast. In Japan, meanwhile, a series of bitter civil wars ended with unification under the Tokugawa shoguns. In western Asia, three Muslim empires arose to dominate the region: the Mughals in India, the Ottomans in Turkey, and the Safavids in Persia.

DECLINE OF THE MING

China 1449–1644

The Ming dynasty's last wave of expansionism ended in 1449 when the Mongols captured Emperor Zhengzhong (ruled 1436–49 and 1457–64). Rejecting further military adventures, subsequent emperors focused on affairs at home.

THE LATER MING RULERS
Emperors such as Jiajing (1531–67) and Wanli (1572–1620) became, however, ever more remote from their subjects, and government fell increasingly under the control of palace eunuchs. With the morale of the regime in decline and a realization

in the provinces that the emperor would do nothing for them, by the 1640s the Ming's hold on power was in desperate trouble. A series of peasant uprisings culminated in April 1644 in the capture of the capital Beijing by the rebel peasant leader Li Zicheng. Li tried to persuade the Ming frontier commander Wu Sangui to join him, but Wu instead allowed the Qing through the frontier (*see facing page*). With his capital lost and his rule overthrown, the last Ming emperor, Chongzhen (ruled 1627–44), committed suicide.

The Temple of Heaven, Beijing is a relic of the Ming dynasty's architectural splendour

THE RISE OF THE QING

China ⌛ 1616–50

northeastern China, an area that lay
side Ming control, a group called the
chens, descendants of the Jin dynasty
15–1234 CE), began, in the late 16th
tury, to absorb their neighbouring
ples. In 1616 their leader
rhaci founded the Later Jin
asty and formally organized
h his people and the Mongol
es of the region. The
ulation was enrolled
four military units
ed banners, each
ntified by the colour of
standard. Nurhaci's
cessor Huang
ji (ruled 1626–43)
oduced Chinese-style
itutions among the

Jurchen, changing the name of his
people in 1636 to Manchu, and restyling
the dynasty in 1637 as Qing. In 1644,
expanding into territory further
south, the Qing took control of the
Ming capital Beijing from rebel
forces (*see facing page*) and
installed six-year-old
Shunzhi as emperor
(ruled 1644–61).
Qing forces went on
sweeping south, crushing
any resistance. By 1650,
apart from isolated holdouts
such as Taiwan, Qing control
over China was complete.

A mounted warrior, typical of the
Qing fighters who fought sporadic
Ming resistance in the 1640s.

CHINA UNDER THE QING

China ⌛ 1644–1795 CE

e Qing bureaucracy in China retained
ny features of the earlier Ming
tem, but caused resentment by
creeing that all Chinese men
pt the traditional Qing hairstyle
shaved forehead and long,
ided ponytail or queue. The
cessors of Shunzhi (*see above*)
Kangxi (ruled 1661–1722),
ngzheng (ruled 1722–35),
d Qianlong (ruled 1736–95) –
sided over the period of greatest
pansion. The Qing absorbed
ter Mongolia, and claimed Tibet
a protectorate in 1750. This was also
me of increasing influences from
side China. Kangxi passed an "edict
toleration" that enabled the spread of
ristian Jesuit missions, while exports of
, silk, and ceramics to Europe burgeoned.

A sinuous dragon coils around a panel from the
Dazheng Hall of the Shenyang Palace in northeast
China, the original residence of the Qing rulers.

JAPAN UNITED AND THE TOKUGAWA SHOGUNATE

Japan   1560–1800

In the mid-1500s, Japan was fragmented into many semi-independent domains, each ruled by a separate *daimyo* (warlord), while the shogun (ruler of the military), and even more so the emperor, were powerless to exert their authority. Gradually, groups of *daimyo* clustered together and, in 1560, the leader of one group, Imagawa Yoshimoto, tried to take control of the royal capital, Kyoto. To do so he had to cross the lands of Oda Nobunaga, who cut his forces to pieces. Nobunaga then entered Kyoto himself, beginning a 40-year process of Japanese unification.

Toyotomi Hideyoshi was one of Nobunaga's chief generals, with considerable military talent.

NOBUNAGA AND HIDEYOSHI

By 1577, Nobunaga had conquered central Japan; he then moved against more distant *daimyo*. His chief general, Toyotomi Hideyoshi, was engaged in a bitter struggle against the powerful Mori clan of northern Honshu when Nobunaga was assassinated in 1582.

Hideyoshi broke off the conflict in order to take over Nobunaga's mantl as head of the unificatio drive. He had still to overcome six major *dai* groupings, finally forcin the capitulation of the most powerful, the Hoj of Odowara, in 1590.

IEYASU COMPLETES THE UNIFICATION

Hideyoshi died in 1598 and a power struggle immediately broke out, from which Tokugawa Ieyasu emerged the victor, smashing his opponents' armies at Sekigahara in 1600. Confiscating vast tracts of land from the defeated *daimyo* he established himself as shogun, but with an unparalleled monopoly on power. Ieyasu made Edo (Tokyo) the new, military capital of Japan. The emperor and his court, although revered, retained only ceremonial stature at Kyoto, and

TOKUGAWA IEYASU

Born Matsudaira Takechiyo in 1542, Tokugawa Ieyasu was a claimant to succeed Oda Nobunaga as shogun in 1582, but was outmanoeuvred by another general, Toyotomi Hideyoshi. Only once Hideyoshi had died, and Ieyasu had won a decisive victory over other rivals at the battle of Sekigahara, did he finally take over the shogunate. His reforms stabilized the power of the Tokugawa shogunate, strengthening it against challenges from regional *daimyo* (warlords). He died in 1616, leaving Japan's unification as his legacy.

nese society became more
ctured. Extensive legislation
blished a hierarchy of four
ses: samurai, farmer,
san, and merchant.

AN TURNS INWARD

der the Tokugawa,
afucian doctrines began
xert a greater influence in
an. With its emphasis on
lty to the political order and
al stability, Confucianism suited
regime well, and went hand-in-hand
a closing inward of Japan. In 1612,
ugawa Hidetada (ruled 1605–23)
firmed a policy of national seclusion
own as *sakoku*) and, in 1614, foreign
le was restricted to the cities of
gasaki and Hirado in southern
shu. By 1639, the Portuguese traders
had been expelled and
the Dutch confined
to a small island
off Nagasaki.

A Japanese mask used in *Noh* theatre. The restraint and elegance of *Noh* appealed to upper-class Japanese Edo society.

Tokugawa rule brought Japan two centuries of relative peace and tranquillity, as well as a cultural flowering. Many of the elements recognized as the keystones of Japanese traditional culture emerged during this period, such as *haiku* poetry, flower arranging, the tea ceremony, the final form of *Noh* theatre, and *Ukiyo-e* ("pictures of the floating world") prints. Yet, for all its unchallenged authority, the later Tokugawa regime was inflexible. Its seclusion from the outside world made Japan ill-prepared to face a resurgent and industrialized Europe in the 19th century that was very different from the Europe it had turned its back on.

The Japanese tea ceremony (*chanoyu*) was refined in the Tokugawa era, becoming a symbol of the delicate etiquette that held together the society of the age.

INDIA UNDER THE MUGHALS

📍 India   ⚔ 1526–1739

Ultimately one of the most powerful states of the 17th century, the Islamic Mughal empire had much more modest beginnings in the efforts of Babur, an ambitious Central Asian princeling who wanted to carve himself a territory near Samarkand. In 1504, Babur seized Kabul in modern Afghanistan and the next year he launched his first raid into India.

BABUR AND HUMAYUN

In 1519, Babur launched a concerted bid to unseat the Lodi sultans of Delhi (*see p.185*). In April 1526, at Panipat, Babur crushed the army of Ibrahim Lodi. He then marched on and took not only Delhi but also Agra, where the Lodi treasury was lodged. Moving west, at Kanua the

BABUR

Founder of the Mughals, Babur (ruled 1526–30) was descended from the Mong conqueror Tamerlane, who had raide Delhi in 1328. Babur outdid him b capturing the city and becomir the first Mughal emperor.

following year he defeat a huge army raised by Rana Sangha of Mewar (in modern-day Rajasth By the time of his death 1530, Babur had consolida his position as master of the rich cities of northern India. His son Humayun, however, met with less success. By 1540, he had lost his fathe kingdom to the Afghan ruler Sher Sha Sur, and was in exile at the Safavid cou in Persia. In 1555, with the support of Persians (*see pp.228–9*), he restored Mug rule by pushing aside Sher Shah's feebl successors. He died soon after, leaving t empire to his 12-year-old son Akbar.

THE REIGN OF AKBAR

At first under the tutelage of the capa regent Bairam Khan, Akbar oversaw a vast extension of Mughal territory. In lifetime Mughal dominion expanded reach from Kashmir in the north and Afghanistan in the northwest to Benga in the east and the Deccan plateau in south. To consolidate his position, Akb established a centralized system of government, administered by warrior-aristocrats (*mansabdars*). The most seni of these were paid with land grants (*jagirs*), and held the right to collect tax from this land. Akbar promoted a poli of religious tolerance. He reduced the

A Mughal miniature of the Battle of Panipat (1526 clearly shows the cannons, part of the arsenal of firearms that was instrumental in Babur's victory.

fluence of the Muslim scholars (*ulama*) government policy, abolished taxes on on-Muslims (*jizya*), and replaced the uslim lunar calendar with a solar one. e thereby avoided dissension among s many non-Muslim subjects.

Akbar's reign also saw a cultural naissance. A new style of north Indian assical music flourished, did an enormously oductive school of ughal painting that mbined Persian and dian styles.

HANGIR AND IAH JEHAN

kbar died in 1605, and as succeeded by his son hangir, who had already ed several times to depose m. In turn, Jahangir faced rebellion in 1623 by his rd son, Khurram, which ded only a year before hangir's death in 1627. civil war instantly erupted tween Jahangir's four sons er the succession.

The victor, Khurram, o took the name Shah han (ruled 1628–58),

The Mughal court excelled in decorative arts, architecture, and producing miniatures.

ntributed some of the Mughal npire's greatest surviving monuments, cluding a new capital at Delhi – which called Shahjahanabad – centred on e Red Fort and the Jama Masjid; and e majestic Taj Mahal at Agra. These ge projects were symbols of Mughal alth gained from flourishing riculture and trade. In 1657, Shah han fell gravely ill. Without waiting to

see the outcome of their father's illness, his sons threw themselves with great gusto into a vicious and damaging civil war, from which Aurangzeb, the third son, emerged victorious in 1660. Shah Jehan had by now recovered, but Aurangzeb locked him away in the palace at Agra, where he died, neglected and bitter, in 1666.

AURANGZEB AND THE DECLINE OF THE EMPIRE

Aurangzeb oversaw the expansion of the empire to its greatest extent, yet he also sowed the seeds of its decline. He was often away on campaigns, and his efforts to defeat the Maratha confederacy of Shivaji in the south, which was seeking to build an empire of its own, met with little success. He was also intolerant in religious matters, reimposing taxes on Hindu pilgrims and, in 1670, reinstating the *jizya* tax on all non-Muslims.

All these moves polarized opinion of him and undermined his support among the vast numbers of Hindus and Sikhs in the Mughal empire.

Aurangzeb died in 1707 and a rapid succession of weak rulers further undermined Mughal power. In 1739, Nadir Shah, the ruler of Persia, sacked Delhi and seized the Mughal treasury. As a serious political force, the Mughal empire was now dead.

The Taj Mahal, at Agra, is Mughal emperor Shah Jehan's stunning mausoleum for his wife Mumtaz Mahal, who died in childbirth in 1631. It is the ultimate Mughal garden tomb, representing paradise on earth, and took from 1632 to 1654 to complete. Shah Jehan is buried there, too.

THE OTTOMAN EMPIRE

⚑ Turkey, Near East, Balkans, N Africa   ⌛ 1453–1739

After their conquest of the Byzantine empire in 1453 under their sultan Mehmet II (*see p.203*), Ottoman armies surged forward into the Balkans. However, failure to capture Belgrade (then in Hungary) in 1456 put a temporary halt to westward expansion. The remnant of Hungary, and a fiercely independent Albanian principality under the rule of the warrior-prince Skanderbeg, kept a watchful eye on their new Turkish neighbours. The Ottomans turned their attention east, where the growing power of Safavid Persia (*see pp.228–9*) threatened to stem or even reverse the Ottoman tide.

THE HEIGHT OF OTTOMAN POWER

It was not until the Battle of Chaldiran in 1514 that Selim I (ruled 1512–20) was able to best the Safavid dynasty. The Ottomans then pushed rapidly forward, capturing the holy sites in Jerusalem and in 1517 overthrowing

> ### SULEYMAN I
>
> Known in the West as "the Magnificent" and to Islamic writers as *Kanuri* ("the lawgiver"), Suleyman (ruled 1520–66) was one of the greatest Ottoman sultans and believed himself to be the spiritual heir of Alexander the Great (*see pp.124–5*) and Julius Caesar (*see p.132*). By the time of Suleyman's death the Ottomans controlled large parts of southeast Europe, the North African coast, and the Middle East.

the Mamluk rulers of Egypt by capturing Cairo. In 1520, Suleyman Selim's son, took charge. In 1523, he captured the island of Rhodes, which was the stronghold of the Knights of St John, a military order of the crusader era.

Having stabilized the situation in Egypt with a new law code in 1525 that appeased local resentment, Suleyman

Ottoman forces equipped with cannons tried to capture Vienna in 1529, but Suleyman's army was unable to dislodge the city's defenders.

orative tilework, often created using
cled material from older structures,
a feature of Ottoman architecture.

ned once more to war with
attack on Hungary. At
hács in 1526, he cut to
ces the army of Louis II
Hungary, resulting in the
ision of the kingdom
ween the Ottomans and
Austrian Habsburgs. In
29, Suleyman attempted to
e by siege the Habsburg
ital of Vienna, but this
rked a watershed in his territorial
bitions, and after only three weeks his
ny, frustrated, retired into Hungary.

E BEGINNING OF DECLINE
leyman's personal life was less
tunate. His two favourite sons,
stafa and Bayezid, were accused

THE DEMISE AND THE TULIP AGE
In the 1650s, Mehmet Koprülü, the
Grand Vizier to Mehmet IV (ruled
1648–87), began a systematic attempt to
root out corruption. He also planned a
resumption of Ottoman conquest, but
died in 1661 before his plans could come
to fruition. His brother-in-law Kara

"I AM GOD'S SLAVE AND SULTAN OF THIS WORLD… IN BAGHDAD I AM SHAH, IN BYZANTINE REALMS THE CAESAR, AND IN EGYPT THE SULTAN."

Inscription of Suleyman the Magnificent on the citadel of Bender, Moldavia, 1538

conspiring against him. To save his
one, Suleyman was forced to have
m both executed (in 1553 and 1562),
ting a shadow over the rest of his reign.
died on a final Hungarian campaign
1566 and the throne fell to his third
Selim, nicknamed "the drunkard",
ose rule was of a very different nature.
Selim's formative experiences were
the enclosed world of the harem of
Topkapi Palace in Istanbul. He
d little or no military training, and
subsequent sultans, relied on
iers (ministers) to control the empire.
cking the sultan's controlling hand, the
pire fell prey to competing elements
the government: the Diwan (supreme
rt); the Grand Vizier (chief minister);
d the janissaries (elite army units).

Mustafa continued Koprülü's ambitions,
besieging Vienna in 1683. Once again,
however, the Turks were forced to
abandon the siege. A steady European
encroachment on Ottoman lands began,
spearheaded by the Habsburgs. Belgrade
and Serbia were lost by the Treaty of
Passarowitz in 1718, but Mahmud I (ruled
1730–54) brought respite by negotiating
the Treaty of Belgrade in 1739.

Amazingly, though the Ottomans were
militarily enfeebled, racked by revolt, and
faced constant threat from, or actual
secession of, its borderlands, the empire
still experienced a golden cultural age in
the late 17th and 18th centuries. A refined
court culture – the "Tulip Age" – belied
the reality of a state that, within 150 years,
would lose most of its European lands.

SAFAVID PERSIA

🏴 Persia   🕮 1501–1736

Following the collapse in 1335 of the Mongol Il-khanate, which had ruled Persia since the 1250s, the country dissolved into a collection of successor states. Then, from the 1370s, Tamerlane, a steppe conqueror in the tradition of Genghis Khan (*see p.166*), built a vast Central Asian empire that, from the 1380s, included much of Persia. After Tamerlane's death in 1405, his descendants continued to rule eastern Persia, while the western portion of the country fell to a group made up of Turkmen dynasties known the Aq Qoyunlu and Kara Qoyunlu.

THE RISE OF THE SAFAVIDS

Beset by civil war in the late 15th century the Aq Qoyunlu were overcome by a new group that had grown up around the Safavids, a Sufi order of Muslim mystic In 1501, the 14-year-old Safavid shah

> ## "NOW THAT I AM KING WE ARE GOING TO FORGET ABOUT THE PRACTICE OF SULTAN MUHAMMAD SHAH; THE KING IS GOING TO MAKE THE DECISIONS NOW."
>
> Safavid ruler Shah Abbas I on his accession to the throne in 1587

The Masjid-e Shah (or Imam Mosque), begun by Shah Abbas I in 1611, forms an imposing centrepiece in Isfahan's Maydan Square.

Ismail I (ruled 1501–24) defeated the Aq Qoyunlu at Alwand, and by 1507 all of western Persia had fallen to the Safavids. Pushing further west still, Ismail's armies met the Ottomans. A protracted struggle culminated at Chaldiran in 1514, where the Ottoman sultan Selim I defeated Ismail and prevented the absorption of eastern Anatolia into the Safavid empire.

THE HEIGHT OF POWER

By 1513, Ismail had created a stable frontier to the ea that restrained his Cent Asian Uzbek neighbou With further westward expansion blocked by the Ottoman empire, Ismail turned his attention to making

An **18th-century hunting scene** reflecting the cultured elegance of the later Safavid court, more inclined to the pursuits of leisure than war.

ofound reforms within the Persian ate. He imposed a new official faith on e country, a variety of Shia Islam that as to dominate Persian religious life to the modern era.

Ottoman and Uzbek aggression and cursions dogged Ismail's descendants til the reign of Shah Abbas I, under nom Safavid rule reached its peak. etween 1587 and 1607 he recaptured st territories, and in 1598, he moved e capital from Qazvin to Isfahan, here he ordered the construction of a zzling array of new buildings, centred the grand Maydan Square.

Abbas I's character had a dark side. 1615, he had his (probably innocent) ir, Safi Mirza, executed on spicion of treasonous plotting, d for similar reasons had s other two sons blinded, squalifying them from cceeding him. On bbas's death in 1629, it as his grandson, Safi I, ho became shah.

SHAH ABBAS I

Aged only 16 when he came to the throne, Shah Abbas I (ruled 1587–1629) proved a determined and able ruler. He embarked on a programme of building that would lead his reign to be regarded as a golden age for Persia.

THE FALL OF THE SAFAVIDS

Despite the loss of Baghdad to the Ottomans in 1638, Safi's able minister Saru Taqi ensured financial stability and the reign of Safi's son Shah Abbas II (1642–66) was peaceful and prosperous. However, his successor Sulayman presided over a gentle decline, as he retreated to the harem and ceased to exert effective power. By 1720, faced with multiple revolts, the Safavid regime fell apart and in October 1722 Shah Husayn surrendered Isfahan to an army led by the rebel Afghan leader Mahmud Ghilzai. Ghilzai did not last long as shah, being murdered in 1725. The country then fell under the control of another tribal leader, Nadir Khan. Ruling through Safavid puppets until 1736, he then declared himself shah and set about an ambitious military programme that included the reconquest of western Persia from the Ottomans and the sacking of Delhi, the Mughal capital, in 1739. However, his cruelty and extortionate tax regimes to fund his campaigns made him deeply unpopular; he was killed in 1747, and Persia once more descended into chaos.

VOYAGES OF DISCOVERY

At the start of the 15th century, Europeans' knowledge of the world
beyond their own continent was limited, and based largely on the
cartography of Ptolemy, a Greek polymath who had died 13 centuries
earlier, in 168 CE. Yet, in little over a century, European horizons
expanded massively as their navigators set sail, opening up new sea
routes to India and the East and discovering the continent of America.

THE FIRST ROUTES

The Portuguese were early
pioneers in endeavours at
sea, concentrating first on
southward voyages around the
African coastline.
In 1486, Diogo
Cão explored the
Congo river, before
making his final
landfall at Cape
Cross in what is now
Namibia. Two years
later, Bartolomeu Dias rounded the
Cape of Good Hope and sailed into
the Indian Ocean, while in 1498
Vasco da Gama crossed over the

Indian Ocean to Calicut in
southern India. The incentive
for these expeditions was largely
a desire to find a sea route to
the sources of the
lucrative spice trade
in eastern Asia.
Not wishing
to be outdone by
their Portuguese rivals,
the Spanish sought an
alternative, westerly
route to Asia and, in
1491, the Genoese-born Christopher
Columbus was able to persuade
Queen Isabella of Castile to support
a voyage across the Atlantic.

Black pepper was one of the precious
commodities that Europeans sought
in pioneering new routes to Asia.

An atlas from *c.*1519 shows details of the coastline of Brazil - a Portuguese discovery.

THE AMERICAS

Columbus set sail in August 1492 with three ships (*see overleaf*). He accepted Ptolemy's calculation of the world's size and so when he sighted land, he believed it to be eastern Asia, not a new continent ripe for expansion. Even a further three voyages did not shake this conviction. Further explorations followed rapidly; within five years, in 1497, John Cabot sailed into North American waters off Newfoundland, while the voyage of Jacques Cartier in 1534 took the French to the Gulf of Saint Lawrence. The Portuguese, meanwhile, began to occupy their own area of the Americas, following the discovery of the Brazilian coastline by Alvares Cabral in 1500.

THE FIRST CIRCUMNAVIGATION

The lure of trade routes to Asia continued to motivate European monarchs and the sailors they funded. In 1519, the Portuguese explorer Ferdinand Magellan set out to sail to the Spice Islands (the Moluccas in Indonesia). He died in 1521 and his deputy completed the voyage; he and his crew were the first Europeans to sail around the world.

King Manuel I of Portugal gives his blessing to Vasco da Gama as he sets out in 1497 on the voyage that would discover a sea route to India.

THE AMERICAS

Soon after Columbus landed in the Americas in 1492, new Spanish expeditions occupied a series of Caribbean islands and toppled the Aztec empire of Mexico and the Inca rulers of Peru. Spain's authority in the New World was soon challenged by other European countries, notably France and England – both of which secured large territories in North America – and Portugal, which gained control of Brazil.

COLUMBUS LANDS IN AMERICA

⚑ The Caribbean   ⚐ 11 October 1492

In 1491, Christopher Columbus won the backing of Queen Isabella of Castile for a voyage that he planned to make to eastern Asia, after an eight-year search for a sponsor. On 3 August the following year, he set sail from the Spanish port of Palos in a small flotilla made up of the *Santa Maria*, *Pinta*, and *Niña*.

SAN SALVADOR
After an arduous voyage, on 11 October one of Columbus's men finally caught sight of land. Columbus named the island – whose exact location is now uncertain – San Salvador, claiming it for Spain. He called the local Arawak natives "Indians" in the firm belief that he had reached the coast of Asia. Three days after reaching San Salvador, Columbus departed, sailing to Cuba and then to Hispaniola, where he established a small colony, the precursor of the massive Spanish settlement to come.

Christopher Columbus landed in the Americas after five weeks at sea. He had wrongly calculated that A was just 4,500km (2,800 miles) west of Europe.

SPAIN CONQUERS MEXICO

Mexico ▪ 1519–1521

nce the Spanish were established in
e Caribbean, they learned of the rich
tec culture on the Mexican mainland.
February 1519, the conquistador
ernán Cortés sailed from Havana,
iba, to find it. Having forced his way
rough the Yucatán peninsula,
16 August he moved inland
th 15 horsemen and 400
fantry. He secured native
ies in the Tlaxcala, bitter
emies of the Aztecs.

HERNÁN CORTÉS

After conquering the Aztecs,
Hernán Cortés became governor
of Mexico, but suffered successive
attempts by the Spanish authorities
to remove him or curb his power. In 1547
he died, wealthy but embittered, in Seville.

THE CAPTURE OF TENOCHTITLÁN

In November 1519, Cortés reached
Tenochtitlán, the Aztec capital, where
the ruler, Moctezuma, received the
Spanish cordially. But Cortés soon had
Moctezuma put under house arrest and,
when the Spanish massacred a
number of Aztec nobles,
Tenochtitlán descended into
chaos. Moctezuma was
killed by his own people,
while the Spanish fought
their way in hand-to-hand
combat out of the city.
Undaunted, in spring 1521,
Cortés returned with fresh
reinforcements to begin a new
siege of Tenochtitlán. This ended
in August the same year with the capture
of the new Aztec ruler, Cuahtemoc, and
the total dissolution of the Aztec empire.

SPAIN CONQUERS PERU

Peru ▪ 1527–1572

1527, a small Spanish expedition, in
arch of the rich land of "Birú" (Peru),
d by Francisco Pizarro, landed at
umbes, an outpost of the Inca empire.
zarro returned in 1531 with 180 men.
e found the Incas recovering from a
vil war, which allowed him to cross the
ndes freely to reach Cajamarca, where
e Inca leader Atahuallpa was camped.

THE FALL OF THE INCA EMPIRE

uring the Inca ruler into a meeting,
zarro took him hostage and then,
July 1533, had him executed. The
panish marched on the capital Cuzco,
hich they took in November. The
estige of the Inca nobility was severely
amaged by their failure to protect

Atahuallpa and they mounted little
coherent opposition. Yet in 1536, Manco
Capac, installed as a puppet ruler, began
a rebellion. Although the Spanish soon
retook Cuzco from the rebels, Inca
resistance continued on the fringes
of Peru until 1572, when their final
stronghold of Vilcamaba fell, and Titu
Cusi, the last Inca ruler, was executed.

ATAHUALLPA

With control of the imperial army in Quito,
Atahuallpa was able to triumph over his
brother Huascar to seize power of the Inca
realm in 1532, ending Peru's civil war. By
the time of this victory, the Spanish had
arrived; they executed Atahuallpa in 1533.

THE SPANISH EMPIRE IN THE NEW WORLD

Central and South America ⚰ 1523–1700

The Spanish faced grave problems governing their vast territories in the Americas, because they lay so far from Spain itself. From 1523, a formal body, the Council of the Indies, was set up to formulate policy for the new colonies. Unfortunately, very few of its members had actual experience of the Americas, and the distances involved led to an unresponsive form of government.

The two hemispheres of the world on this 1744 silver coin symbolize the global nature of Spanish conquest

territories to the north of Panama, and that of Peru had authority over the lands to the south.

The native Americans in the Spanish colonies suffered under the *encomienda* system, which made them the personal "possessions" of Spanish landowners. The obligation on the natives to pay increasing tributes, while at the same time their population was shrinking, caused terrible hardships. The Spanish empire's real economic wealth came, though, from a huge mountain of silver ore discovered at Potosí in Bolivia in 1545, which delivered enormous revenues. Up until 1660, some 16,000 tonnes (17,600 tons) of the metal were shipped to Seville, permitting Philip II of Spain and his successors to conduct a series of long (and expensive) wars.

NEW WORLD SILVER

Later in the 16th century, the Spanish replaced the crown's representatives in the Americas – the governors or captain-generals – with a system of viceroyalties (provinces). That of New Spain supervised the

CHALLENGES TO SPANISH RULE

Spanish control of America was never complete. In eastern South America, Spain competed with Portuguese (and later Dutch) settlements in Brazil; and in the Caribbean, various island were seized by the French and English. In North America, where Spanish control extended into Florida and California, the growing might of France and England put a definitive end to the hopes of an all-Spanish Americas.

With Spanish colonization of the Americas came Catholicism and magnificent church architecture.

EUROPEAN COLONIES IN NORTH AMERICA

North America ⚔ 1584–1724

Though the Spanish had bases in Florida to protect their silver-bullion fleets, it was the English who first attempted to colonize the eastern seaboard of North America. In 1584, English adventurer Sir Walter Raleigh despatched a fleet to establish a settlement on Roanoke Island in Virginia, but the colony disappeared in 1590. After the English defeat of the Spanish Armada in 1588 (*see p.247*), weakening Spanish domination in the North Atlantic, the English made new attempts to colonize North America.

Roanoke island, site of the first English colony (often called the "lost colony"), lies within a chain of barrier islands on which several supply ships came to grief.

ENGLISH RULE AND ITS COMPETITORS

In 1607 the Virginia Company of London established a colony at Jamestown. In 1620, the English established a further settlement at New Plymouth in Massachussetts, spearheaded by a group of Puritans – religious dissenters – who sailed to the New World in the *Mayflower*. From these tiny beginnings, English control spread throughout the eastern seaboard, with colonies established in Maryland in 1634, Rhode Island in 1636, and Pennsylvania (named for its Quaker founder William Penn) in 1682. Further south, the English crown took a more direct role, including establishing a colony in the Carolinas in 1665. Other Europeans joined the scramble, with the Dutch West India Company establishing Fort Orange (now Albany) on the Hudson River in 1623, and a Swedish colony founded in Delaware in 1638. These were eventually swept away by the more powerful English, who, by 1724, controlled the east coast from New England to Georgia. Only in modern Canada to the north were the English challenged – by French colonists. The French had founded Quebec in 1608, and by 1712 controlled a vast area from eastern Canada to the Rocky Mountains, and extending as far south as Louisiana.

"WE WENT BY THE SHORE TO SEEKE FOR THEIR BOATS, BUT COULD FIND NONE..."

Captain John White, on finding the English colony at Roanoke abandoned and the settlers vanished, 1589

TRADING EMPIRES

Parallel to their endeavours of exploration and colonization, many European nations developed large trading empires between the late 15th and 18th centuries, stretching to Africa, Asia, and the Americas. Those established by Spain, Portugal, and France tended to be extensions of monarchical control; by contrast, the maritime empires of England and the Netherlands were more mercantile in nature.

EUROPEAN TRADE

Portugal's experience in pioneering sea routes to the East was matched by its acquisitions there. Forts at Goa (1510), Malacca (1511), and Ormuz (1515) in the Indian Ocean, established by Admiral Afonso da Albuquerque, ensured Portuguese control of the Persian Gulf and the major trade routes leading east. Macau (in southern China) followed in 1517, and by the 1560s, half the spice and three-quarters of the pepper traded in Europe was imported by Portugal.

An Indian cotton wall-hanging from the late-16th century provides an early example of local impressions of European traders.

Spain's American empire yielded vast revenues from silver, shipped to Europe via the Philippines. France, while it benefited from the Canadian fur trade, regarded its empire as a

means for the state to assert power and limit English ambitions, rather than as an enabler of trade.

THE DUTCH AND THE ENGLISH

The empires of Holland and England had their basis in commerce. The Dutch East India Company, or VOC, was founded

The insignia of the VOC, or Dutch East India Company, established to trade with Asia.

in 1602 and established its first outpost at Banten (in Java) in 1604. It expanded to possess a string of factories stretching from Galle in Sri Lanka to southern India, Bengal, Malacca, Taiwan, and Nagasaki in Japan – all controlled from Batavia in northwestern Java. However, from the mid-17th century, trade with Japan waned, and the cost of defending the empire rose. The English encroached on VOC territory with their own East India Company, whilst internal corruption drained finances, and by

the middle of the 18th century, the VOC had become a shadow of its former self.

The English founded its counterpart, the British East India Company, in 1600. After 1615, this company's foothold in Bengal gave it access to crucial resources and allowed it to found bases in Bombay (1668) and Calcutta (1690) in India. In 1694, it was granted a monopoly on trade with India, cementing the company's position and affording it political power. Yet by the mid-19th century the English East India Company was also on the decline, brought down by the costs of military adventures and the heavy burden of corrupt practices – the very problems that had brought down its Dutch rival.

The establishment of Fort St George (the future Madras) in 1639 gave the English East India Company a vital toehold in southeastern India.

ᴇUROPE

By the mid-15th century, Europe, devastated by plague and warfare, had fallen behind other parts of the world both culturally and politically. Yet at this very time a remarkable artistic and literary revolution began in Italy th would resound for centuries to come, while increasingly centralized monarchies emerging in England, France, and Spain were soon ready to build global empires.

HUMANISM

📖 Europe ⌛ *c*.1450–*c*.1550

By the 15th century, education and literature in Europe had been dominated for hundreds of years by the needs and preoccupations of the Christian Church. Although great Classical authors such as Aristotle had formed part of the curriculum taught in universities, their works had been interpreted very much in the light of Catholic teachings. In the mid-15th century this began to change, as scholars in Italy became interested in a wider range of Classical literature, an especially works with a more secular bi that predated the rise of Christianity.

THE SPREAD OF HUMANISM

New Latin works were unearthed, such as those of Vitruvius, whose treatise on Roman architecture profoundly influenced 15th-century Florentine architects such as Filippo Brunelleschi; while other, previously neglected autho such as Cicero and Virgil enjoyed a new vogue. The movement became known as "humanism" for the degree to which its scholarship placed humankind, rather than God, at the centr of its world view. From Italy, the movement spread northwards, producing such towering figures as the Dutch human Erasmus and the English statesman Thomas Mor

ERASMUS (*c*.1466–1526)

The Dutch humanist Gerhard Gerhards (*c*.1466–1526) – known as Erasmus – was an ordained priest, but lived as a scholar. In works such as *In Praise of Folly* (1509), he criticized the corruption of the Church, advocating a life of firm moral and religious principles. His critical scholarship of Biblical texts helped pave the way for the Reformation (see pp.242–3).

THE RENAISSANCE

 Europe 1450–1550

The European Renaissance ("rebirth") refers to a broad movement, beginning in Italy in the early to mid-15th century, that drew inspiration from a new interest in the Classical world to produce astonishing developments in art, architecture, and literature. A prosperous mercantile class became the patrons of the new arts, giving greater freedom to the artists, while the advent of printing enabled the rapid dissemination of ideas.

ARCHITECTURE AND ART

In architecture, a mix of civic pride and firm ambitions to rival the achievements of Roman architecture provided the impetus for remarkable works such as the dome built for the cathedral of Florence (completed in 1436) by Filippo Brunelleschi. In painting and sculpture, the influence of

Sandro Botticelli's *The Birth of Venus* (c.1486) clearly shows the 15th-century's new preoccupation with subjects from Classical mythology.

LEONARDO DA VINCI

Outstanding among the great geniuses of the Renaissance, Leonardo (1452–1519) was apprenticed in 1466 to the sculptor Andrea del Verocchio. He showed a precocious talent in painting, but also embraced engineering and theorized a number of military devices. His artistic works include the innovative *Last Supper*, a mural at the church of Santa Maria delle Grazie in Milan, and the enigmatic portrait *Mona Lisa*.

ancient Greece and Rome was even more apparent; for there was a great interest in the nude human body, as seen especially in the works of Michelangelo Buonarroti. The roll call of Italian artists of this time is awe-inspiring, including such geniuses as Raphael and Leonardo da Vinci. Meanwhile, in literature, the Renaissance produced such famous works as *The Prince* (1532), Machiavelli's eminently secular handbook for rulers.

The ceiling of the Sistine Chapel in the Vatican is a masterwork of the Florentine Michelangelo Buonarroti (1475–1564). Commissioned by Pope Julius I in 1508, the ceiling frescoes depict scenes from the Old Testament and took four years to complete, with the artist working from a scaffold.

THE REFORMATION AND COUNTER-REFORMATION

⚐ Germany, Switzerland, France, Scandinavia, Britain ⌛ 1517–63

On 31 October 1517, Martin Luther (1483–1546), a priest who had become professor of theology at Wittenberg University, Germany, posted a document, his "95 Theses", on the door of the town church. In essence it was a public protest against the sale by priests of "indulgences" – pardons for sins – a practice widely criticized as an abuse of clerical power. This single act was the catalyst for a movement calling for reform of the Catholic Church that was to transform Europe.

Luther went on to attack other precepts of the Church, including the core Catholic dogma of transubstantiation (the belief that the bread and wine at communion transform into the body and blood of Christ) and, crucially, papal supremacy. Attempts were made to reconcile Luther with the religious authorities, until in 1521 he was

Martin Luther translated the Bible into German, a project he undertook to give the German people more direct access to the scriptures.

summoned to present his views at an imperial assembly (*Diet*) at Worms befor the Holy Roman Emperor Charles V. Luther refused to recant and, in respon to the Emperor's outlawing of him and his views, began an autonomous church

THE SPREAD OF PROTESTANTISM

Luther's teachings appealed to Germar princes opposed to imperial dominance they wrote a public letter of protest to the Emperor on Luther's behalf, from which the term "Protestantism" wa born. Throughout the 1520s, the German states of Saxony, Hesse, Brandenburg, and Brunswick one by one took up Lutheranism.

Political struggle turned into outright war, and although the Emperor defeated th Lutherans in battle at Mühlberg in 1547, h could not overcome them politically.

In the *Raising of Lazarus*
(1558), by Lucas Cranach, Luther (in the foreground, left) stands among other Protestant reformers.

The coronation of Charles V as Holy Roman Emperor in 1519. He would preside over a huge empire that marked the pinnacle of Habsburg power.

Calvinism took hold in Scotland, the Netherlands, and large parts of France. Lutheranism had meanwhile spread from large areas of Germany into Scandinavia, and was a factor in English king Henry VIII's break with Rome in the 1530s. The Roman Catholic Church faced crisis.

Charles V was forced to compromise with the Peace of Augsburg in 1555, by which he tolerated Lutheranism in areas where the local prince espoused it. While never recanting his views, Luther abhorred the violence the reform movement had engendered (and indeed had supported the crushing of a revolt in Germany, in 1524, by peasants influenced by his own ideas). But he was followed by more radical reformers, most notably John Calvin (1509–64). Calvin stressed predestination (God's control over all human actions) and a direct relationship with God, devoid of priestly or papal interference.

St Ignatius Loyola served as a soldier in Spain until, in 1522, he took up a more spiritual life.

THE COUNTER-REFORMATION

Yet Catholicism saved itself. Meeting in three sessions at Trent in the Italian Alps from 1545–63, the Catholic hierarchy strengthened both the Church's theology and its political position. Poland, Austria, and Bavaria were won back from Protestantism, although a series of religious wars in Europe from the 1550s put paid to further gains. The Catholic Church also reformed old religious orders and created new ones, most notably the Jesuits, who went on to establish influential schools and missions under the guidance of their founder Ignatius Loyola (1491–1556).

PRINTING

Although printing using reusable and moveable blocks appeared in China as early as 1040, the first effective press for printing books using moveable metal type and oil-based ink emerged in 15th-century Europe. Its invention is attributed to a German craftsman and entrepreneur, Johannes Gutenberg (*c.*1398–1468). The first book printed on this new type of press was the Bible, in 1455.

THE SPREAD OF PRINT

Gutenberg's printing techniques soon spread across Europe. By 1470, there were seven presses in Germany, and this grew to more than 50 by 1499. The first printed book in Italy was produced in 1467; presses were established in Paris by 1470, and in London (by William Caxton) in 1476. The most prestigious early printer, Aldus Manutius, set up the Aldine Press in Venice in 1495 to specialize in Greek, Latin, and early Italian classics.

Printed pamphlets were produced as propaganda during the German Peasants' War of 1524 (*see p.243*).

By 1500, some 35,000 different books were in print. Much cheaper than handwritten works, printed books revolutionized the diffusion of knowledge. The numbers of booksellers and publishers increased, and in the late 15th century, book fairs were held in Lyons, Leipzig, and Frankfurt. As printing became more commonplace, so the types of publications widened. In 1609, the first "news books" (forerunners of newspapers) appeared in Strasbourg (then German), and the first picture book for children was produced in Nuremberg, Germany, in 1658.

Johannes Gutenberg shows the first proofs of his 1455 Latin Bible. There were some 150 different Bible editions printed in the 15th century.

THE ITALIAN WARS

 Italy   1494–1559

 1494, Ludovico Sforza of Milan
couraged Charles VIII of France to
vade Naples, an act that led to six
cades of international warfare over
rritory in Italy involving France, Spain,
d England, as well as the Holy Roman
absburg) and Ottoman
pires. A Habsburg
feat of the French at
via in 1525 seemed to
omise an end to the
nflict, but led only to
e Papacy joining a
o-French alliance. In
urn, Rome was brutally
cked in 1527 by German

mercenaries in the pay of the Habsburgs.
Peace of a sort was restored by the
Treaty of Cateau-Cambrésis in 1559,
by which Henri II of France renounced
all claims to Italy, leaving most of the
peninsula under the influence of Spain.

 Battle of Pavia was the first
gagement in which hand-held
arms played a crucial role.

THE FRENCH WARS OF RELIGION

 France   1559–1598

 the mid-16th century, the Protestant
mmunity in France, known as
uguenots, had grown considerably and
cluded many nobility. The weakness
the French crown during the
gns of the heirs of Henri II
ho died in 1559) left
ective power in the hands
the ducal house of Guise,
atical anti-Protestants
nt on the extermination of
e Huguenots. The powerful
use of Bourbon favoured the
otestants, and war broke out
tween the two in 1562. A brief pause
1563–67 was followed by a further
ut of bloodshed in 1568–70, and the
Bartholomew's Day Massacre of
ousands of Protestants in Paris in
72. More civil strife followed, and

HENRI IV

A Huguenot supporter, in 1589 Henri of
Navarre (1553–1610) had to fight a Catholic
attempt to block his succession to the
French throne. In 1593, he converted
to Catholicism, undermining his
opposition, to rule as Henri IV.

nothing seemed able to
reconcile the two parties,
until the death of Henri III in
1589 left Henri de Bourbon,
Protestant king of Navarre, as
heir to the throne. To accede as king
of France, Henri became a Catholic. This
action, and his guaranteeing of rights to
Protestants in the Edict of Nantes (1598),
cooled tempers and finally brought an end
to France's Wars of Religion.

THE RISE OF SPAIN

⚑ Spain ⚔ 1492–1598

As Europe emerged from the medieval era, Spain was politically and religiously disunited, divided between several competing kingdoms, with many of its territories occupied by Muslim emirates since the 8th century (*see p.181*).

THE EMERGENCE OF A GREAT NATION
In 1469, Queen Isabella of Castile married King Ferdinand of Aragon, uniting the two most important Spanish kingdoms, and in 1492 the royal couple completed the Reconquista – the reconquest of the Muslim-held lands in Spain – with the capture of Granada. The subsequent discovery and conquest of the Americas (*see pp.232–4*) enabled the Habsburg Charles V, the Holy Roman Emperor who became King Charles I of a united Spain in 1519 (*see p.243*), to muster sufficient finances to thrust Spain to the forefront of European

The magnificent El Escorial near Madrid was built the reign of Philip II as a monastery, royal residence and burial place for the monarchs of Spain.

politics. When he died in 1556, the Habsburg realms were split and Philip inherited Spain and the Netherlands.

THE SPAIN OF PHILIP II
Under Philip II (ruled 1556–98), Spain projected its power in all directions. Its naval force defeated the Turks at Lepant in 1571, annexed Portugal in 1580, fought a long war in the Netherlands, and sent a great fleet against England i 1588 (*see facing page*). Yet by the 1590s the flow of silver from the New World was slackening and competition from the French and English in North Americ and the Caribbean was stifling Spain's routes of commerce. In Spain itself a plague in 1599–1600 wiped out around 15 per cent of the population. Although still Europe's most powerful country, the Spain that Philip II inherited in 1598 was dangerously overstretche

A portrait medallion of Philip II of Spain, whose reign saw the height Spanish power, but also sowed the seeds of its decline a century later.

THE SPANISH ARMADA

English Channel 1588

From the mid-16th century, tensions between Europe's Catholic and Protestant rulers threatened to erupt into warfare. Philip II of Spain (*see facing page*) had long been irritated by the interference in Spain's affairs by England's Protestant queen Elizabeth I (ruled 1558–1603), especially her support for an anti-Spanish revolt in the Netherlands (*see below*). In 1588, he ordered a great fleet, the Spanish Armada, commanded by the Duke of Medina Sidonia, to begin an invasion of England. Setting out in May, 130 Spanish ships reached the English coast in late July. English blocking actions, led by Francis Drake and Lord Howard of Effingham, achieved little, until on 7–8 August English fire-ships broke up the Armada and left it vulnerable to an attack that inflicted enormous human casualties on the Spanish. This proved to be Elizabeth's finest hour: Sidonia took the remains of the Armada on a long and costly retreat around Scotland and Ireland back to Spain.

Elizabeth I of England, a powerful Protestant monarch, posed a constant threat to Spain's Philip II.

THE DUTCH REVOLT

Belgium, the Netherlands 1568–1648

Ruled by the Dukes of Burgundy in the 15th century, by the 16th century the Netherlands had fallen into the domains of the Habsburg empire. While its ruler Charles V was perceived as sympathetic to Dutch interests, his successor Philip II of Spain spoke neither Dutch nor French, and was more intolerant of Dutch Protestantism. In 1567, an attempt by the Habsburg governor, the Duke of Alba, to repress religious unrest led to open revolt the following year. Although initially suppressed, the revolt flared up again in 1572. In 1579, a union of provinces loyal to Spain (the Union of Arras) was formed in the south of the Netherlands. This was countered by the Union of Utrecht in the north which, under William of Orange, became, in effect, independent from Spain. Although the Spanish general Parma retook the largest city of the Utrecht union, Antwerp, in 1585, the Spanish could not make any more headway to the north. This was acknowledged in a 12-year truce starting in 1609, and, though the Spanish tried again to recapture the rebellious provinces during the Thirty Years' War (*see p.248*), at its end in 1648 Spain was finally forced to officially recognize Dutch independence.

WILLIAM OF ORANGE

In 1558, Philip II of Spain made William the Silent, Prince of Orange, *stadtholder* (governor) of Holland. But William led the Protestant rebels against Spain in the Dutch Revolt and was assassinated in 1584 by a French Catholic agent.

THE THIRTY YEARS' WAR

Germany   1618–48

In central Europe at the beginning of the 17th century, a watchful calm followed the turmoil of the Reformation (*see pp.242–3*). However, in 1617, Ferdinand of Styria, a devout Catholic, was named king of Bohemia, a mostly Protestant territory. The Bohemian nobility rebelled, and in 1618 threw Ferdinand's representatives from the windows of Hradschin Castle in the "Defenestration of Prague". The nobles then appointed Frederick V as king of Bohemia, but were overcome by an army raised by Catholic German states at the Battle of White Mountain in 1620, and Bohemia reverted to Catholic Habsburg control.

The war spread as other European powers, notably France, the Dutch Republic, and Sweden, tried to thwart Catholic ambition. In the end, fighting dragged on for three decades.

Albrecht von Wallenstein was the Catholic side's most able general, delivering a string of victories in the early 1630s, until he was murdered in 1634.

"GERMANY IS A PLACE OF DEAD MEN'S SKULLS... AND A FIELD OF BLOOD"

Edward Calamy, English preacher, 1641

THE FINAL STAGES

The Swedes under Gustavus Adolphus won a string of battles that seemed to promise victory to the Protestants, but his death at Breitenfeld in 1631 swung power back to the Catholics. The Peace of Prague in 1635 nearly ended the war, but France, displeased with the terms, set it off once more. Only in 1648, by the Peace of Westphalia, was harmony finally restored, with the borders of European states temporarily stabilized, and the Habsburgs' wings firmly clipped.

THE ENGLISH CIVIL WAR

England, Scotland, Ireland 1642–51

uring the late 16th and early 17th
nturies England had evolved a
rong parliament with the right
veto taxation. Charles I (ruled
25–49), a firm believer in the
Divine Right" of monarchs to
le without being limited by any
nstitutional pact with their subjects,
ught to outflank his troublesome
arliament by simply suspending it
r 11 years from 1629. He then
ised revenue through extraordinary
easures such as "Ship Money" –
levy imposed on all the counties of
ngland to fund the navy.

HE FIRST CIVIL WAR

order to raise the funds necessary
quell a Calvinist revolt in Scotland,
harles was forced to recall parliament
1640. Relations between king and
sembly soon deteriorated into open
ostility and, in January 1642, the king
tered parliament with an armed
rce to arrest his leading opponents.
he attempt failed and, fearing for his
wn safety, Charles retired north from
ondon to raise an army.

The ensuing conflict continued for
ur years: an initial inconclusive
ngagement at Edgehill was followed

A clash of swords, following a cavalry charge, was
often the deciding factor in battles of the English
Civil War, despite widespread use of firearms.

by victories for either side during 1643.
The following year, however, the
royalists' fortunes waned, and the
involvement of the Scots in the
anti-royalist coalition further dented
the king's cause. Parliamentary
victories at Marston Moor in 1644
and Naseby in 1645 finally led to the
king's surrender to the Scots in 1646.

THE ROYALIST COLLAPSE

The war was not over, however. The
king made a deal with the Scots to
adopt their Presbyterian form of
church government in England in
return for aid in restoring him to
power. In July 1648, war broke out
again, but the Scottish army was easily
crushed at Preston, dashing Charles I's
hopes of victory. The king was tried
and executed on 30 January 1649 and
England became a "Commonwealth"
or republic. However, there were more
battles to be fought: Charles I's son
(later Charles II) was still at large, and
only his defeat at Worcester in 1651
brought an end to the final phase of
the English Civil War.

OLIVER CROMWELL

Member of Parliament for Huntingdon
from 1628, Oliver Cromwell (1599–1658)
gradually aligned himself with those seeking
constitutional reform in England. Fighting
for the Parliamentarians against the king
in the English Civil War, his instinctive
leadership ability and shrewdness allowed
him to rise in the ranks until, by 1645, he
was the pre-eminent parliamentary
commander. The Parliamentarians won
the Civil War in 1651 and Cromwell was
made Lord Protector – in effect, military
dictator – of England in 1653.

THE EMERGENCE OF MUSCOVY

📕 Russia   ☒ 1462–1725

In the 14th century, the territory of modern Russia, led by the principality of Muscovy, threw off decades of Mongol rule (*see pp.166–7*). Initially occupying a tiny enclave around the city of Moscow itself, Muscovy expanded hugely during the long reign of Ivan III (1462–1505), absorbing almost all of the other Russian principalities.

IVAN THE TERRIBLE
Ivan IV "the Terrible" (ruled 1533–84) consolidated Moscow's power still further. He reformed local government, tightened

> ### PETER THE GREAT
> Peter the Great (ruled 1682–1725) was aged only nine when he became tsar of Russia. For the early part of his reign, his half-sister Sophia exercised power, and then his mother Nataliya took control until her death in 1694. Finally able to rule in his own right, Peter set about a programme of modernization. This bore fruit during the Great Northern War with Sweden (*see facing page*) in Russia's victory at Poltava in 1709. As well as his military and political reforms, Peter established a new Russian capital at St Petersburg in 1703.

"THE GRAND DUKE LEAVES HIS MEN LITTLE REST. HE IS USUALLY AT WAR ..."

German diplomat Sigismund von Herberstein on the Grand Duchy of Muscovy, 1549

royal control over the church, curbed the power of the *boyars* (nobles), and established a more professional army. His military campaigns expanded Muscovy's borders along the Volga river – taking the khanate of Astrakhan – and in the Baltic, where his armies seized much of Livonia. Yet the latter part of his reign descended into tyranny, marked by the slaughter of vast numbers of the nobility. After Ivan's death and the reign of his son Feodor

(ruled 1584–98), Muscovy was rocked by famine, civil war, and invasions from Poland that nearly caused its dissolution. Recovery came under a new dynasty, the Romanovs, who would rule Russia for three centuries from 1613.

THE ROMANOVS
The early Romanovs gradually restored Muscovy's power and in 1667 regained most of the territory in the west that had been lost to Poland. Peter the Great built on these foundations, reconstructing the state according to western models, vastly increasing tax revenues, and waging successful wars against the Ottoman empire (*see pp.226–7*). By the end of Peter's reign in 1725, Russia was one of the most powerful European nations.

The Ivan the Great Bell Tower in the Kremlin is a fortified palace complex that has acted as the seat of the rulers of Russia from the 14th century.

POLAND–LITHUANIA

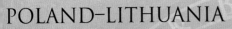

 Poland, Lithuania   1386–1672

 1386, Jogaila of Lithuania converted to
hristianity to marry the Catholic Queen
dwiga of Poland, loosely joining the two
ountries. In 1572, by the Union of
ublin, the federation became the formal
Commonwealth of the Two Nations".
s assembly, the Sejm, had the right to
ect monarchs, but the custom of the
berum veto, by which a single Sejm
ember could veto any measure,
d to stagnation. In 1667, the
ommonwealth lost much eastern
rritory to Russia and was thereafter
rgely at the mercy of the Austro-
Hungarian Habsburg monarchy to the
est and the Russian tsars to the east.

he Polish eagle is part of the coat of arms of the
olish–Lithuanian Commonwealth, which united the
vo countries from 1572 until its dissolution in 1792.

THE RISE OF SWEDEN AND THE GREAT NORTHERN WAR

 Sweden   1528–1719

Gustav Vasa's election as king of Sweden
 1528 marked the start of the country's
se as a great power. Gustav instituted a
ereditary monarchy, centralized
he bureaucracy, and imported
he Reformation *(see
.242–3)*, claiming church
nds and so enriching the
oyal treasury.

After Gustav's death in
560, Sweden underwent
 period of turbulence until
he reign of Gustavus II
dolphus (1611–32). His
eath in the Thirty Years'
see p.248) – during which
weden gained territories
n the southern Baltic –

did not lead to an immediate crisis, yet,
with a weak economy compared to its
European rivals, Sweden's military
successes were brought to an
end in the late 17th century.

In 1700, King Charles XII
(ruled 1697–1718) sparked
off the Great Northern
War with Russia. It ended
in disaster, as Charles was
defeated at Poltava in
1709, spent five years in
exile in the Ottoman
empire, and then died
during a siege near Oslo in
1718, leaving Sweden
vulnerable to a Russian
counter-invasion in 1719.

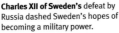

Charles XII of Sweden's defeat by
Russia dashed Sweden's hopes of
becoming a military power.

17TH-CENTURY FRANCE AND ABSOLUTISM

France 1603–1715

The death in 1603 of Henri IV (who had brought religious peace to France), left his nine-year-old son Louis XIII (ruled 1601–43) on the throne. The capable governance of Cardinal Richelieu steered France through the perils of the Thirty Years' War (*see p.248*), and laid the foundations for the great reign of Louis XIV (ruled 1643–1715). Only four years old at the time of his accession, Louis was very much under the sway of his chief minister, Cardinal Mazarin, until Mazarin died in 1661.

THE RULE OF LOUIS XIV

Instead of appointing another minister in the mould of Richelieu or Mazarin, Louis chose to rule in his own right as an absolute monarch. He began a series of wars to secure France's frontiers. From 1688 to 1697, he was at war against a "Grand Alliance" that included England and Holland. After only a brief pause, in

Louis XIV, known as "The Sun King", spent lavishly to enhance France's miltary and cultural prestige.

1700 Louis moved to put a French prince on the throne of Spain, unleashing the War of the Spanish Succession, as other powers sought to avoid the two countries becoming united. The war dragged on until 1714, when the military brilliance of the English general Marlborough thwarted Louis's plans, leading to a peace in whic a French prince became king of Spain, but without uniting the two countries.

Domestically, the wars required a vast improvement in the collection of taxation revenues, which was supervised by Jean-Bapiste Colbert, the director of finances; while Louis enhanced the prestige of the court by establishing a dazzling new palace at Versailles.

The Palace of Versailles, built on the site of a simple royal hunting lodge, was commissioned by Louis XIV in 1669. It became the home of the royal court in 168

THE RISE OF CAPITALISM AND THE SLAVE TRADE

Europe, Africa, the Americas *c*.1600–1865

The birth of businesses such as the English and Dutch East India companies in the early 17th century (*see pp.236–7*) formed the basis for modern capitalist-style economies. These companies enjoyed a much more long-term and independent existence than their precursors, and could build up capital and make longer-term investment plans. Specialist traders now emerged, who arranged the buying and selling of "stock" in the companies (shares in their ownership), making it easier to raise new funds. In Amsterdam, the Amsterdamsche Wisselbank (Amsterdam Exchange bank) was founded in 1609 as a centre for the trade and exchange of stocks, while in London the first listing of share and commodity prices was published in 1698.

Edward Lloyd's coffee house in London became a centre for merchants to discuss investment. It would evolve into the modern-day Lloyds insurance market.

THE SLAVE TRADE

Among the many profitable commercial ventures the new capitalists engaged in was the slave trade. Slaves were gathered, largely in West Africa – often with the co-operation or connivance of local rulers

– and were shipped under inhuman circumstances to the New World. Here, they were exchanged for commodities such as sugar, tobacco, and cotton, which would in turn be sold at a great profit in Europe.

The "Middle Passage", or transit of slaves over the Atlantic, saw some 78,000 slaves a year transported in the 1780s, with up to 600 slaves packed into each ship. They were shackled together in cramped spaces between deck and hold, where disease, damp, and hunger exacted a terrible toll in deaths.

The slave trade was abolished in the British empire only in 1807, although slavery persisted in the USA until 1865.

model of the slave ship *Brookes*, showing the positions into which more than 500 slaves were crammed for the harrowing transatlantic voyage.

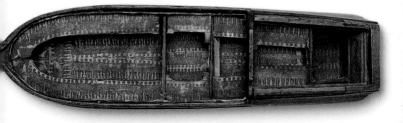

THE SCIENTIFIC REVOLUTION AND THE ENLIGHTENMENT

⚑ Europe   ⌛ 16th–18th centuries

The 16th and 17th centuries saw a metamorphosis in European thinking about the natural world. Just as the Renaissance had transformed art, and the Reformation had loosened the shackles of religious dogma, so now a third revolution produced a new view of the universe.

Improvements in technology began to undermine many long-held theories, the most celebrated casualty being the ancient Earth-centred model of the universe. In 1543, the Polish priest and astronomer Nicolaus Copernicus published a proposal for a sun-centred system – a solar system – with the Earth and five other planets in orbit around it. In 1610, the Italian astronomer Galileo Galilei, using a new, improved telescope, discovered four moons in orbit around Jupiter, thereby definitively showing that the Earth was not, as previously believed, the centre of all motion in the universe.

Copernicus's revolutionary view of the solar system put the Earth in orbit around the sun.

ADVANCES IN MEDICINE

In other areas, too, scientific endeavour made rapid progress. In anatomy, the discovery of a lost text by the Roman medical writer Galen convinced the Flemish scholar Vesalius that Galen had never actually dissected a human body, spurring him to publish his great atlas of anatomy *De Humani Corporis Fabrica* in 1543. Further advances in medical science yielded the first accurate description of the circulation of blood in 1628 by William Harvey, personal physician to Charles I of England. His theory was confirmed in 1661 by the direct observation of capillaries using the recently invented microscope.

THE ENLIGHTENMENT

Just as this scientific revolution had grown from a new freedom in scientific thinking, so the Enlightenment, a radical current

ISAAC NEWTON

In 1609, Johannes Kepler showed that the planets orbited the sun in an elliptical, not a circular, motion, but he could not explain why. The answer was provided by the English polymath Isaac Newton (1643–1727), who realized that the force of "gravity" found on Earth, which caused objects to fall when released, might extend into outer space and be generated by all objects possessing mass. Newton published this theory in his *Principia Mathematica* of 1687, one of the most influential works in scientific history.

intellectual thought,
~~erated philosophy. Rene
~~escartes (1596–1650),
~~e "father of modern
~~ilosophy", was both
~~inker and mathematician,
~~guing that only through
~~ason could mathematical
~~d universal truths be
~~scovered. In the 18th
~~ntury, thinkers known
~~philosophes applied ideas
~~om the advances in
~~ience to challenge the
~~y people thought about
~~vernment and society,
~~eking to replace superstition, tyranny,
~~d injustice with reason, tolerance, and
~~uality. "What does it mean to be free?"

René Descartes argued that logical deduction should be trusted more than sensory perception.

Its aim was to assemble all existing knowledge in clear, accessible prose.

A favourite target for the *philosophes* was royal absolutism. Montesquieu's celebrated treatise *Spirit of the Laws* (1748) proposed a limited monarchy based on a three-way division of powers between the executive (the king), the legislature (parliament), and the judiciary. Such intellectual notions greatly added to the ferment that would, within the next half-century, give rise to both the American and French revolutions.

"THE CONSENT OF THE PEOPLE IS THE SOLE BASIS OF A GOVERNMENT'S AUTHORITY."

Jean-Jacques Rousseau, *Social Contract*, 1762

~~ked François-Marie Arouet (known as
~~oltaire), answering: "To reason correctly
~~d know the rights of man." Jean-
~~cques Rousseau railed against moral
~~cadence and inequality in his essays on
~~e *Arts and Sciences* (1749) and on *Equality*
~~755), arguing that social progress had
~~lped corrupt human nature.

~~E SPREAD OF IDEAS
~~he most influential tool for
~~reading Enlightenment values
~~as Denis Diderot's 28-volume
~~cylopédie, which boasted an
~~pressive array of contributors,
~~cluding Voltaire and Rousseau.

~~n-Jacques Rousseau wrote that "Man ~~born free, and is everywhere in ~~ains", profoundly influencing ~~er French revolutionaries.

THE WORLD OF EMPIRES

THE WORLD IN 1750–1914

The American and French Revolutions transformed Western political expectations. Though the results were contradictory – th USA emerged as a fully functioning democracy, while France wa destabilized for almost a century – demands for political liberati echoed throughout the 19th century. A wave of nationalist uprisin

The world in 1850

—— international border

········ undefined border

Qing empire

Ottoman empire

Britain and possessions

France and possessions

Denmark and possessions

Spain and possessions

Portugal and possessions

Netherlands and possessions

Prussia

Russian empire

Japan

Austrian empire

Persia

United States of America

Napoleon's French Empire 1812

Muhammad Ali's possessions 1840

United Provinces of Central America 1823–38

Great Colombia 1819–30

THE WORLD OF EMPIRES IN 1850

By 1850, the USA spanned the breadth of North America, while most of Latin America had thrown off Spanish and Portuguese rule. Only a few colonies existed in Africa, but Ind had almost entirely become a dominion of th British, who also settled in Australia and New Zealand. A weak Qing dynasty ruled China.

rought independence to much of Latin America and unification to aly and Germany. Elsewhere, however, colonial nations continued o dominate much of the globe, stifling local political development. ven independent regions, such as China and Japan, suffered from gnificant interventions or interference by European powers.

Many of the European powers had suffered nationalist revolutions in 1848, but territorially they remained largely unchanged. By 1850 Italy and Germany, still divided into a number of small states, were just two decades away from unification. In the Balkans, the Ottoman empire still held most of the region, but had lost control of Greece.

THE AMERICAS

By 1750, virtually the whole of the Americas was occupied by the Spanish, Portuguese, French, or British, with the remaining few islands and enclaves occupied by lesser European powers. In contrast, by 1914, only a few areas remained as European colonies, the rest having experienced around a century of independence. In the case of the United States and Spain's American colonies, this was won from the mother country through revolutionary wars.

EUROPEANS IN THE AMERICAS

North America, Caribbean   1750

By the middle of the 18th century, most of the territory of eastern North America had been carved up between the European nations. The British occupied the Thirteen Colonies, an area of the eastern seaboard of what would become the USA, as well as Nova Scotia and an area around Hudson's Bay in modern Canada.

THE FRENCH POSITION
Britain's principal opponents in North America were the French, who held much of modern eastern Canada (or "New France") from their main fortress at Québec. From here, the French had crept south down the Great Lakes and the Ohio river as far as Detroit (founded in 1701), and by 1750 they had a string of fortified positions along these waterways. The goal was to link with their existing possessions around New Orleans in the south to create a north–south corridor of French territory from which to put pressure on the British. At about the same time, British colonists began to move into Ohio, escalating the potential for conflict between Britain and France. Adding to the volatile mix – and so the likelihood of war in eastern North America – were the long-held Spanish positions in Florida and the Caribbean, which they had occupied since the early 16th century.

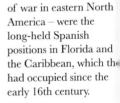

From forts such as San Felipe on Puerto Rico in the Caribbean, Spain defended an arc of territory from seaward invasion.

THE FRENCH AND INDIAN WAR

◆ E North America ⚔ 1754–1760

[Brit]ain and France had sparred [for] decades for control of [the] crucial waterways of [the] Ohio and Mississippi [riv]ers. In 1754, a [ske]rmish near Fort [Du]quesne between the [Fre]nch and Virginian [col]onial troops prompted [the] despatch of a British [exp]editionary force, led by [Ma]jor-General Edward Braddock, who [att]empted to seize the French fort. With [the] help of their Native American [Iro]quois allies, the French routed the [Bri]tish. Native forces were to play a major [par]t on both sides in what became known [as] the French and Indian War.

[TH]E WAR SPREADS

[A s]eries of French victories was halted [onl]y by a setback at Lake St George in [Se]ptember 1755, which saved the [Hu]dson Valley for Britain. By 1756, the [co]nflict had become global (as the Seven [Ye]ars' War; *see pp.270–1*), and the British [be]gan to see that North America was [an] arena in which they could damage [Fre]nch interests and force France to [div]ert resources from Europe. In

A medal struck to commemorate the British capture of Québec in modern Canada from the French in 1759.

1758, the British launched campaigns to thrust north from New York, seize Louisbourg, and march on the French capital in North America, Québec.

THE END OF NEW FRANCE

The French commander, Marquis de Montcalm, fought a series of able blocking actions, but the British took Louisbourg and pushed up the St Lawrence River, so that by June 1759 Montcalm was confined to Québec. General Wolfe's British force took the city, although both commanders were killed in the engagement. In September 1760, the Marquis de Vaudreuil surrendered the last French stronghold at Montréal, ending the North American phase of the Seven Years' War and handing the territories of "New France" over to Britain.

◆ **Marquis de Montcalm** was mortally [wo]unded in the defeat of his forces on [the] Plain of Abraham outside Québec.

THE REVOLUTIONARY WAR

E North America   1775–1783

The British colonies in North America were liable to pay tax to Britain, but without receiving the benefit of representation in parliament, which rankled greatly with the colonists. A series of measures passed from 1763, aimed at raising money for the British government, caused further discontent, and the Stamp Act, a direct tax on paper, provoked riots. In 1773, a group of Bostonians, disguised as Native Americans, threw a cargo of highly taxed East India Company tea into Boston harbour. Their slogan – "no taxation without representation" – struck a deep chord with most colonists.

The **"Boston Tea Party"** protest in 1773, against Britain's three-pence tax on tea, saw American colonists hurl crates of tea into Boston harbour.

THE OUTBREAK OF WAR

In response, the British passed a series of laws in 1774, which the Americans dubbed the "Intolerable Acts". These measures were intended to restore order, but served only to unite the colonies in further protest. A colonial Continental Congress in Philadelphia in September 1774 demanded the repeal of the Intolerable Acts. The appeal fell on dea[f] ears and the British government called on General Thomas Gage, commande[r] of the British forces in Boston, to arres[t] the colonists' troublesome leaders.

The first skirmish, described later as "the shot heard around the world", occurred at Lexington, Massachusetts, on 19 April 1775. Besieged in Boston, Gage then bungled an attempt to dislodge rebel positions at the Battle of Bunker Hill in June, a success that greatly bolstered the Americans'

GEORGE WASHINGTON

Born to a family of Virginia landowners, George Washington (1732–99) served on the British side in the French and Indian War (see p.261), experience that led Congress to appoint him commander of the American military forces in 1775. He came to command widespread respect for his morality and tenacity and, after independence, was president of the Constitutional Convention that drafted the US constitution in 1787. In 1789, he was elected first president of the USA, a position he held for two terms, until 1797.

rale. Soon afterwards, George
ashington became commander of the
wly formed Continental Army. Despite
backs, including the British capture of
w York, in July 1776 the Americans
de a decisive break with Britain.
er a series of difficult negotiations
iong themselves, the American
onies agreed on a Declaration of
dependence, thanks largely to the
ellectual force and literary skills of
omas Jefferson (1743–1826), later to
come the third president of the USA.

E AMERICAN VICTORY

ie British fought on, but Washington's
tory at Saratoga in October 1777
rred the interest of the French, still
nging from their expulsion from
nada (*see p.261*), who formed an
iance with the colonists. The signing
a treaty between the Americans and
e French in February 1778 marked a
ajor turning point in the war. All hope
a British victory ended on 19 October
81 when Lord Cornwallis was forced
surrender the last major British
my at Yorktown, Virginia, after an
-day siege. The British suspended
y further military operations

The Declaration of Independence was adopted on
4 July 1776. Its signatories included John Adams and
Thomas Jefferson, both later US presidents.

against the Americans. In November
1782, they signed a provisional
agreement recognizing American
independence, a decision ratified by
the Treaty of Paris in 1783. George
Washington became the first president
and John Adams the first vice-president
of the new United States of America,
which at the time was often also
referred to as "the Union".

George Washington crossed the Delaware river into
New Jersey in December 1776, at a time when his
army was under severe British pressure.

THE EXPANSION OF THE UNITED STATES

⚐ USA   ☗ 1783–1867

After the Treaty of Paris in 1783, the new USA (the Union) had frontiers along the Mississippi river to the west, where it faced remaining French possessions, and along the Great Lakes to the north, where it bordered British Canada. The USA did not remain confined to these boundaries for long, however. Expansion across the Mississippi began with the 1803 Louisiana Purchase, by which Napoleon, abandoning plans to rebuild a French New World empire, ceded a vast territory that doubled the size of the USA for a mere $15 million.

THE FRONTIER MOVES WEST

A conflict with Britain (the War of 1812) ended in a stalemate and an agreement in 1818 to demarcate the USA's northern border with Canada along the 49th parallel (line of latitude). To the south, the USA acquired Florida from Spain in 1813–19. In 1846, Oregon Country was split with the British, again along the 49th parallel, providing a Pacific frontier.

Texas had become independent from Mexico in 1836, but was annexed by the USA in 1845, which led to war with the Mexicans. In 1848, a victorious USA acquired California, Nevada, Utah, and New Mexico. The Gadsden Purchase in 1853, which added further land from northern Mexico, and the purchase of Alaska from Russia in 1867 completed the growth of the continental Union.

A memorial to the volunteers who died in 1836 at the Alamo, the most famous battle in Texas's fight for independence from Mexico.

LAND OF OPPORTUNITY

As the young nation expanded, large numbers of settlers travelled west to the newly acquired lands. The 1862 Homestead Act, which offered farmers ownership of 65 hectares (160 acres) of land after they had farmed it for five years, accelerated the migration, as did the completion of a transcontinental railroad in 1869. The expansion of the settlement frontier, however, was accompanied by the displacement – often by force – of Native American tribes. The death of General George Custer at Little Big Horn in 1876 was one of the rare conflicts in which Native Americans were the victors.

MERIWETHER LEWIS

Secretary to President Jefferson, in 1803 Meriwether Lewis (1774–1809) was sent to explore the region acquired by the Louisiana Purchase. He and his men reached the Pacific coast in 1805, making them the first Europeans to traverse the width of the USA.

THE SLIDE TO CIVIL WAR

USA   1820–1861

he US Constitutional Convention of
'87 had allowed individual member
ates of the new USA (the Union) to
tain slavery if they wished. The
rthern states abolished slavery,
hile a roughly equal number of
uthern states kept it, leading
constant friction.

E SLAVERY DEBATE

he admission of new
ree" states – which
tlawed slavery – to the
nion threatened to upset
equilibrium. In the
-called "Missouri
ompromise" of 1820, slavery
as forbidden in much of the
est, but this was overturned by the
ansas-Nebraska Act of 1854, while a
preme Court decision in 1857 further
rengthened slavery's status. Still, the
creasing numbers of free territories
stling for statehood alarmed supporters
slavery. After an armed raid in 1859
anti-slavery militant John Brown to
e slaves at Harper's Ferry, Virginia,
is concern turned into active
pposition. In November 1860, the first
epublican Party president, Abraham

> ### ABRAHAM LINCOLN
>
> Kentucky-born Abraham Lincoln (1809–65)
> helped found the anti-slavery Republican
> Party in 1854. Selected as a compromise
> Republican candidate in the 1860 elections,
> his victory in the northern states
> provoked states in the south to
> leave the Union. However, his
> determination saw the Union
> through the ensuing Civil War.
> In 1865, Lincoln signed a
> resolution on the abolition of
> slavery; he was assassinated
> just as the war ended.

Lincoln, was elected on a
platform of opposition to
slavery. The southern states had
opted for a pro-slavery Democrat, John
Breckenridge, and on 20 December
1860, South Carolina voted to leave
the Union. By February 1861, six more
states had also withdrawn, creating a
new body known as the Confederacy.
With tensions between north and south
running so high, it was only a matter of
time before hostilities would break out.

Slave auctions were commonplace in
southern USA; the largest, in Georgia,
involved the sale of over 430 slaves.

THE AMERICAN CIVIL WAR

USA 1860–1865

By the spring of 1861, seven states had seceded from the Union (*see p.265*) to form the pro-slavery Confederacy. On April 12, Confederate forces bombarded Fort Sumter in Charleston harbour, South Carolina, eventually forcing the surrender of its Union troops. The first shots of the Civil War had been fired.

recognition from the Union government. The skill of some masterful Confederate battlefield commanders enabled it to resis in fact, for far longer than could be predicted from its military resources.

The effort devoted by each side to th war was prodigious. Conscription was introduced by the Confederacy in 1862

"GOVERNMENT OF THE PEOPLE, BY THE PEOPLE, FOR THE PEOPLE."

Abraham Lincoln, 1863

The two sides were ill-matched; the Union had vast economic resources and its population was far larger, at 22 million. Even when a further four states joined the Confederacy after the Fort Sumter attack, its population numbered only 9 million, of whom 3.5 million were slaves. The Confederacy's strategy was to defend itself from attack long enough to force

Abraham Lincoln (*right*), US president during the Civil War, was seen as the bringer of liberty to the slaves of the south.

and by the Union the following year. By the conflict's end, some 50 per cent of the eligible population of the Union ha been mobilized, and around 75 per cer in the Confederacy.

THE EARLY COURSE OF THE WAR
Superior Confederate generalship led to early success, with "Stonewall" Jackson two victories at Bull Run, Virginia, seriously endangering the Union's capi at Washington, DC. A further attempt

Soldiers pose for the camera at Fair Oaks, Virginia; the Civil War was one of the first conflicts to be recorded in photographs.

Appomattox Court House on 9 April. Early the following month, the last Confederate forces surrendered in Carolina and Alabama, and the war was over. It had cost the Union side 110,000 battlefield deaths, the Confederacy 93,000, and each side many more from disease or exhaustion. The main outcome was the emancipation of the southern slaves; Lincoln had issued a proclamation to this effect on 1 January 1863, and the USA adopted the 14th amendment, enshrining this in the Constitution in December 1865.

the brilliant Confederate general
bert E. Lee to invade the Union
ded in disaster at Gettysburg in a
ee-day battle in July 1863. This
rked the turning point of the war.
On the western front, Union general
ysses S. Grant won a major victory at
iloh, Tennessee, in April 1862 and
n thrust down the Mississippi river,
ing a strategic position at Vicksburg in
ril 1863 before pushing further south
cut the Confederacy in two – isolating
kansas, Louisiana, and Texas from the
er states. In autumn 1864, Union
eral William Sherman began his
larch to the Sea", moving from the
ssissippi to cut a destructive swathe
ough the Confederacy as far as
lanta on the eastern seaboard.

NFEDERATE SURRENDER
Virginia, meanwhile, Lee sparred for
nths with Grant, the Confederate
eral manoeuvring his forces both
evade capture and to shield
Confederate capital at
chmond. In the end,
spite brilliant rearguard
ions, his resources were
ply drained, his army
luced to barely 8,000.
ter Richmond finally fell
3 April 1865, Lee
rendered to Grant at

RECONSTRUCTION
After the war, the southern states underwent a process of "Reconstruction" intended to prepare them for readmission to the Union. Former Confederate officials were banned from holding public office, and veterans were required to pledge allegiance to the Union. It was a harsh regime that bred resentment in the southern states. Georgia was the last state to be readmitted to the Union, in July 1870, but Reconstruction continued until 1877, when a deal (known as the "Compromise") was struck to allow the withdrawal of the final Federal forces from the south.

nion soldier's portable desk.
markable number of letters
memoirs, written by ordinary
diers, survive from the Civil War.

LATIN AMERICAN INDEPENDENCE

Central and South America   1808–1920

In 1775, Spanish and Portuguese control of their Latin American empires seemed unchallenged. Yet the outbreak of the American and French revolutions provided inspiration for those seeking independence for Central and South America and offered avenues for seeking aid for those already struggling to gain autonomy. When Napoleon turned on his Spanish allies in 1808 during the Peninsular War (*see p.278*), events took a disastrous turn for Spain. With the Spanish king Charles VI and his son, Ferdinand, taken hostage by Napoleon, rebels bent on independence exploited the power vacuum to jostle for power across Spanish America.

SIMÓN BOLÍVAR

Hero of South America's struggle for independence from Spain, Simón Bolívar (1783–1830) began his revolutionary career in Venezuela in 1813. Known as *El Libertador* ("the Liberator"), his hopes of a grand union of the newly independent states were dashed, as the early Republic of Gran Colombia fell apart into its component countries (Columbia, Panama, and Ecuador) shortly before he died of tuberculosis in 1830.

> ## "ALL WHO HAVE SERVED THE REVOLUTION HAVE PLOUGHED THE SEA."
>
> Simón Bolívar, 1830

THE LIBERATION OF SPANISH AMERICA

Revolutionary forces rose from opposite ends of the continent. From the south, José de San Martín, a former Spanish military officer, led 5,000 troops across the Andes from Argentina to strike at a weak point in Chile in 1817. San Martín then liberated the Spanish stronghold of Peru. From the north came Simón Bolívar, whose forces entered Venezuela in 1813; they waged a ferocious campaign, but with limited results. However, in 1817 a larger, revitalized movement for independence emerged to complete the struggle for the north. In 1819, Bolívar was named president of Gran Colombia – a union of Colombia, Panama, and Ecuador.

By 1821 further campaigns had wrested New Granada and Venezuela from Spanish control. In the central Andes, the southern and northern armies crushed

Pancho Villa (*centre*) was a key figure in the Mexican Revolution and the last to lay down his arms, only giving up the fight in 1920.

e remaining loyalist strength. Peru, ïch the Spanish had recaptured, ÿained its independence in 1814.

In Mexico, meanwhile, a movement ÿerged in 1810, led by a radical priest, ïguel Hidalgo y Costilla, who built up ÿ untrained force of 80,000 indigenous ÿhters. Although Hidalgo was captured and executed in 1811, he had badly shaken Spanish control of Mexico, and the country achieved independence in 1822.

leading to the rise of military strongmen (*caudillos*). In 1876, one of these, General Porfirio Díaz, seized power in Mexico and established a dictatorship. Resentment toward him exploded in the Mexican Revolution of 1910, which overthrew Díaz in 1911. His replacement, Francisco Madero, failed to fulfil the expectations of more radical revolutionaries such as Emiliano Zapata and Francisco ("Pancho") Villa, leading the civil war to rumble on until 1920.

A monument, nicknamed El Ángel ("The Angel"), was built in Mexico City in 1910 to commemorate the centenary of the start of Mexico's liberation struggle.

Brazil, the ÿonial upper ÿsses, reliant on ÿrican slavery, wanted to ÿintain ties with Portugal. ÿen, in 1808, the Portuguese ÿurt fled to Brazil to escape ÿpoleon. King John returned to ÿsbon in 1821, leaving his son Pedro in ÿe colony. In 1822, Pedro declared Brazil ÿependent and himself Emperor.

ÿE MEXICAN REVOLUTION

ÿhile Brazil retained its integrity, ÿe former Spanish America split ÿo more than a dozen republics. ÿwever, internal fighting caused the ÿst constitutional governments to fall ÿd Latin America in the mid-19th ÿntury was plagued by instability,

ÿOSÉ DE SAN MARTÍN

ÿrgentinian national hero José de San Martín ÿ1778–1850) joined South America's struggle ÿor independence in 1812. In 1817 he crossed ÿhe Andes to overthrow Spanish control of ÿhile, and won definitive independence for ÿeru in 1821. He died in France.

EUROPE

When France overthrew its monarchy in 1789, the new regime seemed bent on exporting democracy throughout Europe but after two decades of Revolutionary and Napoleonic wars the European status quo remained largely intact. However, Europe was then shaken by a violent upsurge in 1848, fed by new ideals of nationalism that ultimately led to the unifications of Italy and Germany and to independence for a string of Balkan countries.

THE SEVEN YEARS' WAR

Europe　　1756–1763

In 1756, Frederick II of Prussia signed a treaty with Britain to protect British rule in Hanover (in modern Germany). Maria Theresa of Austria used this as a pretext with which to effect a "diplomatic revolution", in which she allied with her former enemy France and firmed up ties with Empress Elizabeth of Russia, making Prussia vulnerable to invasion. Striking first, Frederick sought to occupy Saxony, but was unsuccessful. In 1757, however, he did triumph over the French at Rossbach in Saxony, and then crushed the Austrians in Silesia before inflicting defeat on the Russians at Zorndorf in 1758. The tide turned strongly against Frederick in 1760 and 1761, but the succession of the pro-Prussian Peter in Russia in 1762 brought a new ally. Prussian victory at Freiberg Saxony, in 1762 meant that in 1763 the Treaty of Paris, which brought an end to the Seven Years' War in Europe, restored the status quo.

FREDERICK II

A military genius, Frederick II "the Great" of Prussia (ruled 1740–86) reformed the Prussian army and used it to fight a series of campaigns aimed at gathering the disparate possessions of Prussia into a united state.

THE FIRST GLOBAL WAR

The Seven Years' War broke out in 1756 between Prussia on one side and Austria, France, and Russia on the other. The involvement of Britain, through its holding of Hanover, meant that the war soon gained a global dimension, as France and Britain extended the conflict to their overseas colonies. In the Americas, fighting had erupted in 1755 (*see p.261*), a year before the main war actually began in Europe.

THE WAR IN INDIA

In 1756, the *nawab* (ruler) of Bengal sparked hostilities in India by capturing the British base at Calcutta, and putting his prisoners in the "Black Hole" – a small, dark cell in which many died. The victory of Robert Clive over the *nawab* in June 1757 dramatically revived British fortunes in India (*see p.294*). The failure of a French siege of Madras in 1759, a British victory at Wandiwash in 1760, and the fall of the main French base in India at Pondicherry the following year

A Prussian war banner displaying the imperial eagle and the motto "for glory and fatherland".

meant the end of the Indian phase of the Seven Years' War.

THE WAR ELSEWHERE

In the other main non-European theatres of the war, the British generally had the better of the fighting, capturing Senegal from the French in 1758, seizing the French islands of Guadeloupe and Martinique in 1762, and briefly occupying the Spanish forts at Havana in Cuba and Manila in the Philippines in 1762–63. By the Treaty of Paris, which ended the war, Britain ceded back many of its conquests, but retained French Canada, Spanish Florida, and some French outposts in West Africa.

The British fleet captured Havana in 1762. The occupation was short-lived, as the Treaty of Paris in 1763 gave Florida to Britain in exchange for the city.

THE FRENCH REVOLUTION

France　1789–1796

France's costly involvement in the American Revolutionary War (*see pp.262–3*) put financial reform at the top of the country's political agenda. Bad harvests in 1788–89 aggravated social tensions and fuelled resentment of the *ancien régime* – a system by which 40 per cent of the land was owned by the nobility and clergy, who made up a mere 3 per cent of the population and who were exempt from taxes.

THE ESTATES-GENERAL

After the nobility blocked his attempt to raise revenue, Louis XVI (ruled 1774–92) was forced, in May 1789, to convene the Estates-General – a parliament made up of clergy, nobility, and commoners. The third estate, representing the commoners, insisted on greater voting rights. These were refused

Louis XVI was executed by guillotine on 21 January 1793 on the site that is now the Place de la Concorde in Paris.

and the commoners broke away and took power as a National Assembly – the first step to revolutionary change. Rioting in July 1789 led to the capture of the Bastille prison (*see pp.274–5*), a huge blow against the oppressive forces of the *ancien régime*.

REVOLUTIONARY REFORMS

On 4 August, the National Assembly abolished feudal privileges, sweeping away an entire system of property ownership. For the next two years, the National Assembly passed reforms that further undermined the *ancien régime*, including the "Declaration of the Rights of Man" – which listed citizens' rights – as well as army reforms, and forced the clergy to take a civic oath to the state. In June 1791, Louis XVI, having schemed to undermine the Assembly, attempted to flee abroad, but was captured at Varennes, east of Paris. This apparent abandonment of his people crucially undermined regard for the monarch.

to mete out instant justice, and a Committee of Public Safety (CPS) to wield central power, which it did with mixed success. Internal conflict was rife, and on 2 June 1793, the moderate Girondin faction was expelled from the Convention and the extremist Jacobins seized power under Robespierre. The Jacobins unleashed the "Terror" on France, aimed at purging any remaining anti-Revolutionaries and pro-royalists. In 10 months from September 1793, they executed some 20,000 people, and the Revolution seemed to be consuming itself in violence.

A decisive military victory over Austria in June 1794 eased political pressures and Robespierre and his henchmen were finally toppled in an anti-Jacobin backlash. In 1795, the CPS was replaced by a five-man Directory, which set about the task of restoring faith in the Revolutionary regime.

April 1792, the Assembly declared on Austria and Prussia, who were pathetic to the king, but this caused ic in Paris, and on 20 August a mob med the Tuileries palace and deposed king. In the aftermath, a more radical mbly (the Convention) was elected, France was declared a Republic in tember. In January 1793, the king charged with crimes against the nch nation, convicted, and executed.

TERROR

ed with mounting military and nomic problems, the Convention blished a Revolutionary Tribunal

ROBESPIERRE

Maximilien Robespierre (1758–94), a lawyer, was mocked for his high voice, but respected for his pure principles, which earned him the nickname "The Incorruptible". When he came to power in 1793, his extremism unleashed terror on France, and ultimately led to his execution.

By 14 July 1789, the Bastille prison in Paris housed just seven inmates, but also held vast stores of gunpowder. Weakly defended by a party of *invalides* – troops unfit for active service – it was stormed by a revolutionary mob and its governor, de Launay, was stabbed to death.

FRANCE UNDER NAPOLEON

France ⚑ 1799–1815

The rule of the Directory (1795–99) was a time of great instability and mounting corruption in France. The division of power between five Directors and a two-chamber parliament led to chaos, inaction, and disenchantment with the political process. Into this gap stepped the rising young military star Napoleon Bonaparte. His successes in the Italian campaign of the 1790s lent him an aura of steadiness and invincibility that the fractious Revolutionaries badly needed. In November 1799, having abandoned his army in Palestine, Napoleon arrived back in France to answer his nation's call.

A new civil code for France was one of Napoleon's most enduring legacies, enshrining in law some of the freedoms fought for in the French Revolution.

FROM FIRST CONSUL TO EMPEROR

The Coup of 18 Brumaire (9 November 1799) saw Napoleon and his backers overthrow the Directory, and he became First Consul in the new leadership. His two fellow consuls were soon reduced to powerless nonentities, and in 1802 Napoleon had himself declared First Consul for life. Intelligent, determined, and energetic, Napoleon set to sweeping away the ramshackle amalgam of Revolutionary and feudal systems that had evolved since 1789. In December 1804, he had himself crowned Emperor. Presiding over the ceremony was Pope Pius VII, for Napoleon had made peace with the Catholic Church the previous year in a Concordat that recognized limited papal authority over Catholics in France.

> ## "I HAVE TASTED COMMAND, AND I CANNOT GIVE IT UP."
>
> Napoleon Bonaparte, 1798

DOMESTIC REFORMS

Napoleon's reforms left few spheres of French life untouched. He founded a Bank of France in 1800, and issued a new currency centred around a gold coin, the *napoleon*. He ordered that the educational system be reformed and radically revised the French administrative system, rationalizing the network of *départements* set up in 1790.

A committee of legal experts was formed to bring order to the chaos of legislative codes and temporary expedients. By 1804 it had completed a new civil code that would survive Napoleon's demise as the centrepiece of France's legal system.

THE COST OF WARFARE

The universal conscription and punitive taxation necessitated by Napoleon's constant warfare (*see pp.278–9*) were not popular in France. As victory turned to stalemate, then retreat, after the disastrous 1812 campaign in Russia, support for Napoleon steadily ebbed away. When enemy armies reached Paris in 1814, his power base proved brittle; even

> ### NAPOLEON BONAPARTE
>
> Born into an impoverished Corsican noble family, Napoleon Bonaparte (1769–1821) became a junior artillery officer aged just 16. His subsequent career was characterized by superb opportunism and a tactical brilliance in battle that marked him out from other commanders of the age. It brought him high political office, but the scale of his own ambitions and those of his foreign enemies ultimately brought about his deposition.

long-standing loyalists such as Marshal Ney did nothing to prevent his being deposed. Yet the new Bourbon regime of Louis XVIII was little loved either, and residual affection in France for Napoleon enabled him to return from exile on the Italian island of Elba in May 1815. A final flourish, the "Hundred Days", ended in his defeat at the battle of Waterloo and permanent exile to Saint Helena, an island in the South Atlantic.

At the Committee of Lyon in 1802, Napoleon created the Repubblica Italiana; in 1805, this became the Kingdom of Italy, with the new emperor as its king.

THE NAPOLEONIC WARS

Europe   1802–1815

The French Revolutionary Wars (1792–1802) had been intended to protect France's borders from other European powers eager to stop the spread of revolution. They turned gradually into a more aggressive foreign policy, as France's armies met with a series of successes that stoked its hunger for exporting revolution and acquiring land. The Peace of Amiens, which Napoleon struck with Britain in 1802, promised an end to the wars, but it lasted only a year. By 1805 Britain managed to build an alliance of countries fearful of Napoleon's expansionism – the First Coalition. This was the first of seven such groupings, whose shifting membership would seek to oppose the French emperor and be repeatedly defeated by his armies.

Napoleon wore a hat in a bicorn (two-horned) style that incorporated a badge bearing the French Revolutionary colours of red, white, and blue.

THE FIRST GREAT VICTORIES

Napoleon's great victories in 1805 against Austria at Ulm and an Austro-Prussian army at Austerlitz placed him at the summit of his power. He was thwarted only by naval defeat at Trafalgar (off the southwest coast of Spain) against the

Wellington leads his army from an indecisive encounter at Quatre Bras, in 1815, to the final victory at Waterloo two days later.

British admiral Nelson in October, which scuppered his plans to invade England. However, his insistence on an economic blockade by all the nations under his control as an alternative means to cripple England caused great resentment among the other European countries. Napoleon went on to attack Prussia in October 1806 and within three weeks had defeated its armies at Jena and Austerstädt. He then forced peace on Tsar Alexander I of Russia at Tilsit in July 1807.

THE DOWNFALL OF NAPOLEON

Napoleon's decision to invade Spain and Portugal in 1808, starting the Peninsular War, led to the diversion of badly needed resources into a difficult struggle against

artist's view of Napoleon's planned invasion of [Eng]land in 1805 shows French forces attacking by [sea], air, and tunnelling under the English Channel.

[loc]al guerrillas who were being aided by [Br]itish expeditionary forces. From 1809, [th]e British forces, under the Duke of [We]llington, gradually fought their way [for]ward in a bitter struggle, finally [inv]ading southwest France in 1813–14. [M]eanwhile, in 1812, Napoleon's [de]cision to invade Russia was similarly [mi]sjudged. The Russian army simply

towards Paris, there was little political will to support continued resistance and, betrayed by defections among his senior officers, he was forced to abdicate.

Napoleon was exiled to the island of Elba, but returned the following year, and many flocked back to his standard. The restoration of his regime depended on early, decisive victories, so defeat by the Prussians and British at Waterloo in June 1815 led to his definitive abdication and the end of the Napoleonic Wars.

"HISTORY IS A SET OF LIES... PEOPLE HAVE AGREED UPON."

Napoleon Bonaparte, *Memoirs*, published in 1823

[ret]reated further eastwards, and, [alt]hough Napoleon's Grande Armée did [tak]e Moscow in September, the victory [wa]s hollow. The French were forced to [fa]ll back in a harrowing winter retreat [du]ring which, harassed by the Russians, [th]ey lost more than half a million men.

Both of these campaigns left [Na]poleon vulnerable to a renewed [co]alition against him and, in a massive [ba]ttle at Leipzig in 1813, he suffered his [fir]st major battlefield defeat. Though [Na]poleon fought a brilliant short [ca]mpaign to block the Coalition advance

THE DUKE OF WELLINGTON

In 1808, Arthur Wellesley, 1st Duke of Wellington (1769–1852), was placed in command of a British force despatched to aid Portugal against France. For the next six years he fought his way through the Iberian peninsula, before invading France itself in late 1813. Despite his professed disdain for the common soldier, Wellington had a clear ability to win battles, which inspired great loyalty in his soldiers. After his defeat of Napoleon at Waterloo in 1815, he took to politics, including a stint as British prime minister in 1828–30.

NATIONALISM AND REVOLUTION

Europe ☙ 1804–1878

The Congress of Vienna, which met from 1814 to 1815 to settle the terms by which the Napoleonic Wars would be concluded, ended by sealing a return to more or less the same system of European powers that existed before the French Revolution. For the next quarter-century, the "Congress System" – in which the "Concert of Powers" (Britain, Austria, Russia, and Prussia) met periodically to determine political issues – cast a stifling blanket over any aspirations for change.

Growing in strength all this time were feelings of nationalism – the view that ethnic groups had the right to political self-determination and the right to their own independent states.

Milan Obrenovic's accession as Serbia's first king in 1882 sealed the country's independence.

During the 1848 Revolutions it seemed as if the whole of Europe was in flames. Uprisings in Austria threatened Vienna, heart of the Habsburg empire.

This was a particular problem for the Austro-Hungarian empire, which boasted many such groups, including the Austrians, the Hungarians, and the Czechs. It also posed a threat to the integrity of the Ottoman empire, a similarly multi-ethnic state

NATIONALISM IN THE OTTOMAN EMPIRE

As the Ottoman sultans were decidedly not included in the European Concert of Powers, it is scarcely surprising that it was in their domains that nationalism won its earliest successes. A revolutionary uprising broke out in Greece in 1821, supported by foreign (mainly English) intervention – including the picturesque involvement of the English poet, Lord Byron. The revolutionaries won a great naval victory at Navarino in 1827 and finally forced the Ottomans to

Eugène Delacroix's *Liberty Leading the People* was inspired by the uprising that brought Louis-Philippe to the French throne in 1830, only to be deposed in 1848.

recognize Greek independence in 1832. In Serbia, a revolt sparked off by the reformers Vuk Karadjic and George Petrovic in 1804 secured Russian aid and drove the Ottomans out of the province by 1807. On the defensive after defeat in Greece, the Ottoman sultan finally accepted Serbian autonomy in 1830.

THE 1848 REVOLUTIONS

In central and western Europe, poor harvests in 1846–47 had resulted in appalling hardship for the peasantry. Combined with nationalist frustrations at the seeming impossibility of political change, this produced an astonishing outbreak of revolutionary movements in 1848 that touched almost all parts of Europe. In France, it led to the overthrow of the monarchy of Louis-Philippe and the establishment of the Second Republic.

In the Austro-Hungarian empire, a more obviously nationalist series of uprisings almost overthrew Habsburg power to set up a number of new, ethnically based states. In the end the existing regime won out by offering concessions to the Hungarians, the most significant non-German component of the empire. They established the "Dual Monarchy", in which the ruler was emperor in Austria, but king of a theoretically separate Hungarian state. Popular uprisings in Italy and Germany, which seemed to promise statehood, were similarly premature, and ended in brutal suppressions.

THE DECLINE AND RISE OF NATIONALISM

With this almost total restoration of the status quo, it seemed that the Concert of Powers would continue to run Europe with a conservative fist much as it had done since 1815. Yet within 20 years, the disparate states of Italy and Germany were united as independent countries (*see pp.281–2*), while the dismemberment of the Ottoman empire continued at the Congress of Berlin (1878), which finally recognized the independence of Serbia, Montenegro, and Romania, and began to establish a separate Bulgarian state.

THE UNIFICATION OF GERMANY

🏴 Germany   ⚔ 1864–1871

At the time of the 1848 Revolutions (*see p.281*), Germany was a loose confederation of states, the most powerful among them being Prussia. From 1862, Prussia's Minister-President, Otto von Bismarck, sought to secure the supremacy of Prussia within central Europe by encouraging the other German states to unify under its leadership. The process began in earnest in 1864, when Prussia joined forces with Austria to annex the duchies of Schleswig and Holstein from Denmark. Two years later, war broke out between Prussia and Austria, and a Prussian victory at Königgrätz in 1867 allowed Bismarck to exclude Austria from the German Confederation, and from any say in the constitutional course of the German principalities.

OTTO VON BISMARCK

Prime Minister of Prussia from 1862, Otto von Bismarck (1815–98) wanted to unite Germany under Prussian leadership. His skilful conduct of wars against Denmark and Austria in the 1860s helped secure the infant state; then victory in the Franco-Prussian War (1870–71) persuaded the other German states to join Prussia to form an empire, of which Bismarck became the first chancellor. Though a conservative leader, he did introduce some social reforms aimed at reducing the growing appeal of socialism (*see p.291*).

THE GERMAN EMPIRE

Bismarck was well aware that Napoleon III of France (*see p.284*) would never willingly accept a unified German state on his borders. He attempted to place a German Hohenzollern prince on the throne of Spain to encircle the French. As a result, Napoleon III declared war on Prussia and its German allies. Napoleon was captured after the Battle of Sedan in September 1870, and, though the French continued to resist under a new Republic, Bismarck soon had the victory he desired. In a humiliation of the French, the German empire was proclaimed at the Palace of Versailles on the outskirts of Paris on 18 January 1871, with the Prussian ruler Wilhelm as its first emperor. The new Germany was in principle a federation of 25 states, but there was no doubt that Prussia and Bismarck – champion of the unification – were very firmly in charge.

Wilhelm I was proclaimed first Kaiser (emperor) of the German empire in the Hall of Mirrors at the Palace of Versailles.

THE UNIFICATION OF ITALY

Italy ☒ 1831–1871

e Congress of Vienna in 1814 (*see* 0) confirmed the division of the lian peninsula into a patchwork of es. A revolutionary society known as *Carbonari* (coal-burners) began to ate for unification, and organized a ies of insurrections. In 1831, the lian patriot Giuseppe Mazzini formed movement known as "Young Italy", ich called for one Italian nation, dependent, free, and Republican". lian statesmen were quick to grasp

occupied Sicily and Naples. In 1861, Piedmont established a "Kingdom of Italy" with Victor Emmanuel of Piedmont as its first monarch.

The process of Italian unification was completed with Italy's seizure of the Veneto from Austria in 1866 and, following Napoleon III's withdrawal of the French garrison to fight the Franco-Prussian War, the occupation of Rome in October 1870. Rome officially became the capital of Italy the following year.

> ## "A PEOPLE DESTINED TO ACHIEVE GREAT THINGS FOR THE WELFARE OF HUMANITY MUST ONE DAY OR OTHER BE CONSTITUTED A NATION."
>
> Giuseppe Mazzini, Italian revolutionary and patriot, 1861

ir opportunities. Camillo Cavour, the me minister of Piedmont in northern ly, provoked a war against Austria in 59, and his victory enabled Piedmont take control of most of northern Italy. The next year, Giuseppe Garibaldi aded southern Italy with an army of usands of volunteer "Red Shirts" and

GIUSEPPE GARIBALDI

Having participated in a failed *Carbonari* insurrection in Piedmont in 1834, Giuseppe Garibaldi (1807–82) was forced to flee Italy o South America. In 1849, he returned to command a Roman army established in he wake of the 1848 Revolutions (*see .281*), but on its suppression fled nce more. In 1860, defying more autious mainstream nationalists, e captured most of southern Italy. idelined thereafter, he fought his ast battles in French service during he Franco-Prussian War (*see p.284*).

FRANCE UNDER NAPOLEON III

France 1848–1870

On the restoration of the Bourbon monarchy in France in 1815 (*see pp.276–7*), all members of the Bonaparte family were sent into exile. Napoleon I's nephew, Charles-Louis Napoleon, thus grew up in Switzerland and Germany. However, after the collapse of the "July Monarchy" of Louis-Philippe in 1848, Charles-Louis returned to France, and he was elected president later that year. Then, in 1851, Charles-Louis engineered a coup that resulted in his becoming emperor the following year, as Napoleon III (ruled 1852–70).

Despite his imperial position, Napoleon III saw himself as a social and economic reformer, encouraging the large-scale renovation of Paris – according to a plan devised by the civic planner Baron Haussmann – and overseeing a massive expansion in France's rail network.

NAPOLEON III'S FOREIGN POLICY

Napoleon III joined the British side in the Crimean War against Russia (1853–56), aided the cause of Italian independence by going to war with Austria in 1859, acquired France's first Southeast Asian colony (Cochin-China in 1862, and intervened in Mexico (1862–67) to place a Habsburg emperor on the throne there. It was, however, his quarrel with the German chancellor Otto von Bismarck that led to his defeat and deposition in 1870 during the Franco-Prussian War (*see below*). He died in exile in England in 1873.

THE FRANCO-PRUSSIAN WAR

France 1870–1871

In autumn 1870 France, provoked by plans by German chancellor Otto von Bismarck (*see p.282*) to put a German prince on the Spanish throne, declared war on Prussia. A brief occupation of the Rhineland town of Saarbrücken in August 1870 was France's sole success, and a bloody defeat at Gravelotte on 18 August was followed two weeks later by disaster at Sedan, where Napoleon III was forced to surrender. Although France established a Government of National Defence to continue the country's resistance, its armed forces were shattered and on 28 January 1871 Paris was forced to surrender. France was left in chaos: most of its politicians were discredited; Paris fell briefly under the power of the radical Commune government; and peace with Prussia involved the surrender of Alsace-Lorraine.

On 25 January 1871, frustrated Paris's continued resistance, Bismarck ordered the city to be bombarded with heavy Krupp gu

VICTORIAN ENGLAND

◆ England ⚱ 1837–1901

hen Queen Victoria ascended to the
tish throne in 1837, Britain had not
enjoyed the fruits of its early
ustrialization (*see p.288*), nor recovered
m the loss of its American colonies in
33 (*see p.263*) or the costs of the
poleonic Wars (*see p.278–9*). Yet when
died in 1901, Britain's pre-eminence
an industrial power was unchallenged,
British flag flew in outposts across the
be, and a cultural self-confidence that
w out of this prosperity had moulded
haracteristically "Victorian" Britain.

The Great Exhibition of 1851, held in the Crystal
Palace in Hyde Park, London, was an imperial
showcase for the "works of industry of all nations".

²ANSION ABROAD, REFORM AT HOME
e demise of the East India Company
1858 (*see p.237*) left the British Crown
ontrol of large swathes of India.
th the acquisition of colonies in Africa,

hours of children, and the foundation
of the Salvation Army in 1865 to
encourage charity to London's slum-
dwellers were just a few of the social
developments of Victoria's reign.

> VE ARE NOT INTERESTED
> IN THE POSSIBILITIES
> OF DEFEAT."

Queen Victoria to Arthur Balfour MP, 1899

tain had truly become an imperial
wer, and in 1877 Victoria took the title
mpress of India". At home, there was
ise in reformism: a great increase in
banization inspired a will to tackle the
ial problems it caused. The repeal of
Corn Laws – which had raised the
ce of food – in 1846, the passing of
Factory Acts restricting the working

UEEN VICTORIA

ictoria (ruled 1837–1901) was 18 when
he came to the throne and in 1840 she
arried her German cousin Prince Albert.
heir children married into so many of the
byal families of Europe that Victoria was
nown as the "grandmother of Europe".

RUSSIA IN THE 19TH CENTURY

📖 Russia ⌛ 1801–1905

At the accession of Alexander I in 1801, the Russian empire already stretched from eastern Siberia to Poland, a vast distance that posed almost unsurmountable governance problems to the tsarist administration. Its mainly rural population, largely serfs, laboured under primitive conditions, and although the country had begun to industrialize, it failed to match its western European rivals.

An early Colt revolver shipped to Russia from the USA and used to h the Russians fight the Crimean Wa

ALEXANDER I AND NICHOLAS I

Russia continued to expand in the early 19th century, acquiring Finland from Sweden in 1809, Bessarabia from Turkey in 1812, and the much-diminished state of Poland in 1815. Further acquisitions in the Caucasus, where the Russians finally

A dramatic scene of fighting during the Crimean War between Russia and Turkey and its allies, the first conflict recorded by both artists and photographers.

suppressed a bitter resistance after the surrender of the guerrilla leader Sham in 1859, meant that the Russian empir was roughly half as large again as it ha been under Peter the Great (*see p.251*). It was not a territory that lent itself to central administration: until 1830 there was not even an all-weather road between Moscow and St Petersburg, an the first railway followed only in 1851.

The reigns of Alexander I (1801–25 and Nicholas I (1825–55) were dogged by the issue of serfdom, and whether t serfs should be emancipated. Alexand although liberal in theory, even declari the need for a Russian constitution, di

Vladimir Makovsky's *Death in the Snow* shows the suffering caused by tsarist authorities during the crushing of the 1905 Revolution.

...le in practice, while ...icholas was a more ...aightforward autocrat ...ho ceded little ground. ...e suppressed a revolt in ...land in 1830 and sent ...d to the Habsburgs in ...48 to put down the ...volutions in Austria ...d Hungary. His reign ...ded in disaster, when ...s ambitions to acquire ...rritory from the Ottoman ...npire led to a humiliating defeat at ...e hands of Britain and France in the ...rimean War (1853–56).

TEMPT AT REFORM
...exander II (ruled 1855–81), who ...esided over the expansion of the ...ussian empire into Central Asia, ...stituted a series of liberal reforms, ...ally emancipating the serfs in ...61. Legal reforms enhanced the ...dependence of the judiciary, while in ...64 a system of local government with

oppressive tyranny. One such dissenting group, the "People's Will", finally assassinated the tsar in March 1881.

REPRESSION AND REVOLUTIONARIES
Under Alexander III (ruled 1881–94), a campaign of police terror smothered the revolutionaries, while reforms in 1889 in part back-pedalled on serf emancipation. When Nicholas II came to the throne in 1894, frustration was at boiling point, and the first Marxist party (*see p.291*) was founded in 1898. Russian defeat in the

> # "THE LATE EMPEROR DID NOT ANTICIPATE THIS END, AND THUS DID NOT TRAIN ME IN ANYTHING."
>
> Tsar Nicholas II, 1894

...cted bodies, the *zemstvos*, ...as set up. Yet it was also ...Alexander II's reign ...at there were the first ...volutionary rumblings, ...nong peasants unhappy ...at emancipation had not ...d to prosperity and ...tellectuals who despised ...e tsarist system as an

...holas II reversed many of the reforms ...previous tsars, but this fostered rather ...n extinguished radical sentiment.

Russo-Japanese War (1904–5) increased the clamour for reform to deafening levels, and a wave of revolutionary protest broke out. In response, the tsar allowed the establishment of a state Duma (parliament), and granted basic civil rights. Having satisfied the moderates, he crushed the extremists, ending the Revolution of 1905.

THE INDUSTRIAL REVOLUTION

From the late 18th century in Britain, a wave of industrialization swept across Europe and North America. It transformed the Western world from a rural society into an urban one, and set the foundations for modern capitalism. This "Industrial Revolution" spurred profound social changes, as well as giving rise to innovations in technology that were to fuel vast economic growth.

BRITISH BEGINNINGS

Abundant natural materials such as iron and coal, and a growing middle class eager to invest, allowed Britain to take full advantage of new developments in technology. In the 1770s, James Watts developed an improved steam engine, which could provide the necessary power for various industrial uses, from pumping mines to running machinery in the factories and mills of the early 18th century.

Romanticized depictions of the conditions in the new factories did nothing to stem social unrest.

Textile production mechanized particularly rapidly – by 1835 there were more than 120,000 power looms in textile mills – leading men, women, and children to flock to the towns where the factories were situated. There they endured appalling conditions, working long hours for low pay, until the rise of trade unionism (*see p.290*) began to curb the excesses of factory owners.

THE REVOLUTION SPREADS

The new industrial techniques spread outwards from Britain, taking hold first in Belgium in the 1820s, then spreading fast during the "Second Industrial Revolution" (1840–70) when the building of railways in Germany, Switzerland, and the USA made it easier to move labour and commodities.

In Europe, the abolition of serfdom – in France during the 1790s, in Germany between 1811 and 1848, and in Russia and Poland in the 1860s – assisted industrialization by creating a more readily available workforce. In the USA, large-scale immigration provided the new factories with their employees.

In 1855, Englishman Henry Bessemer invented a new process for making iron into steel – a stronger,

George Stephenson's "North Star" steam engine served on Britain's Great Western Railway, one of the great Victorian railway companies.

more versatile metal than wrought iron. This provided the raw material for new railway lines, improved ships, and more powerful armaments. Demand for steel was almost insatiable – by 1910, Krupp, the leading German steel manufacturer, employed some 70,000 people; in 1846 its workforce had been just 122.

THE THIRD WAVE

From the 1890s, a third wave of industrialization occurred in Russia, Sweden, France, and Italy. This saw the industrialization of chemical and electrical engineering. The Germans now dominated industrial and weaponry production, as Britain's initial lead ebbed away. Fear of what this might mean led Russia, France, and Italy to accelerate investments in arms manufacturing, while Russia improved its rail network specifically for transporting troops. It would be just a few years before Europe would begin fighting the first truly industrialized war – World War I (1914–18) – a war that would destroy those infrastructures that had been so improved by industry.

Developments in engineering technology enabled the building of triumphant monuments to the modern age, such as the Eiffel Tower in Paris.

INDUSTRIALIZATION AND THE LABOUR MOVEMENT

Europe, the USA   *c.*1800–1868

Labour practices in the factories of the Industrial Revolution (*see pp.288–9*) ranged from neglectful to abusive. From the early 19th century, British workers organized themselves into groups to protect their interests, but these "combinations" were illegal and employers often repressed them.

A German socialist banner from the 19th century calls on the workers of the world to unite.

TRADE UNIONISM

In 1824–25, the British government repealed the anti-Combination laws and, for the first time, trade unions became lawful. In 1829, John Doherty established the Grand General Union of the Operative Spinners of Great Britain and Ireland, the first

At the Peterloo Massacre in 1819, British troops fired on unarmed workers protesting at working conditions and lobbying for reforms.

attempt at a national uni[on] – starting a trend that wa[s] followed in the 1830s by other trades. Repression was still commonplace – the deportation of the "Tolpuddle Martyrs", organized agricultural workers, to Australia in 1834 being only the mos[t] famous example.

Rapid economic progress in the 1840s strengthened the hand [of] the unions, and in 1868 the forerunner of the modern Trades Union Congress was established. Meanwhile, the movemen[t] had spread overseas, with the formatio[n] of the National Labour Union in the USA in 1866, and the growth of union[s] in continental Europe following the 18[48] Revolutions (*see pp.280–*

SOCIALISM AND MARXISM

Europe   *c*.1800–1917

he Industrial Revolution inspired
olitical groups to organize workers and
aprove their lot. A philosophy called
ocialism arose that argued that wealth
aould be shared by putting it in the
ands of its creators. Similar sentiments
ad inspired the German Peasants'
evolt in 1532–34 and had also caused

International Working Men's Association
in 1864, which acted as a platform
for the dissemination of his revolutionary
theories. Although he believed that the
full revolution would break out in France
or Germany, it was in the relatively
underdeveloped Russia that Marxists
would finally seize power, in 1917.

"THE HISTORY OF ALL... SOCIETY IS THE HISTORY OF CLASS STRUGGLE."

Karl Marx, *The Communist Manifesto*, 1848

arest in England after the Civil War (*see
.248–9*), but the industrialized Europe of
e 19th century provided the first arena
r these ideas to be put into practice.
  Early 19th-century socialists included
obert Owen, a Welsh industrialist, who
roposed a society in which property was
vned collectively. In France, Henri
aint-Simon advocated a society in
nich there was equal opportunity for
", while his followers wanted an end
 private property. By the early 20th
ntury, many European countries had
tablished socialist parties, including the
abour Party in Britain (1900) and the
ocialist Party in France (1902).

ARXISM AND REVOLUTION

ore radical still were the ideas of
e German-born philosopher and
onomist Karl Marx (1818–83),
ao viewed history as a series of
ass struggles that would lead to
e end of capitalism. Distrusting
e compromises of more
oderate "Social Democrats",
arx helped establish the

l Marx, with Friedrich
gels, wrote *The Communist
unifesto* (1848), setting out
evolutionary socialism.

SCIENTIFIC ADVANCES

The Industrial Revolution (*see pp.288–9*) was accompanied by an explosion in technology, leading to huge developments in transportation (the car and aeroplane), communications (the telephone and wireless signals), and even in domestic life (the electric light bulb and gramophone). In science, British naturalist Charles Darwin overturned the understanding of the world by developing the theory of evolution.

SCIENTIFIC DISCOVERIES

Few men had a greater impact on life in the 19th century than English physicist Michael Faraday, who discovered that moving a magnet through a coil of wire produced an electric current. His experiments in electricity in the 1830s led to dramatic progress in the sphere of communications, with the patenting of the electric telegraph in 1837, and the invention of the telephone by the Scottish-born

The microscope that Charles Darwin took with him on his 1831–36 voyage to the Galapagos Islands in the Pacific.

American scientist Alexander Graham Bell in 1876.

In 1906, the Italian Guglielmo Marconi built on earlier theoretical work by the German scientist Heinrich Hertz to transmit speech wirelessly over the airwaves using radio transmissions. The appearance of the internal combustion engine, patented by Karl Benz in 1879, led to the development of the first practical automobiles by the mid-1880s. The first powered, sustained, heavier-than-air flight

Karl Benz, seated on his 1885 Benz Motorwagen, the first automobile to be available for sale to the general public.

by the Wright brothers in 1903 further revolutionized transportation. Other innovations of the 1890s, such as the gramophone and moving pictures (the latter pioneered by the French inventors the Lumière brothers), were only available at first to small groups, but within decades

Alexander Graham Bell, the inventor of the telephone, made the first long-distance call, from New York to Chicago, in 1892.

1859. Darwin's observation of finches on different islands in the Galapagos group showed they had developed characteristics to suit their particular environments. Darwin

> ## "MAN WITH ALL HIS NOBLE QUALITIES... STILL BEARS IN HIS BODILY FRAME THE INDELIBLE STAMP OF HIS LOWLY ORIGIN."
>
> Charles Darwin, *The Descent of Man*, 1871

the refinement and expansion of these technologies made them accessible to almost everyone.

THE THEORY OF EVOLUTION

The long-held notion that animal species had been created by God and remained essentially unchanged was shaken by the publication of Charles Darwin's *On the Origin of Species* in

argued that through "natural selection" individuals in a species had competed against each other and those stronger or more able survived to pass on their genes. In *The Descent of Man* (1871), Darwin argued that humankind had descended from an ape-like ancestor. Initially bitterly contested, Darwin's theory survived to become scientific orthodoxy.

Asia

The countries of Asia had to contend in the 19th century with increasingly aggressive interventions by European powers, with varying degrees of success. Most of India had fallen under British control by the 1850s, while China had been fatally weakened by the Opium Wars, also fought against Britain. Only Japan had shown that it was more than able to hold its own, by seizing opportunities made possible by industrialization.

THE BATTLE OF PLASSEY

Bengal, India   23–24 June 1757

The British East India Company, which had first established a firm base in Bengal at Calcutta in 1690, struggled for the next half-century with local rulers who were keen to minimize its presence in their territories. In 1756, a major crisis erupted when Siraj-ud-Daula, the new *nawab* (ruler) of Bengal, demanded that the British hand over his wealthy subject Krishna Das, who after embezzling government funds had taken refuge in Calcutta.

THE FALL OF CALCUTTA

Siraj-ud-Daula further demanded that the British demolish the walls of the city, and when they refused, the Bengali army stormed the rather run-down fortifications in June 1757. Some 146 British captives were allegedly then confined in the "Black Hole", the cell of the company barracks, from which it was said only 23 emerged alive. Although exaggerated, the story helped prompt a severe reprisal from the British.

CLIVE WINS AT PLASSEY

The British despatched soldier an statesman Robert Clive and his troops from Madras to punish the *nawab*. After capturing the French headquarters at Chandernagore, Clive defeated Siraj-ud-Daula in a two-day battle at Plassey on 23–24 June. Mir Jafar was made *nawab*, Clive received 28 million rupee on behalf of the East India Company from the royal treasur and the Company's position in Bengal appeared secure.

Robert Clive (1725–74) secure the British position in India as result of his victory at Plassey.

THE BRITISH IN INDIA

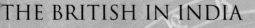

🇮🇳 India   ⏳ 1757–1885

ve's victory at Plassey
1757 (*see facing page*) had
med to cement British
wer in India. But
uble soon erupted
ain with Bengal's next
wab, Mir Kasim, and
his defeat in 1764,
e British East India
ompany effectively
nexed west Bihar. From
en on, the British became
creasingly entangled in
dian affairs, and as they
fended their established interests, they
ined more and more territory.
Through the Anglo-Mysore Wars
'66–99) and the Anglo-Maratha Wars
'72–1818), the Company extended
domains into the south of India to
mplement its near-monopoly of power
the north. It annexed Sindh in 1843,
d conquered the Punjab in two tough
rs in 1845–46 and 1848–49.

Dhuleep Singh, the last maharaja of the
Punjab, was deposed by the British when
they annexed his kingdom in 1849.

of "lapse", which meant
that the lands of Indian
princes who died without
direct heirs simply fell into
British possession. This
was most unpopular with
the native rulers, and
Britain's growing power
fed into the resentment that
sparked the Indian Mutiny in
1857 (*see p.296*). Once the British
had suppressed the mutiny in 1858, the
rights of the East India Company were
transferred to the British Crown.

The next half-century of British rule
in India, known as the Raj, was peaceful,
though the Indian National Congress,
which called for greater political rights
for Indians, was founded in 1885. But
India was the "jewel in the crown" of
the British empire, and the British long
resisted making meaningful concessions
to the Indian nationalists.

E BRITISH RAJ

ne British, under the Governorship of
rd Dalhousie, now began to unify the
ministration of all these disparate
rritories. In the meantime, they
quired more territories by the doctrine

The British Raj
built the spectacular
Victoria Terminus of
the Indian Peninsular
Railway in Mumbai.

THE INDIAN MUTINY

India **1857–1858**

In the 1850s the British East India Company imposed a variety of measures on its *sepoys* – native Indian soldiers – that caused great resentment. Early in 1857, the British introduced a new Enfield rifle into service in India, and the firing drill required the *sepoys* to bite off the tip of the cartridge. Rumours flew that the tip was smeared with animal (pig or cow) fat, offending the religious sensibilities of both Muslim and Hindu troops. A mutiny erupted at Meerut in May 1857 which soon spread to units throughout northern India. The involvement of the aged Mughal emperor Bahadur Shah I seemed to promise the revival of native

Indian power, but the British fought back and, by September 1857, had recaptured lost Delhi, although the last rebels were only suppressed in July the following year.

Indian mutineers massacred the British prisoners at Cawnpore in July 1857, fuelling a desire for revenge among British troops.

THE BURMESE WARS

Burma **1824–1885**

Early relations between the British in India and the neighbouring kingdom of Burma centred on the East India Company's attempts to open trade links. However, when a common frontier was established between Bengal and the Burmese state of Arakan in the late 18th century, tensions led to three wars between the two countries.

THE BRITISH INVASIONS

During the first war (1824–26), the East India Company gained territory in Manipur, Arakan, and Tennasserim. The second Anglo-Burmese war (1852), provoked by minor Burmese violations of the treaty that had

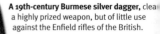

A 19th-century Burmese silver dagger, clea a highly prized weapon, but of little use against the Enfield rifles of the British.

settled the first conflict, ended with Burma's loss of Pegu, the northern section of the country which the British established as the colony of Lower Burma.

For the next 25 years, the Burmese king Mindon Min (ruled 1853–78) fended off furth British advances, but his successo Thibaw (ruled 1878–85) was less able, and in November 1885 a dispute over payment for timber concessions flared up into war. The British advance was swift, and by the end of the month the had captured Thibaw's capital a Mandalay and deposed him.

TURKISH REFORM MOVEMENTS

Turkey ⌛ 1789–1923

form in the Ottoman empire began
th attempts by Selim III (ruled
89–1807) to institute a *Nizam-I cedid*,
"New System" of bureaucratic
ganization, aimed at countering the
action that had contributed to
e Ottoman loss of lands in
rbia and Hungary. His
ccessor Mahmud II
led 1808–39) went
to restore authority to
e central government,
ich had been usurped
powerful local interests.

E YOUNG TURKS

ahmud's successor
odülmecid (ruled 1839–61)
barked on a programme of
odernizing reform that would become
own as *Tanzimat* ("reorganization").
owever, under Abdul Hamid II (ruled
76–1909) the Ottoman empire
ffered a disastrous setback: defeat by
e Russians in 1878 deprived the empire
most of its European territories, and
en, in 1882, it lost Egypt to the British.
nder pressure, Abdul Hamid continued
make educational and military reforms,
t this was not sufficient to satisfy
dical opinion, and in 1902 a meeting
Paris brought together the leadership

e Dolmabahce Palace, overlooking the Bosphorus
Istanbul, was the residence of the last Ottoman
tans in the late 19th and early 20th centuries.

ENVER PASHA

An early leader of the Young Turk
movement, Enver Pasha (1881–1922)
became Turkey's military attaché in Berlin,
a posting that contributed to his
advocacy of a Turkish–German
alliance during World War I.

of the "Young Turks",
a coalition of fervent
nationalists who wished to
rescue Turkey from its
ruinous position. In 1908,
the Young Turks joined a
rebellion in Macedonia and
formed the Committee of
Union and Progress (CUP). They
forced Abdul Hamid to agree to grant a
constitution and establish a parliament.

THE EMPIRE COLLAPSES

The leader of the CUP, Enver Pasha,
pushed forward the reform process –
opening schools to women, for example.
Yet in matters of foreign policy the
Young Turks chose unwisely, entering
World War I on the side of the Germans.
After Germany's defeat in 1918, an
Allied invasion led to British forces
occupying Istanbul by 1920. Turkey was
saved by Kemal Mustafa Ataturk, who
rallied the country's armies and drove
back the Allies in 1922 to become
president of a Turkish Republic in 1923.

QING CHINA

China   1796–1912

In 1796, the White Lotus Rebellion – part tax revolt, part mystical movement, part nostalgia for the rule of the Ming (*see p.165*) – broke out in Qing China. While it was crushed in 1804, the White Lotus weakened the regime of Emperor Jiaqing (ruled 1796–1820) and began a series of debilitating uprisings that would tear China apart.

During the 19th century, European demand for decorative Chinese goods such as silks and porcelain soared.

government to despatch an expeditionary force, sparking off the First Opium War.

THE OPIUM WARS

The conflict was hugely one-sided, and the British soon occupied Hong Kong and Shanghai. The Treaty of Nanjing, which ended the conflict in 1842, ceded Hong Kong to Britain, set limits on the external tariffs China could impose, removed Westerners from Chinese jurisdiction, and opened five "treaty ports" to European traders.

THE OPIUM TRADE

During Jiaqing's reign, huge amounts of opium began to flow into China, largely smuggled in by British traders, which necessitated the export of large quantities of silver to pay for it. Opium addiction became rife and, in 1839, the Chinese government appointed a leading official, Lin Zexu, to suppress trade in the southern port city of Guangzhou. Lin confiscated opium stocks, but also detained several British traders, which prompted the London

Then, in 1856, the Chinese authoriti boarded a British trading vessel, the *Arrow*, and the Second Opium War broke out. This time the French joined in, and after a four-year war that featured the humiliating burning of the

The "Thirteen Factories" (or *hongs*) of Canton (now Guangzhou) were the sole place where foreigners could trade into China until 1842.

> # "AS LONG AS CHINA REMAINS A NATION OF OPIUM SMOKERS, THERE IS NOT THE LEAST REASON TO FEAR THAT SHE WILL BECOME A MILITARY POWER OF ANY IMPORTANCE."
>
> in Zexu, Chinese commissioner at Guangzhou

ng Summer Palace in Beijing, the stern powers (including Russia) were arded 10 further treaty ports, on top enormous financial payments, and the um trade was legalized.

E TAIPING REBELLION

e surrender of the Qing regime in the ium Wars contributed to a rising tide anti-government protests. Largest of se was the Taiping Rebellion.

n 1836, a Christian teacher, Hong uquan, had a series of dreams that led n to believe he had a mission to bring ristianity to China. He made converts ong peasants in Guangzi, south ina, and in January 1851 established e *Taiping Tianguo* – the Heavenly ngdom of Great Peace. In 1853, the iping rebels captured Nanjing, and nned gambling and opium smoking. wever, in 1860, the Western-trained ver-Victorious Army" defeated a iping assault on Shanghai, and in 64 the Qing government recaptured njing. The revolt effectively collapsed.

CIAL REFORM

om 1861, the Qing court was minated by Empress Ci Xi, mother of e Tongzhi emperor. For 47 years she

ruled China, encouraging at first the "Self-strengthening Movement", which permitted limited reforms – including China's first railway, a modern steamship company on the Yangtze river, and a reorganized army. However, China's dramatic defeat by Japan's army and navy in the Sino-Japanese War of 1894–95 over Korea (*see p.301*) undermined support for further reforms.

THE END OF THE QING

Resentment at the growing influence of Christian missionaries in China fed into an uprising by the Boxers, also known as the "Righteous Fists of Harmony", who aimed to expel all foreigners from China. Tacitly supported by Ci Xi, the Boxers marched on Beijing in May 1900, where they besieged the foreign legations for nearly two months. An alliance of eight foreign nations, including Britain, France, the USA, and Japan, sent a relieving force and crushed the rebels. Its credibility compromised, the Qing regime was finally replaced in 1912 by a Republic of China, led by Sun Yat-Sen.

From humble origins as a concubine to the Xianfeng emperor, "Lady Yehonola" became Empress Dowager Ci Xi and controlled China for nearly half a century.

THE MEIJI RESTORATION

🏯 Japan　⚔ 1833–1911

From the early 17th century, the Tokugawa shoguns kept peace in Japan and the population prospered. Yet from the early 19th century, several disasters occurred. A famine in 1833–36 killed many thousands, while, partly in response, a wave of rural riots and urban disorder struck the country.

On top of internal problems, Japan faced new threats from abroad.

The Meiji emperor was restored to power in 1868, leading to the abolition of shogun feudalism.

The country had been virtually closed to foreigners for two centuries, but in the mid-19th century several attempts were made to engage with it. In 1853, the US government sent Commodore Matthew Perry to Edo (Tokyo) with four warships. Perry demanded the opening of Japanese ports for trade, and returned the following year with an even larger flotilla. Powerless to resist such a show of force, the Tokugawa shogun signed the Convention of Kanagawa, opening several ports to the Americans.

THE EMPEROR RESTORED

Similar treaties followed with Britain, France, the Netherlands, and Russia. Japan gradually lost control over its customs dues, and a dispute arose in 1859–60, after foreign merchants discovered that they were able to make a healthy profit buying Japanese gold in the form of relatively undervalued coins, and taking it out of the country. It seemed as if the Tokugawa were ignoring Japan's best interests, and a resistance movement broke out under the slogan of *sonnō jōi* ("honour the emperor, expel the barbarians"). A group of leading *daimyo* (noble) families began to lobby for the return of the emperor to real power, after centuries of powerlessness in Kyoto

1868, a short civil war brought nearly
even centuries of shogun rule to an end:
the emperor was restored and a new era,
the Meiji (1868–1912), began. In 1877,
enraged traditionalists started a major
uprising – the Satsuma Rebellion. A new
conscript army defeated the traditional
samurai forces (*see p.172*), ending their role
in Japanese politics. The emperor set in
train a series of reforms, including the
granting of a formal constitution in 1889.

JAPAN AS A MAJOR POWER

Japan industrialized rapidly and made
use of its new economic strength to build
up its armed forces. In 1894, Chinese
intervention in Korea, where Japan
claimed a sphere of influence, led the
Japanese to declare war. Japanese armies
rapidly proved superior, and they seized
the strategic naval base at Port Arthur in
Manchuria in November. The Treaty of
Shimonoseki (1895), which ended the
conflict, saw China abandon its Korean
interests and cede Taiwan to Japan.
Japan's next military adventure, a
clash with Russia in 1904–5, again over
Korea, resulted in an even more

A great victory parade in Tokyo marked the Japanese victory in the Russo-Japanese War (1904–5), igniting a burst of patriotic fervour.

resounding success. The Japanese
Imperial Navy decimated the Russian
fleet at Tsushima in May 1905, forcing
Tsar Nicholas II to agree in September
to the Treaty of Portsmouth, by which
Russia backed out of Korea and Japan
gained occupation of the Liadong
peninsula. The defeat of a modern
European army by an Asian power sent
shockwaves through Western military
circles. Japan was a force to be reckoned
with, and it renegotiated its treaties to
secure full customs control by 1911.

The Satsuma Rebellion in 1877 was the last (and most serious) of a series of uprisings by traditionalists bent on reversing the reforms of the Meiji Restoration.

OCEANIA

By 1750, the Europeans had explored only a few coastline and scattered islands in the Pacific Ocean, their voyages motivated by the search for the hypothetical *Terra Australis*, or great Southern Continent, but equally impeded by the vast distances involved. Nevertheless, by the early 20th century, European powers had colonized the Pacific islands, while the two largest countries, Australia and New Zealand, had become self-governing dominions.

EXPLORATION IN THE PACIFIC

⚑ South Pacific ⚔ 1642–1770

The Pacific Ocean was first sighted by the Spanish explorer Vasco Nuñez de Balboa in 1513, and soon Spanish and Portuguese ships were crossing its northern reaches. But while Magellan crossed the South Seas in 1520, he completely missed Australia, undermining belief that *Terra Australis*, the "Southern Continent", actually existed. Eventually, the Dutch East India Company made the first sure sightings and exploration of the coast of Australia, with William Janszoon reaching the Gulf of Carpentaria in 1605.

In 1642, the Dutchman Abel Tasman first explored the coastline of Tasmania and also, heading east, made the first European sighting of New Zealand. The Dutch called these lands New Holland but they did not seek to settle there.

COOK'S VOYAGE

The east coast of mainland Australia, however, was first sighted on 20 April 1770 by the British explorer Captain James Cook, whose ship *Endeavour* had been on a voyage tasked with observing the Transit of Venus (a rare astronomical phenomenon), but also motivated by the desire to forestall French ambitions in the South Pacific. On 29 April, Cook made landfall on Australia at Botany Bay, and in August formally claimed possession of the new land for the British Crown.

Native inhabitants of New Guinea, a drawing contemporary with the time of Cook's voyages in the 1770s.

THE FIRST FLEET

New South Wales, Australia 1787–88

[th]e British were at first unsure as to what [to] do about the territory Captain Cook [dis]covered in 1770 (*see facing page*). Then [Lo]rd Sydney, the home secretary, devised [th]e "Heads of a Plan" to solve the twin [pr]oblems of how to prevent the French [est]ablishing their own colony in the new [lan]d, and what to do with the convicts [wh]o would once have been deported to the now-independent Americas. The scheme was to ship a batch of prisoners to Australia. On 13 May 1787, 11 ships (the "First Fleet"), under the command of Captain Arthur Phillip, set off from Portsmouth, England, bearing around 750 convicts, and arrived at Botany Bay on 20 January 1788. Given the name New South Wales, the small colony was reinforced by a Second Fleet in 1790, and a third a year later. At first, survival was the main concern, but within a few years the first settlement, at Sydney Cove, sent out parties to explore their new homeland.

Leg irons and chains shackled the convicts of the First Fleet on their long sea journey.

THE EXPLORATION OF AUSTRALIA

Australia 1798–1861

[A]s Australia's first colony, in New South [W]ales, grew – ably led from 1809 to [18]20 by Governor Lachlan Macquaherie [–] there came a desire to explore the new [co]ntinent. Early attempts concentrated [on] charting the coastline, and included, [in] 1798–99, George Bass and Matthew [Fl]inders' circumnavigation of Tasmania, [pr]eviously believed to be joined to the [m]ainland. But then explorers began to [str]ike inland. In 1813, Gregory Blaxland [cr]ossed the Blue Mountains for the first [ti]me, and in 1828 Charles Sturt explored [M]urray and Darling, reaching the sea [ne]ar present-day Adelaide. By the early [18]40s, new "free" colonies (to which [co]nvicts were not – at least initially – [se]nt) had been founded in Victoria [(1]803), Western Australia (1829), and [So]uth Australia (1836). Gradually, the explorations edged towards the centre of the continent, and in 1845 Sturt reached the fringes of the Simpson Desert. In 1861, John McDouall Stuart, suffering terrible privations along the way, made the first south-to-north crossing of Australia, beginning at Adelaide. His trip established once and for all the continent's extent and the harsh conditions that prevailed in its interior.

Charles Sturt (1795–1869), aged 32 when he arrived in Australia, spent 20 years exploring the continent.

THE FEDERATION OF AUSTRALIA

🏳 Australia　☗ 1872–1901

By the end of the 19th century, the Australian colonies had overcome their early travails, which included conflicts with the Aboriginal peoples, who were gradually pushed out of their lands by European settlers. A growing national self-consciousness emerged, which demanded more than the status of a mere colony of the British Crown. The connection of the six Australian colonies by telegraph in 1872 fuelled the sense of a common destiny and demands for "federation" as a single nation grew. A Federal Council was finally established in 1895, but it had no control over revenue. The 1898 Constitution Bill established a much stronger federal system, and on 1 January 1901, today's Commonwealth of Australia came into being.

The Royal Exhibition Building in the city of Melbourne housed the first session of Australia's Federal Parliament on 9 May 1901.

EUROPEAN SETTLEMENT IN NEW ZEALAND

🏳 New Zealand　☗ 1769–1850

The first contact between Europeans and the Maori of New Zealand (known by the indigenous peoples as *Aoteaoro* – the "land of the long white cloud") – ended unhappily when, in 1642, four Dutch crew members sailing with Abel Tasman (*see p.302*) were killed following a dispute. It was not until Captain Cook's "rediscovery" of New Zealand in 1769 that Europeans encroached once more on Maori possession of the land, and only gradually that sealers, whalers, and missionaries began establishing small coastal enclaves. By 1839, there were probably only 2,500 Europeans on the North and South Islands. The Maori themselves were debilitated by the effects of the epidemic diseases the Europeans brought with them, and by intertribal warfare sparked off by the firearms they bought from foreign traders.

WAITANGI AND EUROPEAN MIGRATION
In 1839, a new New Zealand Company set up a formal colony along the lines of those in Australia, and in February 1840 the British and the Maori chiefs signed the Treaty of Waitangi, which (in the British view) ceded Maori sovereign in exchange for Crown protection. European migration to New Zealand followed, and the settlers founded Auckland and Wellington in 1840, Dunedin in 1848, and Christchurch in 1850. By 1858 the 59,000 Europeans probably outnumbered the Maori.

THE NEW ZEALAND WARS

◀ New Zealand ☎ 1840–73

The Treaty of Waitangi (*see facing page*) did not put an end to friction between the Maori and the British, as the latter sought to expand into new areas. In 1843, open fighting erupted around Nelson, South Island, when armed settlers tried to punish the Maori chief Ngati Toa for resisting further encroachments. The Maori proved competent fighters and beat off the settlers. More fighting erupted in North Island in 1845–46, in part a Maori civil war, and around Wellington, North Island, in 1846.

THE WAIKATO WAR

The Maori, making able use of their *pa* (fortified settlements), beat off most European assaults, and for 15 years calm prevailed. In the 1860s, though, the

The Maori used wooden war clubs, despite also having European firearms.

emergence of a Maori "King Movement", with the selection of the first king Potatau Te Wherowhero, disrupted the balance of power. War flared up again, with the British struggling to break through the Maori network of *pa*. By 1864, a force of almost 14,000 British soldiers had weakened the Maori warriors in the Waikato War, and despite a flare-up in 1872–73, European military supremacy in New Zealand was thereafter largely left unchallenged.

ANTARCTIC EXPLORATION

◀ Antarctica ☎ 1820–1911

Although the Russian expedition of Fabian von Bellinghausen had sighted the Antarctic continent in 1820, and Briton James Ross had explored part of it (including Victoria Land and the Ross Ice Shelf) in 1839–43, most of Antarctica remained a mystery in the 1890s. In 1895, the Sixth International Geographical Conference declared

the Antarctic the world's last great focus for exploration and the race was on to discover and chart its secrets.

THE RACE FOR THE POLE

In prime place among the objectives was to reach the South Pole. In 1908, Sir Ernest Shackleton's expedition reached 88° 23′ south, just 180km (112 miles) short of the Pole. In 1911, however, the competition reached fever pitch with the simultaneous despatch of a Norwegian expedition, led by Roald Amundsen, and a British one, under Robert Scott. Amundsen's better-planned expedition reached the Pole first, on 14 December, beating Scott's group by five weeks.

A photograph of Robert Scott's final five-man party for the assault on the South Pole in 1911, all of whom died on the return trip to their base camp.

AFRICA

In the early 19th century, although Europeans had established settlements at several points along the African coast and North Africa was well known to them, the African interior remained largely uncharted. Yet by 1900, most of the continent had been carved up between European colonial powers, with only a few areas, such as Ethiopia, having been able to resist annexation. Anti-colonial resistance did occur, but in the end European armies always proved too strong.

THE EARLY EXPLORERS

Africa   1805–1871

In 1820, the development of quinine, an effective treatment for malaria, opened up the African interior to proper exploration for the first time. Even so, West Africa was so thoroughly unhealthy for outsiders that it was known as the "White Man's Grave"; Mungo Park's British-sponsored expedition there in 1805 ended in disaster when his party simply disappeared. In 1827, however, the Frenchman René-August Caillié became the first European to reach the fabled desert metropolis of Timbuktu and return alive, and by 1835, Europeans had mapped most of northwestern Africa.

A tropical pith helmet worn by the Scottish missionary David Livingstone (1813–73) as he explored Africa.

over which of the lakes was the source of the Nile. Speke argued (correctly) that it was Victoria, to which he alone had travelled. From the 1840s, the Scottish missionary David Livingstone managed to journey extensively in central and southern Africa. In 1853–56, he made the first known crossing of Africa from east to west, discovering the Victoria Falls on the way, before retiring to a remote station on Lake Tanganyika, where he was in turn famously "discovered" by Henry Morton Stanley in 1871.

By the end of the century, Europeans had charted the courses of the Nile, Niger, Congo, and Zambezi rivers, and the world was well informed of the vast resources that Africa might offer them.

CHARTING THE GREAT RIVERS

An expedition in 1858 by Englishmen Richard Burton and John Hanning Speke located Lake Tanganyika and Lake Victoria, although they quarrelled

THE SCRAMBLE FOR AFRICA

🗺 Africa   ⏳ 1869–1914

1869, the opening of the Suez Canal,
king the Mediterranean to the Red
a and thus to Asia, focused European
ention on Africa's strategic importance.
ropean colonial presence in Africa
s still fragmented. It included Algeria,
o which the French had made inroads
the 1830s; a few Spanish settlements;
rtugal's territory of Angola; and
tish and French trading stations in
st Africa. Britain administered the
pe Colony, bordered by two Boer
rikaners of Dutch origin) states.

E BERLIN CONFERENCE

1884, the German chancellor Otto
Bismarck convened the Berlin
nference to settle rival claims. It was
eed that imperial powers could claim
onies only if they had agreed treaties
h native chiefs and had established an
ninistration there (the "Principle of

Ashanti were one of the few African peoples to
rs strong resistance against European imperialism,
were subjugated by the British in 1900.

CECIL RHODES

Having made his fortune as founder of the
De Beers diamond company in South
Africa, British businessman Cecil Rhodes
(1853–1902) turned to politics. A firm
believer in British imperialism, his British
South Africa Company made treaties
that established a network of control
throughout modern Zimbabwe. As Prime
Minister of the Cape Colony from 1890, he
sponsored the 1895 Jameson Raid, an
attack on the independent Boer Republic
of the Transvaal. However, the attack
failed, ending Rhodes' political career.

Effectivity"). This led European
countries to make effective their claims
in areas they feared others might enter,
setting off a "Scramble for Africa". By
the close of the century virtually all the
continent was under European control.

By 1914, only two areas remained
free: Liberia, which had been settled by
freed American slaves; and Ethiopia,
which still retained its traditional rulers.

EGYPT UNDER MUHAMMAD ALI

📍 Egypt ⏳ 1807–1882

When France and Britain intervened in Egypt during the Napoleonic Wars (*see pp.278–9*) they destabilized the Ottoman regime there, enabling Muhammad Ali – of Albanian origin – to seize power by 1807. He fought on the Ottoman sultan's behalf against a revolt in Saudi Arabia in 1811–12, but then progressively absorbed new territory before launching outright war on the sultan in 1832. An agreement in 1841 removed Muhammad Ali's Syrian conquests to restore peace.

Ali reformed Egypt's army and tried to strengthen the economy by establishing state monopolies. His successors, who took the title Khedive, continued this process, but Ismail Pasha (ruled 1863– overreached himself. His ambitious projects bankrupted the country, allowin the British to occupy Egypt in 1882.

The Suez Canal, one of Ismail Pasha's hugely ambitious projects, was opened by French Empress Eugenie in November 1868.

THE MAHDIST MOVEMENT

📍 Sudan ⏳ 1881–1898

In 1877, the British military officer Charles George Gordon was appointed governor of the Egyptian-controlled Sudan, a post he held until 1880, when ill health forced him to retire.

Around the same time, a mystical Islamic movement arose under Muhammad Ahmad, who declared himself the Mahdi, promised saviour of the Muslim world. The Mahdi's forces annihilated a British expeditionary force under Colonel Hicks at El Obeid, central Sudan, in November 1883. Gordon was sent back to Sudan, but found himself besieged at Khartoum. After prolonged

Lord Charles George Gordon fa down advancing Mahdist rebel on the steps of the British Residence at Khartoum, in 188

resistance, the city was stormed by Mahdists on 26 January 1885, and Gordon was killed.

Although the Mahdi died in June 1885, his successor, the Khalifa 'Abdallahi, continued to rule Sudan until 1898, when a British force un Lord Kitchener invaded the country, bent on revenge for Gordon's death. A Omdurman on 1 September, the Brit armed with the new Maxim gun, tota destroyed 'Abdallahi's army and the Mahdist state collapsed.

THE BOER WARS

📍 South Africa ⚔ 1877–1902

The Dutch were the first Europeans to settle in South Africa, in 1652. From their first colony at Cape Town grew a distinctively Afrikaner, or Boer ("farmer"), society. By 1815, however, the British had acquired possession of the Cape and, in the 1830s, the pressures of their new colonial masters led the Boers to embark on the "Great Trek" inland. A series of Boer republics grew up, including the Orange Free State and the Transvaal. In 1877, Britain annexed the Transvaal, but the Boers declared independence again in 1880 and fought a brief and successful war to secure it. In 1895, the Jameson Raid, a botched British attempt to retake the Transvaal, led to a serious

The Queen's South Africa medal was awarded to British troops for service in the Boer War.

escalation in tensions and the outbreak of the Boer War in October 1899.

WAR BREAKS OUT

The Boers struck first and began protracted sieges of Ladysmith, Kimberley, and Mafeking. A British counteroffensive in early 1900, after defeats at Colenso and Spion Kop in December 1899, required vast reinforcements to push the Boers back. Under serious pressure, the Boers turned to a guerrilla campaign, prolonging the war into 1902, while the British employed ruthless tactics, including the use of concentration camps. The Peace of Vereeniging ended the war in 1902, the Boer republics accepting British sovereignty in return for autonomy.

Guerrilla detachments drawn from the Boer farming community managed to hold off the British army almost two years between 1900 and 1902.

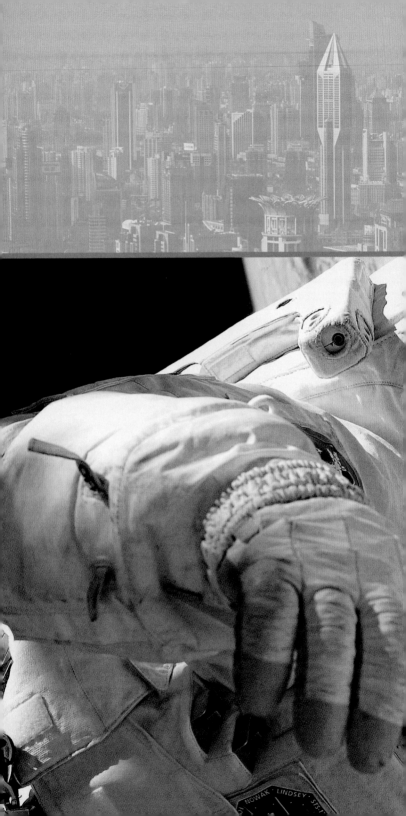

THE MODERN WORLD

THE WORLD IN 1914–PRESENT

Europe began World War I confidently in command of much of
the world's territory. But the conflict's human and economic cost
ushered in a period of turmoil that engulfed the continent, and also
helped spark the Russian Revolution. In the aftermath of World
War II, Europe was forced to abandon most of its colonies and

The world in 1950

——   international border

....   undefined border

◆   United Kingdom
and possessions

◆   France and possessions

  Denmark and possessions

◆   Spain and possessions

●   Portugal and possessions

◆   Netherlands
and possessions

  West Germany

  Japan and possessions

  Norway and possessions

  Belgium and possessions

  Italy and possessions

  New Zealand and possessions

◆   Australia and possessions

◆   US and possessions

  controlled by European Axis
powers 15 Nov 1942

  controlled by Japan
15 Nov 1942

THE MODERN WORLD IN 1950

Though India had regained its independence
from Britain in 1948, much of Africa was still
under European colonial domination in 1950.
However, an ongoing process of large-scale
decolonization was about to take place that
would leave almost no European colonies in
the world by the early 21st century.

nbarked on a process of political unification, while the Cold War – an ideological confrontation between the capitalist USA and ommunist USSR – took centre stage. The end of this struggle the 1990s briefly promised a new era of peace, but soon gave ay to a period of political uncertainty and regional strife.

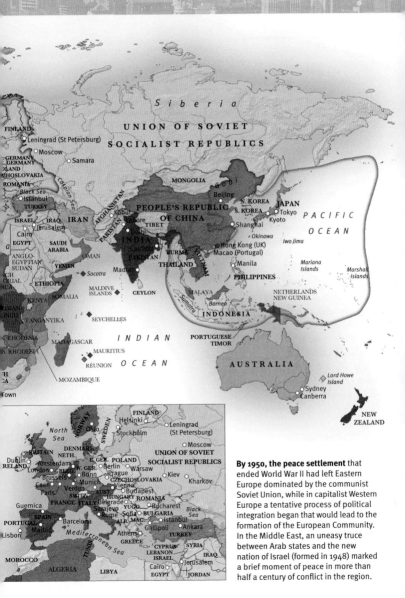

By 1950, the peace settlement that ended World War II had left Eastern Europe dominated by the communist Soviet Union, while in capitalist Western Europe a tentative process of political integration began that would lead to the formation of the European Community. In the Middle East, an uneasy truce between Arab states and the new nation of Israel (formed in 1948) marked a brief moment of peace in more than half a century of conflict in the region.

WORLD WAR I

In 1914, the monarchies that had governed Europe since the end of the Napoleonic Wars a century earlier seemed secure. However, underlying tensions continued to grow, eventually exploding into a war of unprecedented scale and ferocity. In just five years, the war cost the lives of around 10 million soldiers and saw the collapse of the German, Austro-Hungarian, Russian, and Ottoman Turkish empires.

ASSASSINATION AT SARAJEVO

⚑ Sarajevo, Bosnia   ☒ 28 June 1914

The Austro-Hungarian Empire struggled to cope with the end of Ottoman Turkish power in the Balkans in the 19th century (*see p.297*), and to deal with nationalists who sought to stop Austria–Hungary's encroachment into lost Ottoman territories. In 1908, Austria–Hungary annexed Bosnia, riding roughshod over Bosnia's large Serbian population, which felt that it should be a part of Serbia. The two Balkan Wars (1912–13), in which Serbia first defeated the Ottomans and then a coalition of other Balkan states, also raised tensions, as Serbia showed it was a formidable military force.

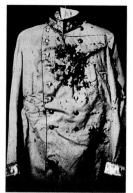

The blood-stained jacket worn by Franz Ferdinand on the day of his assassination in 1914.

DEATH IN THE BALKANS

On 28 June 1914, Archduke Franz Ferdinand, heir to the Austro-Hungarian throne, paid an official visit to Sarajevo to inspect military manoeuvres. A group of pro-Serbian revolutionaries from the "Young Bosnia" movement lay in wait for him. As the royal couple drove to an official reception at the town hall, a bomb was thrown into their car, but it bounced off and only caused injuries in the following vehicles. After the reception, the archduke's route was changed, but by ill-fortune a wrong turn took his driver past one of the Young Bosnian conspirators, Gavrilo Princip, a 19-year-old student. He opened fire, killing the archduke and his wife Sophie. The archduke had been the principal proponent of restraint towards Serbia, and his assassination unleashed a confrontation with Austria–Hungary that would soon engulf the whole of Europe.

ESCALATION INTO WAR

🏴 Europe   ⏳ June–September 1914

en before the murder
Franz Ferdinand (*see
ing page*), there were
ious underlying
ains between the
ajor European powers.
perial ambitions,
stability caused by a
nstant repositioning
alliances, and a
owing arms race all
ded to the potentially
flammable situation.
Anger boiled over in
e Vienna government
er Franz Ferdinand's
sassination, and on 23 July 1914
e Austrians issued an ultimatum to
rbia that would, in effect, have ended
rbian independence. Serbia partially
cepted the treaty, but the Austrians
ere not satisfied and both countries
obilized, with Austria declaring war
1 28 July. Germany had encouraged
ustria–Hungary to act, hoping that
ritain would remain neutral and that
cisive military action would bring a
pid conclusion to the conflict.

British recruiting posters featured the image of Lord Kitchener, veteran of the Boer Wars.

THE CRISIS SPREADS

Russia, fearing that the Austrians might annex its Serbian ally outright, had by now part-mobilized. As a result, the Germans, afraid that Russia might defeat Austria–Hungary, in turn mobilized its own army. Now that Germany might face war with Russia, German military planners thought France could then take advantage and attack Germany's western frontiers. The simple, but terrible, solution was to strike first, and the Germans developed a plan to cross Belgium into France. Germany declared war on Russia on 1 August and on France a day later. On 3 August, German troops crossed the frontiers of Russian Poland and Belgium. The next day Britain entered the conflict on the French side, and World War I had begun.

German soldiers travel in a truck mounted on railway tracks. Such speedy mobilization made the momentum of the July 1914 crisis unstoppable.

THE WESTERN FRONT

W Europe　　1914–15

The shape of the initial fighting in western Europe during World War I was determined by Count Alfred von Schlieffen's German strategic plan of 1905. This called for an attack through Belgium, hooking around French defences and enveloping Paris, in theory provoking France's swift surrender. Yet when the war broke out in early August 1914, Belgian resistance held up the German timetable, giving the French time to consolidate their defences and a British force time to arrive to aid them. In the ensuing First Battle of the Marne, the German thrust reached to within 75km (45 miles) of Paris before being beaten back. The French and German armies

An aerial view of the complex trench system near Fricourt, on the Somme, France.

then raced north toward the English Channel, trying to outflank each other. However, the French infantry could no outpace their opponents and, by late autumn 191 the two sides had dug a system of trenches that stretched from the Nort Sea almost to Switzerlan

WAR IN THE TRENCHES

For the rest of World War I, major advances from these trench lines were the exception rathe than the rule. Life in the trenches was appalling: epidemics of disease easily took hold, with such horrors as "trench foot" (in which damp and infected flesh simply rotted away) becoming an everyday occurrence. The trench syster were also increasingly well defended, so that when soldiers went "over the top", they became entangled in barbed wire

German troops advancing across open ground, a risky strategy that rarely succeeded without heavy casualties for the attacking side.

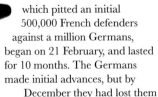

...d were scythed down by fire from ...chine guns – a relatively recent ...vention well adapted to conditions ... the Western Front. Those who ...cceeded in reaching the opposition's ...nch lines found themselves ...adequately supported ...d faced instant ...unterattack from the ...emy's reserve trenches. ...Allied French and ...itish attempts to force ...vances at Neuve ...apelle, Ypres, and Loos ...1915 all failed, with ...ormous casualties. In ... attempt to break the ...adlock, the Germans used ...ison gas (chlorine) at Ypres ...April 1915. This did little

Explosives were often used to detonate mines and so disrupt the enemy's trenches.

...t gain a very localized advantage – ...d at a huge cost, in the suffering ...flicted on the soldiers who inhaled ...is new weapon.

...RDUN AND THE SOMME

...1916, Erich von Falkenhayn, the ...erman Chief of Staff, devised a ...w strategy of attrition – to "bleed ...ance white" by drawing its armies ...to a defence of the hugely strategic ...rtress-city of Verdun. The battle,

which pitted an initial 500,000 French defenders against a million Germans, began on 21 February, and lasted for 10 months. The Germans made initial advances, but by December they had lost them all, at the cost of 700,000 casualties on both sides. Further carnage occurred at the Somme, where, on 1 July, an Anglo–French offensive tried to break the German lines with a huge infantry advance. However, the preliminary artillery bombardment had not cut the German lines of barbed wire nor destroyed their trenches, enabling the Germans to inflict appalling casualties on the British: some 57,000 men on the first day alone. The battle degenerated into a series of costly offensives and counter-offensives that never even remotely delivered the hoped-for breakout from the trench lines. The four months of fighting on the Somme cost 300,000 lives in 1916, and yet in 1917, both high commands still planned to win the war through the same sorts of offensives that had failed so miserably the year before.

THE WAR AT SEA

📕 North Sea, Mediterranean, S Atlantic ⏳ 1914–1918

Naval warfare in World War I was tentative. Both Britain and Germany had a fleet of "dreadnoughts" – heavily armoured battleships – but were keen to avoid a decisive encounter that, if lost, would render them powerless. The British concentrated instead on blockading Germany's North Sea ports to throttle its commerce. The only major fleet-to-fleet encounter, at Jutland (off Denmark) on 31 May–1 June 1916, was indecisive, with both sides suffering significant losses of ships.

The German U-boat campaign, particularly its "unrestricted" phases in 1915 and from 1917, hugely disrupted Allied shipping in the North Atlantic.

Elsewhere, the Germans were initially more adventurous, sending commerce raiders such as the *Emden* to disrupt British and French trade. The German East Asia Squadron, under Admiral von Spee, also threatened trade routes before it was destroyed at the Battle of the Falklands in December 1914. Deprived of more conventional avenues, the Germans turned to submarine warfare, using U-boats to conduct a campaign of "unrestricted warfare" against Allied civilian vessels in 1915. However, the sinking of the cruise liner *Lusitania* in 1915 caused outrage, contributing to the USA joining in the war against Germany.

THE WAR IN EASTERN EUROPE

📕 E Europe ⏳ 1914–1917

During World War I the geography of eastern Europe necessitated different military strategies from those used on the Western Front. More than 1,500km (930 miles) of front, stretching from the Black Sea to the Baltic, rendered building a defensive trench network impractical, so warfare was more mobile than in the west. At Tannenberg and the Masurian Lakes in August–September 1914, the Russians reversed the initial German and Austrian advance. In the Gorlice-Tarnów Offensive of May 1915, however, General von Falkenhayn smashed a Russian army, capturing some 140,000 men and securing Galicia. In June 1916, the Russians recovered and were able to launch the Brusilov Offensive, recapturing much lost ground. But the increasing costs of the war and rising social unrest in the army meant that by June 1917, many Russian army units refused to fight, allowing the Germans to transfer reinforcements to the Western Front.

The German stick grenade was used to clear out stubbornly defended infantry positions. The British nicknamed it the "potato masher".

GALLIPOLI

◢ Gallipoli peninsula, Turkey ⌛ April 1915–January 1916

r a Turkish fleet attacked Russia's
k Sea ports on 29 October 1914,
key allied with Germany. Winston
urchill, British First Lord of the
miralty, immediately lobbied for an
edition to seize control of the
rdanelles – the strategic straits that
ed the Black Sea to the Aegean – to
vent a Turkish blockade that would cut
a vital Russian supply route. But the
ed landings on 25 April 1915 on the

Gallipoli peninsula (overlooking the
straits) were a disaster. The initial day's
objectives were never reached, and a
Turkish counterattack, organized by
Mustafa Kemal (later Atatürk), confined
the Allied forces to enclaves around
Cape Helles in the south and Anzac
Cove in the north. In mid-December, the
Allies evacuated Anzac Cove, and then
withdrew from Cape Helles. By 9 January
1916, their withdrawal was complete.

PALESTINE AND THE ARAB REVOLT

◢ N Saudi Arabia, Palestine, Jordan, Israel, Iraq ⌛ 1915–1918

de from the Gallipoli campaign,
ial British moves against the Ottoman
pire in World War I concentrated on
ing control of Mesopotamia.
r the disastrous surrender
British army at Kut (in
) in April 1916, the focus
ted to a wider area. The
ish attempted to instigate
Arab uprising against
oman rule in northern
bia and the Transjordan,
to link this with a more
ventional military campaign to
control of Palestine. Persuaded by
. Lawrence, Sharif Hussein ibn Ali

T.E. LAWRENCE

Having joined in expeditions in the Near
East, T.E. Lawrence (1888–1935) was a
perfect liaison officer to Britain's
Arab allies. He stirred up the Arab
Revolt of 1916 with a distinctive
flamboyance, giving rise to the
legend of "Lawrence of Arabia".

of Mecca raised a revolt against
the Ottomans in June 1916,
causing enormous disruption in
Sinai and Palestine. General Allenby's
British army entered Jerusalem in
December 1917, and inflicted a
devastating defeat on the Ottoman
army at Megiddo in September 1918,
ending the war in the region.

ral Allenby enters Jerusalem after its capture from
ttomans on 11 December 1917. The damage to
sh morale from its loss was profound.

STALEMATE IN THE WEST

⚑ W Europe   ⚰ 1917

1917 was one of the most difficult years for all those involved in World War I. The Allied naval blockade of Germany led to a shortage of wheat there in the winter, while the German U-boat campaign (*see p.318*) led to hardships in Britain. In April, France's Nivelle Offensive gained barely 500m (1,650ft) in its first day at a cost of 100,000 casualties, and led to widespread mutinies in the French army. Despite enormous losses, British offensives at Arras (in northeastern France) in April and at Messines (west Belgium) in June failed to gain any significant ground. Both sides tried new weapons, the Germans pioneering poi gas artillery shells at Messines, and the British using tanks on a large scale for the first time at Cambrai (northeastern France) in November. Neither weapon contributed to a decisive breakthrough

British troops march towards the front line to relie comrades there. The rotation of units was an atten to mitigate the hardships of trench life.

THE USA ENTERS THE WAR

⚑ W Europe   ⚰ 1917–1918

It was German action that finally broke the 1917 stalemate (*see above*). In February, Germany announced it was resuming unrestricted attacks on foreign shipping. The threat to US trading interests was clear, and was compounded by a telegram written by the German foreign minister encouraging Mexico to attack the USA. President Woodrow Wilson's attempts to maintain neutrality in the conflict, and to act as an honest broker for peace, were over, and in April the USA declared war on Germany.

However, it was not until June that the first US troops arrived in France, under the command of Gener John Pershing, and they were posted t the trenches only in October. The init inexperience of the Americans, and th fact that Pershing at first failed to have his troops operate independently of th allies, meant that for a while their impact was limited. Yet the Germa High Command was we aware that each increase in the numbers of US soldiers fighting with th Allies – which reached four complete divisions 1918 – lessened the cha of a German victory.

In May 1917, the US Congress passed legislation authorizing drafting of men into the army.

DON'T WAIT for the Draft VOLUNTEER

THE END OF THE WAR

◉ W Europe ⌛ 1918

March 1918, Germany
ned a peace treaty
Brest-Litovsk with
e new Bolshevik
vernment of Russia.
is freed up some 44
rman divisions, which
re now shifted to the Western
ont. The German Chief of
aff, Erich Ludendorff, argued
at these divisions should be used
a massive all-or-nothing assault.
21 March, the Germans launched
peration Michael, the first element
their "Spring Offensive". They won
km (45 miles) of ground, but their
gest gains were against the least
istance. As Allied resistance stiffened,
rmany's initial momentum stalled.
dendorff ordered further smaller
acks between April and July, but by
en, with the US presence growing at
0,000 men a month, it was clear that
gamble had failed.

erman army unit returns home in December 1918.
ny soldiers were bitter that the politicians agreed
armistice while they were still able to fight.

Armistice Day on 11 November is marked
by wearing red poppies, the flowers that
bloomed on World War I battlefields.

THE FINAL OFFENSIVE
The Allied counterstroke
came with an attack
along the Marne river
in late July. Another
offensive around Amiens
led to 27,000 German
casualties on 8 August alone,
which Ludendorff dubbed "the black day
of the German army". In the "Hundred
Days Campaign", the Allies then pushed
east, finally breaking through Germany's
trench lines. In a costly series of actions in
September and October, they breached
the Hindenburg line, Germany's last
fortified defence. With its main ally,
Austria–Hungary, having signed an
armistice with Italy after a disastrous
defeat by the Italians in late October,
Germany was under huge pressure, and
a revolution threatened to overthrow the
German Kaiser. Finally, the Germans
signed an armistice on 11 November,
bringing World War I to an end.

American artist John Singer Sargent's harrowing painting *Gassed* evokes the terrible torment inflicted on soldiers who inhaled poison gas. Gas was first used as a weapon by the Germans near Ypres in April 1915, but eventually all sides employed some form of gas warfare.

THE TREATY OF VERSAILLES

Although World War I had ended at the armistice of 11 November 1918, a large number of issues remained. The Western Allies wanted arrangements to ensure that Germany never again posed such a threat to peace, including an adjustment to Germany's borders to reflect its reduced status. Other treaties redrew the map of central and eastern Europe in favour of new nations that had emerged there.

THE PEACE CONFERENCE

On 18 January 1919 in Paris, delegates from more than 20 nations, excluding Germany and Austria–Hungary, gathered to seal peace. The driving forces at the conference were France's prime minister Georges Clemenceau, his British counterpart David Lloyd George, and US president Woodrow Wilson. The French were intent on reducing Germany's capacity for waging war, extracting reparations, and regaining control of Alsace-Lorraine. The British wanted to avoid the anger that extravagant reparations claims might fuel in Germany, and to protect their imperial interests.

French troops disarm German police during their 1923–24 occupation of the Ruhr, western Germany, when Germany refused to pay its reparations.

President Wilson, meanwhile, came armed with his Fourteen Points, the most important of which demanded guarantees of self-determination for the national minorities and the

The Hall of Mirrors at the Palace of Versailles, where the 1919 Treaty was signed.

establishment of an international body to preserve world peace, the League of Nations.

THE SETTLEMENT

By May the outline of a final settlement stated that Germany was to acknowledge its guilt in the war and Kaiser Wilhelm was to be put on trial. Germany was to reduce its army to fewer than 100,000 men, its navy to a token force, and to have no tanks or aircraft. The Rhineland was also to be demilitarized. More galling still was the cession of Alsace-Lorraine to France, part of Schleswig to Denmark, large portions of Prussia and Silesia to Poland, and the occupation of the Saarland region for 15 years by an international force. Any future union of Germany with Austria was also forbidden. Huge reparations (some £11 billion) were to be paid. On 28 June 1919, the German delegation signed the Treaty in its entirety, sowing the seeds of bitterness among the German people that would be a key contributor to the outbreak of World War II just 20 years later. Further treaties imposed conditions on Germany's allies, and contained clauses that also caused considerable political strife in the interwar period.

French Prime Minister Georges Clemenceau signs the Treaty of Versailles on 28 June 1919. His desire to punish Germany harshly caused some debate.

BETWEEN THE WARS

The treaties that ended World War I, such as that signed at Versailles, did little to create a stable political environment in Europe. Resentment at the terms of the peace grew in German and successive governments began to test its limits. In eastern and central Europe, fragile democracies succumbed to dictatorships. More ominously, public unrest in Germany and Italy gave rise to the extremist ideologies of National Socialism and Fascism under Adolf Hitler and Benito Mussolini.

RUSSIA HEADS FOR REVOLUTION

◩ Russia ☗ 1905–1917

After the Revolution of 1905 (*see p.287*), Tsar Nicholas II had been forced to agree a new constitution for Russia, including the formation of an elected Duma (parliament). However, the tsar retained the ability to dissolve the Duma, which he did in 1906 and 1907. Two subsequent Dumas met from 1907–12 and 1912–17, which were in almost constant conflict with Nicholas. Normal political tensions were suspended in the early stages of World War I, but as the war went progressively worse for Russia, rising prices prompted industrial workers to strike. Violence erupted on the streets of Petrograd (St Petersburg) and Moscow in the February Revolution, led by the Petrograd Soviet ("council"), and Nicholas abdicated on 28 February 1917. Power was handed to a Provisional Government under Prince Lvov, but its

Revolutionary officers drive the tsar's confiscated car around the streets of Petrograd. Ironically, it was later to become Lenin's own personal vehicle.

position was contested by the Petrograd Soviet, which was dominated by Vladimir Lenin's revolutionary Russian Bolshevik Party. In July, riots erupted in Petrograd Prince Lvov was replaced as leader of the Provisional Government by Alexander Kerensky, but the possibility of restoring stability would soon be ruined by a tide of revolutionary activity

THE 1917 REVOLUTION

Russia   October 1917

July 1917 Russia's Provisional overnment, under Alexander erensky, suppressed a outbreak of volutionary riots. ladimir Lenin fled Finland, but his llowers received help om an unlikely source.

OLSHEVIK POWER

August 1917, General vr Kornilov, the army mmander in chief,

The Bolshevik hammer and sickle symbolized the unity of industrial and agricultural workers.

dered troops into Petrograd, ostensibly protect the Provisional Government om the Bolshevik threat. Suspecting an tempted coup, Kerensky asked the olsheviks for help, arming the Bolshevik ed Guard militia. Kornilov's alleged attempt to seize power was unsuccessful, but Kerensky's regime was fatally weakened. In September Kerensky attempted to organize a

"Democratic Conference" to rein in the unruly leftist factions baying for power, but this had no effect apart from bringing into disrepute those parties who co-operated with it. In mid-October, the Central Committee of the Bolshevik Party met to plan the seizure of power, fearful that a left-wing coalition of other parties might take power if the Kerensky government collapsed.

On 25 October, Leon Trotsky, the party's chief organizer, launched an almost bloodless coup in Petrograd. Armed squads of pro-Bolshevik revolutionaries occupied key positions such as railway stations and telephone exchanges. Kerensky surrendered and the Bolsheviks moved quickly to push out the other leftists from positions of influence. Their supremacy ensured, the Bolsheviks moved to implement Lenin's revolutionary programme.

LENIN

After his brother was hanged for his part in a plot to kill Tsar Alexander III, Vladimir Ilyich Lenin (1870–1924) became a revolutionary. In 1895, he was exiled to Siberia. On his release, he spent several years in Europe, where he studied Marxism (see p.291). Lenin came to power in the October Revolution of 1917, but he died less than seven years later, his programme for a revolutionary transformation of Russia only partially fulfilled.

THE RUSSIAN CIVIL WAR

Russia   1918–1920

After seizing the centre of power in Petrograd in November 1917, the Bolsheviks fought a multi-sided civil war. Many high-ranking tsarist officers were determined to fight back against the Revolution, and the left-wing parties whom the Bolsheviks had pushed aside were unwilling to let the matter rest. In May 1918, the remaining leaders of the leftist Socialist-Revolutionaries (SR) set

Kolchak in April, but Kornilov's army – now under General Denikin's control following Kornilov's death – captured Kiev, Odessa, and Orel in the summer of 1919, almost threatening Moscow. Yet a devastating counterattack pushed Denik back, and a badly co-ordinated thrust against Petrograd by Yudenich in Octob 1919 failed. The last remaining large White force, under General Wrangel,

"GO WHERE YOU BELONG... INTO THE DUSTBIN OF HISTORY."

Leon Trotsky, dismissing a walkout by the Mensheviks and Socialist-Revolutionaries from the Second All-Russian Congress of Soviets (25–26 October 1917)

up their own government at Samara on the Volga river. Anti-Bolshevik ("White") armies began to form, led by General Kornilov (*see p.327*) in the south, Admiral Kolchak in Siberia, and General Yudenich in the northwest. By late 1918, the situation for the Bolsheviks was critical, with Admiral Kolchak pushing far into the Urals. Trotsky's Red Army defeated

attempted to seize the Crimea, but in la 1920 he evacuated his forces, leaving the Red Army to mop up an assortment of anarchist, nationalist, and Islamic militi which continued to resist reincorporatio by the central government.

Leon Trotsky returned from exile in North America ir 1917 to lead the infant Bolshevik Red Army, instigati proper training to turn it into an effective fighting for

RUSSIA UNDER LENIN AND STALIN

 Russia   1921–1953

When Vladimir Lenin (*see p.327*) came to power after the Russian Revolution, he quickly established a highly centralized system of government, banning all rival political parties and empowering the Communist Party's dominant Central Committee to expel anyone who failed to follow the party line.

From 1921, Lenin promoted the New Economic Policy (NEP), in which peasants were given more control over the levels of agricultural production than strict Bolsheviks would have liked. A federal Union of Soviet Socialist Republics (USSR) was created in 1922.

A 1920 propaganda poster for the Communist Party demands: "Are you a volunteer yet?"

STALINISM

After Lenin's death in 1922, Joseph Stalin – whom Lenin had favoured – removed, tried, or executed his rivals in the Central Committee, and pushed for a tougher line and greater centralized state control. Between 1928 and 1937, he instituted the first of the Five Year Plans – huge schemes that aimed to transform the USSR into an industrialized society. He also enforced a policy of "collectivization", in which land belonging to *kulaks* (prosperous peasants) was given to co-operative farms.

Enormous hardship ensued, including a famine in the Ukraine in 1932–33. A network of prison camps (the *gulags*) was established, and the "Great Terror" of 1936–38 saw the secret police launching waves of purges of the party elite and army. Some 690,000 people were executed, with many more consigned to prison camps. It was only with Stalin's death in 1953 that the icy chill of his oppressive regime began to thaw.

STALIN

Born Joseph Djugashvilli in Georgia in 1878, Stalin (1878–1953) joined the Marxist Social-Democratic Labour Party in 1901, and when this split in 1904 he joined the Bolshevik faction. Stalin became a valued enforcer of Lenin's policies, joining the Bolshevik's policy-making Politburo in 1919. By 1922 he was the party's Secretary General, becoming supreme leader after Lenin's death. In 1926, he expelled Trotsky from the party; he went on to rule the USSR virtually unchallenged for nearly 30 years.

THE GREAT DEPRESSION

Worldwide   1929–1932

During the early 1920s the US economy flourished, but by 1927 the USA was overproducing goods for which it did not have a market. European economies, meanwhile, had failed to adjust to the conditions of peacetime following the end of World War I, and in Germany a savage bout of hyperinflation in 1919–23 had wrecked that country's economy.

A German 1,000 mark note overprinted with the value 1 billion; by December 1922, printing presses were struggling to keep up with hyperinflation.

THE WALL STREET CRASH

Despite the underlying economic gloom, investors on New York's Wall Street stock exchange continued to push up share prices. In October 1929, however, prices began to decline as investor confidence evaporated. On 24 October ("Black Thursday"), panic set in. It was followed by "Black Monday" and "Black Tuesday", on which stock market prices tumbled by 13 and 12 per cent respectively, in a collapse known as the "Wall Street Crash". The decline soon infected the USA's economy, as banks called in loans that could no longer be repaid, and several banks collapsed as panicked savers withdrew their money. A wave of mortgage foreclosures and business

In London, City workers gather after the collapse of British investor Clement Hatry's business empire, which fed into the Wall Street Crash one week later.

nkruptcies led to a downward spiral of employment and homelessness. Many ople were forced to take shelter in antytowns, nicknamed "Hoovervilles" t of resentment against US President erbert Hoover, who declined to extend vernment aid to the unemployed.

E DEPRESSION

 a result of the Crash, US investors thdrew many foreign loans. This used the collapse of the system of ternational loans set up to handle ermany's war reparations and meant at European countries, including ermany, could not pay for their

THE NEW DEAL

Hoover was voted out of office in 1932 when Franklin D. Roosevelt (US president 1933–45) won a landslide victory on the promise of a "New Deal". This was a series of initiatives designed to kick-start the economy and provide emergency relief, new jobs, and agricultural reforms. A series of successful projects, such as the Tennessee Valley Authority – which constructed a large series of dams – did much to alleviate unemployment while the US economy got back on its feet.

The political response in European countries was less constructive. Mass unemployment and poverty led to civil

"I PLEDGE YOU, I PLEDGE MYSELF, TO A NEW DEAL FOR THE AMERICAN PEOPLE."

Franklin D. Roosevelt, Democratic presidential nomination acceptance speech, 1932

ports. Trade between Europe and orth America was badly hit, and the ice of commodities plummeted, by '32 falling to around 45 per cent of eir 1929 values. A wave of economic tionalism erupted as countries sought protect their domestic industries. esident Hoover introduced the noot-Hawley Tariff in 1930, which posed a 42- to 50-per-cent tax on ports, and European governments sponded in kind with similar otectionist measures.

his resulted in the ppling of international ade and in further terioration in the world onomy. In Germany, nemployment more than ubled to over 15 per nt of the workforce – me 4 million people – the end of 1930.

unrest and the rise of right-wing movements. In the 1920s and '30s, many countries in eastern and central Europe became dictatorships – such as Poland, where Marshal Pilsudski's authoritarian regime came to power in 1926. Even in Britain, where in 1930 unemployment had touched 2.5 million (20 per cent of the workforce), Oswald Mosley's Union of British Fascists, founded in 1932, briefly threatened to become a real political force.

rkers widen kerbs, a project of Works Progress Administration Roosevelt's "New Deal".

THE RISE OF FASCISM

The economic hardship and political instability that followed World War I contributed to a climate of violence and lawlessness across much of Europe in the 1920s. This atmosphere, and unresolved disputes about national boundaries and Germany's role within Europe, helped to produce new, right-wing nationalist movements, sharing an ideology that became known as fascism.

MUSSOLINI AND FASCISM

The new right-wing philosophies were fed by loathing and fear of the Union of Soviet Socialist Republics (USSR) and its open desire to export communism. Ironically, the USSR's totalitarian socialist democracy provided a model of government for extreme right-wing nationalists seeking to reform failing democracies in Europe. Mixed with a militaristic ideology, this style of government turned conservatism into fascism.

First of the fascist leaders to rise to power was Italy's Benito Mussolini (1883–1945), who in 1914 joined one of the revolutionary *fasci* (political groups) agitating for social reform. In 1919 he helped found the Fasci Italiani di Combattimento, a group of extreme nationalists. The Fascists became seen as the protectors of law, deploying their informal militia – the

In 1922 Benito Mussolini (fourth from left) led his National Fascist Party in a march on Rome, forcing a handover of power to the Fascists.

"Blackshirts" – to terrorize socialists. In October 1922, Mussolini ordered the Blackshirts to march on Rome and seize power. King Victor Emmanuel III refused his prime minister's request for military support and invited Mussolini to form a government. In 1926, Mussolini assumed power, brutally silencing any political opponents. Known as *Il Duce* ("the leader"), he ruled Italy as a dictator until 1943.

Hitler's book *Mein Kampf* (meaning "My Struggle") was a statement of his political ideology.

NAZISM IN GERMANY

In 1918, Germany's new Weimar Republic faced similar problems. Many Germans and Austrians resented the terms of the Versailles Treaty (*see pp.324–5*). Among them was Adolf Hitler (1889–1945), an Austrian-born former soldier who in 1919 joined a small Munich-based political group – the German Worker's Party, renamed the following year the NDSAP, or Nazi Party. The Nazis had much in common with Mussolini's Fascists, but also had a hankering for a romanticized German past and a dangerous belief in the superiority of the German *Volk* (or race) and of Aryans (white Caucasians), particularly compared to Slavs and Jews. The Nazis aimed to unite all German-speakers in a greater German Reich. Hitler manoeuvred the Nazi Party into power, offering it as the only way to end instability. In 1932, he lost an election for the presidency to Paul von Hindenburg, but the following year Hindenburg offered him the chancellorship, hoping to neutralize the Nazis politically. It was a fatal mistake. In 1933, Hitler pushed through an Enabling Act giving him near-dictatorial powers for a period of four years, and once that time had elapsed the Nazis prevented them from being rescinded.

HITLER IN POWER

Once Führer ("leader") of Germany, Hitler was able to implement his racial and extreme nationalist ideology. This was done with the help of an oppressive state security system bolstered by the Gestapo (political police) and the SS (a paramilitary police force controlled by the Nazis).

Joseph Goebbels was an early follower of Hitler, joining the Nazi Party in 1924. From 1933 to 1945 he was minister in charge of propaganda.

The Nazis had held a party rally in the Bavarian city of Nuremberg as early as 1923, and between 1933 and 1938 it became an annual event. The vast numbers of attendees and the militaristic setting proved the party's power and cemented the cult of Adolf Hitler, the revered Führer.

THE SPANISH CIVIL WAR

Spain   1936–1939

In February 1936, Spain's newly elected left-wing Popular Front government vowed to uphold liberty, prosperity, and justice, but many feared their policies were too progressive. On 19 July 1936, Francisco Franco took control of Spain's armies in Morocco and led them into Spain; the result was civil war.

THE OPPOSING SIDES

The Republicans (government supporters) were composed of liberal democrats, communists, socialists, and anarchists. They faced roughly equal numbers of Franco's Nationalists, who were backed by monarchists, Catholics, and the Falange – the Spanish fascist party. While the Republicans received support from the USSR, Mexico, and socialist and communist volunteers throughout Europe, the Nationalists received military aid from the fascist regimes in Italy and Germany (including the "Condor" legion, armed with tanks).

A 1937 poster by the UGT – a union aligned with the Republicans – urges its members to fight.

THE COURSE OF THE WAR

By 1 November 1936, 25,000 Nationalist troops had begun a three-year siege of the capital, Madrid. In 1937, a campaign to capture the north's Basque provinces led to the aerial bombing of Guernica and many civilian casualties. A disastrous attempt to force a way through to Madrid in March 1938 put the Nationalist central front on the defensive. Further east, however, the Nationalists pushed towards the coast near Valencia in April, cutting the Republican territory in two. At the Battle of the Ebro (25 July– 16 November 1938), Republican forces were all but destroyed. On 26 January 1939, Barcelona fell to Franco's forces, and on 27 March 1939, the Nationalists entered Madrid almost unopposed.

FRANCISCO FRANCO

Born into a military family, Francisco Franco (1892–1975) served in Morocco from 1910 to 1927, becoming the youngest general in Spain. After leading the Nationalist movement to victory in the Spanish Civil War, Franco dominated Spanish politics as head of state for 36 years, though from 1947 he was formally the regent for a restored monarchy in which he chose not to appoint a king. His regime was stifling, militaristic, and conservative – democracy was restored only on his death in 1975.

WOMEN AND THE VOTE

◈ UK, USA, Europe ☻ 1869–1928

ffrage (the right to vote) had been
nsiderably extended during the
th century, particularly in Britain, but
vas still denied to women. In 1903,
iton Emmeline Pankhurst formed the
omen's Social and Political Union
campaign for the vote. Frustrated
the failure to achieve this through

SUFFRAGE IN THE USA AND ELSEWHERE

A similar but more peaceful campaign
began in the USA in the 1840s. The
first state to grant female suffrage was
Wyoming, in 1869; nationally, women
won the vote only in 1920, in part as
recognition of the role they had played
in World War I. Key among the figures

"WOMEN WILL HAVE, WITH US, THE FULLEST RIGHTS."

Stanley Baldwin, prime minister of the UK, 1928

aceful means, the suffragettes, as they
came known, took direct action,
cluding an invasion of the Houses of
rliament. Many suffragettes went on
nger strike, prompting the British
vernment to pass the "Cat and
ouse" Act in 1913, by which the
omen could legally be force-fed. The
mpaign finally achieved success in
18, when women aged 30 and over
tained the vote, although full voting
hts were granted only in 1928.

campaigning for the vote for American
women was Susan B. Anthony, who
co-founded the National Women's
Suffrage Association in 1869.

In the rest of the world, stories of
women's suffrage are mixed. New Zealand
was the first to grant women full suffrage,
in 1893, while some other countries deny
women the vote even today.

The "New Women's Organization" lobbied for
French women to be given the vote – a right
that they received only in 1944.

WORLD WAR II

Adolf Hitler's rise to power in Germany seriously destabilized Europe and, after a series of false alarms, war broke out in September 1939. The conflict became global with the USSR and USA joining the western European powers (the "Allies"), while Japan and Italy joined the German ("Axis") side. By the time the fighting finally ended in 1945, World War II had led to the deaths of some 25 million military personnel, and at least as many civilians.

GERMANY'S PATH TO WAR

Poland   September 1939

Throughout the late 1930s, the chancellor of Germany, Adolf Hitler, had steadily chipped away at the restrictions placed on his country by the Treaty of Versailles (*see pp.324–5*); he had restarted conscription, established an airforce and, in March 1936, remilitarized the Rhineland. In March 1938, he went further, sending German troops into Austria and proclaiming its *Anschluss* ("union") with Germany.

THE CZECH AND POLISH CRISES

In September 1938, Hitler demanded concessions for the German-speakers of Czechoslovakia's Sudetenland, and the Munich Conference (involving German, Britain, France, and Italy) granted him occupation of Sudetenland. The German foreign minister, von Ribbentrop, brokered a deal with the USSR to divide eastern central Europe into two spheres of influence, leaving western Poland in German hands. On the pretext that Poland refused to allow Germany to occupy the once-German port of Danzig, on 1 September 1939 Hitler ordered German forces to invade Poland, marking the beginning of World War II.

The Germans used propaganda to support their annexations, such as this postcard proclaiming that the once-Polish town of Danzig "is German".

BLITZKRIEG AND THE FALL OF FRANCE

◩ Scandinavia, Belgium, the Netherlands, France ⌛ September 1939–June 1940

1939 the British and French
vernments had guaranteed
otection for Poland against
rman aggression, so when
rman forces invaded
and on 1 September,
y responded by
claring war. Germany's
sault had begun with
Luftwaffe (airforce)
nket-bombing roads,
vns, and villages.
st-moving mobile units,
arheaded by Panzer (tank)
isions, thrust deep into the Polish
rtland. It was a new form of warfare,
vid and devastating, which became
own as *Blitzkrieg*.

After French surrender in June 1940,
Philippe Pétain led a regime that
governed southern France from Vichy.

of "Phoney War": the Allies
built up weapons stocks,
but made no move against
Germany. Then Hitler
invaded Denmark and
Norway in April 1940,
occupying both nations.

THE SURRENDER OF FRANCE

On 10 May, Hitler pushed
west towards France, overrunning
the Netherlands, Belgium, and
Luxembourg. German forces broke
through the Ardennes, and reached
Abbeville on the northern French coast,
trapping the British Expeditionary Force
(BEF) sent to aid France. As the German
army surged towards Paris, the British
prime minister Winston Churchill
ordered the BEF, who were hemmed in
around the port of Dunkirk, to evacuate.
The German army entered Paris on 19
June, and three days later the French
signed an armistice with Germany.

E FALL OF POLAND AND SCANDINAVIA

thin a week, Warsaw was under siege.
Soviet invasion on 17 September dealt
fatal blow, and Polish resistance ended
28 September. There followed months

successful removal by sea of some 338,000
ed soldiers from Dunkirk in May 1940 preserved
core of an army that could resist Germany.

THE BATTLE OF BRITAIN

Britain ☗ August–October 1940

Having overcome France in June 1940, Adolf Hitler turned his attention to Britain, the one remaining country of significance that resisted him. He laid plans for the invasion of southern England ("Operation Sealion"), but before they could be put into effect, the Germans needed to achieve dominance of the skies. The aerial conflict that raged between August and October 1940 became known as the Battle of Britain, and it pitted Germany's Luftwaffe, under the command of Herman Göring, against the Fighter Command of the British Royal Air Force (RAF), led by Air Marshal Hugh Dowding.

WINSTON CHURCHILL

First Lord of the Admiralty during World War I, Winston Churchill (1874–1965) warned against German rearmament in the 1930s. When he became Britain's prime minister in May 1940, his strong resolve and wooing of US support helped to ensure Britain's final victory in World War II.

THE FIRST GERMAN ATTACKS

Dowding linked the new technology of radar to a system of battle groups and sectors that was able to respond rapidly to German raids. Although the Luftwaffe had superiority in numbers of aircraft, they were often close to their extreme flight range and so could operate for only a short time in British airspace. On 12 August 1940, concerted German attacks on British airfields began, but an attempt the following day (*Adlertag*, or "Eagle Day") to overwhelm the RAF with a mass attack failed.

THE RAF WINS OUT

The Germans assumed that the main force of the RAF was spent, and that they would soon achieve by attrition what they could not with a single blow. The RAF, however, proved resilient, and by early September had some 738 Spitfire and Hurricane fighter aircraft – more than at the start of the campaign. Instead, it was the Luftwaffe that was suffering a steady stream of losses. At the start of September, Hitler ordered a change of tactics and the bombing of London, which started in earnest on 7 September. Although the Battle of Britain carried on until October, in effect the German chances of destroying the RAF had already ended.

The single-engine Supermarine Spitfire formed the backbone of Fighter Command during the Battle of Britain.

AIR POWER IN WORLD WAR II

World War II was the first major conflict in which air power played a
determining role. During the Polish campaign in 1939, the Luftwaffe
deployed some 1,500 aircraft to pulverize Poland and smash its lines
of communication. From then on, almost every campaign used air
support, with an increasing emphasis on strategic bombing, aiming
to destroy the opponent's industries and undermine its morale.

STRATEGIC BOMBING

The Battle of Britain (*see facing page*)
seemed to indicate that there was no
decisive strategic advantage in using
air power, but both sides continued
to deploy massive numbers of aircraft
in a tactical role. From 1941, with the
arrival of more efficient bombers such

German Dornier 217 bombers attack London
during the Battle of Britain in 1940, foreshadowing
later, much larger attacks on Germany itself.

however, and the chances of hitting
a specific military or industrial
target were remote, so Harris
ordered larger raids, containing up
to 1,000 bombers. At the attack on

> "BOMB THE ENEMY SOFT UNTIL
> A COMPARATIVELY SMALL LAND
> FORCE... CAN OVERCOME HIS
> REMAINING RESISTANCE."
>
> Air Vice Marshal Arthur ("Bomber") Harris, January 1943

as the Vickers Wellington, the British
were able to bomb German cities on
a large scale, a tactic championed by
Arthur Harris, the controversial chief
of Bomber Command from 1941.
The bombers were inaccurate,

Hamburg on 27–28 July, the sheer
weight of Allied bombing caused a
firestorm and 40,000 to 45,000
people died. By 1944, the Luftwaffe's
resistance had almost disappeared,
and the Allies could bomb at will.

THE GERMAN INVASION OF THE USSR

USSR June–December 1941

Ever since the 1920s, Hitler had viewed the western USSR as a possible area for German expansion to provide *Lebensraum* ("living space") for a growing population. By 1941, Hitler also feared that the USA might join the war on the British side and so, although an uneasy peace had prevailed in eastern Europe since the defeat of Poland in September 1939, he decided on an invasion of Britain's last possible European ally, the USSR.

German army helmets were the only part of their ge suitable for the harsh temperatures in the USSR, a the German soldiers suffered terribly from the cold

OPERATION BARBAROSSA

The force that Hitler had assembled for the planned invasion, Operation Barbarossa, was truly prodigious, including around four million German troops and their allies, and some 11,000 tanks. At around dawn on 22 June 1941, the German army crossed into the USSR, the invasion having been delayed by several crucial months to deal with a crisis in Yugoslavia. The Soviet Red Army was caught almost completely by surprise and was hampered by a military strategy that insisted on defending every metre of ground, leaving few reserves to contain the intense, rapid attacks of the German *Blitzkrieg* tactic.

THE BATTLE FOR MOSCOW

The German armoured columns sped forward, in the north reaching Leningr by 19 August and on the central front surrounding Minsk on 18 June, where they would capture some 300,000 prisoners – a sign of the large-scale collapse of the Soviet defensive effort. By December 1941, Moscow itself was under threat. The most advanced German units reached the outer suburb on 2 December. But the offensive ground to a halt in the face of fanatical Soviet resistance and the effects of winter, which froze the lubricant in German tanks On 5 December, the Soviet commander, General Zhukov ordered a counterattack and within a month, the Germans had been driven back from Moscow.

A Soviet border garrison surrenders in June 1941. Few Red Army units could defend themselves against swift German forces.

THE BATTLE OF STALINGRAD

 Stalingrad, USSR   June 1942–February 1943

he industrial city of
talingrad stood on the
est bank of the Volga
ver in southern Russia,
ontrolling the vital river
nd rail connections that
rried oil supplies to the
mament factories of
ntral Russia. Thwarted
his desire to capture
loscow the previous
inter (*see facing page*),
litler ordered a thrust in
e spring and summer of 1942 to
pture Stalingrad and the oil reserves
rther south in the Caucasus.

German troops surrendered at Stalingrad in early
February 1943, after holding out for more than
two months against besieging Soviet forces.

PERATIONS BLUE AND URANUS

he general German offensive,
peration Blue, began on 29 June
942, and General Paulus's 6th Army
on moved to secure Stalingrad itself.

somehow clinging on to a small strip
along the Volga when Soviet General
Zhukov ordered a counterattack,
Operation Uranus. The Soviet forces
crashed through the weaker Romanian
armies and within four days had the Axis

"THE GOD OF WAR HAS GONE OVER TO THE OTHER SIDE."

Adolf Hitler, February 1943

ustained air attacks on 23 August
egan the main assault, and the same
ay German troops reached the Volga
orth of the city. But this was the limit of
eir success – an astonishingly tenacious
oviet resistance bogged the 6th Army
own in house-to-house fighting. On
9 November, the Red Army was still

side surrounded. Confounding Zhukov's
expectation of an attempt at breakout,
Paulus settled down for a siege. But after
a German attempt to relieve Paulus
failed in December, any hope of victory
was gone, and the remnants of the 6th
Army finally surrendered on 2 February
1943, at a cost of around 170,000 dead.

osin-Nagant M91/30 rifles were
sed by the Red Army as sniper
les from 1932, to devastating
fect on the streets of Stalingrad.

THE WAR IN NORTH AFRICA

North Africa　June 1940–May 1943

The vast North African desert provided a theatre of war unlike any other in World War II; one in which tanks played a crucial role. Yet the relative strength of the armies deployed there was tiny compared with other fronts. Italy declared war on the Allies on 10 June 1940, and in September, General Graziani – the Italian commander in chief in North Africa – launched an attack towards British-held Egypt.

At the Battle of El Alamein, Rommel lost more than 400 tanks, a loss from which the German war effort in North Africa was never really able to recover.

THE WESTERN DESERT CAMPAIGN

After initial successes, by December 1940 Graziani's force was driven back as far as Tripolitania in Libya – the first of the swings in fortune that characterized the desert fighting. By 22 January 1941, the British had taken the strategic city of Tobruk, but the Germans had started to send reinforcements to bolster their Italian allies and, under the command of General Rommel, the German Afrika

Korps commenced a dramatic advance eastwards. A British counteroffensive (Operation Crusader) forced the German back in December, but in June of the following year, Rommel captured Tobruk and threatened to push towards the Egyptian capital Cairo. In a 12-day battle at El Alamein in October 1942, the new British commander, General Montgomery (*see p.348*), wore down the Afrika Korps and then struck west.

OPERATION TORCH

Rommel now retreated into Tunisia, but on 8 November 1942 a series of Anglo–American landings (Operation Torch) in Morocco and Algeria tightened the noose on the German and Italian armies in North Africa. Despite stubborn resistance, Rommel's position grew steadily worse. He flew out to Germany in March 1943, and on 13 May the last Axis armies in Tunisia surrendered.

ERWIN ROMMEL

An early proponent of mobile warfare, Erwin Rommel (1891–1944) led a Panzer unit during the Battle of France in 1940. After his failed North Africa campaign of 1941–43 he was sent to France, where he committed suicide after being implicated in a plot to kill Hitler.

General Rommel (far left) was a master of armoured warfare, which played a vital part in Germany's efforts in the North African desert.

THE WAR IN ITALY

Italy   July 1943–May 1945

At the Casablanca Conference in January 1943, the Allies decided to exploit imminent victory in North Africa (see facing page) by launching a new front in Italy. This would enable them to threaten Germany itself from the south, using Sicily as a springboard for the assault. On 10 July "Operation Husky" began. The Allied advance was sluggish, however, and allowed time for Germany's General Kesselring to evacuate more than 100,000 of his soldiers back to the Italian mainland on 11–12 August.

In June 1944 US general Mark Clark entered Rome, a German-declared "open city" that escaped bombing.

SALERNO

The fall of Mussolini's regime on 25 July brought forward Allied plans to invade southern Italy. By the time an armistice with the new Italian government was announced on 8 September, British forces had already crossed over into southern Italy. The following day they made a larger amphibious landing at Salerno, south of Naples. However, the Germans had been pouring reinforcements into Italy and resistance was stiffer than the Allies had expected, very nearly pushing their forces back into the sea.

THE END OF THE ITALIAN CAMPAIGN

The Allied campaign never regained its momentum, and stalled trying to breach a series of strong German defensive lines. A new Allied amphibious landing at Anzio, south of Rome, in December 1943 became bogged down, while it required an enormous effort and almost five months (January to May 1944) to clear the Germans from their positions around Monte Cassino. Even after they finally reached Rome on 4 June 1944, the Allies failed to exploit their victory, and the Germans finally surrendered in Italy only on 2 May 1945, at the very end of the war.

The military cemetery at Monte Cassino is overlooked by the ruins of the abbey that was destroyed by Allied bombing in February 1944.

PEARL HARBOR

⚑ Hawaii ☠ 7 December 1941

Throughout 1940, US president Roosevelt looked on with alarm as the Japanese steadily encroached on new territory, occupying northern Indochina in July 1940. Meanwhile, the powerful Japanese naval lobby pressed for a pre-emptive strike against the USA to cripple its military capacity before it could react to Japan's advances. Finally, on 1 December 1941, Japanese emperor Hirohito approved the order for an attack on the main US Pacific naval base at Pearl Harbor in Hawaii.

This Japanese military flag inscribed with prayers is an example of the potent mix of nationalism and religious sentiments that inspired Japanese soldiers

THE JAPANESE ATTACK

Although intercepted intelligence had given indications that an attack of some sort might occur, the Americans were totally unprepared when the large Japanese task force, including six aircraft carriers, began its attack on 7 December. The Japanese commander, Admiral Nagumo, launched two waves of bombers and fighters against the US base, an hour apart. Some 18 US naval vessels were sunk, including eight battleships, and nearly 400 aircraft were destroyed (with the loss of just 29 Japanese planes). The only consolation for America was that its two aircraft carriers were – by chance – absent from Pearl Harbor that day. The following day in Congress, President Roosevelt described the Japanese attack as a "date which will live in infamy" and declared war on Japan. Germany and Italy declared war on the USA three days later.

The US battleships West Virginia and Tennessee ablaze after Japan's attack on Pearl Harbor. The West Virginia was repaired and returned to service in 1944.

THE JAPANESE ADVANCE

SE Asia, Pacific islands December 1941–March 1942

The Japanese bombing of Pearl Harbor (*see facing page*) was followed by an attack on the British-held territories of Malaya and Singapore. Japan's armies rapidly swept aside British defences in Malaya, using surprise and mobility to compensate for a lack of heavy equipment such as tanks. By 12 February 1942, Japanese forces had landed in Singapore, a fortress-city that was supposedly the British bastion in Southeast Asia. Three days later its commander, Lieutenant-General Arthur Percival, surrendered his 100,000-man command, the largest surrender in British military history.

British troops surrender to the Japanese at Singapore. Large numbers would be used by the Japanese on labour projects in Southeast Asia.

THE PHILIPPINES AND BURMA

At the same time, the Japanese moved against the Philippines – American-held since 1898 – from bases on Taiwan. By late December, Japanese air superiority had forced the US general Douglas

the British evacuated their remaining positions in Burma in late April, but the Allies' fighting retreat prevented any large-scale Japanese move into India.

In the early part of 1942, the Japanese made a series of amphibious attacks on Allied colonies in the Pacific, occupying the Dutch East Indies and the British-held portion of Borneo, and on 8 March

"THE WORST DISASTER AND LARGEST CAPITULATION IN BRITISH HISTORY."

Winston Churchill on the surrender of Singapore to the Japanese, 1942

MacArthur to order a retreat to the island of Corregidor. The US defence, though spirited, proved hopeless, and on 5 May the last American troops surrendered.

To complete their defensive perimeter, the Japanese moved to secure Burma in the west and a string of Pacific islands to the east. They captured the Burmese capital Rangoon on 8 March 1942, and

landing in New Guinea. It now seemed conceivable that they might even invade Australia from the north, and the catastrophic Japanese defeat of a joint Allied fleet at the Battle of the Java Sea on 27 February made the situation seem even more irrecoverable. In the event, however, this would prove to be the high tide of the Japanese advance.

D-DAY AND THE WAR IN THE WEST

⚑ France ⌛ June–August 1944

After almost four years of planning, a combined American, British, Canadian, and Free French force launched Operation Overlord to wrest control of Europe from Germany. It began on "D-Day", 6 June 1944, on the coast of northern France. The Germans believed that any Allied landings would occur near Calais, on the eastern north coast, so were underprepared when the attack came in Normandy.

More than 7,000 Allied naval vessels were involved in the preliminary bombardment of German positions and the subsequent landings. The largest of the five assault areas was at Coleville-sur-Mer, codenamed Omaha Beach. Heavy Allied air and naval bombardment, effective at the four other landing points (Utah, Gold, Juno, and Sword), had made little impact on the well-prepared German positions at Omaha, and the US 1st and 29th

US army field telephones enabled rapid communications from the front line to headquarters units.

Infantry Divisions suffered enormous casualties. By early afternoon, the US had secured a small strip of beach, 9.7km (6 miles) wide and about 3.2km (2 miles) deep, but at the cost of 3,000 casualties.

THE BEACHHEAD EXPANDS

Meeting with less resistance at the other beaches, the Allies landed 130,000 troops by nightfall. Six days later, they had linked together the five beachheads into a continuous front and could land armoured vehicles, heavy artillery, and a stream of troops. Despite these reinforcements, the campaign in Normandy went slowly. Allied forces under the British general Bernard Montgomery stalled in front of Caen,

BERNARD MONTGOMERY

A veteran of World War I (who was severely wounded in France in 1914), Montgomery (1887–1976) took command of the British 8th Army in North Africa during World War II. His meticulous planning led to the defeat of the German field marshal Rommel at El Alamein in October 1942. Montgomery could be overcautious, which hampered his operation to take Caen after D-Day. Confident of his own importance, he quarrelled with General Eisenhower, the US commander in chief in western Europe, which almost led to his dismissal in 1945.

he French city of Caen in ormandy was largely destroyed by lied bombing and the fighting at took place in its streets.

hich had been a D-Day bjective, and it took a najor offensive to secure he city's fall on 18 July. he Germans had efended well, but their osses, including 2,000 anks, made victory npossible. Hitler refused o sanction tactical vithdrawals, demanding that every inch f ground be defended. The Allies, in urn, were hampered by the difficult Normandy terrain and by bad weather, vhich prevented them from effectively mploying their more than ten-to-one uperiority in aircraft.

HE FALAISE POCKET

On 25 July the US 7th Army advanced outh through St Lô, clearing the way for n advance towards Paris. A German ounteroffensive ended with almost all he German troops in Normandy enned into a pocket around Falaise.

When Hitler did allow a retreat, on 16 August, it was too late for the 25,000 German soldiers who were taken prisoner.

On 19 August, the first Allied units crossed the Seine, threatening German control of Paris. A second Allied landing in France, on the southern Riviera, captured Toulon and Marseilles by the end of August. By pushing north towards Lyons, this advance threatened to trap German forces between its forces and the advance from Normandy.

US troops disembark in Normandy in June 1944. By 30 June, some 850,000 men, 148,000 vehicles, and 570,000 tons of supplies had been put ashore.

THE DEFEAT OF GERMANY

France, Germany, Russia, Ukraine, Belarus   January 1943–May 1945

The Allies won a morale-boosting victory in France with the recapture of Paris on 24 August 1944, symbolically spearheaded by a Free French unit. Yet any hope that the war might soon be over in western Europe was dashed by a German recovery. German units in

and into the vital German industrial heartland of the Ruhr. During the operation, elements of a British airborne division became trapped at Arnhem and 6,000 men surrendered on 21 September. In December, Hitler made his last throw of the dice in the

"WE WILL FIGHT ON TO THE LAST."

General Krebs, German army Chief of Staff on 1 May 1945, the day before the final surrender of Berlin

Normandy began to regroup and a series of strategic miscalculations hampered the Allies' progress.

The Allies captured the Belgian port of Antwerp on 4 September, but then stalled. British general Montgomery suggested an operation called Market Garden to push across the lower Rhine

west, with a massive assault on the Rhine in the "Battle of the Bulge". More than 500,000 men took part in the advance, which began on 16 December. Though initially caught off-balance by the sheer weight of German numbers, the Americans held out at Bastogne, counterattacking to

On 24 August 1944, a small force of the 2nd French Armoured Division under Captain Raymond Dronne liberated Paris.

VIVE DE GAUL

The Soviet hammer and sickle flag was raised on the Reichstag building in central Berlin during the final German surrender.

of German defenders. The German positions collapsed, and by July the Red Army was in Poland. Pausing on the Vistula in autumn 1944, while Polish insurgents perished in a failed anti-German uprising in Warsaw, Soviet forces finally took Warsaw on 17 January 1945, and then began the race for Berlin. In mid-April the final assault began, with two million Soviet troops spearheaded by General Zhukov's 1st Belorussian Army. The one million German defenders, many of them untrained units and some soldiers little more than boys, showed a fanatical determination to resist, but by 30 April even Hitler despaired and committed suicide. Two days later the Berlin garrison surrendered. On 7 May, Hitler's successor government at Flensburg in northwest Germany signed a document of surrender. The Allies designated the following day – 8 May – as Victory in Europe (VE) Day.

arrow the neck of the "bulge" of erman troops, and on 8 January 1945 e Germans finally retreated. They had ffered 100,000 casualties and lost 000 aircraft. The Allies finally crossed e Rhine in force on 24 March, and ;ainst only patchy resistance reached e Elbe, where on 25 April they met up ith the Russian Red Army who had en advancing westwards.

IE TRIUMPH OF THE RED ARMY

fter its sensational victory at Stalingrad January 1943 (*see p.343*), the Red Army d endured mixed fortunes. They were iven back at Kharkov following a rapid lvance westwards, but at ursk on 12–13 July, they won e largest tank battle in story (more than 6,000 tanks ere engaged). By 6 December 43 the Red Army had taken e Ukrainian capital Kiev.

After a lull in the fighting cessitated by a harsh winter, alin ordered a new offensive, peration Bagration, to clear e German Army Group entre from Belorussia. On June 1944, the Red Army unched a vast assault around 'insk, with some 2.4 million en facing half that number

e Red Army's advance into Germany used a mass exodus of civilians, such these refugees seeking desperately escape from Berlin.

THE HOLOCAUST

Among the most pernicious aspects of German National Socialist ideology was its view that Aryans (white Caucasians) were racially superior and that other groups, most especially the Jews, were inferior. The practical consequence of this belief was the Holocaust – the deliberate attempt to annihilate the Jewish population of Europe, which resulted in the murder of some six million Jews by 1945.

EARLY ANTI-JEWISH MEASURES

When Hitler took power in Germany in January 1933, he began a slow process of reducing the civil rights and economic position of the country's half-million Jews. They were excluded from state office and from many professions in 1933–34. In September 1935, the Nuremberg Laws stripped Jews of their German citizenship and prohibited marriage or sexual relations between German Jews and Aryans. In November 1938, widespread violence broke out in a pogrom (anti-Jewish riot) known as *Kristallnacht* that destroyed some 7,500 Jewish businesses and killed 91 Jews.

The German invasion of Poland in September 1939 and of the USSR in June 1941 tragically transformed Germany's anti-Semitic policies. With 3.1 million

Half-starved survivors of the camp at Ebensee – liberated by the USA on 7 May 1945 – to which many former inmates of Auschwitz had been sent.

Jews in Poland and 2.7 million in the western USSR – as well as more than a million in occupied France, the Low Countries, Scandinavia, and the Balkans – Nazi authorities took drastic measures to "clear" Jewish populations. In Poland, the *Einsatzgruppen* (action groups made up from the SS – the elite paramilitary units of the Nazi Party) herded Jews into restricted areas of towns known as ghettoes.

The Star of David, once a symbol of hope for a Jewish homeland, was used in Nazi Germany as a badge to single out Jews.

Top Nazi leaders faced trial at the Allied Military Tribunal in Nuremberg in January 1946 for atrocities against the Jews.

Thousands more went to labour camps to work for the German war effort. As German troops swept in to the USSR, the SS shot or gassed (in mobile vans) as many Jews as they could find. In Kiev, 33,771 Jews were marched out to the Babi Yar ravine and shot on 29–30 September 1941.

THE "FINAL SOLUTION"

On 20 January 1942, Reinhard Heydrich, head of the Gestapo, summoned senior bureaucrats to a villa at Lake Wannsee in Berlin to ensure their support for a "Final Solution" to the Jewish question. Jews would be transported to camps in eastern Europe, to be worked to death or killed on the spot by mass gassing in sealed chambers. The bodies were to be burned in huge crematoria staffed by Jews themselves. Trainloads of Jews arrived at the death camps – Auschwitz, Belzec, Chelmno, Majdanek, Sobibór, and Treblinka – from occupied and Axis Europe (except Bulgaria, whose king refused to co-operate). Only when the Soviet Red Army advanced westward in 1944–45 did the camps cease work. Even then the suffering was not over. Many thousands died in "Death Marches", during which they were herded, starving and freezing, deeper west into Germany.

After the war the Allies tried 22 leading Nazis at Nuremberg in 1945–46 for the atrocities. Twelve were sentenced to death and six to long periods of imprisonment. Of the European Jews who had suffered the Holocaust, only around 300,000 survived, and many of these would not return to their homeland, choosing instead to emigrate to the new Jewish State of Israel (*see p.384*).

Railway tracks lead to the main gates of the Auschwitz concentration camp, in which around a million Jews were murdered.

THE DEFEAT OF JAPAN

 SE Asia, Pacific islands March 1942–August 1945

In early 1942, the Japanese sought to complete their outer perimeter in the southern Pacific by seizing the remainder of southern New Guinea. A large Japanese naval force set out in May 1942, but at the Battle of the Coral Sea the Americans turned them back with large losses. A far more significant setback came at the Battle of Midway in early June. The Japanese admiral Yamomoto intended to surprise the US fleet at the American-held Midway Islands. However, US intelligence had cracked the Japanese message codes, and the US Navy was well prepared for their arrival. Yamamoto, moreover, had wrongly calculated that the two US aircraft carriers would not be present at Midway. In the ensuing battle, Japan lost four aircraft carriers and hundreds of pilots (some 70 per cent of its total). At the end of 1942, Japanese success on land also petered out as US naval superiority

The Burma Star was a medal awarded to Commonwealth military personnel who served in Burma between 1941 and 1945.

pushed Japan out of Guadalcanal in the Solomon Islands by February 1943.

Later in 1943 the tide of war in the Pacific turned even more in favour of the Allied powers, largely because Japan struggled to match the extraordinary military and industrial resources of the USA. In June 1943, General MacArthur ordered Operation Cartwheel, designed to neutralize Japan's bases on New Guinea and the nearby island of New Britain. Although Japanese troops held out until the end of the war, they were confined to the mountains and posed no real further threat to the Allies.

ISLAND-HOPPING

In November 1943, the Americans continued their "island-hopping" strategy with the conquest of the Gilbert Islands, although the fierce resistance of even very small garrisons there showed the difficulties the USA might face in pressing its campaign to a successful conclusion. They then continued on to seize the Gilbert and Marianas islands, from where they could launch direct air attacks against Japan.

During 1944 and 1945, US power at sea and in the air began to have a decisive effect. A sea blockade of Japan cut off all imports, strangling the Japanese war economy. Another pivotal US naval victory at the Battle of Leyte Gulf in October 1944 opened the way for the USA to regain the Philippines. Landings at Leyte on 20 December met only light resistance, and by March 1945, the USA had liberated the Philippine capital of

A US-supplied M5 tank manned by a Chinese crew in northern Burma in 1944. Long-time adversaries of the Japanese, the Chinese fought for the Allies in Burma.

GENERAL DOUGLAS MACARTHUR

The Supreme Allied Commander in the Pacific, US general Douglas MacArthur (1880–1964) was born into a military family and began his military career in World War I. He rose to the rank of Army Chief of Staff in the interwar years. At the end of World War II, he became Supreme Allied Commander in Japan, overseeing its reconstruction and the drafting of a new Japanese constitution. In 1950–51, he led United Nations forces in Korea, but after a disagreement with President Truman was relieved of his command in April 1951.

anila. Meanwhile, in January 1945, the ritish advanced back into Burma and early May had secured the entire ntral area of the country.

O JIMA TO SURRENDER

February 1945, the USA invaded Iwo ma. It secured the island in several rd-fought weeks, and at the cost of ,000 Marine casualties, to provide base for fighters to support US bombing raids on mainland Japan. The USA now launched

Marines
se their national g on top of Mount ribachi after the US pture of the island of o Jima in February 1945.

a series of devastating strikes on Tokyo, which on 9–10 March caused a firestorm that killed around 100,000 Japanese citizens.

Japan's island-garrisons were isolated and picked off one by one by the USA, but although it could clearly no longer win the war, Japan was refusing to accept defeat. The fanatical resistance on the small island of Okinawa, where 120,000 Japanese troops – of whom just 7,500 survived – fought back from 26 March to 30 June, demonstrated how bloody the invasion of the Japanese home islands might be. It was this resistance that led President Truman to sanction the dropping of atomic bombs on the Japanese cities of Hiroshima and Nagasaki on 6 and 9 August 1945 (*see pp.356–7*). As a direct result of these bombings, the Japanese signed an unconditional surrender on 2 September aboard the USS *Missouri* in Tokyo Bay.

THE ATOM BOMB

Scientists discovered the awesome power of nuclear fission just before World War II, and warring countries raced to develop the first atomic bomb. The world became aware of America's scientific victory when it dropped bombs on two Japanese cities – Hiroshima and Nagasaki – destroying them within seconds. The development of these weapons was to play a large part in the ensuing Cold War (*see pp.360–61*).

THE NUCLEAR RACE

In 1938, German scientists Otto Hahn and Fritz Strassmann had split uranium atoms by bombarding them with neutrons. Known as "nuclear fission", this process had obvious military uses, and scientists in the UK and USA grew concerned that Germany might use it to make bombs. In August 1939, Albert Einstein wrote to President Roosevelt urging him to take action. The president set up the Uranium Committee to pursue research, and after the USA entered the war in December 1941, he established the Manhattan Project to accelerate US development of an explosive nuclear device.

The "Fat Man" plutonium bomb dropped by the B-29 bomber *Bock's Car* on Nagasaki was just 1.5m (5ft) in diameter, but killed tens of thousands.

THE FIRST BOMBS

The decision to use nuclear force in World War II was taken by US president Harry S. Truman, who was frustrated at Japan's resistance to final surrender and conscious of the huge casualties – on both sides – that would result from a direct invasion of Japan. He chose Hiroshima for its industrial and military significance. On 6 August 1945, a US B-29 bomber plane named *Enola Gay* dropped "Little

The first nuclear artillery shell – designed for firing from ground-based guns – was tested in the Nevada Desert on 25 May 1953.

The ruins of Hiroshima's Museum of Science and Technology in the aftermath of the atomic bomb, which totally destroyed 48,000 buildings.

Boy" over the city of Hiroshima. The bomb exploded 600m (1,950ft) above the city with a blast equivalent to 13 kilotons of TNT. An estimated 90,000 people were killed instantly; another 50,000 died later from wounds or radiation poisoning. Around 90 per cent of Hiroshima's buildings were damaged or destroyed in the blast.

The second bomb was destined for the town of Kokura, but this was shrouded in cloud on the morning of 9 August 1945, so the US bomber headed for the city of Nagasaki instead. At 11:02am its "Fat Man" bomb delivered 22 kilotons of explosive force over Nagasaki, leading to 70,000 deaths by the end of the year.

WORLDWIDE DEVELOPMENT
The USA quickly lost its nuclear monopoly after the war, as the USSR, Britain, France, and China developed nuclear weaponry. The stockpiling of large nuclear arsenals in the USSR and USA created a balance of terror between the two powers that was to play a large part in the Cold War, which dominated world politics from the late 1940s to the early 1990s. Israel, India, Pakistan, and North Korea went on to develop nuclear bombs and arsenals by the early 21st century.

"I AM BECOME DEATH, THE DESTROYER OF WORLDS."

Robert Oppenheimer, physicist and director of the Manhattan Project, quoting from the *Bhagavid Gita* on the first testing of the atomic bomb, 1945

EUROPE AFTER WORLD WAR II

For much of the 20th century after World War II, Europe seemed irrevocably divided into two parts: a democratic, capitalist West, and a communist Eastern bloc. The problems of national self-determination and democratic aspirations were smothered rather than solved by this new order. When communist regimes collapsed from the late 1980s, Europe erupted in a series of savage civil wars.

THE MARSHALL PLAN

◧ W Europe   ⚔ 1948–1952

In 1945 the Allied powers met at Yalta in the Crimea and Potsdam in Germany to shape post-war Europe. Stalin's insistence that the Soviet sphere be extended to cover eastern Poland and the Baltic states raised anxieties about his expansionist ambitions.

HARD TIMES

Concern over Stalin's intentions had led the British government to support Greek anti-Communist rebels in the Greek Civil War that erupted in December 1944. Yet economic hardship in the devastated Western economies threatened to secure communist influence just as much as Stalin's more direct diplomatic thuggery. Shortages were dire in 1947, partly due to the shattered state

George C. Marshall was awarded the Nobel Peace Prize in 1953 for his development of the Marshall Plan.

of European post-war industry, and France and Italy suffered strikes.

THE PARIS CONFERENCE

Allied plans to revive western Germany were opposed by the USSR, which wanted to leech reparations from Germany's economy, not to repair it. US Secretary of State George C. Marshall announced a new European Recovery Program (the "Marshall Plan") in May 1948, offering economic aid to speed Europe's recovery. Stalin forbade Eastern European countries from participating, so only western European nations assembled in Paris in July to discuss the plan. The US was ultimately to disburse some $12 billion of aid to the 16 participating countries by 1952.

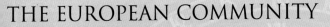

THE EUROPEAN COMMUNITY

⚑ W and S Europe   ⌛ 1957–1986

After World War II, it was clear to many politicians that Europe needed a mechanism to co-ordinate its economies, and, among idealists and pragmatists alike, a desire emerged to build a political structure to ensure that no further war between the major European powers would ever again devastate the continent. In 1950, Jean Monnet devised the "Schuman Plan", which led to the founding of the European Coal and Steel Community (ECSC) in 1950. This pooled the coal and steel resources of France, Germany, Italy, Belgium, Luxembourg, and the Netherlands.

In 1957, the Treaty of Rome established the European Economic Community (EEC), with these countries as founder members. The EEC allowed free movement of goods, services, and labour between member states and promoted greater economic integration. Initially Britain stood aside, suspicious of ceding control over its own economic affairs, but it finally joined in 1973, and by 1986 the EEC had 12 members.

THE EASTERN BLOC IN EUROPE

⚑ E Europe   ⌛ 1947–1968

Although Communist parties had actively resisted German occupation in some countries of Eastern Europe, their pre-eminent role from the late 1940s onwards owed as much to Stalin's brutal suppression of other political groups as to their real level of popular support.

THE IMPOSITION OF COMMUNISM

In January 1947 the Peasants' Party of Poland was robbed of probable election victory by falsified results. Stubborn anti-Soviet resistance in Czechoslovakia was subdued by the mysterious death of two leading anti-Communist ministers early in 1948. For almost 40 years, most central and Eastern European countries lived under brutal Communist regimes.

Following Stalin's death in 1953, some countries made bids for greater independence. In 1956,

the Hungarian leader Imre Nagy announced the end of one-party rule by the Communists, the expulsion of Soviet troops, and Hungary's withdrawal from the Warsaw Pact (*see p.361*) – but Hungarian hardliners and Soviet forces soon snuffed out his revolution. Similarly, in 1968, Alexander Dubček tried to implement economic and political reforms in Czechoslovakia. His "Prague Spring" was suppressed in August; Warsaw Pact troops invaded Czechoslovakia and imposed a more amenable regime.

Czech demonstrators mount a Soviet tank following the Warsaw Pact invasion in August 1968.

THE COLD WAR

Tensions over the post-World War II settlement between Britain and the USA on one hand, and the USSR on the other, led one Soviet official to state in 1947 that the world was now split between Western imperialists and socialist anti-imperialists. Countries around the world aligned themselves with one of the two groupings, beginning a Cold War – a state of political hostility that stopped short of actual warfare.

EARLY CONFRONTATIONS

The first real crisis of the Cold War almost brought the two sides to open warfare. Early in 1948, the Western Allies proposed to unite their sectors of Berlin (which was isolated deep inside the Soviet zone of occupation in Germany) into a single unit. The Soviets retaliated by cutting off land routes into those sectors. Far from capitulating, however, Britain, France, and the USA decided to launch an airlift, and for 11 months they delivered enough supplies to feed West Berlin's two million people.

During the Berlin airlift, the Western Allies delivered some 2.3 million tons of food to the city on more than 277,000 flights.

THE COLD WAR GROWS

In April 1949, 12 Western countries formed the North Atlantic Treaty Organization (NATO), a mutual self-defence pact clearly aimed at the USSR, and a month later the Western Allies announced the formation of the Federal Republic of Germany. The Cold War rift between the USA and USSR now seemed irresolvable; furthermore, it was given a new edge by the USSR's first atomic weapons test in August 1949.

As each side's sphere of influence in Europe solidified, the Cold War spread globally to areas where the two "superpowers" – the USSR and the USA – could operate through proxies. The victory of Mao Zedong's Communists in the Chinese Civil War in 1949 opened up yet another front – one that was to lead to enormous problems for the US side. Mao began to enact his own foreign policy initiatives, into which the USA would become entangled during the Korean War (*see p.394*) and the Vietnam War (*see p.395*).

Cold War allies Fidel Castro (*left*) and Nikita Khrushchev show fraternal solidarity during the Cuban leader's visit to Moscow in 1963.

THE CUBAN MISSILE CRISIS

Although Nikita Khrushchev, Soviet leader from 1953, sought to promote a policy of "peaceful coexistence" with the West, it did not prevent him from founding the Warsaw Pact in 1955 as a military organization to confront NATO. In 1962 a serious crisis developed when Khrushchev despatched nuclear missiles to bases in Cuba, then controlled by Fidel Castro's communist regime. This posed a very real threat to the USA, which considered invading Cuba or launching air strikes in response. Two weeks of knife-edge negotiations finally convinced the Soviets to back down and withdraw their weapons.

THE END OF THE COLD WAR

The superpowers continued to stockpile nuclear missiles throughout the 1970s and '80s. A period of easing tension in the 1970s, when the two sides ceased to posture quite so openly, was not matched by any reduction in the destructive power of their arsenals. A series of Strategic Arms Limitations Talks (SALT) had begun in the late 1960s, but agreement on real reductions was reached only in the early 1990s, when the USSR was finally on the verge of collapse and the Cold War was at last coming to an end.

> # "FROM STETTIN IN THE BALTIC TO TRIESTE IN THE ADRIATIC, AN IRON CURTAIN HAS DESCENDED ACROSS THE CONTINENT."
>
> Winston Churchill, in a speech at Fulton, Missouri, USA, 5 March 1946

The US Navy Trident missile gave reality to the idea of Mutual Assured Destruction, in which warring sides would both be destroyed by a nuclear conflict.

IRELAND AND THE TROUBLES

⚐ Northern Ireland ☠ 1968–1997

In April 1916, the Easter Rising in Dublin helped spark war between the nationalist Irish Republican Army (IRA) and the British authorities. In 1922 Britain sanctioned an independent Irish Free State (later the Irish Republic), which excluded the areas in the north of Ireland that had a Protestant (and pro-British) "Unionist" majority; these were retained within the UK.

THE YEARS OF VIOLENCE

In 1968–69, rising tensions between Catholic and Protestant communities led to renewed violence. A new nationalist group, the Provisional IRA, emerged in 1969 to push for the violent expulsion of the British authorities from Northern Ireland. It was matched by Protestant paramilitary groups, such as the Ulster Volunteer Force (UVF), established in 1966. Two decades of violence followed, including "Bloody Sunday" on 30 January 1972, when British security forces shot dead

13 Catholic protestors, and the IRA bombing of a Birmingham pub on 21 November 1974, killing 21 people.

Normal political life did not return to the province until the late 1990s. The Provisional IRA declared a final ceasefir

> ## "BLOODY SUNDAY ...WAS SHEER UNADULTERATED MURDER."
>
> Coroner Major Hubert O'Neill, 21 August 1973

in 1997 and began negotiations that would finally lead to a power-sharing government with Protestant Unionists. The "Troubles", though, had left in their wake more than 3,000 dead and a legacy of sectarian mistrust.

A mural in a Protestant district of Belfast, Northern Ireland's capital, shows the "loyalist" group that fought nationalist paramilitaries

UFF MEMBER

UDU MEMBER

UDA MEMBER

ULSTER DEFENCE UNION EST. 1893

ULSTER DEFENCE ASSOCIATION EST. 1972

ETA

⚑ Spain   ☲ 1959–present

Nationalists in Basque Spain had claimed independence in the 19th century, but the region suffered under Franco's repressive regime (*see p.336*). Extremists formed the armed group ETA (*Euskadi ta Askatana*, or "Homeland and Liberty") in 1959 to fight for independence.

At first attacking the local infrastructure, in 1968 ETA moved on to violent terrorist attacks, killing a police chief in August that year. In 1973, the group assassinated Admiral Luis Carrero Blanco, Franco's designated successor. After Franco's death, some autonomy was granted to the Spanish provinces, with particularly wide powers ceded to the government of the Basque region. ETA, though, did not cease its violent campaign, continuing to demand full independence. Abortive ceasefires from 1998 have always been followed by new bombings and shootings, some of them fatal.

PERESTROIKA

⚑ USSR, E Europe   ☲ 1985–1991

In 1964, Leonid Brezhnev became Soviet leader, succeeding Nikita Khrushchev. Under his governance, the Soviet economy stagnated, and there were often shortages of manufactured goods. Senior party officials had access to privileges unattainable to many people, and although the Soviet security forces – notably the KGB – relentlessly persecuted dissidents, by the late 1980s the system seemed on the point of collapsing beneath the weight of its own inefficiency and corruption.

British prime minister Margaret Thatcher met Mikhail Gorbachev in Moscow in 1987. He was, she once remarked, a man "we can do business with".

THE FAILURE OF REFORM

Mikhail Gorbachev became Soviet leader in 1985, and at once publicly acknowledged the faults in the system. While never questioning Lenin's view of the prime importance to Russia of the Communist Party, he argued that *perestroika* ("restructuring") was needed to streamline it and that a new openness (*glasnost*) was needed to allow a debate on how best to repair the Communist regime. Cautious reforms included limited rights for private enterprise (introduced in 1987–88), but talk of change provoked demands for more, and Gorbachev was overtaken by events. In 1988, the Eastern bloc countries threw off communism and in 1991 Gorbachev, who had made himself president with executive powers the previous year, was overthrown.

THE COLLAPSE OF COMMUNISM

⚑ E Europe, the USSR   ⌛ 1989–1991

In 1980 striking shipyard workers in Gdansk, Poland, forced the Communist government to allow workers to form an independent trade union – Solidarity – led by Lech Walesa. The state struck back in December by declaring martial law, and suppressed Solidarity. The USSR could have intervened but chose not to, and by 1988, with the economic situation deteriorating badly, Poland's government

Lech Walesa, leader of Solidarity, is carried in triump through the streets of Krakow, shortly after the Augus 1980 accord that legalized the trade union.

> "THE SOVIET UNION COULD NOT EXIST WITHOUT THE IMAGE OF THE EMPIRE!"
>
> Boris Yeltsin, *The Struggle for Russia*, 1994

opened talks with the trade unionists and agreed to hold elections in June 1989. These were meant to yield a coalition rule, but ended in Solidarity's victory. A non-communist – Tadeusz Mazowiecki – became prime minister, dismantling the pillars of communist power.

In May 1989, streams of East Germans disenchanted at being denied even the gradual change occurring elsewhere in the Eastern bloc, began to take refuge in gently reformist Hungary – the only country they could go to without a visa. Hardline East German leader Erich Honecker demanded Soviet action, but Soviet leader Mikhail Gorbachev had enough on his hands keeping the USSR together, and refused to give Honecker any assistance. Mass demonstrations broke out, and the East German government panicked. First it tried to

BORIS YELTSIN

A member of the Communist Central Committee in Sverdlovsk from 1981, Boris Nikolayevich Yeltsin (1931–2007) became the party's chief in Moscow in 1985–87, but was sacked amid allegations of alcoholism. Yeltsin bounced back and by 1990 was chairman of the Russian component of the USSR. After the USSR dissolved, he became President of Russia, but constitutional crises, Russian losses in two invasions of Chechnya, economic problems, and corruption all tarnished his reputation and he resigned in 1999.

urge its own hardliners, and then on
November it announced that the Berlin
Wall, which had divided the Eastern and
Western sectors of the city since 1961,
would be opened. East Germany
collapsed, and became reunited with
West Germany the following August.

The spread of anti-communism was
uncontrollable. In early December, a
"Velvet Revolution" overthrew the
communists in Czechoslovakia,
while towards the end of
the month the communist
dictator of Romania, Nicolae
Ceaucescu, was toppled
in a much bloodier coup.

THE COLLAPSE OF THE USSR

Waves of dissent now began to lap
at the USSR itself. Throughout 1990
Gorbachev struggled to stop the
Union dissolving. He still believed he
could "de-Leninize" the Communist
Party, and held a referendum in
March 1991 in which 78 per cent of
voters said the USSR (in a modified
form) should stay. However, on
19 August 1991, a committee of
communist hardliners staged a
coup, arresting Gorbachev and his
advisers, and declaring a return to
old-style Soviet rule. Boris Yeltsin,
President of the Russian Republic
(part of the USSR), rallied opinion
against the coup and it collapsed.
Yet nothing was ever the same
again. On 1 December, Ukraine
declared its independence, and
Gorbachev resigned. At midnight
on 31 December 1991, the
USSR ceased to exist.
The Communist Party,
at the heart of public
life since 1917, had
been banned eight
weeks earlier.

colossal statue
Vladimir Lenin was
removed from the
Romanian capital of
Bucharest in March
1980, at the end of
communist rule.

On 9 November 1989, after weeks of civil unrest, the East German Communist government announced that it would permit travel into West Berlin. Within hours 50,000 East Germans climbed and crossed the Wall, and even started to destroy it; by 1991 it had been demolished.

THE WAR IN YUGOSLAVIA

▣ Former Yugoslavia   ⚑ 1991–1995

Josip Tito, the communist dictator of Yugoslavia from 1945 to his death in 1980, reorganized the state in 1946 into six socialist republics – Serbia, Croatia, Slovenia, Bosnia-Herzegovina, Montenegro, and Macedonia – in an effort to balance Yugoslavia's potentially explosive mixture of religions and ethnic groups.

After the collapse of communism in 1990, free elections led to nationalist governments in Slovenia and Croatia, which demanded independence. The president of the Serbian republic, Slobodan Milosevic, stridently opposed this notion and whipped up pro-Yugoslav (fundamentally Serb) sentiment. When Slovenia declared its independence from Serbia in June 1991, the Serb-dominated army intervened, but after a short campaign were forced to withdraw.

Smarting from this rebuff, the Serbian army moved in greater force into Croatia, which had also declared its

General Ratko Mladic, commander of the Bosnian Serb forces during the civil war there in 1992–95.

independence. A bloody campaign ensued in eastern Slavonia, where the cities of Vukovar and Vinkovci were destroyed and many Croat civilians massacred. Only in 1992 did a UN-brokered ceasefire bring peace. By then Bosnia, an even more ethnically mixed republic – around 43 per cent Muslim, 31 per cent Serb, and 17 per cent Croat – was sliding into civil war. The vicious conflict saw Europe's worst fighting since World War II, including a brutal siege of Sarajevo conducted by the Bosnian government, and the massacre of thousands of refugees at a UN "safe haven" in Srebrenica. The violence only ended in August 1995, when a NATO bombing campaign induced Slobodan Milosevic to withdraw support for the Bosnian Serbs and to sign the Dayton peace accord in December.

The Croatian city of Vukovar suffered a two-month siege by Yugoslav army forces and Serb paramilitaries between September and November 1991.

NEW CHALLENGES FOR EUROPE

Europe   1992–present

urope had spent nearly
of the 20th century
vided by war, but as the
old War ended, most
uropean leaders looked
rward to a new period
peace and prosperity.
vents, however, did not
fold quite as they
pected. The rapid
llapse of communism
Eastern Europe and
e USSR (*see pp.364–5*)
ened up the prospect of
Europe without fear, but
e equally rapid descent of Yugoslavia
to civil strife (*see facing page*) suggested
at lasting peace was illusory.

Crowds filled the streets of Kiev in support of the
Ukrainian opposition leader Viktor Yuschenko during
the "Orange Revolution" of December 2004.

ROPEAN UNION
he European Community (*see p.359*)
formed itself in 1992 by means of the
aastricht Treaty, in which it gave itself
eater powers, and a new name – the
ropean Union (EU). A process of
largement then began, first with the
mission of Sweden, Finland, and

the organization had 27 member states,
making it a large and fractious family
in which agreeing any further changes
seemed an almost impossible challenge.

FURTHER HURDLES
An ethnic civil war had erupted in Kosovo
in 1997–99, leaving the region in a legal
limbo – neither independent nor a part

"WE NEVER WANT TO WAGE WAR AGAINST EACH OTHER… THAT IS THE MOST IMPORTANT REASON FOR A UNITED EUROPE."

Former German chancellor Helmut Kohl, 1 May 2004

ustria into the Union in 1995, and then
th the strategically more significant
dditions of ten further countries in 2005,
cluding many former Eastern bloc
tions (such as Poland and Hungary) and
e former Soviet republics of Estonia,
tvia, and Lithuania. By 2007, when
lgaria and Romania joined the EU,

of Serbia – and the EU uncertain as to
whether or not to recognize the territory.
Similarly, Ukraine had overthrown its
old-guard communist regime in late 2004;
encouraging the new state to join the EU
might provide political stability, but it
would alienate the Russian government.
Europe still faced many challenges.

THE AMERICAS

In the second half of the 20th century, the Americas were marked by extremes of wealth and poverty. The USA was the richest and most powerful nation on Earth, but it also struggled with social divisions and prejudices, such as the exclusion of black citizens from the political process. In South America, political and economic crises – combined with occasional direct interventions by the USA – created an environment in which stability was hard to achieve.

US ECONOMIC GROWTH

⚑ USA ☗ 1945–1960

The USA experienced an economic boom during World War II, as its industries expanded to cope with wartime production. This growth continued in peacetime, and the country's buoyant economy created a new middle class that spent its money on consumer goods – some 83 per cent of homes in the USA had a television by 1958. As a result of an improved diet, American children were on average 5–8cm (2–3in) taller in 1950 than their grandparents had been in 1900, and life expectancy for women rose from 51 to 71 years old. There was a large-scale migration to the suburbs, accompanied by a building programme to erect a massive 13 million new houses in the ten years between 1948 and 1958. There was consumer choice as never before, and the USA developed a "youth culture" for the first time, which fed into a cultural renaissance in the 1960s.

However, the country's growing prosperity had done nothing to halt racial segregation. Many cities became "doughnut-shaped", with a rich business centre surrounded by poorer African-American inner suburbs, and then a more prosperous, and largely white-inhabited, outer zone.

Increasing affluence fuelled the technological innovation of consumer "must-haves", such as this 1955 portable TV.

McCARTHYISM

USA ⌛ 1950–1954

The growing tensions of the Cold War between the USA and the USSR (*see pp.360–1*) soon fed back into US politics, as fears arose that the Soviets would encourage communist subversion or even outright revolution in America. On 9 February 1950, Republican senator Joseph McCarthy gave a speech in which he claimed to have the names of 205 communists working in the US State Department. A political furore erupted in which, to defend himself, McCarthy issued further accusations of communist infiltration.

Senator Joseph McCarthy testifies to the Senate Foreign Relations Subcommittee in March 1950.

Bodies such as the House Committee on Un-American Activities investigated alleged communist activity, while McCarthy himself, as Chair of the Senate Permanent Subcommittee on Investigations in 1953–55, sought to root out communists in all walks of life, particularly in the film industry and among labour activists. Yet when he turned to attacks on the army, he overplayed his hand: public sympathy for him waned, and in December 1954 his activities were condemned by a vote in the Senate.

THE ASSASSINATION OF JFK

Dallas, Texas ⚰ 22 November 1963

On Friday 22 November 1963, President John F. Kennedy visited Dallas, Texas, to drum up support for his re-election in the 1964 US presidential race. As the motorcade drove through Dealey Plaza, at least three gunshots rang out, killing the president instantly.

THE INVESTIGATION

The assassination became the subject of huge controversy. A lone gunman, Lee Harvey Oswald, was arrested shortly after the shooting and charged with murder. However, two days later he was shot dead while in police custody by Jack Ruby, a gangster who later gave contradictory motives for the killing. Kennedy's successor, vice-president Lyndon Johnson, rapidly established the Warren Commission to investigate the assassination. It concluded there was no wider conspiracy to kill Kennedy.

President Kennedy and his wife Jacqueline smile at the Dallas crowds, minutes before his assassination on 22 November 1963.

CIVIL RIGHTS

By the 1950s, discrimination against African-Americans had become entrenched in many southern US states. From the 1870s onwards, discriminatory laws had been passed depriving African-Americans of the right to vote, and legalizing a system of segregation in which black people were denied access to whites-only schools and universities, and even from choosing where they might sit on public transport.

THE MONTGOMERY BUS BOYCOTT

In the mid-1950s, years of anger and frustration triggered a concerted reaction against discrimination. In December 1955, Rosa Parks refused to give up her seat to a white man on a segregated bus. Her arrest ignited a movement for civil rights. Local activists, including members of the NAACP (the National Association for the Advancement of Coloured People), which had long lobbied for African-American rights, organized a boycott of Montgomery's public transport system, which ended in November 1956 with a Supreme Court ruling that the buses must be desegregated.

Rosa Parks in the front of a bus, after the abolition of segregation on the Montgomery buses.

MARTIN LUTHER KING

An organizer of the Montgomery boycott, and the first African-American to climb aboard a bus when it ended, Martin Luther King Jr (1929–68) was a young Baptist pastor who would soon become the public face and abiding inspiration of the civil rights movement. Unswerving in his pledge to non-violence, he followed the lead of Mahatma Gandhi (*see p.380–1*) in encouraging civil disobedience to highlight unjust laws.

In 1954, the Supreme Court had ruled that education must be desegregated. This remained largely untested until nine African-American students attempted to attend a high school in Little Rock, Arkansas, in September 1957. The National Guard had to protect them, but they were able to attend class.

SIT-INS AND FREEDOM RIDES

In February 1960, black students from Greensboro, North Carolina, staged the first "sit-in" by refusing to move

Martin Luther King delivers his "I have a dream" speech. In 1964, he received the Nobel Peace Prize; four years he later was assassinated in Tennessee.

from seats at lunch counters reserved for whites, demonstrating how basic rights were still denied to black Americans. In 1961 groups of black and white people set out to ride buses together – these "Freedom Rides" tested the ruling on desegregated travel. All the while a campaign grew to promote the voter registration of southern African-American citizens. Martin Luther King organized a mass rally in Birmingham, Alabama, in April 1963 and a "March on Washington" in August, in which he made his iconic speech, "I have a dream…", from the Lincoln Memorial to 250,000 people. Under intense pressure, the government buckled and in 1964 passed the Civil Rights Act, making many forms of discrimination illegal. The achievements of the civil rights movement were crowned 45 years later with the election of Barack Obama, the first African-American president of the USA.

The raised fist of the "Black Power" movement, popularized by radical activists in the 1960s.

THE SPACE RACE

Earth's orbit, the Moon   1957–1969

At the end of World War II, both the USA and the USSR scrambled to secure the expertise of German scientists who had created the first ballistic missile, the V2. This knowledge could be used to develop rockets capable of reaching space and satellites that would orbit the Earth. A "Space Race" grew out of the Cold War (*see pp.360–61*), with both sides wishing to exploit the propaganda and military benefits of making the first forays beyond the Earth's surface and atmosphere.

Soviet cosmonaut Yuri Gagarin on his mission to become the first human in space in April 1961.

The USSR won the early victories in this race, putting the first artificial satellite, *Sputnik 1*, into Earth orbit on 4 October 1957. This was followed by the US *Explorer* in January 1958. Then a Soviet cosmonaut, Yuri Gagarin, became the first human in space, on 12 April 1961. The USA got their first astronaut (Alan Shepard) aloft 23 days later.

Piqued by the failure of the USA to match its apparently technologically inferior rival, President John F. Kennedy announced in May 1961 that, within a decade, an American would land on the moon and come safely home. So began the Apollo programme that culminated in *Apollo 11*. At 10:56pm on 20 July 1969, Neil Armstrong became the first man to stand on the moon. All the astronauts made it back to Earth, and the USA declared the space race won.

US astronaut Buzz Aldrin, the second man to stand on the moon, makes his historic walk during the *Apollo 11* mission on 20 July 1969.

THE CUBAN REVOLUTION

Cuba   1953–1959

The military regime of Fulgencio Batista, which had ruled Cuba since 1933, came under increasing pressure in the 1950s. In 1955, it released a group of political dissidents who had attacked a military

> ## "EACH AND EVERY ONE OF US WILL PAY ON DEMAND HIS PART OF SACRIFICE."
>
> Ernesto "Ché" Guevara (1928–67),
> Cuban revolutionary leader

barracks in 1953. This turned out to be a disastrous miscalculation: among them was Fidel Castro, a young revolutionary activist. On 2 December 1956, Castro – who had left Cuba – returned with a group of around 80 fellow revolutionaries aboard the *Granma*. Three days later, Batista's soldiers attacked and most of the revolutionaries were killed, but Castro and a few others, including Ernesto "Ché" Guevara, escaped into the hills. Kept together by Castro's determination, the band grew larger. In 1958, the orthodox Communist Party of Cuba gave its backing to Castro's revolutionaries and, as Batista's forces continually failed to dislodge him, in August 1958 Castro decided on an offensive of his own. Encountering surprisingly light resistance, by 31 December he had taken the strategic central city of Santa Clara.

Batista panicked and fled Cuba, leaving Castro to enter the capital, Havana, on 8 January 1959. With his idiosyncratic brand of communism, he dominated the country's political life for the next half-century.

Fidel Castro and some of his revolutionaries in 1957, at a time when they were still in hiding in Cuba's Sierra Maestra hills, under pressure from Batista's army.

ALLENDE AND PINOCHET

Chile   1970–1988

Since 1938, a succession of civilian governments in Chile had struggled to cope with increasing economic hardship and the aspirations of landless peasants. In 1970, a left-wing front led by Salvador Allende tapped into these feelings to win an election, but before long his coalition began to fracture. The USA raised concerns when Allende established diplomatic relations with China and other communist regimes. In 1973, General Augusto Pinochet seized power in a US-backed coup. Although Pinochet restored economic order, thousands of political opponents "disappeared". Finally, after losing a referendum on the extension of his term of presidency, in 1990 Pinochet stepped down and civilian rule was restored to Chile.

A photo-montage of the *desaparecidos*, more than 3,000 political opponents of Pinochet who were killed or "disappeared" during his dictatorship.

PERÓN AND ARGENTINA

Argentina   1946–1974

Popular with trade-union leaders and the poor, Juan Domingo Perón became president of Argentina in 1946. He immediately embarked on economic reform, nationalizing banks and expanding education. His following, and that of his first wife Eva, was enormous – but there were negative aspects to his rule: he vigorously suppressed all opposition, and sheltered Nazi war criminals fleeing from justice. He also offended the Catholic Church by legalizing divorce.

Peron's populist "Third Way" foreign policy aimed to avoid alienating either side in the Cold War (*see pp.360–61*). But

Former actress Eva Maria Duarte married Juan Perón in 1945, and later became his vice-president.

it was too radical for some in the armed forces and in 1955, the last in a series of military coups unseated him. However, his supporters remained numerous and their effective exclusion from political participation in the 1960s destabilized a series of military-led governments. In 1972 Perón returned from exile to Argentina and in 1973 was elected president, aged 78. His austerity measures calmed inflation, but he died in 1974, leaving his third wife Isabela to complete the last two years of his term.

THE USA IN LATIN AMERICA

📖 Latin America ⌛ 1952–present

Ever since 1823, when President James Monroe sought to exclude the European powers from expanding their hold in the Americas, the USA had actively desired to keep the sphere of influence in Latin America purely American. At times this meant intervention: in 1898, war with Spain resulted in US occupation of Cuba. As the Cold War flared up, the USA sought to exclude communism from its sphere, signing a series of bilateral defence pacts with Latin American countries from 1952.

Panama's Manuel Noriega waves to crowds in October 1989 after the suppression of a coup against him.

THE SANDINISTAS

The Cuban Revolution of 1959 marked both the failure of US exclusion policy and the sharpening of US attempts to contain the spread of communism. In 1979, the Marxist Sandinista movement overthrew the Nicaraguan dictatorship of Anastasio Somoza. The new regime, led by Daniel Ortega, had strong ties to Cuba and the USA tried for years to destabilize it. Ultimately, though, it was a peace plan brokered by other Latin American countries which laid down free elections that finally brought down the Sandinistas in 1990.

NORIEGA AND PANAMA

Fears of a different kind emerged over Panama, which contained the strategic Canal Zone. Manuel Noriega, commander of Panama's armed forces, had become increasingly involved in the illegal drugs trade, which was channelled through Central America.

In 1989, the USA finally lost patience and launched an invasion of Panama. Noriega's forces put up little resistance, and the commander was seized, flown to the USA, and put on trial. He was sentenced to 40 years' imprisonment for drug trafficking.

Sandinista fighters advance along a road during the Nicaraguan Civil War (1972–79), which ended in the overthrow of Somoza's dictatorship.

DEMOCRACY RETURNS TO LATIN AMERICA

Latin America   1982–present

The 1980s saw the end of many dictatorships in Latin America, beginning in 1982 with the fall of the Argentinian military government (*junta*) and the restoration of civilian rule to Chile in 1988 (*see p.376*). Democracy provided no easy answers, but produced some strong-minded populists. In 1990, Peru elected as its president Alberto Fujimori, whose "Fujishock" policies tamed hyperinflation and won plaudits from the International Monetary Fund (IMF). Yet his violations of the constitution and

President Hugo Chávez initiated a "Bolivarian Revolution" of democratic socialism in Venezuela

suspicions of corruption led to his overthrow in 2000. Hugo Chávez, a former army chief, became president in Venezuela in 1998. He initiated laws to empower the poverty-stricken majority, but ruthlessly stamped down any opposition. His attempts to forge alliances with other radical Latin American presidents, such as Fidel Castro (Cuba) and Evo Morales (Bolivia), were met with suspicion in the USA.

THE FALKLANDS WAR

Falkland Islands   April–June 1982

Argentina and the UK had long disputed the ownership of the Falkland Islands in the western Atlantic. Talks between the two countries on the islands' future broke down in early 1982, and on 2 April the Argentines launched an invasion of the Falklands. They overwhelmed the small British garrison, but the Argentine military government under General Leopoldo Galtieri underestimated the British resolve to recover the islands. Prime Minister Margaret Thatcher ordered the despatch of a large task force which landed British soldiers on the Falklands on 21 May. The British units fought their way east to the Falklands' capital, Port Stanley, by 14 June, where they took 11,000 Argentine prisoners, reclaiming the islands and ending the war.

The Argentine cruiser *General Belgrano* was sunk after an attack by a British nuclear-powered submarine on 2 May 1982, with the loss of 321 lives.

NAFTA

North America   1992–present

In November 1992, the leaders of the USA, Canada, and Mexico established a North American Free Trade Area (NAFTA). This promoted the freedom of movement of goods and services – and labour, but only to a very limited extent – across the borders of their respective countries. NAFTA became active on 1 January 1994. Central American countries (and others, such as Chile) hoped that they might also be included, but they met strong opposition from US politicians, who were already concerned that products from a lower-wage economy such as Mexico would now be freely available in the USA.

US president Bill Clinton speaks at a public meeting in November 1992 to promote NAFTA.

MEXICO AND CANADA

The economic benefits in Mexico were to a great extent confined to the north of the country, where low-cost factories proliferated along the border with the USA. However, Mexico was still vulnerable to economic shocks, as demonstrated by a devaluation of its currency in 1994. Panic set in and the country needed $50 billion of loans, secured against its oil reserves. This situation in turn contributed to the loss of political dominance by the Institutional Revolutionary Party, which had ruled Mexico unchallenged since 1929.

The USA's other NAFTA partner, Canada, was generally a model of economic stability, but it suffered persistent political crises over the aspirations for autonomy of its mainly French-speaking province, Québec. First winning elections in the province in 1976, the separatist Parti Québecois was never, however, quite strong enough to force a referendum on the issue.

The border between the USA and Mexico. NAFTA has freed trade between the two, but Mexican immigrants remain a huge political issue in the USA.

$\mathscr{A}$sia and the Middle East

Asia faced a series of political upheavals after World War II. First the aftermath of British withdrawal from Israel and India turned bloody, then the long-term effects of the communist victory in China's civil war led to violent struggles in Korea and Southeast Asia. Nevertheless, in the latter half of the 20th century, economic growth in East and Southeast Asia helped improve upon this troubled legacy.

THE INDIAN NATIONAL CONGRESS

🏴 India   ⚰ 1885–1945

In 1885, Western-educated Indians campaigning for greater rights founded the Indian National Congress (INC). Although in principle the congress represented all Indians, its members were mainly Hindu, and in 1906 some Muslims broke away from the INC to form the Muslim League.

GANDHI'S PROTEST MOVEMENTS

The 1909 Government of India Act allowed a greater number of Indians to sit on legislative councils alongside the British. However, the changes were deemed to be insufficient, and in March 1919 Mahatma Gandhi launched his *satyagraha* protests – a mass nonviolent movement to force British concessions. At one meeting in Amritsar, the British authorities opened fire on protestors, killing nearly 400 of them. Gandhi did not answer violence with violence, although sporadic riots erupted in the 1920s. In 1930, he symbolically declared Indian independence and conducted a "salt *satyagraha*", marching to the sea

A line of workers lie down to block strikebreakers from entering a workshop gate in 1930, as part of Gandhi's *satyagraha* protest movement.

near Gujarat to make salt, which was illegal because manufacture of salt was a government monopoly.

Another Act in 1935 allowed more Indians to vote, but still this did not satisfy Gandhi and the INC. World War II suspended the main independence drive, but by its end calls for Indian independence swelled again, with a force almost impossible for Britain to resist.

THE PARTITION OF INDIA

India, Pakistan, Bangladesh 14–15 August 1947

In 1945, the British government sent a delegation of Cabinet ministers to India to try to secure agreement between the Hindu-dominated Indian National Congress (INC; *see facing page*) and the Muslim League on terms for the country's independence. They failed, and communal tensions between Muslims and Hindus festered: on 16 August 1946, the Muslim League leader, Muhammad Ali Jinnah, organized a "Direct Action Day" in a bid to secure a separate state for Muslims. The ensuing riots led to the deaths of thousands.

The British will to remain in control of the country had by now ebbed away, and they realized that the only way they were going to be able to withdraw from India was to partition the country and transfer power to two separate

Three policemen lie injured following riots in the Punjabi city of Lahore over the decision to incorporate it within the borders of the new state of Pakistan.

governments. In July 1947, the British government passed the Indian Independence Act, ordering the demarcation of India and Pakistan.

POST-INDEPENDENCE MASSACRES

On 14–15 August 1947, the two new states gained their independence, sparking an exodus of millions of Hindus, Muslims, and Sikhs who found themselves on what they saw as the wrong side of the border. Fighting erupted between India and Pakistan over the disputed region of Kashmir. As many as two million died in the appalling carnage of inter-community violence that tarnished the first days of the infant countries.

MAHATMA GANDHI

Born in Gujarat, India, Mohandas K. Gandhi (1869–1948) studied law in London. He moved to South Africa in 1893, where he helped found the Natal Indian Congress to lobby for greater civil rights for Indians. Returning to India in 1915, he became involved in the INC. His insistence on nonviolence and a united India sometimes put him at odds with other independence leaders, but he earned the name Mahatma ("great soul") for his calm devotion to the cause. He was assassinated in 1948 by a Hindu extremist.

DECOLONIALIZATION

At the end of World War II, European powers, in particular the British, French, Portuguese, and Dutch, still controlled large colonial empires, and there was mostly no timetable for granting the colonies their independence. Yet within ten years, most of Asia – and in a further 20 years, almost all of Africa – had achieved freedom, leaving only small islands or other isolated territories under European colonial rule.

ASIAN INDEPENDENCE

In Asia, it was mostly weakening colonial control as a result of World War II that sparked independence movements, especially in India (*see p.381*). In Indochina the French struggled to beat back the rise of nationalists such as Ho Chi Minh, whose Vietminh fighters had occupied much of Vietnam. In the French Indochina War (1946–54), the French army failed to dislodge the Vietminh from the north of Vietnam, and had to accept a division of the country into communist northern and capitalist southern states (*see p.395*).

King Muhammad V of Morocco returned home from French-imposed exile late in 1955.

INDEPENDENCE FOR AFRICA

In 1956, the USA forced the French and British to back down from occupying the Suez Canal area in Egypt, and their will to hold on to their African possessions seemed to evaporate. Britain had already granted independence to Ghana in 1957, after which many former British colonies in Africa became sovereign nations: Tanganyika (now Tanzania) in 1961, Uganda in 1962, Kenya in 1963, and Zambia in 1964. Eventually only Rhodesia remained, to become Zimbabwe in 1980 (*see p.397*).

A breathtaking firework display marked the transition from British to Chinese rule in Hong Kong on the night of 30 June–1 July 1997.

Political prisoners were freed on to the streets of Ghana's capital, Accra, in 1966.

colonial authorities staged a coup to prevent a perceived "weak" French government from granting concessions to the Algerian separatist group, FLN. Although the coup was put down by General Charles de Gaulle, fighting raged on until, in 1962, Algeria achieved independence.

French colonies in Africa followed a similar path to independence, though France initially sought to impose a conditional form of freedom in which it continued to control the currency, defence, and foreign affairs of former colonies. However, full independence was granted to most colonies in 1960. Only in Algeria, with its large minority of French settlers (the *pieds noirs*), did there seem any prospect of Paris retaining control. In 1958, the French

THE LAST OUTPOSTS

Britain handed Hong Kong back to China in 1997, and the Chinese took Macao from the Portuguese in 1999. By 2000 only a handful of colonial territories worldwide were still deemed unable to govern themselves. The colonial era was at an end.

"THE WIND OF CHANGE IS BLOWING THROUGH THIS CONTINENT."

British prime minister Harold Macmillan to the South African parliament, 3 February 1960

THE BIRTH OF ISRAEL

Israel 1917–1949

From the 1880s, many Jews emigrated to Ottoman-controlled Palestine with the aim of creating a Jewish state there. This goal was given focus when the First World Zionist Congress convened in Switzerland in 1897. In 1917, the British government drew up a new policy, the Balfour Declaration, that recognized the Zionist aim of a Jewish homeland.

An ancient symbol of Judaism, the Star of David was adopted in 1948 as the emblem on the flag of the new State of Israel.

THE BRITISH MANDATE

The League of Nations granted Britain formal control of Palestine following the collapse of the Ottoman empire after World War I. However, the British struggled to reconcile the very different political agendas of Arab and Jewish groups. Jewish–Arab violence also troubled Britain's authorities, who in 1939 called the St James Conference to reconcile the two sides. This failed, and the British subsequently conceded to Arab demands for restrictions on Jewish immigration. However, Jewish fortunes were reversed when the question of allowing Jews to migrate to Israel became a moral rather than political issue following the Holocaust of World War II (*see pp.352–3*). In 1946 US president Harry S. Truman endorsed a proposal to issue 100,000 entry permits to Jews from Europe, and the British determination to hold on to

A Jewish family at a *kibbutz* (agricultural commune) near Haifa in 1948. The formation of the State of Israel fulfilled dreams of a Jewish homeland.

The bombing by Jewish extremists of Jerusalem's King David Hotel on 22 July 1946 crushed the morale of the British in Palestine.

report in August that proposed partitioning the territory into an Arab zone of some 44 per cent of the land, with a Jewish state receiving around 56 per cent. Jerusalem and Bethlehem were to remain UN-controlled in this complex, and in truth unworkable, mosaic.

CIVIL WAR

The British announced they would withdraw on 15 May 1948 and fighting erupted as the Jewish and Arab sides sought to gain control of the areas

...eir mandate cracked. A concerted ...ampaign of violence to evict the British ...om Palestine was also having its effect, ... part spearheaded by the Haganah ... the official Jewish paramilitary force – ...s well as more extremist groups such as ...gun Zvai Leumi and the Stern Gang.

...HE UNSCOP PLAN

...y February 1947 the British despaired ...f working out a plan for Palestine, and ...anded matters over to the United ...ations (UN), whose Special Committee ...n Palestine (UNSCOP) produced a

assigned to them in the plan. On 14 May, Zionist leader David Ben-Gurion declared the formation of the State of Israel, but already there was full-scale civil war. The fledgling Israeli state also beat back an invasion by six Arab countries that had intervened to support the Palestinian Arabs. By November Jewish forces had secured not only the sector assigned to them, but large additional areas. This sent a stream of at least 500,000 Arab refugees into neighbouring Arab states, where many of them and their descendants remain.

DAVID BEN-GURION

Born David Grün in Russian-controlled Poland, David Ben-Gurion (1886–1973) was involved in Zionist activities by his mid-teens. In 1906, he arrived in Palestine, establishing the first workers' agricultural commune. Deported by the Ottoman authorities in 1915, Ben-Gurion spent World War I in New York, before returning to help establish a Zionist trade union movement in Palestine. He held the office of prime minister of Israel twice (from 1948 to 1953 and from 1955 to 1963) before finally retiring from political life in 1970.

THE ARAB–ISRAELI CONFLICT

⚑ Middle East   ⌛ 1948 to present

By July 1949, Israel had signed armistice agreements with the Arab countries that had invaded in 1948 (*see p.385*), but as a result the Palestinians, who had fled their homes during the fighting, were deprived of any prospect of immediate return. In their refugee camps, mostly in Lebanon and the area on the West Bank of the Jordan, they became the responsibility

1967, a mutual defence pact between Egypt, Lebanon, and Syria looked likely to turn into an invasion of Israel, which provoked the Israelis to a pre-emptive strike. In the ensuing Six Days' War, the Israelis destroyed much of the Egyptian Air Force on the ground and made large territorial gains in the Sinai from Egypt, took much of the West Bank (including

> ## "I COME BEARING AN OLIVE BRANCH IN ONE HAND, AND THE FREEDOM FIGHTER'S GUN IN THE OTHER."
>
> Yasser Arafat, PLO chairman, November 1974

of the United Nations Relief and Works Agency (UNRWA), which operated programmes to relieve their plight.

CONTINUED FIGHTING

Bitterness between Israel and Arab countries broke out into open warfare on a number of further occasions. In 1956, the Israelis joined in the Anglo–French operation to occupy the Suez Canal after its nationalization by Egyptian president Nasser, and they briefly occupied much of the strategic Sinai Desert. In May

East Jerusalem) from Jordan, and seized parts of the Golan Heights from Syria. These areas became known as the Occupied Territories. In 1973, Egypt and Syria launched an attack on Israel on Yom Kippur – the Jewish Day of Atonement – when they knew much of the Israeli military would be at religious observances. The Arab forces made significant early advances, but the Israeli Defence Force (IDF) struck back, pushing their opponents back beyond the 1967 lines. After the conflict, Israel was left with small territorial gains in the Golan Heights; the Arabs with nothing.

THE PLO

Resorting to terrorist and guerrilla tactics, in 1964 the Palestinians founded the Palestine Liberation Organizatio

Israeli soldiers fire shells at Syrian positions on the Golan Heights during the Yom Kippur War in October 1973.

Palestinian youths confront the Israeli army, angered by a Jewish settler's massacre of 29 Arabs in the main mosque in Hebron, the West Bank, in February 1994.

LO), which for the next 40 years aimed help Palestinians realize their hopes of storing some of their 1948 losses.

Under the leadership of Yasser Arafat om 1969, the PLO sponsored guerrilla ids on Israeli and military targets. It so hijacked international aircraft and urdered members of the Israeli Olympic am at the 1972 Munich games. Setbacks curred when Jordan expelled ilitant Palestinians in 70, and when PLO hters were pushed out Lebanon in 1985–88.

Yasser Arafat led the Palestine Liberation Organization from 1969 until his death in 2004.

OVES FOR PEACE

ael evacuated the Sinai 1979 following the mp David Accords, ned by presidents dat of Egypt and Begin Israel, but hopes for nore permanent tlement proved illusory. 1987, a low-level surrection broke out nong the Palestinians in aza and in the other Occupied rritories, eventually leading the Israeli vernment to soften its reluctance to gotiate with the Palestinian leadership. his led to the Oslo Accords of ptember 1993, which allowed the

creation of a Palestinian Authority – led by Yasser Arafat – and the Palestinians' gradual assumption of power over much of the Occupied Territories.

However, opposition from extremists on both sides frittered away the chance for lasting peace. Suicide bombers from the radical Islamist Hamas movement struck several times in Israel in 1993–95, and on 4 November 1995 a Jewish extremist killed the Israeli prime minister Yitzhak Rabin. A new Palestinian *intifada*, or uprising, erupted in autumn 2000, and since then, peace processes have offered the Palestinians less and less. The Israeli government has sponsored settlements on formerly Palestinian land and built a security wall isolating those Palestinian enclaves it does not seek to control directly. Radicalism has flourished on the Palestinian side, with Hamas taking power in Gaza in 2007. The 60-year Arab–Israeli conflict looks set to continue for a long time yet.

OIL AND POLITICS

The awareness among oil-producing nations that they could use the threat of cutting off oil exports as an economic weapon became much stronger after the foundation of the State of Israel in 1948, with one major oil embargo being put into place since then. Outside powers have also sought to exert political or direct military influence over oil-producing nations in a bid to ensure vital fuel supplies.

THE 1973 OIL CRISIS

An oil embargo formed part of the Arab response to the Six Days' War with Israel in 1967 (*see p.386*), but was largely ineffective due to a lack of solidarity between the oil-producing countries. This led to the foundation, in 1968, of the Organization of Arab Petroleum Exporting Countries (OAPEC), a body whose purpose was to co-ordinate and control the use of oil as a political weapon.

The Yom Kippur War of 1973 saw OAPEC flex its political muscles for the first time, as Saudi Arabia and Egypt put an embargo on shipments of crude oil to Western nations that were providing aid to Israel; this trebled world oil prices and sent the world into recession.

US president Jimmy Carter greets Sheikh Ahmed Yamani, Saudi Arabia's Minister of Oil and an architect of the OAPEC oil embargo of 1973.

But the oil weapon has never again been used to such conspicuous effect: some members have always been tempted – by the higher profits that could be made – into sidestepping any restrictions or embargo.

In the early 21st century, control of energy reserves and the means of their transmission remains an area of supreme concern for industrialized powers. Russia (which has massive natural gas fields) has become increasingly ready to threaten to cut off supplies or raise prices to countries whose foreign policies are not to its taste.

A large queue for petrol in Nigeria, which exports most of its crude oil, leaving little for domestic use.

THE IRANIAN REVOLUTION

Iran ⚱ 1979

the 1960s, Mohammed Reza Pahlavi, ah (monarch) of Iran since 1941, nbarked on a programme of economic d social modernization, bolstered by an's vast oil reserves. In Iran's mosques, e teachings of the cleric Ayatollah ihollah Khomeini – in exile since 1964 were gaining ground. He preached an d to the Iranian monarchy, with its rceived insensitivity to traditional Shia lam, and the installation of a theocracy guided by clerics. By 1978, demonstrations against the monarchy had erupted, but were brutally suppressed by martial law.

FROM MONARCHY TO THEOCRACY

Fearing imminent revolution, the Shah fled Iran on 16 January 1979. Khomeini returned on 1 February, and a popular referendum voted for an Islamic Republic. A new constitution named Khomeini as Iran's supreme leader, and appointed clergy to run many state institutions. Relations between the new regime and the USA deteriorated sharply when the US government permitted the Shah to enter the USA for cancer treatment in October 1979. Demanding the Shah's return to Iran to face trial, student radicals invaded the US embassy in Teheran, taking 63 hostages and holding them for over a year. Thirty years later, diplomatic relations between Iran and the USA have still not been restored.

Iranian women demonstrators carry a placard bearing Ayatollah Khomeini's portrait just after his return to Teheran.

THE SOVIET INVASION OF AFGHANISTAN

🏳 Afghanistan ⏳ 1973–1988

Muhammad Zahir Shah was deposed as king of Afghanistan in a Marxist-led coup in 1973. The People's Democratic Party of Afghanistan (PDPA) government of Nur Muhammad Taraki and Hafizullah Amin then began a programme of secularization that offended conservative Muslims and brutally suppressed dissent. When 50 Russian advisors were murdered in the Afghan city of Herat, the USSR invaded to restore order on 24 December 1978. An Islamic resistance group then declared a *jihad* (holy war) against the USSR and the PDPA. These Islamist *mujahideen* guerrillas fought off the Soviet troops, and even began to threaten Soviet aircraft. The war was vastly expensive for the USSR, and, in February 1988, under firm international pressure, President Mikhail Gorbachev announced the withdrawal of Soviet troops, leaving the *mujahideen* and PDPA in a stalemate.

A Soviet-made AK-47 Kalashnikov assault rifle used by both Soviet soldiers and Afghan *mujahideen* fighters during the 1978–88 conflict in Afghanistan.

INDO–PAKISTAN WARS

🏳 India–Pakistan border ⏳ 1947–1999

When the British withdrew from India in 1947 (*see p.381*), the partition of the Indian subcontinent between India and Pakistan left a question over the future of the princely state of Kashmir and Jammu. Faced with a Pakistani invasion of Poonch, part of his territory, the maharaja appealed to India for help and Indian forces secured the capital Srinagar and eastern Kashmir. The ensuing war continued until a ceasefire was agreed in January 1949. The frontlines solidified into a "Line of Control" across which the two sides occasionally skirmished, fighting two low-level wars there (in 1968 and 1999). A major Indo–Pakistan war erupted in 1971 when the breakaway regime of East Pakistan (now Bangladesh) successfully bid for independence from the Pakistani government, with significant military assistance from India

Child refugees fleeing for safety from fighting in East Pakistan during the 1971 Indo–Pakistan war, which led to the region's independence as Bangladesh.

THE IRAN–IRAQ WAR

📍 Iran–Iraq border ⚔ 1979–1988

In 1979, Saddam Hussein (*see p.413*) became president of Iraq, following an internal coup in the ruling Ba'ath party. A man of unbridled ambition, he sought to reassert Iraq's position as a strategic power in the Gulf region. The Iraqi regime was concerned about the possibility of Iran exporting its religious revolution (*see p.389*) to Iraq's large Shia minority, while a festering dispute over territorial rights in the Shatt al-Arab waterway threatened to erupt anew.

Sensing a moment of weakness in Iran, Saddam ordered his forces across the border on 22 September 1980. The war, however, was not the walkover that he had expected. The Iranians defended fanatically, and by March 1981 the Iraqi offensive had stalled. By June 1982, the Iranians had recovered almost all the lost ground. Thereafter, however, neither side was able to deliver a knockout blow and the war degenerated into a series of offensives that gained little ground at huge cost, as well as sparking the "War of the Cities" – missile attacks on major cities. Finally, both sides accepted that neither could force a victory and agreed a ceasefire in August 1988, with little to show for the war's 1.5 million casualties.

THE FIRST GULF WAR

📍 Kuwait, Iraq ⚔ August 1990–February 1991

In August 1990, the Iraqi president Saddam Hussein invaded the small Gulf sheikhdom of Kuwait. He claimed it as a province of Iraq, with more than half an eye on the country's vast oil reserves, which might help him cover the $100 billion cost of the war with Iran in 1980–88 (*see above*). The Iraqi army faced precious little resistance to its invasion and the Kuwaiti emir fled.

As the Iraqi forces retreated from Kuwait they set off a series of fires in the oilfields, which took weeks to extinguish and caused severe environmental damage.

OPERATION DESERT STORM

The international community were not prepared to acquiesce, and a series of United Nations Resolutions demanded Iraqi withdrawal. US President George Bush (president 1989–93) built an international coalition, including many Arab countries. On 15–16 January 1991, the coalition forces launched Operation Desert Storm, an air offensive that destroyed military and strategic targets. This was followed by a massive land assault on 24 February known as Operation Desert Sabre. Within less than a week the Iraqi army had retreated from Kuwait and coalition forces had penetrated southern Iraq; then they pulled out, leaving Hussein still in power.

COMMUNIST CHINA

China ⌛ 1949–present

In October 1934, Chinese Communists, largely confined by their rivals in the nationalist KMT party to rural areas, abandoned their Jianxi base, broke through a nationalist blockade, and began the "Long March" to find a safer refuge. A trek of around 10,000km (6,200 miles) ensued, and by the time the Communists established a new headquarters at Yan'an in October 1935, only around a tenth of the 80,000 marchers survived. The Communists, now led by Mao Zedong, regrouped and in July 1946 launched a civil war to wrest control of China from the nationalists.

Despite serious initial setbacks, Mao's forces were able to recruit reinforcements and in the winter of 1947 made gains in Manchuria. The nationalists' best armies perished there and throughout 1948 were in retreat. Finally, in January 1949, Mao entered Beijing in triumph, while the remaining nationalists fled to the

Actors during the Cultural Revolution (1966–76) perform a play criticizing Confucius, who was seen as symbolic of traditional conservative thinking.

island of Taiwan to establish a Republic of China, with the aim of rivalling the Communist People's Republic of China (PRC). Initially the PRC aligned itself politically with the USSR, agreeing a Treaty of Alliance and Mutual Assistance in 1950. But in the 1960s Chinese resentment at the cost of the Korean War (*see p.394*), in which Stalin

MAO ZEDONG

Born into a peasant family in Hunan, Mao Zedong (1893–1976) moved to Beijing in 1919 and encountered communism for the first time. He joined the Chinese Communist Party at its inception in 1921 and, in 1927, led the abortive "Autumn Harvest" communist uprising. He took control of the party in 1935. His long tenure as leader of China from 1949 to 1976 left an indelible stamp on the country.

President Nixon's visit to China in 1972 was the start of an improved relationship between the USA and the communist Chinese government.

Deng Xiaoping, who introduced a series of measures aimed at turning the Chinese economy away from centralized planning, increasing the volume of foreign trade, and encouraging foreign investment into China. These new policies reaped spectacular rewards, with the Chinese economy growing at a rate often around 10 per cent each year.

When other communist regimes collapsed one by one in 1988, China experienced its own pro-democracy movement, which for a time in June 1989 seemed as if it might even dent the party's political monopoly. But Premier Li Peng ordered the army to act, and on 4 June 1989, troops opened fire on the protestors in Beijing's Tiananmen Square, killing some 400 to 800 of them. No opposition movement on a similar scale emerged again. The implicit bargain with the Chinese people became that in exchange for economic wellbeing, there would be no modification of the Communist Party's central role and that all dissent would be suppressed.

ad encouraged Chinese involvement and a territorial dispute that erupted into military clashes in March 1969 with the USSR itself – strained the relationship.

Domestically, Mao encouraged a radical programme of industrialization, in 1958 beginning the "Great Leap Forward", in which industrial and agricultural co-operatives were amalgamated into communes and industrial targets raised. At first it seemed as if China had achieved spectacular increases in output, but later evidence showed that these policies had caused disastrous famines. In 1966, the Cultural Revolution was launched, with the aim of cleansing the country of "bourgeois" influences. Children were recruited as Red Guards, and were encouraged to inform on schoolteachers and relatives who showed any signs of dissent against the regime.

After Mao's death in 1976, his wife Jiang Qing and a party faction known as the "Gang of Four" tried to seize power, but were arrested and jailed. Instead, for the following 5 years China was led by

The People's Liberation Army (PLA) is the third-largest army in the world, with over 2.25 million service personnel in its army, navy, and air forces.

THE KOREAN WAR

Korea   1950–1953

Korea, annexed by Japan in 1910, was partitioned following Japan's surrender in World War II. The division line, at latitude 38°N, was known as the "38th parallel". Soviet forces occupied land north of this line, while the US held the south. In 1949, both Soviet and US forces withdrew, and tensions between North and South Korea began to rise. Finally, on 25 June 1950, the communist leader of North Korea, Kim Il Sung, ordered an invasion of the south. A United Nations Command (UNC) made up mostly of US forces was sent to assist the south, but they and the South Korean troops were soon penned in to a small area in the southernmost tip of the peninsula. In September, General Douglas MacArthur, commander of the UNC forces, landed troops 240km (150 miles) further north at Inchon, catching the North Koreans off-guard. By October, UNC forces had crossed the 38th parallel and moved north to the Chinese border. The Chinese government quickly launched a counteroffensive, and pushed the UNC forces back south of the 38th parallel.

THE END OF THE WAR

The war dragged on for a further two years. Finally, in July 1953, the two sides signed an armistice, leaving the dividing line between the two Koreas close to the 38th parallel, more or less exactly where it had been before the war had started.

US Marines prepare to disembark at Inchon, Korea, in September 1950. The offensive drove pro-communist forces back to the Chinese border.

THE FIRST INDOCHINA WAR

Indochina   1947–1954

At the end of World War II, northern Vietnam came under the control of Ho Chi Minh's communist Vietminh movement, while the French re-established their administration over what they had named "Indochina" only in the south. Attempts to reach political accord failed; there was fierce fighting throughout 1947–48, which flared up again in 1950. The able Vietminh general Vo Nguyen Giap thwarted all French offensives and then delivered a final blow at the Battle of Dien Bien Phu, where a heavily fortified French position was overrun in May 1954.

THE GENEVA CONFERENCE

The French will to resist was shattered. On 21 July 1954, a peace conference held in Geneva agreed a formal partition of Vietnam along the 17th parallel, dividing the country between a communist north and a Western-aligned south.

THE VIETNAM WAR

⚑ Vietnam   ⌛ 1963–1973

The division of Vietnam in 1954 did not bring the country peace. Fearing the spread of communism in the region during 1955, US President Dwight Eisenhower (1890–1969) helped the anti-communist Ngo Dinh Diem to take power in the south via dubious elections, and sent the government hundreds of military advisers. The North Vietnamese reacted by encouraging those in the South who opposed Diem – the Vietcong – to take up arms against the South.

Dog tags were used by the US armed forces in Vietnam as an easy means to identify soldiers who had been killed in battle.

THE US MILITARY CAMPAIGN

The USA became drawn ever deeper into the conflict, despatching more than $500 million of US aid to South Vietnam by the end of 1963. In August 1964, US president Lyndon B. Johnson used an attack by North Vietnamese boats on a US military vessel in the Gulf of Tonkin as a pretext to authorize retaliatory raids on North Vietnam. The first US Marines arrived in South Vietnam in March 1965, and by July they exceeded 50,000. At the peak of the US deployment, in April 1969, there were 543,000 US troops in Vietnam (as well as 47,000 Australians and a New Zealand contingent). A formidable US bombing campaign, Operation Rolling Thunder, failed to dent the Vietcong resistance, and growing US casualties sapped support at home for continued involvement.

A bold series of attacks by the Vietcong on South Vietnamese cities in January 1968 (the "Tet Offensive") also unnerved the Americans, and in August 1969 they began to "Vietnamize" the conflict by withdrawing their forces. On 27 January 1973, the USA signed the Paris Peace Accord by which US forces would leave Vietnam within 60 days. Deprived of US backing, the South Vietnamese regime survived until April 1975, when the southern capital Saigon fell to the Vietminh.

The Vietnam War was the first conflict in which helicopters played an important role. Here, a US Chinook resupplies US forces.

JAPAN, CHINA, AND THE TIGER ECONOMIES

East Asia ⚊ 1945–present

After World War II, Allied forces led by US General MacArthur occupied Japan for six years. MacArthur worked with Prime Minister Shigeru Yoshida to draft a new democratic constitution for Japan and reconstruct the Japanese economy.

AN ECONOMIC MIRACLE

From the mid-1950s, the Japanese economy entered a period of rapid growth.

A Sony Walkman personal stereo is a typical product of Japanese 1970s technological innovation.

Having established heavy industries, such as coal, iron, and steel, the emphasis in Japanese industry shifted in the 1960s to specialist high-tech production, including a lucrative role in the new computing industry. The 1973 Oil Crisis (*see p.388*) caused a temporary setback, but by the 1990s Japan's economy was second in size only to that of the USA. The long economic boom came to an end in the late 1990s, as an overvalued currency and excessive lending by banks finally resulted in a dramatic slowdown that lasted more than a decade.

THE ASIAN TIGERS

From the mid-1960s, Japan's economic record had been matched by South Korea, Taiwan, Singapore, and Hong Kong – a group that was nicknamed "the tigers". In the 1990s a second wave of tigers included Thailand, Malaysia, and also China, whose rapid growth in the 1990s placed it in the first rank of world economic powers.

However, Thailand was to overstretch itself, and in 1997, foreign investors began rapidly withdrawing funds, leading to the collapse of the Thai currency. Panic in the financial sector spread to other parts of the Asian economies, as investors offloaded their Asian assets. It took some years for the tigers to recover, but they did so, confounding expectations. Unfortunately, just a decade later they were to run into the global economic storm that began in 2008.

The skyline of Pudong in China, with its modern, high-tech buildings, is a dramatic contrast to Asian cities of even a few decades earlier.

AFRICA

The modern history of most African states has been troubled. Decolonialization created nations that cut across ethnic divides, in many cases leading to civil war. Despite Africa's rich reserves of oil, diamonds, and some metals (including gold), inadequate infrastructures hampered attempts to develop modern economies, while many African leaders chose dictatorship over democracy, doing little to enable their countries to compete on the global market.

RHODESIA AND UDI

📕 Rhodesia (now Zimbabwe)   ⌛ 1962–present

In 1962 elections in Southern Rhodesia put the right-wing (pro-white) Rhodesian Front back in power. In 1964, its leader Ian Smith made a show of negotiating with Britain over independence for Rhodesia, on terms that would reflect the will of its black majority. In reality, Smith had no intention of allowing black Rhodesians any real political power, and on 11 November 1965 confronted the British with a unilateral declaration of independence (UDI).

Ian Smith gives a press conference in London shortly before the end of talks that hoped to avert UDI.

Ndabaningi Sithole, came to realize that merely lobbying for black majority rule was futile, and were prepared to fight. Smith faced a growing guerrilla insurgency, which placed enormous strain on Rhodesia's resources.

MODERN ZIMBABWE
Isolated by the collapse of Portuguese rule in Mozambique and Angola in 1973, and with the insurgency reaching the heart of the country by 1976, the Rhodesian government finally agreed to a new constitution in 1978. A moderate black nationalist faction under Bishop Abel Muzorewa took power in 1979, but elections in February 1980 returned the hard-line Robert Mugabe, by then leader of ZANU, who remained Zimbabwe's leader for the following three decades.

THE UDI REGIME
The British government instantly isolated the rebel colony, and the UN condemned the UDI as the act of "a racist minority". But despite the imposition of sanctions, Ian Smith continued to rule. African nationalist groups, notably ZANU, under

POST-COLONIAL AFRICA

⚐ Africa ⏳ 1960–present

The end of European rule in Africa left more than 50 independent countries facing myriad challenges, often exacerbated by years of colonialism or created by the legacy of the borders that colonial powers had imposed.

The advent of the Cold War (*see p.360–1*) in the 1940s had aggravated Africa's problems, as the continent became a proxy battlefield between the superpowers. In the Horn

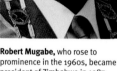

Robert Mugabe, who rose to prominence in the 1960s, became president of Zimbabwe in 1987.

of Africa, Cold War tensions exploded into open warfare, as Ethiopia saw the overthrow in 1973 of Emperor Haile Selassie by a Marxist group, the Derg, led by Colonel Mengistu Haile Mariam. With Soviet and Cuban backing, Mengistu secured most of Ethiopia. He also became involved in a war in the Ogaden Desert with Somalia in 1977, a country that then became a US ally until it dissolved into total chaos after 1991.

FAMINE AND CIVIL WAR

A growing insurgency against the Derg and the regime's policies of agricultural centralization contributed to severe famines in Ethiopia in 1984–85, in which as many as a million may have died. Climate change (*see pp.408–9*) and continued instability in the region have meant that government policy continues to be dominated by crisis responses to famine rather than long-term solutions.

Marxist groups also seized power in Angola and Mozambique after the Portuguese government abruptly decided to withdraw its colonial control in 1973.

In both cases, long-running civil war broke out. In Angola, conflict between the Marxist MPLA and the anti-communist UNITA movement of Jonas Savimbi finally ended only with Savimbi's death in 2002.

The dubious worth of Europe's legacy to Africa was demonstrated in the Belgian Congo, which achieved independence in 1960 under Patrice Lumumba, but almost instantly suffered the secession of the copper-rich province of Katanga. The Belgians sent back troops to Congo, intervening on the side of the Katangan leader Moise Tshombe, before a United Nations force displaced

Refugees of the inter-ethnic fighting in Rwanda in 1994, in which thousands of Tutsis were slaughtered. Large numbers of Hutus also died in its aftermath.

em. Out of this
ppalling mess the real
inner was Joseph
Mobutu, the army Chief
f Staff, who obtained
he presidency in 1965,
a post he held until
1997. In common with
many African dictators,
he viewed the country's
treasury as his personal
cash cow, sequestering
huge sums that impoverished his nation
through both the direct losses and the
corruption that it encouraged.

A sign warns of land mines in Mozambique, a hazard that persisted years after the end of the civil war there in 1992.

RWANDA AND ZIMBABWE

Rwanda had been French-administered
from the end of World War I to its
independence in 1964, and the colonial
regime had done nothing to ease tensions
between the two main ethnic groups:
Hutu and Tutsi. A Hutu massacre of
Tutsis in 1964 foreshadowed the genocide
of 1994, when Hutu Interahamwe
militias slaughtered some 500,000 Tutsis
as the Tutsi-led RPF fought its way to the
capital of Kigali. The RPF, led by Paul

Kagame, took power,
but many Hutus fled
to Zaire, where they
became involved in a
multi-sided civil war.

Zimbabwe had
entered independence
as one of the stronger
African economies, but it suffered a
dramatic deterioration in fortunes under
Robert Mugabe, whose regime became
increasingly autocratic. From 2000,
"veterans" of the struggle for
independence seized many white-owned
farms, crippling the agricultural economy.
By 2008, the economy was in tatters,
basic services had seized up, and inflation
reached almost unmeasurably high levels.
Mugabe and Morgan Tsvangirai, leader
of the opposition Movement for
Democratic Change, signed a power-
sharing agreement in September 2008,
but, in reality, the prospects for the
country look grim.

THE END OF APARTHEID

South Africa ⚓ 1958–1999

Dr Hendrik Verwoerd, South Africa's prime minister between 1958 and 1966, drew up the system of apartheid – an Afrikaans word meaning "separateness" – in which legalized segregation discriminated against the country's non-white population. Apartheid controlled where non-whites could live and work, as well as their movements, and denied them political rights. Initially, European powers, still the masters of colonial holdings in Africa, did nothing to oppose the inequalities this created.

In 1960 police turned their guns on a nonviolent demonstration held by the anti-apartheid group the Pan Africanist Congress (PAC) in Sharpeville, killing 69 people and injuring 180 more. The massacre triggered a shift to more militant tactics among activists. In 1961, Nelson Mandela became leader of the military wing of the African National Congress (ANC) Party, beginning a campaign of sabotage against government installations. He and other ANC members were arrested and sentenced to life imprisonment.

APARTHEID PERSISTS

As the 1970s and 1980s progressed, violence escalated and resentment grew at a system of Bantustans – impoverishe

> "NEVER, NEVER, AND NEVER AGAIN SHALL IT BE THAT THIS BEAUTIFUL LAND WILL AGAIN EXPERIENCE THE OPPRESSION OF ONE BY ANOTHER."

Nelson Mandela, 9 May 1994

NELSON MANDELA

Born in the Eastern Cape, South Africa, Nelson Rolhlahla Mandela (1918–) was an early anti-apartheid activist, and after the Sharpeville Massacre in 1960 joined in the ANC's move to a more violent struggle. He was arrested in August 1962 and served 27 years in prison. Mandela emerged in 1990 to become a powerful voice arguing for peaceful reconciliation between South Africa's communities, and served as the country's first non-white president from 1994 to 1999.

Corrugated iron shacks in the Soweto township are characteristic of the living conditions of many black South Africans during apartheid, and beyond.

nclaves to which Blacks were relocated s a substitute for any real rights. The olice force and military clamped down n dissent, habitually violating human ghts. A series of anti-government riots, hich began in Soweto in June 1976, nded 16 months later after between 00 and 700 people had been killed.

Two events weakened South frica's position. First, its hodesian allies lost power in 979 (*see p.397*) and second, in 986, the international ommunity imposed conomic sanctions on ie country. Yet still the overnment shied away om real reform.

HE END OF APARTHEID

took a new government dministration to open ie way for change. In 989, the country elected W. de Klerk as president, nd he soon lifted bans on the ANC and ther opposition groups. On 11 February 990, Nelson Mandela was released from ie Robben Island prison where he had een held since 1963 and, setting aside ny bitterness from nearly 30 years of

South Africa's ANC flag displays a spear – a symbol of resistance to colonial and apartheid rule.

incarceration, he began talks with the de Klerk government on ways to achieve a transition to Black majority rule. There were grave obstacles, including the question of how to reconcile different views from political and tribal factions among the Black community, and strong opposition to change from many Whites.

A Convention for a Democratic South Africa met on 20 December 1991 to thrash out the issues, and a referendum among Whites in March 1992 – which delivered a 68-per-cent vote for change – bolstered de Klerk.

After 11 months of hiatus, negotiations resumed in March 1993 and finally, on 26–28 April 1994, South Africa held its first-ever elections open to universal suffrage. On 10 May 1994, Nelson Mandela became President of South Africa, a post he held until 1999, as the last vestiges of the apartheid system were swept away.

Of South Africa's **22.7 million** registered voters, some 19.7 million voted in the national elections on 26–28 April 1994; a turnout of 86 per cent, which caused massive queues in many areas. The ANC, as expected, was the overwhelming winner, receiving 62.6 per cent of the vote.

NEW CHALLENGES

In the early 1990s, following the collapse of communism and the end of the Cold War, it seemed for some that "history had ended" and the world had overcome the challenges it once faced. Yet soon, the advent of dangerous new diseases, an awareness of impending environmental disaster, and the rise of radical Islamic international terror networks – combined with a resurgence of more old-fashioned political problems – created a challenging environment for 21st-century governments.

BIOTECHNOLOGY

⚑ Global   ☆ 1945–present

The founding of the United Nations Food and Agriculture Organization (FAO) in 1945 signalled an international desire to enhance crops and eradicate hunger. In 1960, the International Rice Research Institute was established in the Philippines to improve rice production. Its work has helped rice farmers to increase output by an average of 2.5 per cent each year since 1965. Known as the Green Revolution, this transformation has gone a long way to support the burgeoning population of less developed countries.

GM FOODS AND CLONING
In the 1990s, scientists developed the technique of Genetic Modification (GM) to alter plants' genetic material and so create crops with better disease and pest resistance. In late 1996 and early 1997, it emerged that the US company Monsanto had been shipping soya containing GM material to European ports, resulting in a storm of controversy and strong public fears in Europe about

Scientists tend to a greenhouse of GM crops. The problem of cross-contamination of non-GM crops by pollen from GM crops has caused great controversy.

the long-term effects of consuming GM foods. In February 1997, a sheep ("Dolly") that had been grown from an adult sheep cell (or cloned) was born, giving rise to concerns that the science of biotechnology had far outrun any consideration of the ethical aspects of such manipulations.

MEDICAL ADVANCES AND NEW DISEASES

Global   1967–present

The past century has produced astonishing advances in medicine, most notably the discovery of penicillin – the first antibiotic – by Alexander Fleming in 1928. By the 1950s, antibiotics were being used to provide treatments for many killer diseases, such as syphilis and tuberculosis.

ADVANCES AND CHALLENGES

Scientists pushed forward other medical boundaries, too. In 1967, surgeons carried out the first successful human heart transplant. However, while some infectious diseases were eradicated (the last recorded case of naturally occurring smallpox was in Somalia in 1977), many old killers, such as cholera and typhoid, have persisted in

Since the early 1990s, the red ribbon has become a symbol for HIV/AIDs awareness.

A doctor in Kenya vaccinates a small child. Programmes of mass vaccination have played a key role in reducing the spread of infectious diseases.

underdeveloped countries. As many as 40,000 people a day die from diseases caught by drinking water contaminated by sewage.

THE RISE OF "NEW" DISEASES

The sexually transmitted disease AIDS, caused by the HIV virus, was first identified among homosexual men in the USA in 1981. HIV spread globally, and by 2007, AIDS had caused 2.1 million deaths worldwide, with a further 33 million people infected with HIV. Outbreaks of the acute respiratory disease SARS in 2002–03, and Mexican "swine 'flu", a strain of the influenza virus that crossed over from pigs to humans in 2009, have provoked fears that it is only a matter of time before a pandemic occurs on the scale of the "Spanish Flu" that killed up to 20 million people just after World War I.

GLOBALIZATION

The increasing interconnectedness of the world economy, with multinational companies cutting across many different jurisdictions, has been termed "globalization". Global consumption of uniform products has led to concerns about the erosion of different cultures and the fear that individual governments have become almost powerless in comparison to the enormous power wielded by global corporations.

THE GROWTH OF GLOBAL TRADE

The process of globalization has, in once sense, been going on ever since agricultural villages began trading with more distant neighbours in the Neolithic age. The events of the mid- to late 20th century, however, were of an entirely different order. In 1944, representatives of 45 nations met at Bretton Woods in the USA to establish the International Monetary Fund (IMF) to increase world trade through co-operation between nations. It was a first sign that the world needed an international approach to tackle the globalization of the world economy.

Barcodes first appeared on products in the USA in 1974, and are now a powerful tool for tracking goods as they make their way across the world.

From the 1980s onwards, many governments began to liberalize their economies, privatizing state assets and encouraging "open" competitive markets. The volume of goods traded worldwide each year in the early 21st century was approximately 16 times larger than that in 1950. Global bodies such as the World

A car lot outside a Toyota factory near Derby, UK. The Japanese car company began assembling vehicles overseas in 1964.

Trade Organization – established in 1995, and with 153 member countries by 2008 – set ground rules for international trade and solved disputes between governments. The idea behind these organizations was that easier international trade would result in greater growth in the world economy and greater prosperity for its people. The advent of the Internet and digital communications from the 1990s added new dimensions to the world's economic infrastructure, making international trade quicker and more efficient and the exchange of information almost instantaneous.

A McDonald's restaurant in Kuwait City. The "golden arches" are a potent symbol of globalization.

ANTI-GLOBALIZATION

However, globalization has potentially negative effects, too. Multinational companies can shift production to countries where labour costs are lower or health-and-safety legislation is less stringent, cutting their costs and increasing profits. By the 21st century many service jobs – such as those in customer service call centres – had been transferred from high-cost Western countries to lower-wage developing countries. Moves such as this have led to an anti-globalization movement, protesting at international agreements that appear to ignore the interests of people in both industrialized and developing nations. Consistent growth since World War II, the protestors argued, had come at the cost of causing long-term economic, social, and environmental disaster.

Globalization, though, no matter the violent protests against it, now seems an unstoppable phenomenon. The question may not be how to halt it, but rather how best to manage it.

CLIMATE CHANGE AND THE GREEN MOVEMENT

Global   1988–present

Since the Industrial Revolution (*see pp.288–9*), average global temperatures have risen by about 0.8°C (1.44°F). This warming has accelerated in the last four decades, so that between 1995 and 2007 the world experienced ten of the warmest years on record. Many experts believe human activity is to blame for this change in the Earth's climate, and are calling for urgent action to prevent a global crisis and protect the planet for future generations.

A recycling symbol, a sign of increasing efforts worldwide to reduce the burden of waste.

THE GREENHOUSE EFFECT
The Intergovernmental Panel on Climate Change (IPCC) was set up in 1988 to investigate climate change. In 2007, the IPCC produced a report that projected rises in temperature of between 1.8 and 4°C (3.2 and 7.2°F) by the end of the 21st century. The report concluded that a raised atmospheric concentration of the gas carbon dioxide (CO_2) has intensified a natural phenomenon known as the "Greenhouse Effect". This is a process by which the surface and atmosphere of the Earth are warmed as heat radiation from the sun is absorbed by "greenhouse" gases, including methane and CO_2. This effect is magnified as the climate of the Earth changes, because the warming oceans are less able to remove CO_2 from the atmosphere. Increasing industrialization has caused a rapid acceleration in the production of CO_2 emissions. Coal-burning power stations generate CO_2, as do air, sea, and road traffic; for example,

"FUTURE GENERATIONS MAY WELL HAVE OCCASION TO ASK THEMSELVES, 'WHAT WERE OUR PARENTS THINKING?' "

Al Gore, *An Inconvenient Truth*, 2006

Wind turbines can generate electricity with comparatively little impact on the environment.

Each of the 232 million cars in the USA produces more than five tonnes of the gas each year.

There are several signs that global warming is starting to severely impact upon our environment, such as a dramatic retreat of glaciers in non-polar regions, a diminution in sea ice around the Arctic, and a break-up of many ice shelves in the Antarctic. Changes in rainfall patterns in many regions of the world – tens of millions suffered from drought in Africa in the 1980s – and an increase in the number of severe weather events, such as hurricanes, floods, and droughts, are believed to be a result of climate change.

EXTINCTIONS AND DEFORESTATION

Many animal species are now in danger of extinction. The World Conservation Union (WCU) considers 688 African fish, bird, and mammal species to be under threat – 201 of them "critically endangered". This situation has been aggravated by habitat loss, caused not only by the expansion of human populations into new areas – a process promoted by overpopulation – but also by environmental degradation caused at least in part by climate change. The world's tropical forests play an important part in holding back global warming too, as they "inhale" CO_2. Yet many of these forests are in retreat, having become the victims of over-logging or simply clearance for agricultural expansion.

THE GREEN MOVEMENT

Many fear that climate change is becoming irreversible, though there is much lobbying for social change to help slow the trend, and perhaps even reverse it. Investment is increasing in renewable sources of energy, such as tidal, wind, and solar power; and in many developed economies, there is a push for consumers to recycle goods.

Many policy makers continue to dispute the findings of global-warming experts, or at least shy away from radical action that might alienate them from their electorates. Yet without urgent action, an increasing consensus believes that climate change will produce an environmental catastrophe.

As rainfall levels have fallen in many areas, desertification – encroachment by deserts – has become an increasing problem.

THE COMMUNICATIONS REVOLUTION

🏴 Global ⌛ 1958–present

Since World War I, advances in technology have transformed global communications and transport systems. A journey that once took weeks by land or sea can now be made by air in hours, while huge amounts of data can be transmitted almost instantaneously across the world, at the click of a computer mouse.

The Apple iPhone, released in 2007, put computer-processing power into a mobile handset.

ROAD AND AIR TRAVEL

The 20th-century boom in travel was largely a result of advances in engine technology that permitted ever more powerful automobiles. Global statistics predict that by 2030 there will be 1.2 billion motor vehicles in use worldwide, operating on a network of roads that cross the land throughout the globe. More dramatic still has been the explosive growth in air travel since World War II, reaching almost 4.5 billion passengers in 2008. In the Classical era,

travelling from Rome to London would have taken weeks and enormous expense, but in the 21st century the journey can be made by air in fewer than three hours and for less than a day's average wage in either country.

THE REBIRTH OF COMMUNICATION

By the early 20th century, technological advances were making it possible to exchange messages instantly across the world by radio and telephone (see pp.292–3). Then, in 1958, the development of the microchip dramatically transformed the world of communications. Microchips provide the "brains" for computers, personal communications, and cellular phones, allowing the storage and transmission of vast amounts of data, often merely at the touch of a button. A precursor of the Internet became operational in 1969, and the World Wide Web was made available to the public in 1991; while the first mobile telephone network went live in Chicago, USA, in 1978. Both of these innovations have given citizens global communications tools of previously unimaginable scope and power.

Mobile phone technology provides communication to remote villages where the cost of installing fixed telephone cables is prohibitive.

9/11

⚑ Global   ⚏ 1958–present

On 11 September 2001, Islamic extremists launched successful attacks on the World Trade Center in New York City and the Pentagon in Washington DC.

THE USA UNDER ATTACK

At 8:46am American Airlines Flight 11 crashed into the World Trade Center's north tower, followed by an attack on the south tower just 16 minutes later by a hijacked United Airlines Flight 175. In all, more than 2,500 people died. Then, at 9:37am, American Airlines Flight 77 crashed into the Pentagon, killing a further 184 people, and at 10:03am another 40 died when United Airlines Flight 93, probably bound for the Capitol Building or the White House in Washington DC, ploughed into a field near Shanksville, Pennsylvania.

OSAMA BIN LADEN

From a wealthy Saudi Arabian family, Osama bin Laden (1957–) joined the *mujahideen* fight in Afghanistan in the 1980s (*see p.390*). Around 1988 he founded al-Qaeda ("the base"), using extreme terror to oppose US policy toward Muslims.

There had never been such a damaging terrorist attack on US soil. The attackers had used comparatively simple methods – knives and the threat of bombs – to take over the aircraft, but the logistics of the operation were well thought out and clearly required months of planning. It took very little time for the prime suspect to emerge as al-Qaeda, an extremist Islamic terrorist network with bases in Afghanistan, led by Osama bin Laden.

"TODAY, OUR FELLOW CITIZENS, OUR WAY OF LIFE, OUR VERY FREEDOM, CAME UNDER ATTACK."

President George W. Bush, 11 September 2001

Smoke billows out from the World Trade Center, New York City, after the al-Qaeda terrorist attack on 11 September 2001.

THE AFGHAN WAR

Afghanistan   October 2001–present

The withdrawal of Soviet troops from Afghanistan in 1988 (*see p.390*) was followed by a bitter civil war, as the *mujahideen* commanders fought for control of the country. In reaction to this chaos, a new political faction arose, the Taleban (meaning "students"), who originated in the *madrassas* (religious schools) of the conservative southern province of Kandahar. From August 1994, the Taleban militia won victory after victory, finally capturing the Afghan capital Kabul in September 1996.

The Taleban, under their leader Mullah Omar, instituted a regime of harsh Islamic rigour, gravely curtailing the rights of women and banning activities such as the playing of music or kite-flying, with

Taleban fighters near Kabul in February 1995, after their rapid advance northwards from Kandahar.

severe (including capital) punishment for offenders. Only in the north of the country did a Northern Alliance resist, but they controlled only 10 per cent of Afghanistan by 2000. From 1997, the Taleban regime played host to the al-Qaeda movement of Osama bin Laden (*see p.411*), which used its Afghan safe haven as a base to plan terrorist attacks against US interests.

THE US CAMPAIGN IN AFGHANISTAN

Once it became clear that al-Qaeda had carried out the 9/11 attacks against the USA (*see p.411*), the US government demanded that the Taleban hand over Osama bin Laden. Mullah Omar refused and on 7 October the Americans began to bomb Afghan cities. The Americans also started to provide military aid to the Northern Alliance, who began an offensive southwards. The Taleban, faced with US carpet-bombing, largely melted away. Kabul fell on 13 November and the Taleban stronghold of Kandahar at the end of the month. However, Osama bin Laden and much of the al-Qaeda leadership managed to slip away.

THE TALEBAN RETURN

Despite the subsequent despatch of a multinational armed force to stabilize the country, the Taleban regrouped. The new Afghan government of Hamid Karzai wavered between supporting international offensives against the resurgent Taleban and seeking compromise with more moderate elements.

By 2009, large rural areas of southern Afghanistan were again under Taleban rule, hundreds of the international force had been killed, and peace for Afghanistan seemed ever distant.

THE WAR IN IRAQ

🏴 Iraq   ⏳ March 2003–present

From 1993, the Iraqi president Saddam Hussein had been forced to allow the United Nations (UN) to inspect his armaments industries to ensure he did not acquire "weapons of mass destruction" (WMD), such as nuclear, chemical, or biological weaponry. US President George W. Bush (president 2001–09) exploited Saddam's often patchy compliance with this directive, encouraging the international community throughout late 2002 to pressure the Iraqi government to come clean about its weapons stocks. Saddam blustered, realizing too late that Bush had boxed him into a corner.

The Americans were unable to secure a definitive UN resolution authorizing force, but maintained that previous resolutions contained implicit approval

Flames light up Baghdad on the second night of the US bombing of the Iraqi capital on 23 March 2003, an attack the Americans described as "shock and awe".

for military action. On 20 March 2003, US air strikes against Baghdad began. In contrast to the first Gulf War (*see p.391*), a land attack began almost immediately, with US-led coalition forces landing near the southern port of Basra on 22 March. As the invasion force pushed northwards, many Iraqi units failed to resist or melted away and the USA took Baghdad on 9 April, with the last major city, Tikrit, falling four days later.

IRAQ AFTER THE WAR

Postwar Iraq descended into chaos, with the breakout of an insurgency against US occupation, mostly by Sunni Muslims, that killed hundreds of US soldiers. The previously supportive Shia population turned against the coalition, too, and a vicious set of civil wars erupted between the two communities, with the loss of thousands of lives. In 2009, the US government announced its intention to withdraw its forces by August 2010, leaving the Iraqi government to rebuild a nation in which the bitterness of the post-war violence had made communal harmony almost impossible to achieve.

SADDAM HUSSEIN

A member of the Iraqi Ba'ath party from 1957, Saddam Hussein (1937–2006) played a key role in the coup that brought the party to power in 1968. He ruled Iraq from 1979 with brutal force at home and abroad. The Americans toppled him in 2003.

BEYOND THE NATION STATE

As early as the 1920s, there was an awareness that the world's nations needed a more international approach to policy making to avoid the kind of tensions that had led to World War I. Despite this knowledge, the League of Nations, which first met in 1920, failed the challenge of keeping the peace, while its successor, the United Nations, was hampered by the outbreak of the Cold War in the late 1940s.

FAILED STATES AND TERRORISM

When the Cold War (*see pp.360–61*) ended in the 1990s, many saw it as heralding the "End of History" or a "New World Order", both notions that proved hugely over-optimistic. Nation states with widely varying political traditions could not – or refused to – impose Western democratic systems; while others simply fell apart either as a result of years of misrule or because funding to their governments was removed when they were no

The Taj Mahal hotel in Mumbai, India, was targeted during the terrorist attacks on the city in November 2008.

longer required as Cold War allies. The phenomenon of "failed states" (such as Somalia) arose; in such nations, no effective government exists, leading to civil war and warlordism. Enforcing world norms (such as the repression of piracy) is simply impossible on a failed state's national territory.

The world has faced the growth of a new sort of international terrorism, exemplified by al-Qaeda, whose agenda is not a nationalistic one (such as that of the IRA for a united, independent Ireland, or ETA for

Somali children line up for a meal at a refugee centre. In 2007, there were an estimated 31.7 million refugees worldwide.

Bill Gates (left) and Warren Buffett (right) have given a total of over $52 billion in aid for health and education. Private funding plays a growing role in world development.

Basque independence in northern Spain), but aims instead to establish its own new (Islamic) world order. Incidents such as the 9/11 attack on the USA (*see p.411*), or the 2008 attacks on hotels in Mumbai in India, demonstrated a threat that – because it was able to undermine the safety of a huge number of countries – could not be dealt with by one nation acting alone.

WORLD PROBLEMS WITH GLOBAL SOLUTIONS

The leaders of the 21st century face challenging problems. Large-scale population shifts – such as the vast numbers of migrants seeking to enter the European Union illegally from African countries – as well as climate change, threaten the livelihoods of millions. Globalization is increasing the interdependence of the world economy, so that a fiscal crisis in one country can soon translate into factory closures or banking chaos in another, as happened in 2008–09.

If the most powerful countries can set aside their individual self-interests, or if global bodies such as the UN can forge an international consensus to address these problems, then the 21st-century world may avoid crises far more profound and devastating than those of the previous century. The alternative is a situation in which non-state bodies, such as regional alliances, global corporations, and terrorist groups, set the political agenda in a world far less stable than the one we know.

DIRECTORY

KINGS & RULERS

Whether leadership is achieved through heredity, democracy, or sheer brute force, leaders make decisions that determine how history will judge their time in power. Great leaders have been the salvation of their people, while weak leaders have been responsible for bringing mighty empires to their knees.

LONGEST-REIGNING MONARCHS			
NAME	**PLACE**	**DATES OF REIGN**	**DURATION**
Pepi II	New Kingdom Egypt	2278–2184 BCE	94 years
Taejo	Koguryo (Korea)	53–146 CE	93 years
Sobhuza	Swaziland	1899–1982	83 years
Jangsu	Koguryo (Korea)	413–91 CE	78 years
Tai Wu	China (Shang Dynasty)	1486–1411 BCE	75 years
Louis XIV	France	1643–1715	72 years
Trieu Vu Vuong	Vietnam	207–136 BCE	71 years
Johannes II	Liechtenstein	1858–1929	70 years
Pandukhabaya	Rajarata (Sri Lanka)	437–367 BCE	70 years
Shapur II	Sassanid Persia	309–79 CE	70 years
Ponhea Yat	Khmer Empire (Cambodia)	1393–1463	70 years
Kinich Yanab Pakal	Palenque	615–83	68 years
Franz Josef I	Austria–Hungary	1848–1916	68 years
Rameses II	New Kingdom Egypt	1279–1213 BCE	66 years
Ferdinand III	Sicily	1759–1825	65 years
Sultan Ibrahim	Johor (Malaysia)	1895–1959	64 years
Amoghavarsha	Rashtrakuta Empire (India)	814–78	64 years
Victoria	United Kingdom	1837–1901	63 years
James I	Aragon	1213–76	63 years
Bhumibol Adulyadej (Rama IX)	Thailand	1946–	63 years (as of 2009)
Hirohito	Japan	1926–89	62 years
Kangxi	China (Qing Dynasty)	1661–1722	61 years
Saqr bin Mohammad al-Qassimi	Ras Al Khaimah (United Arab Emirates)	1948–	61 years (as of 2009)

Emperor Kangxi – who ascended to the throne at the age of seven – was the architect of one of the greatest periods of Chinese expansion during his 61-year reign.

EGYPTIAN PHARAOHS

PERIOD	DYNASTY	NOTABLE PHARAOHS
Early Dynastic Period (2920–2649 BCE)	1st dynasty (2920–2770 BCE)	Narmer
		Menes (Aha)
		Den
	2nd dynasty (2770–2649 BCE)	Peribsen
Old Kingdom (2649–2150 BCE)	3rd dynasty (2649–2575 BCE)	Djoser (2630 BCE-2611 BCE)
	4th dynasty (2575–2465 BCE)	Snefru (2575–2551 BCE)
		Khufu (Cheops) (2551–2528 BCE)
		Menkaure (Mycinerus) (2490–2472 BCE)
		Shepseskaf (2472–2467 BCE)
	5th dynasty (2465–2323 BCE)	Userkaf (2465–2458 BCE)
		Sahure' (2458–2446 BCE)
		Neuserre' (2416–2392 BCE)
		Djedkare' (2388–2356 BCE)
		Wenis (Unas) (2356–2323 BCE)
	6th dynasty (2323–2150 BCE)	Teti (2323–2291 BCE)
		Pepi I (2289–2255 BCE)
		Merenre (2255–2246 BCE)
		Pepi II (2246–2152 BCE)
First Intermediate Period (2150–2040 BCE)	7th & 8th dynasties (2150–2134 BCE)	Numerous ephemeral kings, as central authority collapsed
	9th & 10th dynasties (2134–2040 BCE)	Power struggle between minor rulers of Upper and Lower Egypt
	11th dynasty (at Thebes) (2134–2040 BCE)	Inyotef II (2118–2069 BCE)
		Mentuhotep II (2061–2040 BCE)
Middle Kingdom (2040–1640 BCE)	11th dynasty (all Egypt) (2040–1991 BCE)	Mentuhotep II (2040–2010 BCE)
		Mentuhotep III (2010–1998 BCE)
		Mentuhotep IV (1998–1991 BCE)
	12th dynasty (1991–1783 BCE)	Amenemhet I (1991–1962 BCE)
		Senwosret I (1971–1926 BCE)
		Amenemhet II (1929–1892 BCE)
		Senwosret III (1878–1841 BCE)
		Amenemhet IV (1799–1787 BCE)
	13th dynasty (1783–c.1640 BCE)	Minor rulers
	14th dynasty (c.1730–c.1640 BCE)	Minor rulers
Second Intermediate Period (1640–1532 BCE)	15th dynasty (Hyksos) (1640–1532 BCE)	Apophis (c.1585–c.1542 BCE)
	16th dynasty (1640 –1532 BCE)	Minor Hyksos rulers contemporary with the 15th dynasty
	17th dynasty (at Thebes) (1640–1550 BCE)	Kamose (1555–1550 BCE)

EGYPTIAN PHARAOHS (continued)

PERIOD	DYNASTY	NOTABLE PHARAOHS
New Kingdom (1550–1070 BCE)	18th dynasty (1550–1307 BCE)	Ahmose (1550–1525 BCE)
		Amenophis I (1525–1504 BCE)
		Tuthmosis I (1504–1492 BCE)
		Tuthmosis II (1492–1479 BCE)
		Tuthmosis III (1479–1425 BCE)
		Hatshepsut (1473–1458 BCE)
		Amenophis II (1427–1401 BCE)
		Tuthmosis IV (1401–1391 BCE)
		Amenophis III (1391–1353 BCE)
		Amenophis IV/Akhenaten (1353–1335 BCE)
		Smenkhare (1335–1333 BCE)
		Tutankhamun (1333–1323 BCE)
		Ay (1323–1319 BCE)
		Horemheb (1319–1307 BCE)
	19th dynasty (1307–1196 BCE)	Rameses I (1307–1306 BCE)
		Seti I (1306–1290 BCE)
		Rameses II (1290–1224 BCE)
		Merneptah (1224–1214 BCE)
	20th dynasty (1196–1070 BCE)	Rameses III (1194–1163 BCE)
		Rameses V (1156–1151 BCE)
		Rameses XI (1100–1070 BCE)
Third Intermediate Period (1070–712 BCE)	21st dynasty (1070–945 BCE)	Smendes (1070–1044 BCE)
		Psusennes I (1040–992 BCE)
		Osorkon I (984–978 BCE)
		Psusennes II (959–945 BCE)
	22nd dynasty (945–712 BCE)	Shoshenq I (945–924 BCE)
		Osorkon II (924–909 BCE)
		Shoshenq III (835–783 BCE)
		Osorkon V (735–712 BCE)
	23rd dynasty (c.828–712 BCE) 24th dynasty (724–712 BCE) 25th dynasty (770–712 BCE)	Competing lines of lesser rulers at Hermopolis Magna, Leontopolis, and Tanis
Late Period (712–332 BCE)	25th dynasty (Nubia and all of Egypt) (712–657 BCE)	Shabaqa (712–698 BCE)
		Taharqa (690–664 BCE)
	26th dynasty (672–525 BCE)	Necho I (672–664 BCE)
		Psammetichus I (664–610 BCE)
		Apries (589–570 BCE)

An ornament from Tutankhamun's tomb featuring the scarab beetle, symbol of resurrection, and the protective Eye of Horus.

In 525 BCE Egypt was conquered by the Persian king Cambyses, and, apart from a brief period when native Egyptian rulers regained power, remained part of the Persian empire until 332 BCE when it was conquered by Alexander the Great. In 30 BCE it became part of the Roman empire.

ROMAN EMPERORS

In 27 CE Octavian, on becoming Rome's first emperor, renamed himself Gaius Julius Caesar Augustus, and from then on Roman emperors took the honorific title Augustus for the duration of their reign. Until 286 CE this was normally a title unique to one individual, but there were periods of joint rule, usually when the imperial succession was disputed, or the emperor's nominated heir was too young to rule alone following his predecessor's death. However, the emperor Diocletian instigated a different system, the Tetrarchy, under which four individuals ruled the empire, two as Augustus, and two as Caesar – a kind of "junior emperor". This use of titles persisted until 395 CE, when the eastern and western portions of the empire split from each other permanently.

NAME	REIGN	NAME	REIGN
Augustus	27 BCE–14 CE	Pertinax	193 CE
Tiberius	14–37 CE	Didius Julianus	193 CE
Gaius Caligula	37–41 CE	Septimius Severus	193–211 CE
Claudius	41–54 CE	Caracalla (co-Augustus 198–211)	198–217 CE
Nero	54–68 CE	Geta (co-Augustus)	209–11 CE
Galba	68–69 CE	Macrinus	217–18 CE
Otho	69 CE	Diadumenianus (co-Augustus)	218 CE
Vitellius	69 CE	Elagabalus	218–22 CE
Vespasian	69–79 CE	Alexander Severus	222–35 CE
Titus	79–81 CE	Maximinus Thrax	235–38 CE
Domitian	81–96 CE	Gordian I & Gordian II	238 CE
Nerva	96–98 CE	Pupienus & Balbinus	238 CE
Trajan	98–117 CE	Gordian III	238–44 CE
Hadrian	117–38 CE	Philip I	244–49 CE
Antoninus Pius	138–61 CE	Philip II (co-Augustus)	247–49 CE
Marcus Aurelius	161–80 CE	Decius	249–51 CE
Lucius Verus (co-Augustus)	161–69 CE	Herennius Etruscus (co-Augustus)	251 CE
Commodus	180–92 CE		

The Roman amphitheatre at El Djem, in modern Tunisia, was built during the rule of the provincial governor Gordian, who became emperor in 238 CE.

ROMAN EMPERORS (continued)

NAME	REIGN	NAME	REIGN
Trebonianus Gallus	251–53 CE	Severus (Caesar 305–06, co-Augustus 306–07)	306–07 CE
Hostilianus (co-Augustus)	251 CE		
Volusianus (co-Augustus)	251–53 CE	Licinius	308–24 CE
Aemilianus	253 CE	Maximin Daia (Caesar 305–10, co-Augustus 310–13)	310–13 CE
Valerian	253–60 CE		
Gallienus (co-Augustus 253–60)	253–68 CE	Constantine I (Augustus 306, Caesar 306–07, co-Augustus 307–24)	306–37 CE
Claudius Gothicus	268–70 CE		
Quintillus	270 CE		
Aurelian	270–75 CE	Constantine II (Caesar 317–37, co-Augustus 337–40)	337–40 CE
Tacitus	275–76 CE		
Florian	276 CE	Constantius II (Caesar 324–37, co-Augustus 337–50)	337–61 CE
Probus	276–82 CE		
Carus	282–83 CE	Constans (Caesar 333–37, co-Augustus 337–50)	337–50 CE
Numerian	283–84 CE		
Carinus (co-Augustus 283–84)	283–85 CE	Julian (Caesar 355–60)	360–63 CE
Diocletian	284–305 CE	Jovian	363–64 CE
Maximian (Caesar 285–86, co-Augustus 286–305)	286–305 CE	Valentinian I (co-Augustus)	364–75 CE
		Valens (co-Augustus)	364–78 CE
Constantius I Chlorus (Caesar 293–305, co-Augustus 305–06)	305–06 CE	Gratian (co-Augustus)	367–83 CE
		Valentinian II (co-Augustus)	375–92 CE
Galerius (Caesar 293–305, co-Augustus 305–11)	305–11 CE	Theodosius I (co-Augustus 379–92)	379–95 CE

WESTERN EMPIRE

NAME	REIGN	NAME	REIGN
Honorius	395–423 CE	Libius Severus	461–65 CE
Constantius III (co-Augustus)	421 CE	Anthemius	467–72 CE
Valentinian III	424–55 CE	Olybrius	472 CE
Petronius Maximus	455 CE	Glycerius	473–74 CE
Avitus	455–56 CE	Julius Nepos	474–75 CE
Majorian	457–61 CE	Romulus Augustulus	475–76 CE

EASTERN EMPIRE

NAME	REIGN	NAME	REIGN
Arcadius	395–408 CE	Leo I	457–74 CE
Theodosius II (co-Augustus 405–08)	405–50 CE	Zeno (deposed)	474–75 CE
		Basiliscus	475–77 CE
Marcian	450–57 CE		

BYZANTINE EMPERORS

NAME	REIGN	NAME	REIGN
Zeno	477–91	Nicephorus II Phocas	963–69
Anastasius	491–518	John I Tzimisces	969–76
Justin	518–27	Basil I "the Bulgar-slayer"	976–1025
Justinian	527–65	Constantine VIII (co-emperor to 1025)	976–1028
Justin II	565–78		
Tiberius II	578–82	Romanus III Argyrus	1028–34
Maurice	582–602	Michael IV the Paphlagonian	1034–41
Phocas	602–10	Michael V Calaphates	1041–42
Heraclius	610–41	Constantine IX Monomachus	1042–55
Heraclonas	641	Zoe (co-ruler as Empress)	1042–50
Constantine III	641	Theodora (sole ruler as Empress)	1055–56
Constans II	641–68		
Constantine IV	668–85	Michael VI Stratioticus	1056–57
Justinian II (deposed)	685–95	**COMNENID DYNASTY**	
Leontius	695–98	Isaac I Comenus	1057–59
Tiberius III	698–705	**DUCID DYNASTY**	
Justinian II (restored)	705–11	Constantine X Ducas	1059–67
Philippicus	711–13	Romanus IV Diogenes	1068–71
Anastasius II	713–15	Michael VII Ducas	1071–78
Theodosius III	715–17	Nicephorus III Botaniates	1078–81
Leo III the Isaurian	717–41	**COMNENID DYNASTY**	
Constantine V Copronymos	741–75	Alexius I Comnenus	1081–1118
Leo IV	775–80	John II	1118–43
Constantine VI	780–97	Manuel I	1143–80
Irene (Empress)	797–802	Alexius II	1180–83
Nicephorus I	802–11	Andronicus I	1183–85
Stauracius	811	**ANGELID DYNASTY**	
Michael I	811–13	Isaac II Angelus	1185–95
Leo V the Armenian	813–20	Alexius III	1195–1203
Michael II	820–29	Isaac II (restored)	1203–04
Theophilus	829–42	Alexius IV (co-Emperor)	1203–04
Michael III	842–67	Alexius V Mourzouphlos	1204
MACEDONIAN DYNASTY		**LASCARID DYNASTY (AS EMPERORS OF NICAEA)**	
Basil I the Macedonian	867–86	Theodore I Lascaris	1204–22
Leo VI ("the Wise")	887–912	John III Vatatzes	1222–54
Alexander	912–13	Theodore II	1254–58
Constantine VII Porphyrogenitus	912–59	John IV	1258–61
		PALAEOLOGID DYNASTY	
Romanus I Lecapenus (co-Emperor)	919–44	Michael VIII (to 1261 as Emperor of Nicaea)	1259–82
Romanus II	959–63	Andronicus II	1282–1328

BYZANTINE EMPERORS (continued)

NAME	REIGN	NAME	REIGN
Michael IX (co-Emperor)	1293–1320	John V (restored)	1379–91
Andronicus III	1328–41	Manuel II	1391–1425
John V	1341–76	John VII (regent)	1399–1402
John VI (co-Emperor)	1347–54	John VIII	1425–48
Andronicus IV	1376–79	Constantine XI	1448–53

OTTOMAN EMPERORS

NAME	REIGN	NAME	REIGN
Osman I	1299–1326	Murad IV	1623–40
Orkhan	1326–59	Ibrahim	1640–48
Murad I	1359–89	Mehmet IV	1648–87
Bayezid I	1389–1403	Suleyman III	1687–91
Suleyman I (rival claimant)	1403–10	Ahmad II	1691–95
Mehmet I (rival claimant to 1410)	1403–21	Mustafa II	1695–1703
		Ahmad III	1703–30
Murad II	1421–44	Mahmud I	1730–54
Mehmet II	1444	Osman III	1754–57
Murad II (restored)	1444–51	Mustafa III	1757–74
Mehmet II (restored)	1451–81	'Abdul Hamid I	1774–89
Bayezid II	1481–1512	Selim III	1789–1807
Selim I the Grim	1512–20	Mustafa IV	1807–08
Suleyman II the Magnificent	1520–66	Mahmud II	1808–39
Selim II	1566–74	'Abdul–Majid I	1839–61
Murad III	1574–95	'Abdul–'Aziz	1861–76
Mehmet III	1595–1603	Murad V	1876
Ahmad I	1603–17	'Abdul–Hamid II	1876–1909
Mustafa I	1617–18	Mehmet V	1909–18
Osman II	1618–22	Mehmet VI	1918–22
Mustafa I (restored)	1622–23	'Abdul-Majid II (caliph)	1922–24

The Ottoman emperor Bayezid II (seated, far right) gave sanctuary to Jews exiled by the Spanish Inquisition.

RULERS OF THE HOLY ROMAN EMPIRE

NAME	REIGN	NAME	REIGN
Charlemagne	800–14	**HOHENSTAUFEN DYNASTY**	
Louis I	814–40	Conrad III	1138–52
Lothair I	840–55	Frederick I Barbarossa	1155–90
Louis II	855–75	Henry VI	1191–97
Charles II	875–77	Philip of Swabia	1198–1208
Charles III	884–87	**GUELPH DYNASTY**	
Guy of Spoleto	891–94	Otto IV of Saxony	1209–15
Lambert of Spoleto	894–96	**HOHENSTAUFEN DYNASTY**	
Arnulf	896–99	Frederick II	1215–50
Louis III	899–911	Conrad IV	1250–54
Berengar I	915–24	William of Holland	1254–56
OTTONIAN SAXON DYNASTY		Alfonso X of Castile	1267–73
Conrad I of Franconia	911–18	Rudolf I of Habsburg	1273–91
		Adolf of Nassau	1292–98
Henry I the Fowler	919–36	Albert I of Austria	1298–1308
Otto I the Great	962–73	Henry VII	1312–13
Otto II	973–83	Louis IV of Wittelsbach	1328–47
Otto III	996–1002	Charles IV of Luxemburg	1347–78
Henry II Of Saxony	1014–24	Wenzel of Luxemburg	1378–1400
SALIAN FRANKISH DYNASTY		Rupert II of the Palatinate	1400–10
Conrad II of Franconia	1027–39	Sigismund of Luxemburg	1433–37
		HABSBURG DYNASTY	
Henry III	1046–56	Albert II	1437–39
Henry IV	1084–1105	Frederick II of Styria	1440–93
Henry V	1111–25	Maximilian I	1493–1519
SUPPLINGBURGER DYNASTY		Charles V	1519–56
Lothair III	1133–37	Ferdinand I	1556–64
		Maximilian II	1564–76
		Rudolf II	1576–1612
		Matthias	1612–19
		Ferdinand II of Styria	1619–37
		Ferdinand III	1637–58
		Leopold I	1658–1705
		Charles VI	1711–40
		WITTELSBACH DYNASTY	
		Charles VII of Bavaria	1742–45
		HABSBURG-LORRAINE DYNASTY	
		Francis I	1745–65
		Joseph II	1765–90
		Leopold II	1790–92
		Francis II	1792–1806

The double-headed eagle became the central motif of the Holy Roman Empire with the accession of the Austrian Habsburg Dynasty.

EMPERORS OF AUSTRIA

NAME	REIGN	NAME	REIGN
Francis (Holy Roman Emperor Francis II)	1804–35	Franz Joseph	1848–1916
		Charles	1916–18
Ferdinand	1835–48		

KINGS OF PRUSSIA

NAME	REIGN	NAME	REIGN
Frederick I	1701–13	Frederick William III	1797–1840
Frederick William I	1714–40	Frederick William IV	1840–61
Frederick II the Great	1740–86	William I	1861–71
Frederick William II	1786–97	(from 1871 German Emperor)	

EMPERORS OF GERMANY

NAME	REIGN	NAME	REIGN
William I (King of Prussia)	1871–88	Frederick	1888
		William II (Kaiser Wilhelm)	1888–1918

William II (centre), the last German emperor, abdicated after his country's defeat in World War I. He died in exile in the Netherlands in 1941.

KINGS OF SARDINIA

NAME	REIGN	NAME	REIGN
Victor Amadeus II	1718–30	Charles Felix	1821–31
Charles Emmanuel III	1730–73	Charles Albert	1831–49
Victor Amadeus III	1773–96	Victor Emmanuel II	1849–61
Charles Emmanuel IV	1796–1802	(from 1861 King of Italy)	
Victor Emmanuel I	1802–21		

KINGS OF ITALY

NAME	REIGN	NAME	REIGN
Victor Emmanuel II (of Sardinia)	1861–78	Victor Emmanuel III	1900–46
		Umberto II	1946
Umberto I	1878–1900		

KINGS OF FRANCE

After the fall of Rome, a number of barbarian groups vied for power in Gaul. The Franks, led by the Merovingian ruler Childeric, emerged victorious, uniting France under Childeric's son Clovis. On Clovis's death his kingdom was partitioned between his four sons and their descendants until Pepin, first of the Carolingians, was anointed king of all the Franks by Pope Zachary in 751.

NAME	REIGN	NAME	REIGN
MEROVINGIAN DYNASTY		Childeric III	743–51
Childeric I	c.457–81	**CAROLINGIAN DYNASTY**	
Clovis I	481–511	Pepin the Short	751–68
Theoderic I (Rheims)	511–34	Charlemagne (Charles I)	768–814
Chlodomir (Orléans)	511–24	Carloman (co-ruler)	768–71
Childebert (Paris)	511–58	Louis I the Pious	814–40
Chlotar I (Soissons)	511–61	Charles II the Bald	840–77
Theudebert I (Austrasia)	534–48	Louis II the Stammerer	877–79
Theodebald (Austrasia)	548–55	Louis III	879–82
Charibert I (Paris)	561–67	Carloman II	879–84
Guntram (Burgundy)	561–92	Charles the Fat	884–87
Sigebert (Metz)	561–75	Odo	887–98
Chilperic I (Soissons)	561–84	Charles III the Simple	898–923
Childebert II (Austrasia)	575–95	Robert I	922–23
Chlotar II (Soissons; sole king 613–23)	584–629	Raoul	923–36
		Louis IV	936–54
Theudebert II (Austrasia)	595–612	Lothair	954–86
Theoderic II (Burgundy; Austrasia 612–13)	595–613	Louis V	986–87
		CAPETIAN DYNASTY	
Dagobert I (Austrasia 623–34, Neustria 629–39)	623–39	Hugh Capet	987–96
		Robert II the Pious	996–1031
Charibert II (Aquitaine)	629–32	Henry I	1031–60
Sigebert II (Austrasia)	634–59	Philip I	1060–1108
Clovis II (Neustria and Burgundy)	639–57	Louis VI the Fat	1108–37
		Louis VII the Young	1137–80
Dagobert II (Austrasia)	659–61	Philip II Augustus	1180–1223
Chlotar III (Neustria)	657–73	Louis VIII	1223–26
Childeric II (Austrasia)	661–75	Louis IX the Saint	1226–70
Theoderic III (Neustria; Austrasia)	673–90	Philip III the Bold	1270–85
		Philip IV the Fair	1285–1314
Dagobert II (Austrasia)	676–79	Louis X	1314–16
Clovis III	690–954	John I	1316
Childebert III	685–711	Philip V	1316–22
Dagobert III	711–15	Charles IV the Fair	1322–28
Chilperic II (Neustria)	715–21	**HOUSE OF VALOIS**	
Chlotar IV (Austrasia)	718–19	Philip VI the Fortunate	1328–50
Theoderic IV	721–37	John II the Good	1350–64

KINGS OF FRANCE (continued)

The arrest, trial, and execution of Louis XVI during the French Revolution marked a turning point in European history.

NAME	REIGN	NAME	REIGN
Charles V the Wise	1364–80	Louis XIV	1643–1715
Charles VI	1380–1422	Louis XV	1715–74
Charles VII	1422–61	Louis XVI	1774–92
Louis XI	1461–83	**FRENCH REPUBLIC**	1792–1804
Charles VIII	1483–98	**FIRST EMPIRE**	
HOUSE OF VALOIS		Napoleon I (Bonaparte)	1804–14, 1815
Louis XII	1498–1515	**HOUSE OF BOURBON**	
Francis I	1515–47	Louis XVII	1814–15, 1815–24
Henry II	1547–59		
Francis II	1559–60	Charles X	1824–30
Charles IX	1560–74	**HOUSE OF BOURBON–ORLÉANS**	
Henry III	1574–89	Louis–Philippe	1830–48
HOUSE OF BOURBON		**SECOND FRENCH REPUBLIC**	1848–52
Henry IV of Navarre	1589–1610	**SECOND EMPIRE**	
Louis XIII	1610–43	Napoleon III	1852–70

DUKES OF NORMANDY

NAME	REIGN	NAME	REIGN
Rolf Ganger	911–32	Robert II	1087–1106
William I	932–42	Henry I (of England)	1106–35
Richard I	942–96	Stephen	1135–44
Richard II	996–1027	Geoffrey of Anjou	1144–50
Richard III	1027–28	Henry II (of England)	1150–89
Robert I	1028–35	Richard IV (I of England)	1189–99
William II (I of England)	1035–87	John (of England)	1199–1204

KINGS AND QUEENS OF SPAIN

The northern Spanish kingdoms of Castile and Leon were joined by marriage in 1037, and were formally united in 1230. In 1469, Isabella of Castile married Ferdinand of Aragon, and when both succeeded to their respective thrones, they united their domains to form the Kingdom of Spain.

KINGS AND QUEENS OF CASTILE–LEON

NAME	REIGN	NAME	REIGN
Ferdinand I	1037–65	Ferdinand IV	1295–1312
Sancho II	1065–72	Alfonso XI	1312–50
Alfonso VI	1065–1109	Peter the Cruel	1350–66
Urraca	1109–26	Henry II	1366–67
Alfonso VII	1126–57	Peter the Cruel (restored)	1367–69
Sancho III (Castile)	1157–58	Henry II (restored)	1369–79
Ferdinand II (Leon)	1157–88	John I	1379–90
Alfonso VIII (Castile)	1158–1214	Henry III	1390–1406
Alfonso IX (Leon)	1188–1230	John II	1406–54
Henry I (Castile)	1214–17	Henry IV	1454–74
Ferdinand III (Castile, Leon from 1230)	1217–52	Isabella	1474–1504
		Joanna	1504–16
Alfonso X the Wise	1252–84	Philip I	1504–06
Sancho IV	1284–95	Ferdinand V (II Of Aragon)	1506–16

KINGS OF ARAGON

NAME	REIGN
Ramiro I	1035–63
Sancho	1063–94
Peter I	1094–1104
Alfonso I	1104–34
Ramiro II	1134–37
Petronilla	1137–62
Alfonso II	1162–96
Peter II	1196–1213
James I the Conqueror	1213–76
Peter III	1276–85
Alfonso III	1285–91
James II	1291–1327
Alfonso IV	1327–36
Peter IV	1336–87
John I	1387–95
Martin	1395–1410
Ferdinand	1412–16
Alfonso V	1416–58
John II	1458–79
Ferdinand II (V of Castile)	1479–1516

Ramiro I, the illegitimate son of Sancho II of Navarre, inherited the county of Aragon, which was to expand into a major Iberian kingdom.

KINGS AND QUEENS OF SPAIN (continued)

KINGS AND QUEENS OF UNITED SPAIN

NAME	REIGN	NAME	REIGN
HABSBURG DYNASTY		**HOUSE OF BONAPARTE**	
Charles I	1516–56	Joseph Bonaparte	1808–13
Philip II	1556–98	**BOURBON DYNASTY**	
Philip III	1598–1621	Ferdinand VII (restored)	1813–33
Philip IV	1621–65	Isabella II	1833–68
Charles II	1665–1700	**HOUSE OF SAVOY**	
BOURBON DYNASTY		Amadeus of Savoy	1870–73
Philip V	1700–24	**FIRST SPANISH REPUBLIC**	1873–74
Luis	1724	**BOURBON DYNASTY**	
Philip V (restored)	1724–46	Alfonso XII	1874–85
Ferdinand VI	1746–59	Alfonso XIII	1886–1931
Charles III (of Naples)	1759–88	**SECOND SPANISH REPUBLIC**	1931–39
		FRANCOIST SPAIN	1939–75
Charles IV	1788–1808	**BOURBON DYNASTY**	
Ferdinand VII	1808	Juan Carlos	1975–

KINGS AND QUEENS OF PORTUGAL

NAME	REIGN	NAME	REIGN
Henry of Burgundy (count)	1097–1112	Philip II (III of Spain)	1598–1621
Afonso I (count until 1139)	1112–85	Philip III (IV of Spain)	1621–40
Sancho I	1185–1211	**BRAGANZA DYNASTY**	
Afonso II	1211–23	John IV	1640–56
Sancho II	1223–46	Afonso VI	1656–83
Afonso III	1246–79	Peter II	1683–1706
Diniz	1279–1325	John V	1706–50
Afonso IV	1325–57	Joseph	1750–77
Pedro I	1357–67	Maria	1777–1816
Ferdinand	1367–83	Peter III (co-ruler)	1777–86
AVIZ DYNASTY		John VI	1816–26
John I	1385–1433	Peter IV	1826
Edward	1433–38	Maria II	1826–28
Afonso V	1438–81	Miguel	1828–34
John II	1481–95	Maria II (restored)	1834–53
Manuel I	1495–1521	Peter V	1853–61
John III	1521–57	Luis	1861–89
Sebastian	1557–78	Charles	1889–1908
Henry	1578–80	Manuel II	1908–10
HABSBURG DYNASTY			
Philip I (II of Spain)	1580–98		

KINGS AND QUEENS OF ENGLAND

NAME	REIGN	NAME	REIGN
HOUSE OF WESSEX		**Stephen**	1135–41
Egbert	802–39	**Matilda**	1141
Ethelwulf	839–55	**Stephen (restored)**	1141–54
Ethelbald	855–60	**HOUSE OF PLANTAGENET**	
Ethelbert	860–66	Henry II of Anjou	1154–89
Ethelred I	866–71	Richard I the Lionheart	1189–99
Alfred the Great	871–99	John	1199–1216
Edward the Elder	899–925	Henry III	1216–72
Athelstan	925–39	Edward I	1272–1307
Edmund	939–46	Edward II	1307–27
Edred	946–55	Edward III	1327–77
Edwy	955–59	Richard II	1377–99
Edgar	959–75	**HOUSE OF LANCASTER**	
Edward the Martyr	975–78	Henry IV Bolingbroke	1399–1413
Ethelred II the Unready	978–1013	Henry V	1413–22
HOUSE OF DENMARK		Henry VI	1422–61
Sweyn Forkbeard	1013–14	**HOUSE OF YORK**	
HOUSE OF WESSEX		Edward IV	1461–70
Ethelred II (restored)	1014–16	**HOUSE OF LANCASTER**	
Edmund Ironside	1016	Henry VI (restored)	1470–71
HOUSE OF DENMARK		**HOUSE OF YORK**	
Canute	1016–35	Edward IV (restored)	1471–83
Harold I Harefoot	1035–40	Edward V	1483
Harthacnut	1040–42	Richard III	1483–85
HOUSE OF WESSEX		**HOUSE OF TUDOR**	
Edward the Confessor	1042–66	Henry VII	1485–1509
Harold II Godwinson	1066	Henry VIII	1509–47
HOUSE OF NORMANDY		Edward VI	1547–53
William I the Conqueror	1066–87	Mary I	1553–58
William II Rufus	1087–1100	Elizabeth I	1558–1603
Henry I	1100–35	**HOUSE OF STUART**	
		James I (VI of Scotland)	1603–25
		Charles I	1625–49
		COMMONWEALTH (REPUBLIC)	1649–60
		HOUSE OF STUART	
		Charles II	1660–85
		James II	1685–88
		William III	1689–1702
		Mary II (co-ruler)	1689–94
		Anne (of Great Britain from 1707)	1702–14

The Crown of Mary of Modena, Queen Consort of James II.

KINGS AND QUEENS OF SCOTLAND

NAME	REIGN	NAME	REIGN
HOUSE OF ALPIN		Alexander III	1249–86
Kenneth MacAlpin (of Dalriada)	843–58	Margaret of Norway	1286–1300
		HOUSE OF BALLIOL	
Donald I	858–62	John Balliol	1292–90
Constantine I	862–77	**HOUSE OF BRUCE**	
Aed	877–78	Robert I the Bruce	1306–29
Eochaid	878–89	David II	1329–71
Donald II	889–900	**HOUSE OF STUART**	
Constantine II	900–42	Robert II	1371–90
Malcolm I	942–54	Robert III	1390–1406
Indulf	954–62	James I	1406–37
Dubh	962–66	James II	1437–60
Culen	966–71	James III	1460–88
Kenneth II	971–95	James IV	1488–1513
Constantine III	995–97	James V	1513–42
Kenneth III	997–1005	Mary I (Queen of Scots)	1542–67
Malcolm II	1005–34	James VI (I of England from 1603)	1567–1625
HOUSE OF DUNKELD			
Duncan I	1034–40		
Macbeth	1040–57		
Lulach	1057–58		
Malcolm III Canmore	1058–93		
Donald III Bane	1093–94		
Duncan II	1094		
Donald III Bane (restored)	1094–97		
Edgar	1097–1107		
Alexander I	1107–24		
David I	1124–53		
Malcolm IV	1153–65		
William the Lion	1165–1214		
Alexander II	1214–49		

Mary Stuart was only six days old when her father James V died, making her queen of Scotland.

KINGS AND QUEENS OF GREAT BRITAIN

NAME	REIGN	NAME	REIGN
HOUSE OF HANOVER		**HOUSE OF SAXE–COBURG–GOTHA**	
George I	1714–27	Edward VII	1901–10
George II	1727–60	**HOUSE OF WINDSOR**	
George III	1760–1820	George V	1910–36
George IV	1820–30	Edward VIII	1936
William IV	1830–37	George VI	1936–52
Victoria	1837–1901	Elizabeth II	1952–

HIGH KINGS OF IRELAND

NAME	REIGN	NAME	REIGN
Niall Noigiallach	376–405	Sechnassach	665–69
Niath Í	405–28	Cenn Faelad	670–73
Loeguire	428–58	Finsnechta Fledach	674–93
Ailill Molt	459–78	Lingsech mac Oengus	694–701
Lugaid mac Loeguiri	479–503	Congal Cennmagair	702–08
Muirchertach mac Erca	504–27	Fergal Mac Maele Duin	709–18
Tuathal Maelgarb	528–38	Fogartach mac Neill	719
Diarmait mac Cerbrbel	539–58	Cinaed mac Irgalaig	720–22
Domhnall Ilchegach and Fearghus of Ailech	559–61	Flaighbertach mac Loingsig	723–29
		Aed Allan mac Fergal	730–38
Eochaid of Ailech and Baetan mac Ninnid	562–63	Domnall Midi	739–58
		Nial Frossach	759–65
Ainmuire mac Setnae	564–66	Donnchad Midi	766–92
Baetan mac Ninnedo	567	Aed Ordnide	793–817
Aed mac Ainmuire	568–94	Conchobar mac Donnchada	818–31
Aed Slaine and Colman Rimid	595–600	Nial Caille	832–46
Aed Uaridnach	601–07	Mael Sechnaill I mac Maele Ruaniad	846–60
Mael Coba mac Aed	608–10		
Suibne Menn	611–23	Aed Finliath	861–76
Domnall mac Aed	624–39	Flann Sinna	877–914
Cellach and Conall Cael	640–56	Niall Glundub	915–17
Diarmait mac Aed and Blathmac mac Aed	657–64	Donnchad Donn	918–42
		Congalach Congba	943–54
		Domnall Ua Neill	955–78
		Mael Sechnaill II mac Domnaill	979–1002
		Brian Boruma (Boru)	1002–14
		Mael Sechnaill II mac Domnail (restored)	1014–22
		Unrecorded high kings	1022–72
		Tairrdelbach Ua Briain (Turlough O'Brian)	1072–86
		Muirchetrach Ua Briain (Murtough O' Brian)	1086–1119
		Domnall Ua Lochlain (Donnell O'Loughlin) (rival claimant)	1090–1121
		Tarrdelbach Ua Conchobar (Turlough O'Connor)	1119–56
		Muirchertach mac Lochlainn (Murtough MacLoughlin)	1156–66
		Ruadri Ua Conchobar (Rory O'Connor)	1166–83

The assassination of Brian Boru (right), an Irish national hero, led to the restoration of Mael Sechnaill II as the High King of Ireland in 1014.

RULERS OF RUSSIA

NAME	REIGN	NAME	REIGN
RURIKID DYNASTY		**SHUISKII DYNASTY**	
PRINCES OF MOSCOW		Vasili IV	1606–10
Daniel	1283–1303	**ROMANOV DYNASTY**	
Yuri	1303–25	Michael	1613–45
Ivan I	1325–40	Alexei	1645–76
Simeon the Proud	1340–53	Feodor III	1676–82
Ivan II	1353–59	Ivan V	1682–96
GRAND PRINCES OF MOSCOW–VLADIMIR		Peter I the Great (emperor from 1721)	1696–1725
Dmitri Donskoi	1359–89		
Vasili I	1389–1425	Catherine I	1725–27
Vasili II the Blind	1425–62	Peter II	1727–30
Ivan III the Great	1462–1505	Anna	1730–40
Vasili III	1505–33	Ivan VI	1740–41
TSARS OF RUSSIA		Elizabeth	1741–62
Ivan IV The Terrible (tsar from 1547)	1533–84	Peter III	1762
		Catherine II the Great	1762–96
Feodor I	1584–98	Paul I	1796–1801
GODUNOV DYNASTY		Alexander I	1801–25
Boris Godunov	1598–1605	Nicholas I	1825–55
Feodor II	1605	Alexander II	1855–81
Dimitri II	1605–06	Alexander III	1881–94
		Nicholas II	1894–1917

Grand Prince Dimitri Donskoi was blessed by Saint Sergius before marching to war against the Mongols at the Battle of Kulikovo in 1380.

EMPERORS OF CHINA

NAME	REIGN	NAME	REIGN
QIN DYNASTY		Zhongzong	684
Qin Shi Huangdi	221–210 BCE	Ruizong	684–90
Er Shi	210–207 BCE	Wu Zetian	690–705
WESTERN HAN DYNASTY		Zhongzong (restored)	705–10
Gaodi	206–195 BCE	Ruizong (restored)	710–12
Huidi	195–188 BCE	Xuangzong	712–56
Lu Hou (regent)	188–180 BCE	Suzong	756–62
Wendi	180–157 BCE	Daizong	762–79
Jingdi	157–141 BCE	Dezong	779–805
Wudi	141–87 BCE	Shunzong	805
Zhaodi	87–74 BCE	Xianzong	805–20
Xuandi	74–49 BCE	Muzong	820–24
Yuandi	49–33 BCE	Jingzong	824–27
Chengdi	33–7 BCE	Wenzong	827–40
Aidi	7–1 BCE	Wuzong	840–46
Pingdi	1 BCE–6 CE	Xuanzong	846–59
Ruzi	7–9 CE	Yizong	859–73
HSIN DYNASTY		Xizong	873–88
Wang Mang	9–23 CE	Zhaozong	888–904
EASTERN HAN DYNASTY		Aidi	904–07
Guang Wudi	25–57 CE	**FIVE DYNASTIES AND TEN KINGDOMS PERIOD**	907–60
Mingdi	57–75 CE		
Zhangdi	75–88 CE	**NORTHERN SONG DYNASTY**	
Hedi	88–106 CE	Taizu	960–76
Shangdi	106 CE	Taizong	976–97
Andi	106–25 CE	Zhenzong	998–1022
Shundi	125–44 CE	Renzong	1022–63
Chongdi	144–45 CE	Yingzong	1064–67
Zhidi	145–46 CE	Shenzong	1068–85
Huandi	146–68 CE	Zhezong	1086–1101
Lingdi	169–89 CE	Huizong	1101–25
Xiandi	189–220 CE	Qinzong	1126
PERIOD OF DISUNITY	220–581 CE	**SOUTHERN SONG DYNASTY**	
SUI DYNASTY		Gaozong	1127–62
Wendi	581–604	Xiazong	1163–90
Yangdi	604–17	Guangzong	1190–94
Gongdi	617–18	Ningzong	1195–1224
TANG DYNASTY		Lizong	1225–64
Gaozu	618–26	Duzong	1265–74
Taizong	626–49	Gongzong	1275
Gaozong	649–83	Duanzong	1276–78

EMPERORS OF CHINA (continued)

Thirteen of the Ming dynasty emperors are buried in a magnificent tomb complex near their capital, Beijing.

NAME	REIGN	NAME	REIGN
Bing Di	1279	Chenghua	1464–87
YUAN DYNASTY		Hongzhi	1487–1505
Shizu (Kublai Khan)	1279–94	Zhengde	1505–21
Chengzong (Temur Oljeitu)	1294–1307	Jiajing	1521–67
Wuzong (Khaishan)	1308–11	Longqing	1567–72
Renzong (Ayrbarwada)	1311–20	Wanli	1572–1620
Yingzong (Shidebala)	1321–23	Taichang	1620
Taiding (Yesun Temur)	1323–28	Tiangqi	1620–27
Wenzong (Tugh Temur)	1328–29	Chongzhen	1628–44
Mingzong (Khoshila)	1329	**QING DYNASTY**	
Wenzong (restored)	1329–32	Shunzhi	1644–61
Shundi (Toghon Temur)	1332–68	Kangxi	1661–1722
MING DYNASTY		Yongzheng	1722–35
Hongwu	1368–98	Qianlong	1735–96
Jianwen	1399–1402	Jiajing	1796–1820
Yongle	1403–24	Daoguang	1820–50
Hongxi	1425	Xianfeng	1850–61
Xuande	1426–35	Tongzhi	1861–75
Zhengtong	1436–49	Guangxu	1875–1908
Jingtai	1449–57	Puyi	1908–11
Zhengtong (restored)	1457–64		

INDIAN RULERS

The Indian subcontinent has seen the rise and fall of many kingdoms and empires. The Mauryan empire encompassed almost all of South Asia; the Gupta empire formed a wide band across northern India; while the Chola empire stretched across Southeast Asia. At their height, the Muslim Delhi Sultanate and Mughal empire controlled virtually all of modern India and Pakistan.

MAURYA EMPIRE (321–180 BCE)

NAME	DATE	NAME	DATE
Chandragupta Maurya	321–297 BCE	Salisuka	215–202 BCE
Bindusara	297–272 BCE	Devadharma	202–195 BCE
Ashoka	272–232 BCE	Satamdhanu	195–187 BCE
Dasaratha	232–224 BCE	Brihadratha	187–180 BCE
Samprati	224–215 BCE		

GUPTA INDIA (c.275–550 CE)

NAME	DATE	NAME	DATE
Gupta	c.275–300 CE	Kumaragupta II	c.467–77 CE
Ghatotkacha	c.300–20 CE	Budhagupta	c.477–95 CE
Chandragupta I	c.320–50 CE	Chandragupta III	c.495–500 CE
Samudragupta	c.350–76 CE	Vainyagupta	c.500–15 CE
Chandragupta II	c.376–415 CE	Narasimhagupta	c.515–30 CE
Kumaragupta	c.415–55 CE	Kumaragupta III	c.530–40 CE
Skandagupta	c.455–67 CE	Vishnugupta	c.540–50 CE

CHOLA INDIA (c.846–1279)

NAME	DATE	NAME	DATE
Viyayalaya	c.846–71	Aditya II (co-ruler)	957–69
Aditya I	c.871–907	Madurantaka Uttama	973–85
Parantaka I	907–53	Rajaraja I	985–1016
Rajaditya I (co-ruler)	947–49	Rajendra I	1016–44
Gandaraditya	953–57	Rajadhiraja I	1044–54
Arinjaya (co-ruler)	956–57	Rajendra II	1054–64
Parantaka II	957–73	Raja Mahendra (co-ruler)	1060–63
		Virarajendra	1064–69
		Adirajendra	1069–70
		Rajendra III Kulottunga Chola	1070–1122
		Vikrama Chola	1122–35
		Kulottunga Chola II	1135–50
		Rajaraja II	1150–73
		Rajadhiraja II	1173–79
		Kulottunga III	1179–1218
		Rajaraja III	1218–46
		Rajendra IV	1246–79

Chola king Rajaraja I built the great temple of Brihadisvara at Thanjavur in southern India.

INDIAN RULERS (continued)

DELHI SULTANATE (1206–1526)

NAME	DATE	NAME	DATE
SLAVE MAMLUK DYNASTY		**TUGHLUQID DYNASTY**	
Aibak	1206–10	Tughluq I	1321–25
Aran Shan	1210–11	Muhammad II	1325–51
Iltutmish	1211–36	Firuz Shah III	1351–88
Firuz Shah	1236	Tughluq II	1388–89
Radiyya Begum	1236–40	Abu Bakr	1389–90
Bahram Shah	1240–42	Muhammad III	1390–94
Mas'ud Shah	1242–46	Sikandar I	1394
Mahmud Shah	1246–66	Mahmud II	1394–13
Balban	1266–87	Daulat Khan Lodi	1413–14
Kai-Qubadh	1287–90	**SAYYID DYNASTY**	
Kayumarth	1290	Khidr Khan	1414–21
KHALJI DYNASTY		Mubarak II	1421–34
Firuz Shah II	1290–96	Muhammad IV	1434–45
Ibrahim I	1296	Alam Shah	1445–51
Muhammad I	1296–1316	**LODI DYNASTY**	
'Umar	1316	Bahlul Lodi	1451–89
Mubarak I	1316–20	Sikandar II	1489–17
Khusraw	1320	Ibrahim II	1517–26

MUGHAL EMPIRE (1526–1858)

NAME	DATE	NAME	DATE
MUGHAL DYNASTY		Bahadur Shah I	1707–12
Babur	1526–30	'Azim-ush-Sha'n	1712
Humayun	1530–40	Jahandar Shah	1712–13
SURID DYNASTY		Farrukhsiyar	1713–19
Shir Shah Sur	1540–45	Rafi' ud-Darajat	1719
Islam Shah	1545–53	Shah Jahan II	1719
Muhammad 'Adil	1553–55	Nikusiyar	1719
Ibrahim III	1555	Muhammad Ibrahim	1719–48
Sikandar III	1555–56	Ahmad Shah	1748–54
MUGHAL EMPERORS		Alamgir II	1754–59
Humayun (restored)	1555–56	Shah Alam II	1759–88
Akbar I the Great	1556–1605	Baidar Bakht	1788
Jahangir	1605–27	Shah Alam II (restored)	1788–1806
Shah Jahan I	1628–58	Akbar II	1806–37
Aurangzeb	1658–1707	Bahadur Shah II	1837–58
Azam Shah	1707		

INCA EMPERORS

NAME	REIGN
Manco Capac	c.1100
Sinchi Roca	unknown
Lloque Yupanqui	unknown
Mayta Capac	unknown
Capac Yupanqui	c.1200
Inca Roca	unknown
Inca Yupanqui	unknown
Viracocha	unknown
Inca Urco	1438
Pachacuti	1438–71
Tupac Yupanqui	1471–93
Huayna Capac	1493–1526
Huascar	1526–32
Atahuallpa	1530–33
Tupac Hualpa	1533
Manco Inca Yupanqui	1533–45
Sayri Tupac	1545–60
Titu Cusi Yupanqui	1560–71
Tupac Amaru	1571–72

Atahuallpa, Inca emperor of Peru, was captured by the Spanish conquistador Francisco Pizarro, who executed him for heresy against Christianity.

AZTEC EMPERORS

NAME	REIGN	NAME	REIGN
Acampichtli	1372–91	Tizoc	1481–86
Huitzilihuitl	1391–1415	Ahuitzotl	1486–1502
Chimalpopoca	1415–26	Moctezuma II Xocoyotzin	1502–20
Itzcoatl	1426–40	Cuitlahuac	1520
Moctezuma I Ilhuicamina	1440–68	Cuauhtemoc	1520–21
Axayacatl	1468–81		

A relief carving shows the feathered serpent deity, Quetzalcoatl, descending between Aztec year-symbols. These, when decoded, enabled rulers' reigns to be dated.

PRESIDENTS OF THE UNITED STATES OF AMERICA

NAME	TERM	NAME	TERM
George Washington	1789–97	Benjamin Harrison	1889–93
John Adams	1797–1801	Grover Cleveland	1893–97
Thomas Jefferson	1801–09	William McKinley	1897–1901
James Madison	1809–17	Theodore Roosevelt	1901–09
James Monroe	1817–25	William Howard Taft	1909–13
John Quincy Adams	1825–29	Woodrow Wilson	1913–21
Andrew Jackson	1829–37	Warren G. Harding	1921–23
Martin Van Buren	1837–41	Calvin Coolidge	1923–29
William Henry Harrison	1841	Herbert Hoover	1929–33
John Tyler	1841–45	Franklin D. Roosevelt	1933–45
James Knox Polk	1845–49	Harry S. Truman	1945–53
Zachary Taylor	1849–50	Dwight D. Eisenhower	1953–61
Millard Fillmore	1850–53	John F. Kennedy	1961–63
Franklin Pierce	1853–57	Lyndon B. Johnson	1963–69
James Buchanan	1857–61	Richard Nixon	1969–74
Abraham Lincoln	1861–65	Gerald Ford	1974–77
Andrew Johnson	1865–69	James ("Jimmy") Carter	1977–81
Ulysses S. Grant	1869–77	Ronald Reagan	1981–89
Rutherford B. Hayes	1877–81	George H. W. Bush	1989–93
James A. Garfield	1881	William ("Bill") Clinton	1993–2001
Chester A. Arthur	1881–85	George W. Bush	2001–09
Grover Cleveland	1885–89	Barack Obama	2009–

Theodore Roosevelt, the 26th president of the USA, was an extremely popular political figure, affectionately nicknamed "Teddy" by the public.

WARS & BATTLES

The human story is one of conflict. Disputes over territory, religion, and governance have escalated into war throughout history, and while the stories of great battles and great commanders make compelling reading, the tragic consequences of war should never be forgotten.

ADVANCES IN MILITARY TECHNOLOGY

The earliest spears and bows were used to hunt food, but humans soon turned their weapons against each other in intertribal conflict. From these early beginnings, advances in military technology have shaped the way peoples and nations wage war against each other.

INVENTION	DATE	INVENTION	DATE
Wheeled chariot	c.3500 BCE	Periscope	1854
Flamethrower	c.650	Breech-loading artillery; hand-rotating machine-gun	1859
Stirrup	c.700		
Crossbow	c.1100	Magazine rifle	1860
Longbow	c.1150	Anti-aircraft gun	1870
Gunpowder	c.1040	Cordite	1875
Rockets	c.1250	Semi-automatic machine-gun	1885
Cannon (at Battle of Crécy)	1345	Armoured car	1899–1901
Hand-held firearms	c.1350	Plastic explosive	1899
Matchlock firing mechanism	c.1425	Rigid airship	1900
Mortar	1451	Dreadnought battleships	1905
Pistol	c.1485	Shipborne aircraft	1910
Wheel-lock firing mechanism	c.1515	Poison gas; depth charge	1915
Flintlock for use in small arms	c.1556	Tank	1916
Ironclad warships	1592	Sonar	1918
Musket	c.1600	Radar	1933
Puckle machine-gun	1718	Helicopter	1937
Submarine (man-powered)	1776	Jet aircraft	1939
Shrapnel ammunition	1786	Nerve gas	1942
Percussion cap	1805	Atomic bomb	1945
Steam-powered warships	1813	Hydrogen bomb	1953
Screw-propelled boats	1837	Nuclear-powered submarine	1955
Repeater rifle	1852	Laser	1960

American troops disembark on a Normandy beach following the D-Day landings of World War II.

GREEK–PERSIAN WARS (490–448 BCE)

OPPOSING FORCES Coalition of Greek city-states including Athens and Sparta *v.* Persia

The Persian ruler Darius I attempted to conquer mainland Greek city-states after they had given assistance to a revolt by Persian-ruled Greek cities in Ionia. The invasion was renewed by Darius's son, Xerxes I. After the Greek victory at Plataea in 479 BCE, mainland Greece was not invaded again, but fighting continued in the Aegean and Ionia.

MAJOR BATTLES	DATE	DESCRIPTION	OUTCOME
Eretria	490 BCE	siege	Persian victory
Marathon	490 BCE	land battle	Greek victory
Thermopylae	August 480 BCE	land battle	Persian tactical victory, Greek strategic victory
Artemisium	August 480 BCE	naval battle	Persian victory
Salamis	480 BCE	naval battle	Greek victory
Plataea	June 479 BCE	land battle	Greek victory
Mycale	June 479 BCE	naval battle	Greek victory
Eurymedon	466 BCE	land battle	Greek victory
Salamis (Cyprus)	450 BCE	land battle	Greek victory

The war was concluded by the Peace of Callias (448 BCE), by which the Persians agreed to respect the autonomy of the Ionian Greeks and not to base warships in the Aegean. *See also p.117.*

PELOPONNESIAN WAR (431–404 BCE)

OPPOSING FORCES Athens and allies *v.* Sparta and allies

The Greek city-state of Sparta, in the Peloponnese, attempted to challenge the growing maritime superiority of the Athenian empire. The war fell into several phases, beginning with a failed Spartan siege of Athens (the Archidamian War). This was followed by an Athenian land-based invasion of Spartan territory from 425 BCE, and then a disastrous Athenian expedition to Sicily (415–13 BCE). Athens then rebuilt its naval forces, but in 405 BCE its fleet was destroyed at Aegospotami and Athenian power was broken.

MAJOR BATTLES	DATE	DESCRIPTION	OUTCOME
Archidamian War	431–430 BCE	siege of Athens	stalemate, Athenian strategic victory
Pylos	425 BCE	land battle	Athenian victory
Sphacteria	425 BCE	land/naval battle	Athenian victory
Delium	424 BCE	land battle	Boeotian (Spartan ally) victory
Amphipolis	422 BCE	land battle	Spartan victory
Mantinea	418 BCE	land battle	Spartan victory
Syracuse	415–413 BCE	siege	Syracusan/Spartan victory
Cyzicus	410 BCE	naval battle	Athenian victory
Notium	406 BCE	naval battle	Spartan victory
Arginusae	406 BCE	naval battle	Athenian victory
Aegospotami	405 BCE	naval battle	Athenian victory

After Aegospotami, Athens' fleet was reduced to a mere 12 ships and surrendered the next year. The city was stripped of its overseas possessions and its walls were demolished, but the Spartans resisted pressure to raze the city entirely. *See also p.122.*

The Persian king Darius III was routed by Alexander the Great at Issus, despite commanding troops that outnumbered Alexander's by two to one.

ALEXANDER THE GREAT'S CONQUESTS (334–323 BCE)

OPPOSING FORCES Macedonia *v.* Persian empire

After destroying the power of rival Greek states (especially Thebes) in 336–334 BCE, Alexander invaded the Persian empire in 334 BCE, defeating Darius III in a series of brilliant tactical battles and conquering the whole Persian empire, including Egypt. He then invaded northwestern India, before pulling back in 325 BCE after his army refused to proceed further.

BATTLE	DATE	DESCRIPTION	OUTCOME
Granicus	334 BCE	land battle	Macedonian victory
Issus	333 BCE	land battle	Macedonian victory
Gaugamela	331 BCE	land battle	Macedonian victory
Hydaspes	326 BCE	land battle	Macedonian victory against Indian ruler Porus

On his return from India, Alexander planned a campaign in Arabia, but died of a fever at Babylon in 323 BCE. *See also pp.124–5.*

PUNIC WARS

OPPOSING FORCES Rome and allies *v.* Carthage and allies

FIRST PUNIC WAR (264–241 BCE)

As the Romans' interests in the western Mediterranean grew with the extension of their territory, they clashed with the established power of Carthage, particularly in Sicily. The war was principally a naval one, won against the odds by the establishment of Rome's first fleet.

BATTLE	DATE	DESCRIPTION	OUTCOME
Mylae	260 BCE	naval battle	Roman victory
Ecnomus	256 BCE	naval battle	Roman victory
Drepana	249 BCE	naval battle	Carthaginian victory
Aegates Islands	241 BCE	naval battle	Roman victory

After the defeat at Aegates, Carthage surrendered, and agreed to evacuate Sicily and not to assist its former Sicilian allies against Rome.

▶

PUNIC WARS (continued)

SECOND PUNIC WAR (218–202 BCE)

Seeking revenge for its losses in the Second Punic War, the Carthaginians, bolstered by a new land empire in Spain, launched a land assault on the Italian peninsula led by the general Hannibal. A string of victories foundered in strategic stalemate, and in 204 BCE the Romans counter-invaded Africa, forcing Hannibal's recall to Carthage.

MAJOR BATTLE	DATE	DESCRIPTION	OUTCOME
Trebia	218 BCE	land battle	Carthaginian victory
Lake Trasimene	217 BCE	land battle	Carthaginian victory
Cannae	216 BCE	land battle	Carthaginian victory
Syracuse	212 BCE	siege	Roman victory
Metaurus	207 BCE	land battle	Roman victory
Illipa	207 BCE	land battle	Roman victory
Zama	202 BCE	land battle	Roman victory

After the defeat at Zama, Carthage surrendered, and Rome took control of Spain, while the Carthaginian fleet was reduced to ten ships.

THIRD PUNIC WAR (149–146 BCE)

A war between Carthage and the Numidian king Massinissa offered Rome a pretext to intervene. Encouraged by the leading senator Cato, Roman forces landed in Africa, and after a brief campaign set siege to Carthage.

MAJOR BATTLE	DATE	DESCRIPTION	OUTCOME
Carthage	149–146 BCE	siege	Roman victory

After a bitter three-year siege, Roman forces stormed the city, and sold off the survivors as slaves. Carthaginian power was utterly destroyed. *See also pp.130–1.*

Hannibal is thought to have used rafts to ferry his war elephants across the Rhône river in France en route from Spain to Italy.

ROMAN CIVIL WARS (49–31 BCE)

FIRST CIVIL WAR (49–44 BCE)

OPPOSING FORCES Julius Caesar *v.* Pompey the Great

Political competition in the late Roman Republic so destabilized the state that a senatorial party sought to prevent Julius Caesar from gaining supreme power. Even with the backing of Pompey the Great, the senatorial group failed to prevent Caesar entering Italy and then winning a decisive victory against Pompey in Greece.

MAJOR BATTLE	DATE	DESCRIPTION	OUTCOME
Pharsalus	48 BCE	land battle	Caesarian victory
Thapsus	46 BCE	land battle	Caesarian victory against followers of Pompey and Numidian allies
Munda	46 BCE	land battle	Caesarian victory

The remaining followers of Pompey were wiped out in campaigns in Africa and Spain.

SECOND CIVIL WAR (33–31 BCE)

OPPOSING FORCES Octavian (Augustus) *v.* Mark Antony

After Caesar's assassination in 44 BCE, his heir Octavian joined forces with Mark Anthony to defeat the assassins at Philippi in 42 BCE. However, shifting alliances eventually led to a confrontation between Octavian and Antony, his former ally. After Antony abdicated control of the western provinces, he and his Egyptian ally Cleopatra were decisively defeated.

MAJOR BATTLE	DATE	DESCRIPTION	OUTCOME
Actium	33 BCE	naval battle	Octavian victory

After the defeat at Actium, Antony and Cleopatra fled back to Egypt, where they both committed suicide. Egypt was annexed and Octavian, now virtually unchallenged, assumed supreme power over the Roman state, becoming emperor in 27 BCE. *See also p.132.*

The short sword, or *gladius*, used in hand-to-hand combat, was the key weapon of the Roman soldier.

BYZANTINE–SELJUK WARS (1064–71, 1110–17, 1158–76)

OPPOSING FORCES Byzantines *v.* Seljuk Turks

After military successes in the Balkans and Asia Minor (modern Turkey) in the late 9th and early 10th centuries, the Byzantine empire faced a new enemy, the Muslim Seljuk Turks, who invaded Asia Minor in the mid-11th century. A disastrous defeat at Manzikert in 1071, in which the Emperor Romanus was captured, led to the loss of much of central Asia Minor to the Turks. After a partial recovery, Byzantine control was again shattered after a defeat at Myriocephalon.

MAJOR BATTLE	DATE	DESCRIPTION	OUTCOME
Manzikert	1071	land battle	Seljuk victory
Myriocephalon	1176	land battle	Seljuk victory

Most of Asia Minor fell to the Seljuks, leaving a weakened Byzantine empire with little option but to appeal to the western European Christian states for help.

THE CRUSADES (1095–1272)

OPPOSING FORCES Various western European Christian armies *v.* Muslim states of the eastern Mediterranean and Egypt

In 1095, Byzantine Emperor Alexius I Comnenus appealed to the west for help, leading Pope Urban II to call for a war to retake the Holy Land from the Muslims. This First Crusade was the precursor to a series of religion-driven military campaigns.

MAJOR BATTLE	DATE	DESCRIPTION	OUTCOME
FIRST CRUSADE (1095–99)			
Dorylaeum	1097	land battle	Crusader victory
Jerusalem	1099	siege	Crusader victory
SECOND CRUSADE (1147–49)			
Edessa	1144	siege	Muslim victory
THIRD CRUSADE (1189–92)			
Hattin	1187	land battle	Muslim victory
Arsouf	1191	land battle	Crusader victory
FOURTH CRUSADE (1202–04)			
Constantinople	1204	siege	Crusader victory, although their original target was Jerusalem
FIFTH CRUSADE (1217–21)			
Damietta	1218–21	siege	Muslim victory
SIXTH CRUSADE (1228–29)			
SEVENTH CRUSADE (1248–54)			
Mansoura	1250	land battle	Muslim victory
EIGHTH CRUSADE (1270)			
Tunis	1270	land battle	Muslim victory

After the failure of the 13th-century Crusades to provide relief to the states the Crusaders had established in the eastern Mediterranean, their fortresses fell one by one. In 1291, Acre, the last significant stronghold, was captured by the Egyptian Mamluks. *See also pp.198–9.*

MONGOL CONQUESTS (1206–1405)

OPPOSING FORCES Mongols *v.* various European and Asian peoples

After the Mongols united under Genghis Khan in 1206, their armies conquered much of central Asia and northern China before his death in 1227. They then invaded Europe (1237–42), but did not conquer it. Their attempts to subdue the Middle East suffered a setback in 1260 and they were thereafter confined in the region to Persia.

MAJOR BATTLE	DATE	DESCRIPTION	OUTCOME
Kalka River	1223	land battle	Mongols defeat Russians
Legnica	1241	land battle	Mongols defeat Poles and Germans
Ain Jalut	1260	land battle	Egyptian Mamluks defeat Mongols
Yamen	1279	land battle	Mongols defeat Southern Song

Although they completed the conquest of China in 1279, the Mongol empire fragmented in the late 13th century. Under Timur (ruled 1370–1405), the Mongols carried out a last campaign of conquest in central Asia, Russia, northern India, and modern Turkey. *See also pp.168–9.*

Knights from allied kingdoms joined the opposing English and French sides at the Battle of Crécy.

HUNDRED YEARS WAR (1337–1453)

OPPOSING FORCES English (and Burgundians) v. French

In 1337, King Edward III of England asserted his claim to the French throne, invading France and winning a series of victories. A 1360 treaty by which the English gained Aquitaine broke down in 1368, leading to large-scale English losses. In 1412 the war broke out again, and by 1420 the English had gained almost all of northern France. Reinvigorated by Joan of Arc in the late 1420s, the French struck back and by 1453 had reduced the English to controlling only Bordeaux.

MAJOR BATTLE	DATE	DESCRIPTION	OUTCOME
Sluys	1340	naval battle	English victory
Crécy	1346	land battle	English victory
Poitiers	1356	land battle	English victory
Najera	1367	land battle	English victory
Agincourt	1415	land battle	English victory
Orléans	1429	siege	French victory
Castillon	1453	land battle	French victory

The English were almost wholly driven out of France, but did not lose their last French possession, Calais, until 1558. *See also p.201.*

ONIN WAR (1467–77)

OPPOSING FORCES Yamana clan v. Hosokawa clan

A dispute over the succession to the Ashikaga shogunate in Japan escalated into open civil war. Both the main protagonists, Yamana Mochitoyo and Hosokawa Katsumoto, died in 1473, but the war dragged on for four more years.

MAJOR BATTLE	DATE	DESCRIPTION	OUTCOME
Kyoto	1477	siege	stalemate

The war left central authority weakened and Japan divided between many competing clans, a situation which would not be resolved for more than a century.

THE ITALIAN WARS (1494–95, 1521–25, 1526–30, 1535–38, 1542–44)

OPPOSING FORCES Italian city-states and Holy Roman Empire *v.* French and Italian allies

In 1494, the Milanese, fearing an attack from Naples, invited Charles VIII of France to intervene. This set off more than half a century of warfare, in which the German Emperor Charles V also became involved.

MAJOR BATTLE	DATE	DESCRIPTION	OUTCOME
Fornovo	1495	land battle	Italian victory
Bicocca	1521	land battle	Imperial victory against French and Swiss
Pavia	1525	land battle	Imperial/Italian victory
Rome	1527	siege	City sacked by mutinous German mercenaries
Ceresole	1544	land battle	French victory

The war was ended by the Peace of Crespy (1544), but Italy was not able to escape partial foreign dominance until the late 19th century. *See also p.245.*

WARS OF JAPANESE UNIFICATION (1560–1603)

OPPOSING FORCES Oda Nobunaga, Toyotomi Hideyoshi, Tokugawa Ieyasu and allies *v.* opposing *daimyo* clans

After the Onin Wars (*see p.449*), Japan was divided between competing *daimyo* clans. The *daimyo* of Owari, Oda Nobunaga, set out on a campaign to reunite Japan, in alliance with the Tokugawa clan. He was assassinated in 1582, but by 1584 most of Japan was at peace and united under his ally Toyotomi Hideyoshi. *See also pp.220–21.*

MAJOR BATTLE	DATE	DESCRIPTION	OUTCOME
Okehazama	1560	land battle	Nobunaga victory
Nagashino	1575	land battle	Nobunaga victory
Sekigehara	1600	land battle	Tokugawa Ieyasu victory

Hideyoshi died in 1598, and Tokugawa Ieyasu assumed his mantle. After defeating rival claimants, in 1603 he took the title of shogun and Japan's unification was in effect complete.

Japanese warriors upheld a code of honour (*bushido*) in which death was preferable to the shame of defeat.

EIGHTY YEARS WAR ("THE DUTCH REVOLT", 1568–1648)

OPPOSING FORCES Dutch *v.* Philip II of Spain and allies in southern Netherlands

Resentment at oppressive Spanish rule led the provinces of Holland and Zeeland to rebel. Under the leadership of William of Orange, the rebels gained ground in the 1570s, but by 1579 the Spanish had reconquered the south, forming the Union of Arras. The northern states (the Union of Utrecht) declared independence in 1581 and fought various Spanish attempts to suppress them.

MAJOR BATTLE	DATE	DESCRIPTION	OUTCOME
Jemmingen	1568	land battle	Spanish victory
Leiden	1574	siege	Dutch victory
Nieuwpoort (The Dunes)	1600	land battle	Dutch victory
Ostend	1601–04	siege	Spanish victory
Breda	1625	land battle	Dutch victory
The Downs	1639	naval battle	Dutch victory

In 1648, Dutch independence was recognized by the Peace of Westphalia. *See also p.247.*

WAR OF THE THREE KINGDOMS (THE ENGLISH CIVIL WAR, 1642–51)

OPPOSING FORCES Charles I and Royalists *v.* Parliamentarians

Friction over British king Charles I's need for money to wage war in Ireland and his desire to circumvent parliament's control over taxation led to outright hostility. Both sides achieved successes, but by 1644 the more professionally trained parliamentary armies won major victories. In 1646 the king fled to Scotland from where he sought to foment a new war. Although Charles was captured by parliament, an invading Scottish army renewed the war. But it was defeated, and the king was hanged for treason in 1649.

Charles I (ruled 1625–49) engaged in a struggle for power with the English parliament which was to lead to his overthrow, trial, and execution.

MAJOR BATTLE	DATE	DESCRIPTION	OUTCOME
Edgehill	1642	land battle	stalemate
Lansdown	1643	land battle	Royalist victory
Newbury	1643	land battle	Parliamentary victory
Marston Moor	1644	land battle	Parliamentary victory
Naseby	1645	land battle	Parliamentary victory
Preston	1648	land battle	Parliamentary victory
Worcester	1651	land battle	Parliamentary victory

After his father's execution, Charles II carried on the struggle, invading England from Scotland. After his defeat at Worcester in 1651, he fled to Europe. He was only finally restored to the English throne in 1660. *See also p.249.*

THE THIRTY YEARS' WAR (1618–48)

OPPOSING FORCES Imperial Catholic alliance *v.* mainly Protestant powers plus France

Tensions between Catholic and Protestant European powers, together with the desire of German princes to assert themselves against the Holy Roman Empire, exploded into war in 1618 after an anti-Imperial revolt in Protestant Bohemia. By 1629, the Catholic allies of the Holy Roman Empire were in the ascendant, but the intervention of Protestant Sweden in 1629 prolonged the war. Seeing a chance to damage its Habsburg rivals in Spain and Austria, Catholic France entered the war on the Protestant side in 1635, and the war was to last another 13 years.

MAJOR BATTLE	DATE	DESCRIPTION	OUTCOME
White Mountain	1620	land battle	Imperial victory
Breitenfeld	1631	land battle	Swedish/Protestant victory
Lutzen	1632	land battle	Swedish/Protestant victory; Gustavus Adolphus killed
Nördlingen	1632	land battle	Spanish/Imperial victory
Rocroi	1643	land battle	French victory
Jankau	1645	land battle	Swedish/Protestant victory

After three years of negotiation, the Peace of Westphalia finally ended the war in 1648. The Holy Roman Emperor was stripped of many of his powers over German princes, Protestantism was to be tolerated in the empire and France, and Sweden gained territories. *See also p.248.*

THE GREAT NORTHERN WAR (1700–21)

OPPOSING FORCES Sweden *v.* Denmark, Saxony, Poland–Lithuania and Russia

Charles XII of Sweden (1697–1718) faced threats from Denmark, Saxony, and Russia, who each sought to acquire Swedish territory. In 1700, Charles invaded Denmark, forcing the Danes to sue for peace. He then pushed the Saxons out of Livonia and Lithuania, and invaded Poland. War with Russia went badly, though, and a disastrous defeat in 1709 led to Charles's exile. Sweden's enemies regrouped and forced an end to the war by 1721.

MAJOR BATTLE	DATE	DESCRIPTION	OUTCOME
Narva	1700	land battle	Swedish victory (against Russians)
Pultusk	1703	land battle	Swedish victory (against Saxons)
Poltava	1709	land battle	Russian victory
Stralsund	1715	land battle	Danish victory

The Treaty of Nystad (1721) which ended the war left many of Sweden's former Baltic possessions in Russian hands. *See also p.251.*

Small arms utilizing a true flintlock mechanism were in widespread use in European conflicts from around the mid-17th to the early 19th century.

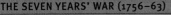

THE SEVEN YEARS' WAR (1756–63)

OPPOSING FORCES Great Britain and Prussia *v.* France, Austria, Russia, Saxony, Sweden

Rivalry between Austria and Prussia over the succession to the Austrian throne spilled over into a global conflict involving Britain and its allies on one hand, and France and its supporters on the other. The war had three main theatres of conflict. In Europe, much of the fighting was between Austria and Prussia, as Frederick the Great of Prussia invaded Saxony in 1756, but after initial successes, his capital Berlin was captured by Russia in 1760. Once British support for Prussia waned, and Russia dropped out after the tsar was assassinated in 1762, the war petered out.

The Austrian field marshal Baron Ernst von Laudon (1717–90) destroyed an entire corps of Frederick the Great's army at the Battle of Landshut.

THE WAR IN EUROPE

MAJOR BATTLE	DATE	DESCRIPTION	OUTCOME
Rossbach	1757	land battle	Prussian victory (against French/Austrians)
Leuthen	1757	land battle	Prussian victory (against Austrians)
Minden	1759	land battle	British victory (against French)
Kunersdorf	1759	land battle	Austrian/Russian victory (against Prussians)
Liegnitz	1760	land battle	Prussian victory (against Austrians)
Landshut	1760	land battle	Austrian victory (against Prussians)

THE WAR IN THE AMERICAS

In North America – where the war is called "The French and Indian War" – the British and French struggle for supremacy ended in the British acquisition of French Canada. Britain had similar successes against Spain in Cuba and the Philippines.

MAJOR BATTLE	DATE	DESCRIPTION	OUTCOME
Quebec	1759	land battle	British victory (against French)

THE WAR IN INDIA

In India, long-running tensions ignited into war between colonial France and Britain. Robert Clive captured Calcutta and ousted Bengal's nawab, a French ally, at the Battle of Plassey, and with the capture of the French capital Pondicherry in 1761, British victory was complete.

MAJOR BATTLE	DATE	DESCRIPTION	OUTCOME
Plassey	1757	land battle	British victory (against French/Indian allies)
Wandiwash	1759	land battle	British victory (against French)

The Treaty of Paris (1763) brought the Seven Years' War to an end. Great Britain gained Minorca, Canada, and Florida, while Spain acquired Louisiana from France. Prussia managed to retain Silesia, one of the main battlegrounds of the war. *See also pp.261, 270–1, 294.*

AMERICAN REVOLUTIONARY WAR (1775–83)

OPPOSING FORCES Great Britain *v.* American colonists (and French allies)

Resentment at British rule in its 13 North American colonies grew in the 1760s, and in 1775 fighting broke out between colonial militias and British regular forces. In July 1776 the Americans declared independence. An American victory at Saratoga in 1777 brought France in on their side, while the British were unable to wear down American resistance marshalled by George Washington. British successes in the south from 1778 came to naught and their main army was trapped in Yorktown, Virginia, where in mid-October 1781, they surrendered.

MAJOR BATTLE	DATE	DESCRIPTION	OUTCOME
Lexington and Concord	1775	land battle	American victory
Bunker Hill	1775	land battle	British victory
Trenton	1776	land battle	American victory
Saratoga	1777	land battle	American victory
1st Savannah	1778	land battle	British victory
Camden	1780	land battle	British victory
Yorktown	1781	siege	American victory

By the Treaty of Paris (1783) that ended the war, Britain recognized the independence of the United States; Britain and France restored possessions they had captured from each other in India; and Spain acquired Florida and Minorca from Britain. *See also pp.262–3.*

The Battle of Bunker Hill, on 17 June 1775, was the first large-scale engagement between British troops and colonists in the American Revolutionary War.

FRENCH REVOLUTIONARY WARS (1792–1802)

OPPOSING FORCES France *v.* varying coalitions including Britain, Austria, Prussia, Russia

Alarmed at the prospect of the French Revolution being exported, Austrian and Prussian armies invaded France but were pushed back. The French then invaded the Austrian Netherlands in 1792, and also subdued Switzerland. In Italy, from 1796, Napoleon Bonaparte fought a series of campaigns which ended in French occupation of most of the region by 1797. A new anti-French coalition struggled, and despite British victories in Egypt in 1798, it fell apart by 1802, and the Peace of Amiens seemed to end the struggle. *See also pp.272–3.*

MAJOR BATTLE	DATE	DESCRIPTION	OUTCOME
Valmy	1792	land battle	French victory (against Prussians)
Castiglione	1796	land battle	French victory (against Austrians)
Arcole	1796	land battle	French victory (against Austrians)
The Nile	1798	naval battle	British victory
Marengo	1800	land battle	French victory (against Austrians)
Hohenlinden	1800	land battle	French victory (against Austrians)

The pause was only temporary, however, and in 1803, the Napoleonic Wars began.

THE NAPOLEONIC WARS (1803–1815)

OPPOSING FORCES France *v.* varying coalitions including Britain, Austria, Prussia, Russia

The immediate pretext for the start of the Napoleonic Wars was the British occupation of Malta in 1803. The Third and Fourth Coalitions against Napoleon fell apart in 1807–09, but the Austrians, fearing French occupation, fought back. Britain invaded the Iberian peninsula in the Fifth Coalition of 1808, beginning the Peninsular War. Napoleon disastrously invaded Russia in 1812; seriously weakened, he was then badly beaten at Leipzig in 1813 and fell back on the defence of France. After Paris fell to the Sixth Coalition in March 1814, he abdicated and was exiled to Elba. Napoleon soon escaped, restored himself to the throne, and fought a brief campaign ("The Hundred Days") that ended in his final defeat by the Prussians and British in June 1815.

MAJOR BATTLE	DATE	DESCRIPTION	OUTCOME
Trafalgar	1805	naval battle	British victory
Austerlitz	1805	land battle	French victory (against Austrians/Russians)
Jena-Auerstadt	1806	land battle	French victory (against Prussians)
Wagram	1809	land battle	French victory (against Austrians)
Talavera	1809	land battle	British victory
Badajoz	1812	land battle	British victory
Salamanca	1812	land battle	British victory
Borodino	1812	land battle	French victory (against Russians)
Bautzen	1813	land battle	inconclusive (Russian/Prussians *v.* French)
Leipzig	1813	land battle	Russian/Prussian/Swedish/Austrian victory
Toulouse	1814	land battle	British victory
Quatre Bras	1815	land battle	inconclusive (British *v.* French)
Waterloo	1815	land battle	British/Prussian victory

After the Napoleonic Wars, France lost its position as the pre-eminent European military power, which it was never to recover. *See also pp.278–9.*

CRIMEAN WAR (1853–56)

OPPOSING FORCES Russia *v.* Ottoman Turkey, Britain, France

Russia's claims to have rights of protection over the Holy Land and Orthodox Christians in the Balkans led to tensions with Ottoman Turkey. In 1853 Russia invaded the principalities of Wallachia and Moldavia in the Balkans, leading to war with Turkey. England and France entered the war on Turkey's side, and sent an expeditionary force to the Crimea. It fought there for two years, engaging in the long and bloody siege of Sevastopol (finally captured in September 1855). Fighting also took place between Russia and Turkey in the Caucasus.

MAJOR BATTLE	DATE	DESCRIPTION	OUTCOME
Alma	1854	land battle	British/French victory
Sevastopol	1854–55	siege	British/French victory
Balaclava	1855	land battle	inconclusive
Inkerman	1854	land battle	British/French victory
Kars	1855	siege	Russian victory (against Turks)

The Congress of Paris (1856) ended the war. Russia gave up its claim to protect Christians in the Ottoman empire, the shore of the Black Sea was neutralized, and the autonomy of Moldavia and Wallachia was recognized.

The charge of the Light Brigade at Balaclava proved a disastrous tactical error by the British.

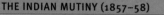

THE INDIAN MUTINY (1857–58)

OPPOSING FORCES British *v.* native Indian forces

The extension of British territories in India brought fears that Indian religious sensibilities were being ignored. Mutiny by many Indian soldiers in British service spread throughout northern India, with many native rulers joining its ranks and British garrisons being massacred. The aged Mughal emperor in Delhi (previously politically powerless) was brought on board as a figurehead for an independence movement. The British struck back, recapturing Delhi and relieving a siege of Lucknow in 1858.

MAJOR BATTLE	DATE	DESCRIPTION	OUTCOME
Cawnpore	1857	siege	Indian victory
Delhi	1857	siege	British victory
Lucknow	1857–58	siege	British victory
2nd Cawnpore	1857	land battle	British victory
Jhansi	1858	land battle	British victory

After the mutiny, rule over India was transferred from the East India Company, a private venture, to the British crown. The last Mughal Emperor was deposed. *See also p.296.*

AMERICAN CIVIL WAR (1861–65)

OPPOSING FORCES The Union *v.* the Confederacy

Tensions built over several decades between the southern and northern states of the United States, particularly over the issue of slavery. When the northern Democrat Abraham Lincoln was elected president in 1860, South Carolina seceded from the Union, followed within five months by 10 other states. For four years the new group (the Confederacy) fought the Union, with particularly fierce fighting in northern Virginia, the "Eastern Theater", where Richmond (the Confederate capital) was within striking distance of Washington DC. A push by Confederate general Robert E. Lee into Pennsylvania was defeated at Gettysburg in July 1863, and the Confederacy was thereafter on the defensive.

The battle flag of the Second Battalion Hilliard's Alabama Legion, riddled with Union bulletholes.

THE EASTERN THEATER

MAJOR BATTLE	DATE	DESCRIPTION	OUTCOME
Fort Sumter	1861	siege	Confederate victory
1st Bull Run	1861	land battle	Confederate victory
Seven Days	1862	land battle	Union victory
Antietam	1862	land battle	Union victory
Fredericksburg	1862	land battle	Confederate victory
Chancellorsville	1863	land battle	Confederate victory
Gettysburg	1863	land battle	Union victory

THE WESTERN THEATER

Meanwhile, from 1862 to 1863 Union General Ulysses S. Grant advanced down the Mississippi river, the "Western Theater" of the war, cutting the Confederacy in two. In late 1864, Grant engaged in a "march to the sea" to Savannah, Georgia.

MAJOR BATTLE	DATE	DESCRIPTION	OUTCOME
Shiloh	1862	land battle	Union victory
Vicksburg	1863	siege	Union victory

THE DEFEAT OF THE SOUTH

The Confederacy had defended Virginia bitterly, but with the Union forces advancing now from the south, became encircled. Richmond fell and the last Confederate field armies surrendered in April 1865 at Appomattox Courthouse, Virginia and Bennett Place, North Carolina.

MAJOR BATTLE	DATE	DESCRIPTION	OUTCOME
Wilderness	1864	land battle	inconclusive
Cold Harbor	1864	land battle	Confederate victory

In the aftermath of the war, the Confederate government was dissolved, slavery was abolished, and a process of "Reconstruction" was set in place that was intended to re-establish central control in the south and supervise the restoration of political rights. Southern states were gradually readmitted to the Union, with Georgia the last to rejoin in July 1870. *See also pp.266–7.*

FRANCO–PRUSSIAN WAR (1870–71)

OPPOSING FORCES France *v.* Prussia

Tension rose between France and Prussia over the latter's attempt to unite the German states under its leadership and the Prussian Chancellor Bismarck's plan to put a German prince on the Spanish throne (so encircling France with pro-Prussian states). Napoleon III of France was provoked into war, invading Germany, but his armies were soon pushed back and the Prussians advanced into France. After a disastrous French defeat at the Battle of Sedan in September, where Napoleon III was captured, Paris was besieged. It surrendered in January 1871.

MAJOR BATTLE	DATE	DESCRIPTION	OUTCOME
Gravelotte	1870	land battle	Prussian victory
Metz	1870	siege	Prussian victory
Sedan	1870	land battle	Prussian victory
Paris	1870–71	siege	Prussian victory

By the Treaty of Frankfurt (May 1871), the border territories of Alsace and Lorraine were handed over to Prussia, and France paid a huge indemnity (five billion francs). French ambitions to regain Alsace-Lorraine would play a part in the outbreak of World War I. *See also p.284.*

TAIPING REBELLION (1850–64)

OPPOSING FORCES Chinese central (Qing) government *v.* Taiping rebels

In 1851, a Christian teacher, Hong Xiuquan, declared the establishment of the *Taiping Tianguo*, the "Heavenly Kingdom of Great Peace", and fought off attempts by the Qing government to suppress his utopian society. In 1853, the Taiping rebels captured Nanjing, but gradually foreign powers intervened to help the Qing. In 1860, a Taiping assault on Shanghai was defeated by the Western-trained "Ever-Victorious Army". In 1864, the Qing government recaptured Nanjing and the last Taiping rebels were easily mopped up. *See also pp.298–9.*

MAJOR BATTLE	DATE	DESCRIPTION	OUTCOME
Nanjing	1853	land battle	Taiping victory
Shanghai	1860	land battle	Qing victory
Nanjing	1864	siege	Qing victory

The Taiping rebels attacked Peking (modern Beijing) after their 1853 capture of Nanjing.

BOER WARS (SOUTH AFRICAN WARS, 1880–1, 1899–1902)

OPPOSING FORCES British *v.* Boers (Afrikaners)

The fears of Boer (Dutch Afrikaner) settlers in South Africa about British encroachment on their territories were realized in 1877 when Britain annexed the independent Boer Republic of the Transvaal. A short war ensued in which the Boers regained their autonomy. Relations deteriorated again in the 1890s and another war broke out in 1899 between the British and the Boer South African Republic and its ally the Orange Free State. Initial Boer successes were pushed back in 1900, and by June the main Boer armies were defeated and a series of besieged "British" towns relieved. Guerrilla resistance continued for another year, but British blockades, and their introduction of concentration camps, broke the final Boer resistance.

MAJOR BATTLE	DATE	DESCRIPTION	OUTCOME
Mafeking	1899–1900	siege	British victory
Ladysmith	1899–1900	siege	British victory
Colenso	1899	land battle	Boer victory
Spion Kop	1900	land battle	Boer victory
Bloemfontein	1900	siege	British victory

By the 1902 Treaty of Vereeniging the Orange Free State and Transvaal became part of British-ruled South Africa, with only limited guarantees of autonomy. *See also p.308.*

Boer soldiers at Spion Kop, a battle that resulted in a major victory for the Afrikaners.

BALKAN WARS (1912–13)

OPPOSING FORCES (First) Bulgaria, Greece, Serbia, Montenegro *v.* Ottoman Turkey
(Second) Bulgaria *v.* Turkey, Serbia, Greece, Romania

In March 1912 Bulgaria, Greece, and Serbia allied, intent on gaining territory from an Ottoman Turkey whose control over the Balkans was clearly weakening. Greek forces advanced from the south, and the Serbs made large gains in the north, while Bulgaria invaded Thrace in the east. Ottoman resistance crumbled, but within months fighting broke out again as Serbia, Greece, and Romania sought to prevent Bulgaria gaining too much territory. With Turkey beginning to recapture territory lost in the first war, the other countries rapidly agreed a peace.

MAJOR BATTLE	DATE	DESCRIPTION	OUTCOME
Monastir	1912	land battle	Serb victory
Lule Burgas	1912	land battle	Bulgarian victory
Adrianople	1913	land battle	Turkish victory

Bulgaria was forced to give up most of its gains from the first war, including Adrianople, which was retained by Turkey. Nonetheless, Turkey had lost four-fifths of its pre-war Balkan lands, mostly to Serbia, Greece, and Romania. *See also p.314.*

WORLD WAR I (1914–18)

OPPOSING FORCES "Entente" (Britain, France, Italy, Russia, United States, and others) *v.*
"Central Powers" (Germany, Austro-Hungary, and others)

THE WESTERN FRONT

Long-standing tensions between European powers exploded into war in autumn 1914 following the assassination of an Austrian archduke in Sarajevo by Serbian nationalists. Fearing an attack from France, Germany struck first, almost reaching Paris before being driven back in early September. Both sides engaged in a "race to the sea", each trying to outflank the other. Neither was successful, and the opposing armies then dug complex networks of trenches, the Western Front, which from late 1914 to early 1918 proved almost impermeable to a series of appallingly costly offensives. Finally in 1918, the Germans broke through, but their offensive petered out, and they were pushed back beyond their defensive lines and sued for peace.

MAJOR BATTLE	DATE	DESCRIPTION	OUTCOME
1st Marne	1914	land battle	Entente victory
1st Aisne	1914	land battle	indecisive
1st Ypres	1914	land battle	Entente victory
Verdun	1916	land battle	Entente (French) victory
1st Somme	1916	land battle	indecisive
Vimy Ridge	1917	land battle	Entente victory
Messines	1917	land battle	Entente victory
Passchendaele	1917	land battle	Entente victory
Cambrai	1917	land battle	indecisive
2nd Marne	1918	land battle	Entente victory

THE EASTERN FRONT

The war was more mobile on other fronts, especially on the Eastern Front in central and Eastern Europe, where Austria and Germany faced Russia.

MAJOR BATTLE	DATE	DESCRIPTION	OUTCOME
Tannenberg	1914	land battle	Central Powers victory (against Russia)
Gorlice-Tarnow	1915	land battle	Central Powers victory (against Russia)

The collapse of the Russian tsarist government after the Russian Revolution of November 1917 brought the war on the Eastern Front to an end.

THE WAR IN THE MIDDLE EAST

In Palestine and Mesopotamia, the British and their allies sought to undermine the German-aligned Ottoman Turkish government; despite losses at Kut and Gallipoli they were eventually successful.

MAJOR BATTLE	DATE	DESCRIPTION	OUTCOME
Kut-al-Amara	1915–16	siege	Turkish victory (against British, Indians)
Gallipoli	1915–16	land battle	Turkish victory (against British, Australians, New Zealanders)
Megiddo	1918	land battle	Entente victory (against Turks)

Germany signed an armistice on 11 November 1918 bringing fighting to an end in western Europe. A series of peace treaties changed the face of Europe and the Middle East. *See also pp.314–25.*

RUSSIAN CIVIL WAR (1918–21)

OPPOSING FORCES Bolsheviks v. "White" Russians

The seizing of power by the Bolsheviks in the 1917 Russian Revolution was opposed by significant political and military forces. Fighting broke out in summer 1918, with anti-Bolshevik "White" forces based in Siberia under General Kolchak (supported by the "Czech legion" of former prisoners of war); in the Caucasus under General Denikin; and near Petrograd under General Yudenich. British, French, Japanese, and American forces also intervened in the north to block Bolshevik ports. Under Leon Trotsky, the Bolshevik Red Army defeated the three main White Armies, capturing Omsk in November 1919. A White Army managed to hold out in the Crimean peninsula until November 1920.

Leon Trotsky (centre) reviews his troops in Moscow's Red Square.

MAJOR BATTLE	DATE	DESCRIPTION	OUTCOME
Tsaritsyn	1919	land battle	Bolshevik victory
Petrograd	1919	land battle	Bolshevik victory

Secure in power, the Bolsheviks mopped up residual resistance in 1921–22 and in 1922 established the USSR, a communist state that would dominate international politics for nearly 70 years. *See also p.328.*

SPANISH CIVIL WAR (1936–39)

OPPOSING FORCES Nationalists v. Republicans

In the 1920s, Spain was destabilized by faction fighting between left-wing and right-wing extremists. When the leftist Popular Front won elections in 1936, elements of the army, led by General Franco, launched a coup to stop it taking power. These Nationalists took over much of the south and west of Spain in 1936, and then aimed for the capital, Madrid.

The government Republican forces defended Madrid doggedly, but with Italian and German military aid the Nationalists went on the offensive in 1938, capturing the strategic town of Teruel in February, and then seizing Barcelona in January 1939. Madrid surrendered to the Nationalist forces in March and the war came to an end.

MAJOR BATTLE	DATE	DESCRIPTION	OUTCOME
Guadalajara	1937	land battle	Republican victory
Teruel	1937–38	land battle	Nationalist victory
Ebro	1938	land battle	Nationalist victory
Barcelona	1939	siege	Nationalist victory
Madrid	1939	siege	Nationalist victory

After the official end of the war, guerrilla war was waged on an irregular basis well into the 1950s, gradually evaporating due to military defeats and the scant support from an exhausted population.

WORLD WAR II (1939–45)

OPPOSING FORCES "Allies" (British, French, and others) *v.* "Axis" (German, Japanese, Italians to 1943, and others)

BLITZKRIEG

In 1938, in a flagrant breach of the settlement that ended World War I, Germany, under Adolf Hitler, annexed Austria and part of Czechoslovakia. In September 1939 he invaded Poland; Britain and France declared war on Germany in response. After a lull, in 1940 Germany invaded Belgium, the Netherlands, and Scandinavia in a "lightning war" (Blitzkrieg), then invaded and occupied France. Britain averted a planned German invasion by winning the Battle of Britain in 1940.

MAJOR BATTLE	DATE	DESCRIPTION	OUTCOME
Defeat of Poland	1939	land battle	German victory
Battle of France	1940	land battle	German victory
Battle of Britain	1940	aerial battle	British victory

THE WAR IN THE MEDITERRANEAN

Italy joined Germany in the war in June 1940, and when both moved on British-held Egypt, land operations became focused on North Africa. The British were victorious (latterly with American help), and in 1943 invaded Sicily and mainland Italy. The Italians sued for peace but the German army continued a dogged resistance in the Italian peninsula until 1945.

MAJOR BATTLE	DATE	DESCRIPTION	OUTCOME
El Alamein	1942	land battle	Allied victory
Anzio	1944	land battle	Allied victory
Monte Cassino	1944	land battle	Allied victory

INVASION OF RUSSIA

The German invasion of the USSR in autumn 1941 opened another front, where the Germans were rapidly successful, almost taking Moscow in November–December, but then stalling. In 1942 they became bogged down in a siege of Stalingrad, but when that failed they were relentlessly pushed back by the Soviet army, until by 1944 they were back in Poland.

MAJOR BATTLE	DATE	DESCRIPTION	OUTCOME
Leningrad	1941–44	siege	Allied (Soviet) victory
Moscow	1941–42	land battle	Allied (Soviet) victory
Stalingrad	1942–43	siege	Allied (Soviet) victory
Kursk	1943	land battle	Allied (Soviet) victory

GERMANY DEFEATED

In western Europe, the Allies landed in Normandy in June 1944 and pushed east towards Germany, while the Red Army advanced in early 1945 into eastern Germany. In April–May 1945, the Soviets reached Berlin and after a huge battle the city capitulated and the Germans surrendered.

MAJOR BATTLE	DATE	DESCRIPTION	OUTCOME
Normandy Landings	1944	land/naval battle	Allied victory
Arnhem	1944	land battle	German victory
Berlin	1945	land battle	Soviet victory

WORLD WAR II (1939–45) (continued)

WAR IN THE PACIFIC

In 1941, Japan attacked the US fleet at Pearl Harbor, bringing the US in on the Allied side, and Japan on the Axis side. The Japanese overran British and Dutch possessions in Southeast Asia in 1941–42 and pushed the Americans out of the Philippines, but the US regrouped and pushed the Japanese back. The Japanese continued to resist after the defeat of Germany, until nuclear bombs dropped on Hiroshima and Nagasaki prompted Japan's surrender on 2 September 1945.

A naval attack prepared the way for the US invasion of the island of Okinawa and the seizing of its Japanese airfields.

MAJOR BATTLE	DATE	DESCRIPTION	OUTCOME
Philippines	1941–42	land battle	Japanese victory
Singapore	1942	siege	Japanese victory
Coral Sea	1942	naval battle	American victory
Guadalcanal	1942–43	land battle	Allied (American) victory
Midway	1942	naval battle	Allied (American) victory
Leyte Gulf	1944	land battle	Allied (American) victory
Philippine Sea	1944	naval battle	Allied (American) victory
Iwo Jima	1945	land battle	Allied (American) victory
Okinawa	1945	land battle	Allied (American) victory

No formal treaties were signed marking the end of World War II. The Cold War (see pp.360–1) which erupted in its wake left Europe divided between a communist east and a capitalist west. Japan underwent several years of US occupation before independence was restored under a democratic government in 1952. See also pp.338–359.

CHINESE CIVIL WAR (1945–49)

OPPOSING FORCES Communists v. Nationalists (Kuomintang)

After the defeat of Japan in World War II, Chinese Communist forces and their Nationalist foes rushed to occupy the area the Japanese had formerly occupied. The Communist leader Mao Zedong seemed willing to compromise with his Nationalist opponent Chiang Kai-Shek, but Chiang, buoyed by early Nationalist victories, refused. In October 1948 the Nationalists suffered a major defeat in Manchuria, and the Communist forces fanned out into central and southern China, capturing the Nationalist capital Chungking in November 1949. Chiang and his remaining forces fled to Taiwan.

MAJOR BATTLE	DATE	DESCRIPTION	OUTCOME
Manchuria campaign	Oct–Nov 1948	land battle	Communist victory
Huai-Hai	1949	land battle	Communist victory
Beijing	1949	land battle	Communist victory

Mao Zedong proclaimed the People's Republic of China in 1949, but the Nationalists continued to hold out in Taiwan, where Chiang declared the rival Republic of China in 1950 – a political split that remained into the 21st century. See also pp.392–3.

KOREAN WAR (1950–53)

OPPOSING FORCES North Koreans and Chinese *v.* South Koreans and UN force
(including Americans, Australians, and British)

At the end of World War II, Korea was divided along the 38th parallel between a communist-aligned zone supported by China and a southern area supported by the United States. The North Koreans invaded the south in June 1950. A United Nations expeditionary force pushed the North Koreans back almost to the Chinese border by November. The Chinese reacted with a counteroffensive and took the South Korean capital Seoul in January 1951. The UN forces recovered, and the front lines solidified close to the 38th parallel until the end of the war in 1953.

MAJOR BATTLE	DATE	DESCRIPTION	OUTCOME
Pusan Perimeter	1950	land battle	inconclusive
Inchon	1950	land battle	UN/South Korean victory
Imjin River	1951	land battle	North Korean/Chinese victory
Heartbreak Ridge	1951	land battle	UN/South Korean victory

An armistice signed in July 1953 recognized a demarcation line more or less where it had been before a war that cost some 3 million casualties. Korea remains divided. *See also p.394.*

FRENCH INDOCHINA WAR (1946–54)

OPPOSING FORCES French *v.* Vietnamese nationalists (Vietminh)

Following World War II, the French only succeeded in restoring their colonial authority in Vietnam over the south of the country. The north was taken over by Ho Chi Minh's communists. In December 1946, his forces, the Vietminh, attacked French garrisons and began a guerrilla war, which the French struggled to contain. Despite efforts to broker a political settlement with moderates, the French could not budge the Vietminh. In March 1954, the fall of the strategic French garrison of Dien Bien Phu persuaded them to make peace.

MAJOR BATTLE	DATE	DESCRIPTION	OUTCOME
Hoa Binh	1951–52	land battle	Vietminh victory
Dien Bien Phu	1954	land battle	Vietminh victory

The Geneva Conference in July 1954 formally partitioned Vietnam between a communist north and capitalist south. French influence in Southeast Asia was totally undermined. *See also p.294.*

Trench warfare reminiscent of
World War I characterized the
Battle of Dien Bien Phu.

ARAB–ISRAELI WARS (1948–73)

OPPOSING FORCES Israel *v.* Egypt, Syria, Jordan, Lebanon, Iraq, and Palestinians

The declaration of the State of Israel in 1948 was strongly opposed by its Arab neighbours who invaded in May 1948. Israel halted the Arab advance, and then managed to occupy an area 50 per cent larger than its previous territory. In 1956 Israel fought Egypt in support of the British and French landings in the Suez Canal, but withdrew from their gains in the Sinai.

THE SINAI WAR

MAJOR BATTLE	DATE	DESCRIPTION	OUTCOME
Operation Kadesh	1956	land battle	Israeli victory (against Egyptians)

In 1967, Israel launched pre-emptive strikes against its neighbours, and in the Six-Day War, rapidly destroyed Arab air forces, and seized land in the West Bank (from Jordan), the Gaza Strip (from Egypt), and the Golan Heights (from Syria).

THE SIX-DAY WAR

MAJOR BATTLE	DATE	DESCRIPTION	OUTCOME
Abu Ageila	1967	land battle	Israeli victory (against Egyptians)

In October 1973 Arab forces attacked again (the Yom Kippur War), with Egyptian armies moving across the Suez canal, and Syrian forces pushing from the northeast. Israel pushed back all these offensives and almost reached the Syrian capital Damascus before a ceasefire.

THE YOM KIPPUR WAR

MAJOR BATTLE	DATE	DESCRIPTION	OUTCOME
1st Mount Hermon	1973	land battle	Syrian victory
Chinese Farm	1973	land battle	Israeli victory (against Egyptians)
2nd Mount Hermon	1973	land battle	Israeli victory (against Syrians)

Israel evacuated the Sinai in 1979 following the Camp David Accords, but hopes for a more permanent settlement proved illusory and the conflict continues. *See also pp.386–7.*

VIETNAM WAR (1961–75)

OPPOSING FORCES South Vietnamese, Americans, and Australians *v.* North Vietnamese (Vietcong)

Ho Chi Minh's North Vietnam communists encouraged a civil war in the South to overthrow its US-backed regime. In 1964, after Northern patrol boats attacked US naval vessels, American combat troops were despatched to Vietnam. Using guerrilla tactics, the Vietcong caused large numbers of US casualties. After the Tet Offensive in 1968 the Americans began to run down their operation, and had withdrawn by 1973. The South Vietnam government continued to resist until 1975 when a Vietcong offensive pushed south, taking the capital, Saigon.

MAJOR BATTLE	DATE	DESCRIPTION	OUTCOME
Ia Drang Valley	1965	land battle	inconclusive
Long Tan	1966	land battle	Australian victory
Hill 881	1967	land battle	American victory
Tet Offensive	1968	land battle	South Vietnamese victory (but Vietcong propaganda victory)
Saigon	1975	land battle	Vietcong victory

The fall of Saigon led to the reunion of Vietnam under communist rule. *See also p.395.*

IRAN–IRAQ WAR (1980–88)

OPPOSING FORCES Iraq *v.* Iran

Disputes between Iran and Iraq led the Iraqi leader, Saddam Hussein, to invade Iran in September 1980. Iraq made immediate gains, but the offensive stalled and by June 1982 the Iranians had recovered the lost ground. An Iranian offensive in early 1984 looked close to capturing the key Iraqi port of Basra and pushing towards Baghdad. Support from other Arab countries stiffened Iraqi resistance and the war bogged down in a stalemate characterized by mass infantry attacks with high casualties. Iraqi gains early in 1988 persuaded the Iranians to make peace.

MAJOR BATTLE	DATE	DESCRIPTION	OUTCOME
Dezful	1981	land battle	Iraqi victory
Khorramshahr	1982	land battle	Iranian victory
Al Faw	1986	land battle	Iranian victory
2nd Al Faw	1988	land battle	Iraqi victory

Despite the enormous economic and human cost, the war left the borders between the countries unchanged. In 1990, as war with a Western-backed coalition loomed, Saddam recognized Iranian rights over the strategic Shatt al-Arab waterway – one of the causes of the war. *See also p.391.*

GULF WARS (1990–91, 2003)

OPPOSING FORCES Iraq *v.* international coalition led by United States

THE FIRST GULF WAR (1990–91)

In August 1990, Iraqi leader Saddam Hussein ordered his forces to invade Kuwait, hoping to use its oil wealth to help offset the crippling costs of the Iran–Iraq War. He hoped international response would be muted, but was mistaken, for the Americans, with UN-backing, assembled a huge force in Saudi Arabia. In January 1991, large-scale air attacks on Iraq began, and on 25 February a land offensive rapidly swept the Iraqi army out of Kuwait and pushed deep into Iraq. The coalition forces withdrew from Iraq, however, and Saddam put down revolts against him.

MAJOR BATTLE	DATE	DESCRIPTION	OUTCOME
Kuwait	1990	land battle	Iraqi victory
Operation Desert Storm	1991	land battle	coalition victory
Khafji	1991	land and air battle	coalition victory

Following the war, Saddam was forced to submit to a regime of weapons inspections to ensure he did not obtain "weapons of mass destruction".

Bombing raids launched from aircraft carriers by the US Marine Corps supported ground operations.

GULF WARS (1990–91, 2003) (continued)

THE SECOND GULF WAR – THE WAR IN IRAQ (2003–)

In 2002, tensions mounted between Iraq and the United States over Saddam's constant breaches of the inspection and disclosure regime imposed after the first Gulf War. Although not backed by the same support in the United Nations for military action, the United States assembled a smaller coalition and in March 2003, after a brief air campaign, coalition forces entered Iraq. Resistance by the Iraqi army was patchy and many units simply disbanded. Baghdad fell on 9 April and the last Iraqi towns a few weeks after that.

MAJOR BATTLE	DATE	DESCRIPTION	OUTCOME
Umm Qasr	2003	land battle	coalition victory
Nasiriyah	2003	land battle	coalition victory
Baghdad	2003	land battle	coalition victory
Najaf	2003	land battle	coalition victory
Fallujah	2004	land battle	insurgent victory
Ramadi	2004	land battle	coalition victory

Although the Iraqi regime had fallen, plans for the post-war fate of the country did not take account of a large-scale insurgency which broke out against US occupation. At first insurgents came mainly from the Sunni community which had done best out of Saddam's regime, but the insurgency spread to the majority Shia population of the south of the country. Casualties amongst coalition forces mounted and bombings killed thousands of civilians. Despite the best efforts of the United States and the Iraqi government, the insurgency, although at times contained, could not be eradicated. The Americans ceded increasing powers back to the Iraqi government, and in 2009 announced that their forces would withdraw by 2010. *See also p.413.*

AFGHANISTAN WAR (2001–)

OPPOSING FORCES US-led coalition *v.* Taleban

The refusal of Mullah Omar, head of the extreme Islamist Taleban government of Afghanistan, to hand over Osama bin Laden, leader of al-Qaeda – implicated in the attacks on the United States on 11 September 2001 – led the American government to assist anti-Taleban rebels with air strikes and special forces. Kandahar fell in early December and the Taleban leadership (and its al-Qaeda allies) slipped away, many, it is believed, to Pakistan. There, the Taleban gathered its strength and began to infiltrate the south of Afghanistan once more. Despite a growing international force (ISAF), the coalition casualties mounted. Operations to sweep the Taleban out of areas often found them back in control there within weeks or even days.

MAJOR BATTLE	DATE	DESCRIPTION	OUTCOME
Mazar-I-Sharif	2001	land battle	coalition victory
Herat	2001	land battle	coalition victory
Tora Bora	2001	land battle	coalition victory
Kunduz	2001	land battle	coalition victory
Musa Qala	2007	land battle	coalition victory
Eagle's Summit	2008	land battle	coalition victory

Counter-insurgency operations in Afghanistan continue. An increase in US troop numbers from 30,000 to almost 50,000 was announced in February 2009, in a bid to stem the rising tide of Taleban attacks ahead of any possible American disengagement from the country. *See also p.412.*

HISTORICAL LANDMARKS

While rulers, military commanders, and politicians shape our world, human civilization is also the result of the creativity, innovation, and achievements of the scientists, artists, explorers, inventors, and thinkers who help to drive society and knowledge forward.

CALENDAR SYSTEMS

Most of the world uses the Gregorian calendar for noting day-to-day activities and historical landmarks, but many cultures use more ancient calendars for marking events of ritual and cultural significance. Historians must take account of older dating systems when analysing source material.

CALENDAR	BASIS	SYSTEM
Hebrew	Lunisolar	12 months of 29/30 days and an intercalary (leap) month added seven times in a 19-year cycle. Era begins 3761 BCE.
Maya	---	260-day and 365-day cycles combined to form "Calendar Round" of approximately 52 years.
Chinese	Lunar	12 months of 29/30 days, with a leap month every 2–3 years. Beginning of era disputed; either 2697 or 2637 BCE.
Ancient Egyptian	Solar	365 days, with 12 months of 30 days, and 5 intercalary days at the end of the year.
Attic (ancient Athens)	Lunisolar	354 days, with 12 months of 28/29 days and a leap month of 30 days every third year.
Ancient Rome	Solar	355 days, 12 months of 28–30 days, with a leap month added periodically. Era dated from 753 BCE (date of foundation of the city of Rome).
Japanese	Lunisolar	A system similar to the Chinese calendar was in official use to 1873. Era dated from 660 BCE.
Gregorian	Solar	365 days, with a leap day every four years. Era begins at 1 CE.
Ethiopian/Ge'ez	Solar	12 months of 30 days, with a leap month of 5–6 days. Era begins at 9 CE.
Coptic (Egypt)	Solar	Similar to Ethiopian, but era begins at 284 CE.
Islamic	Lunar	354 days (12 months of 29/30 days). Era begins 622 CE (date of the *Hegira* – Muhammad's flight from Mecca).

Albert Einstein, best known for his Special Theory of Relativity, received the Nobel Prize for Physics in 1921.

GREAT EXPLORERS

The "discoveries" of many early explorers were actually of lands that had thriving indigenous societies, which often led to disastrous results. Yet we can still admire the imagination and tenacity of those who risked their lives journeying into territory completely unknown to them.

NAME	LIVED	ORIGIN	EXPEDITIONS/DISCOVERIES
Hanno	*fl.* 5th century BCE	Carthage	Sailed down the west coast of Africa (*c.*470 BCE).
Erik the Red	*c.*950–1002 CE	Norway	Explored the coast of Greenland (985 CE).
Leif Eriksson	*fl.* 11th century CE	Norway	Discovered Vinland, part of North America (*c.*1000 CE).
Marco Polo	1254–1324	Italy	Travelled extensively in China and along the Silk Road (1275–92).
Ibn Battuta	*c.*1304–68	Morocco	Explored the Sahara, Arabia, India, Central Asia, China, and Southeast Asia.
Dinís Diaz	*fl.* mid-15th century	Portugal	Discovered the Cape Verde islands off the west coast of Africa (1445).
Bartolomeu Dias	*c.*1450–1500	Portugal	Rounded Africa's Cape of Good Hope (1488).
Vasco da Gama	*c.*1469–1524	Portugal	Sailed round Africa's Cape of Good Hope and reached India (1497–98).
Christopher Columbus	1451–1506	Italy	Discovered the Americas, landing in the Bahamas (1492); discovered the mainland of South America (1498).
John Cabot	*c.* 1450–1499	Italy	Discovered mainland North America (1497).
Pedro Álvarez Cabral	*c.*1467–1520	Portugal	Discovered Brazil (1500).
Amerigo Vespucci	1454–1512	Italy	Explored the coastline of South America (1501).
Afonso de Albuquerque	1453–1515	Portugal	Reached India via Zanzibar (1503–04).
Vasco Núñez de Balboa	1475–1519	Spain	First European to navigate the South Sea (Pacific Ocean), from Panama (1513).
Juan Ponce de Leon	*c.*1460–1521	Spain	Discovered Florida (1513).
Hernán Cortes	1485–1547	Spain	Led the conquest of the Aztec empire in Mexico (1518–22).
Ferdinand Magellan	*c.*1480–1521	Portugal	Explored the Philippines; partially circumnavigated the globe (1520–21).
Francisco Pizarro	1475–1541	Spain	Led the conquest of the Inca empire in Peru (1530–33).
Francisco Vásquez de Coronado	1510–54	Spain	Led the first major expedition to the southwest of the modern United States (1540–42).

GREAT EXPLORERS (continued)

NAME	LIVED	ORIGIN	EXPEDITIONS/DISCOVERIES
García López de Cárdenas	fl. 1540s	Spain	Reached the Grand Canyon in 1540.
Richard Chancellor	d. 1556	England	Voyaged to Russia via the North Cape (1553–56).
Martin Frobisher	c.1535–94	England	Reached the Frobisher Strait (Canada) while searching for the Northwest Passage (1576).
Francis Drake	c.1540–96	England	Circumnavigated the globe (1580).
Walter Raleigh	1552–1618	England	Undertook numerous voyages to America; attempted, unsuccessfully, to found a colony in Virginia (1584).
Cornelis de Houtman	1565–99	Netherlands	Led first Dutch expedition to the East Indies; sailed the south coast of Java (1598).
Samuel de Champlain	1567–1635	France	Explored the St Lawrence River (1603); founded Quebec (1608).
Henry Hudson	c.1565–1611	England	Discovered Hudson Bay (Canada) (1610).
William Baffin	1584–1622	England	Explored Baffin Bay, part of the Northwest Passage (1616).
Abel Tasman	1603–c.1659	Netherlands	Reached New Zealand and Tasmania (1642).
William Dampier	1651–1715	England	Crossed the Pacific Ocean (1683).
Vitus Bering	1681–1741	Denmark	Explored Siberia (1733–41).
James Cook	1728–79	Britain	Mapped the New Zealand and Australian coasts (1769); made first Australian landfall, at Botany Bay, New South Wales (1770).
James Bruce	1730–94	Britain	Explored the Blue Nile; claimed to have found the source of the Nile (1768–74).

Francis Drake was knighted by Queen Elizabeth I on the deck of his ship, the *Golden Hind*, upon his return to England.

GREAT EXPLORERS (continued)

NAME	LIVED	ORIGIN	EXPEDITIONS/DISCOVERIES
Antoine Bruni d'Entrecasteaux	1739–93	France	Surveyed the South Pacific (1791–93).
Mungo Park	1771–1806	Britain	Explored the Niger River (1795–96).
George Bass	1771–1803	Britain	Explored the coastline of southeastern Australia (1795–98).
Friedrich Alexander von Humboldt	1769–1859	Germany	Explored modern Venezuela and the Orinoco River (1799–1800).
Matthew Flinders	1774–1814	Britain	Circumnavigated Australia (1801–03).
Meriwether Lewis	1774–1809	USA	Led the first transcontinental expedition across the United States (1804–05).
William Clark	1770–1838	USA	Co-leader of expedition with Lewis (*above*).
Alexander Gordon Laing	1793–1826	Britain	First European to reach Timbuktu, in Mali (1826).
David Livingstone	1813–73	Britain	Discovered the Victoria Falls on the Zambezi river (1855).
Robert O'Hara Burke	1820–61	Ireland	Led an ill-fated expedition to explore the Australian interior (1860–61).
Richard Francis Burton	1821–90	Britain	Travelled in Arabia and reached Medina and Mecca (1853).
Henry Morton Stanley	1841–1904	Britain	Undertook voyages down the Congo (1874).
Fridtjof Nansen	1861–1930	Norway	Crossed Greenland (1888).
Aurel Stein	1862–1943	Hungary	Explored Central Asia and located an ancient complex at Dunhuang (1906–08).
Francis Younghusband	1863–1942	Britain	Led an expedition which reached Lhasa in Tibet (1903–04).
Sven Hedin	1865–1962	Sweden	Explored Central Asia and discovered lost cities in the Taklamakan desert (1893–97).
Wilfred Thesiger	1910–2003	Britain	Intrepid traveller who twice crossed the Empty Quarter of Arabia.
Jacques-Yves Cousteau	1910–97	France	Marine ecologist who dedicated his life to deep-water oceanic exploration.
Thor Heyerdahl	1914–2002	Norway	Sought to prove theories of prehistoric migration by sea with long-distance voyages using rafts built from natural materials.
Edmund Hillary	1919–2008	New Zealand	Completed the first ascent of Mount Everest in the Himalayas (1953).
Yuri Gagarin	1934–68	USSR	First person in space (1961).
Neil Armstrong	1930–	USA	First person to set foot on the moon (1969).

Ernest Shackleton's ship, *Endurance*, became locked in the ice in Antarctica.

POLAR EXPLORERS

NAME	LIVED	ORIGIN	EXPEDITIONS/DISCOVERIES
John Davis	c.1550–1605	England	Explored Greenland, discovered the Davis Strait (1585) while searching for the Northwest Passage.
Willem Barents	1550–97	Netherlands	Searched for the Northeast Passage (1594–97).
Fabian von Bellingshausen	1778–1852	Estonia	Early explorer of the Antarctic (1819–21).
John Franklin	1786–1847	Britain	Searched for the Northwest Passage; never returned from his expedition (1847).
William Edward Parry	1790–1855	Britain	Made an early attempt to reach the North Pole overland (1827).
James Clark Ross	1800–62	USA	Made an extensive exploration of the Antarctic, discovering the Ross Sea and Ross Ice Shelf (1841).
Salomon Andrée	1854–97	Sweden	Attempted to balloon over the Arctic; disappeared during the flight (1897).
Otto Nordenskjöld	1869–1928	Sweden	Spent the winter in Antarctica (1901–03).
Robert Peary	1856–1920	USA	Claimed to have reached North Pole (1909).
Robert Falcon Scott	1868–1912	Britain	Lost out to Roald Amundsen in the race to reach the South Pole (1911–12).
Roald Amundsen	1872–1928	Norway	First man to reach the South Pole (1911).
Ernest Shackleton	1874–1922	Britain	Led an expedition to cross Antarctica, but became stranded for four months on Elephant Island (1914).
Richard Byrd	1888–1957	USA	Completed the first overflight of the North Pole (1926).
Vivian Fuchs	1908–99	Britain	Completed the first land crossing of the Antarctic continent (1958).

INVENTIONS AND DISCOVERIES

The modern world is very different from the world of our ancestors. Over the course of human existence, basic human needs – from the need to survive to the urge to obtain knowledge – have produced tens of thousands of inventions and discoveries. These have transformed both the way we function and the way we think, and have made us distinct from the rest of the animal kingdom. *See also* Advances in Military Technology, *p.443*; Great Advances in Medicine, *p.478*.

INVENTION/DISCOVERY	DATE	ORIGINATOR	PLACE OF ORIGIN
Stone tools	c.2.75 MYA	early humans	Africa
Control of fire	c.500, 000 YA	early humans	Africa
Boat	c.50, 000 YA	early migrants	Australasia
Mining	c.40, 000 YA	paleolithic humans	Europe
Permanent shelters	c.28, 000 YA	paleolithic humans	eastern Europe
Farming	c.10, 000 BCE	Middle Eastern peoples	Mesopotamia
Pottery vessels	c.10, 000 BCE	Jōmon people	ancient Japan
Irrigation	c.5500 BCE	Middle Eastern peoples	Mesopotamia
Horse domestication	c.4500 BCE	Andronovo culture	Europe/Asia
Plough	c.4000 BCE	Sumerian people	Mesopotamia
Writing	c.3200 BCE	Sumerian people	Sumer/Egypt
Wheeled transport	c.3200 BCE	Sumerian people	Sumer
Calendar	c.3000 BCE	Babylonians	Babylonia
Silk weaving	c.2700 BCE	Chinese peoples	ancient China
Plumbing	c.2700 BCE	Indus Valley civilization	Indus (Pakistan)
Papyrus scroll	c.2600 BCE	Imhotep (attributed)	ancient Egypt
Law code	c.1755 BCE	King Hammurabi	Babylonia
Alphabet	14th century BCE	Semitic peoples (slaves of the Egyptians)	ancient Egypt
Magnetism	c.1000 BCE	Thales of Miletus (attrib.)	ancient Greece
Coinage	c.600 BCE	Lydian people	ancient Turkey
World map	6th century BCE	Babylonians	Babylonia
Planetary models	c.360 BCE	Eudoxus of Cnidus	ancient Greece
Rotation of the Earth	c.350 BCE	Heraclides Ponticus	ancient Greece
Steel production	c.200 BCE	Han dynasty	India/China
Compound pulley	c.200 BCE	Archimedes	ancient Greece
Encyclopaedia	77 CE	Pliny the Elder	Roman empire
Paper	c.105 CE	Cai Lun	ancient China
Compass	250	Chinese peoples	ancient China
Concept of zero/decimal system	c.590–650	Brahmagupta	India
Astrolabe	c.800	Muhammad al-Fazari	Arabia
University	859	Fatimah al-Fihri	Morocco
Star chart	c.1000–50	Abu Rayhan Biruni	Persia
Pendulum	c.1000	Ibn Yunus	Egypt
Magnifying glass	c.1021	Ibn al-Haytham	Persia

INVENTIONS AND DISCOVERIES (continued)

INVENTION/DISCOVERY	DATE	ORIGINATOR	PLACE OF ORIGIN
Movable type	c.1045	Bi Sheng	China
Mechanical clock	1088	Su Song	China
Algebra	1202	Fibonacci	Italy
The scientific method	c.1220–35	Robert Grosseteste	England
Printing press	c.1445	Johannes Gutenburg	Germany
Terrestrial globe	c.1490	Martin Behaim	Bohemia
Sun-centred universe	1503–43	Copernicus	Italy
Compound microscope	c.1595	Hans Lippershey, Zacharias Janssen	Netherlands
Laws of planetary motion	1609–19	Johannes Kepler	Germany
Newspaper	1609	Johann Carolus	Germany
Refracting telescope	1609	Galileo Galilei	Italy
Mechanical calculator	1642	Wilhelm Schickard	Germany
Barometer	1643	Evangelista Torricelli	Italy
Atmospheric pressure	1647–48	Blaise Pascal	France
Microscopic life	1673	Antoni van Leeuwenhoewk	Netherlands
Laws of motion	1687	Sir Isaac Newton	England
Seed drill	1701	Jethro Tull	England
Steam piston engine	1712	Thomas Newcomen	Britain
Marine chronometer	1735	John Harrison	Britain
Lightning rod	1752	Benjamin Franklin	USA
Watt steam engine	1776	James Watt	Britain
Oxygen	1777	Antoine Lavoisier	France
Hot air balloon	1783	Montgolfier brothers	France
Threshing machine	1786	Andrew Meikle	Britain
Battery	1800	Alessandro Volta	Italy
Bicycle	1818	Karl Drais	Germany
Permanent photography	c.1820	Joseph Nicéphore Niépce	France
Braille alphabet	1821	Louis Braille	France

Martin Behaim (standing, centre) demonstrates his terrestrial globe.

INVENTIONS AND DISCOVERIES (continued)

Thomas Edison was one of the most prolific inventors in history, registering over 1,000 US patents, including the phonograph.

INVENTION/DISCOVERY	DATE	ORIGINATOR	PLACE OF ORIGIN
Electric motor	1821	Michael Faraday	Britain
Programmable computer	1822	Charles Babbage	Britain
Electromagnet	1823	William Sturgeon	Britain
Internal combustion engine	1826	Samuel Morey	USA
Water turbine	1827	Claude Burdin, Benoît Fourneyron	France
Steam locomotive	1829	George Stephenson	Britain
Electrical generator	1831	Michael Faraday	Britain
Refrigerator	1834	Jacob Perkins	USA/Britain
Vulcanization of rubber	1837	Charles Goodyear	USA
Polystyrene	1839	Eduard Simon	Germany
Undersea telegraph cable	1858	Charles Wheatstone	Britain
Theory of evolution	1859	Charles Darwin	Britain
Pasteurization	1862	Louis Pasteur, Claude Bernard	France
Laws of heredity	1866	Gregor Mendel	Austria
Dynamite	1867	Alfred Nobel	Sweden
Periodic Table	1869	Dmitri Mendeleev	Russia
Telephone	1876	Alexander Graham Bell	Britain
Phonograph	1877	Thomas Edison	USA
Incandescent light bulb	1878	Joseph Wilson Swan	Britain
Automobile	1885	Karl Benz	Germany
Petrol engine	1886	Gottlieb Daimler	Germany
Wireless communication	1893	Nikolai Tesla	Austria-Hungary
Radio telegraph	1895	Guglielmo Marconi	Italy
Cinematography	1895	Auguste & Louis Lumière	France
Radium	1898	Marie & Pierre Curie	Poland/France
Quantum theory	1900	Max Planck	Germany

INVENTIONS AND DISCOVERIES (continued)

INVENTION/DISCOVERY	DATE	ORIGINATOR	PLACE OF ORIGIN
Rigid dirigible airship	1900	Ferdinand Graf von Zeppelin	Germany
Aeroplane (controlled powered flight)	1903	Wright Brothers	USA
Conditioned reflexes	1904	Ivan Pavlov	Russia
Theory of relativity	1905	Albert Einstein	Switzerland
Bakelite plastic	1909	Leo Baekeland	Belgium
Stainless steel	1913	Harry Brearley	Britain
Structure of the atom	1913	Niels Bohr	Denmark
Television	1925	John Logie Baird	Britain
Law of the expanding universe	1929	Edwin Hubble	USA
Nylon	1935	Wallace Carothers	USA
RADAR	1935	Robert Watson-Watt	Britain
Jet engine	1937	Frank Whittle	Britain
Ball-point pen	1938	László Bíró	Hungary
Nuclear reactor	1942	Enrico Fermi	Italy /USA
Aqualung	1943	Jacques Cousteau, Emile Gagnan	France
Atomic bomb	1945	J. Robert Oppenheimer	USA
Photosynthesis	1946	Melvin Calvin	USA
Commercial jet airliner	1948	Vickers	Britain
Radiocarbon dating	1949	Willard Libby	USA
Big Bang theory	1949	George Gamow, Ralph Alpher, Robert Herman	USA
Structure of DNA	1953	Francis Crick, Rosalind Franklin, James D. Watson	Britain/USA
Communications satellite	1958	Kenneth Masterman-Smith	USA
LASER	1960	Theodore H. Maiman	USA
Plate tectonics	1967	Dan McKenzie	Britain
Microprocessor	1969	Intel	USA
E-mail	1971	Ray Tomlinson	USA
Genetic modification	1973	Stanley Norman Cohen, Herbert Boyer	USA
Personal computer	1973	Xerox PARC	USA
Mobile telephone	1973	Martin Cooper (Motorola)	USA
Compact disc	1980	Philips Electronic/Sony Corporation	Netherlands/Japan
World Wide Web	1990	Tim Berners-Lee	Britain
Global Positioning System	1995	US Department of Defense	USA
Genetic cloning	1996	Ian Wilmut, Keith Campbell	Britain
Portable media player	2001	Apple	USA

GREAT ADVANCES IN MEDICINE

Prehistoric cave art in the Lascaux caves in France depicts the use of plants as healing agents, and throughout history, physicians and scientists have continued to work to understand the human body, heal injury, and combat illness. Today, many of the world's most dreadful diseases have been conquered, but newly evolving ones continue to challenge us.

DATE	MEDICAL MILESTONE
*c.*420 BCE	Hippocrates of Cos, originator of Hippocratic oath, active.
170 CE	Galen, greatest physician of Roman times, describes the nervous system.
570–71 CE	Gregory of Tours, France, gives first description of smallpox.
918	First psychiatric hospital opened, Baghdad.
1000	First recorded use of oral anaesthesia, by the Arab physician Abu al-Qasim.
1037	Death of Avicenna (Ibn Sina), great Arab physician.
1080	Medical school founded at Salerno, Italy.
1123	St Bartholomew's, London's oldest hospital, founded.
*c.*1250	First anatomy demonstrations at Salerno.
1284	Eyeglasses (early spectacles) in use, invented by Salvino d'Armate, Italy.
1288	Santa Maria Nuova, Italy's oldest hospital, founded in Florence. Death of Ibn an-Nafis, first to describe the circulation of the blood through the heart and lungs.
*c.*1315	Dissection of human corpses takes place, Bologna University, Italy.
1543	Andreas Vesalius's *De Humani Corporis*, first great work on anatomy, published.
1603	Girolamo Fabrizio publishes study on discovery of valves in veins.
1628	William Harvey describes the systemic circulation of the blood.

The stethoscope (invented 1816) at first consisted of a wooden "listening tube" with an earpiece.

DATE	MEDICAL MILESTONE
*c.*1630	Invention of obstetrical forceps.
1653	Description of the liver by Francis Glisson, England.
1663	Marcello Malpighi publishes work on the lungs, describing capillaries.
1672	Regnier de Graaf publishes description of human reproductive organs.
1677	Cinchona bark first described as a fever treatment.
1701	First recorded inoculation against smallpox.
1714	First mercury thermometer invented, by Gabriel Fahrenheit, Netherlands.
1730	First tracheotomy (surgery to open the windpipe) recorded.
1736	First successful appendectomy performed, by Claudius Amyand, London.
1761	Percussion technique (tapping) for diagnosing chest disorders developed.
1795	Nitrous oxide ("laughing gas") first used, by Humphry Davy, London.
1796	Edward Jenner develops first vaccination against smallpox.
1816	Stethoscope invented by René-Théophile-Hyacinthe Laennec, France.
1829	First clinical description of the blood disorder haemophilia.
1831	Chloroform discovered simultaneously in USA, France, and Germany.
1840	Elizabeth Fry founds the Institute of Nursing in London.

GREAT ADVANCES IN MEDICINE (continued)

DATE	MEDICAL MILESTONE
1844	Nitrous oxide used as anaesthetic in dental procedure.
1846	US dentist William Thomas Green Morton uses ether as an anaesthetic.
1849	First woman to qualify as a doctor in the UK (Elizabeth Blackwell).
1858	General Medical Council established in the UK.
1861	Louis Pasteur discovers anaerobic bacteria, preventing spoilage in milk through heat treatment ("pasteurization") designed to kill microorganisms.
1869	First description of a skin graft.
1876	Link between pancreas and diabetes discovered.
1880	Malaria parasite identified by French doctor Charles Louis Alphonse Laveran.
1882	Tuberculosis bacterium isolated; first gall bladder removal operation.
1885	Louis Pasteur develops rabies vaccine.
1890	Tetanus and diphtheria vaccines developed.
1893	First open-heart surgery.
1895	X-ray machine invented by Wilhelm Röntgen, Germany.
1899	London School of Hygiene and Tropical Medicine founded.
1900	Four major human blood groups described.
1905	First direct blood transfusion; first artificial hip joints.
1912	Term "vitamin" first used.
1921	Insulin (hormone that regulates blood sugar levels) first isolated, Canada.
1928	Alexander Fleming discovers penicillin (first antibiotic).
1935	First prefrontal lobotomy to treat mental illness.
1937	Yellow fever vaccine developed.
1943	First kidney dialysis machine.
1948	World Health Organization established. National Health Service established in UK.
1952	Amniocentesis test (for foetal abnormalities/infections) developed.
1954	First successful kidney transplant performed.
1957	Live polio vaccine developed.
1962	First laser eye surgery.
1967	First human heart transplant performed by Christian Barnard, South Africa.
1972	CAT scans (digital medical imaging) introduced.
1978	First "test-tube baby" born.
1981	AIDS first identified.
1982	Artificial heart developed, by Dr Robert Jarvik, USA.
2003	First draft of complete human genome sequence published.

Elizabeth Fry (1780–1845) campaigned for social reform and better healthcare for the poor.

MASTERS OF WESTERN ART

Most art of the past had a purpose: depictions of historical and Biblical events ennobled society's origins; courtly and military set-pieces glorified rulers and their generals; bucolic portraits flattered the landed gentry, and pastoral scenes decorated the homes of an urbanized bourgeoisie. But in the modern era, artists, free from patronage, have pursued their own, often shocking, agendas.

NAME	LIVED	ORIGIN	STYLE/KEY WORK
Giotto di Bondone	c.1267–1337	Italy	Brought a new level of realism to medieval art. *The Lamentation of Christ* (c.1305).
Jan van Eyck	c.1390–1441	Netherlands	Painter of the merchant class and bourgeoisie. *The Arnolfini Marriage* (1434).
Rogier van der Weyden	c.1399–1464	Netherlands	The greatest northern painter of his day. *The Deposition* (c.1435–40).
Piero della Francesca	1415–92	Italy	A master of perspective. *The Resurrection of Christ* (c.1463).
Alessandro Botticelli	1445–1510	Italy	A key Florentine painter of religious pictures. *La Primavera* (c.1482).
Hieronymus Bosch	c.1450–1516	Netherlands	Medieval painter of fantasy scenes. *The Garden of Earthly Delights* (c.1510–15).
Leonardo da Vinci	1452–1519	Italy	Unrivalled artist and inventor. *The Last Supper* (1495–7); *Mona Lisa* (1503–06).
Albrech Dürer	1471–1528	Germany	The greatest artist of the Northern Renaissance. *The Four Horsemen of the Apocalypse* (c.1497–98).
Michelangelo Buonarroti	1475–1564	Italy	Outstanding sculptor, painter, and architect. *David* (1501–04).
Raphael (Raffaello Sanzio)	1483–1520	Italy	A great master of the High Renaissance. *The Coronation of the Virgin* (1502–03).
Titian (Tiziano Vecellio)	c.1487–1576	Italy	The supreme master of the Venetian School. *Venus and Adonis* (1553).
Hans Holbein (the Younger)	c.1497–1543	Germany	One of the greatest portraitists of the 16th century. *Portrait of Henry VII* (1536).

The Creation of Adam is perhaps the most famous detail from Michelangelo's vast fresco on the ceiling of the Vatican's Sistine Chapel.

MASTERS OF WESTERN ART (continued)

NAME	LIVED	ORIGIN	STYLE/KEY WORK
Pieter Bruegel (the Elder)	c.1525–69	Flanders	The leading Flemish artist of his day. *The Wedding Feast* (c.1567–68).
El Greco	1541–1614	Spain/ Greece	An intense, spiritual painter. *The Resurrection* (1584–94).
Caravaggio	1571–1610	Italy	An exponent of realism. *The Supper at Emmaus* (1601).
Peter Paul Rubens	1577–1640	Flanders	The most influential figure in northern European Baroque. *Samson and Delilah* (c.1609).
Nicolas Poussin	1594–1665	France	The founder of French Classical painting. *Arcadian Shepherds* (c.1648–50).
Gianlorenzo Bernini	1598–1680	Italy	A sculptor with a free, visionary style. *Apollo and Daphne* (1622–24).
Diego de Velázquez	1599–1660	Spain	The greatest Spanish painter of the 17th century. *Las Meninas* (1656).
Rembrandt van Rijn	1606–69	Netherlands	The greatest of the Dutch masters. *Jacob Blessing the Children of Joseph* (1656).
Jan Vermeer	1632–75	Netherlands	Finest of the Dutch genre painters. *Girl with a Pearl Earring* (c.1660–61).
Giambattista Tiepolo	1696–1770	Italy	The last of the great Venetian decorators in the Renaissance tradition. *Queen Zenobia Addressing her Soldiers* (c.1730).
Giovanni Antonio Canaletto	1697–1768	Italy	Most famous Venetian view painter of the 18th century. *The Basin of San Marco on Ascension Day* (c.1740).
William Hogarth	1697–1764	England	Printmaker and satirist, credited with pioneering western sequential (comic) art. *A Rake's Progress* (1735).
Francisco Goya	1746–1828	Spain	A portrait painter of great intensity and introspection. *The Clothed Maja* (c.1800).
Jacques-Louis David	1748–1825	France	Founder of French Neo-Classical painting. *Napoleon Crossing the Alps on 20th May 1800* (1803).
J. M. W. Turner	1775–1851	Britain	The master of Romantic landscape and seascape. *The Fighting Téméraire* (1839).
Eugène Delacroix	1798–1863	France	Leading French Romanticist. *Scenes from the Massacre of Chios* (1824).
Gustave Courbet	1819–77	France	The Father of French Realism. *Burial at Ornans* (1850).
Edouard Manet	1832–83	France	Father-figure of the avant-garde. *Olympia* (1863).

▶

MASTERS OF WESTERN ART (continued)

NAME	LIVED	ORIGIN	STYLE/KEY WORK
Edgar Degas	1834–1917	France	A master draughtsman and painter of dancing scenes. *The Star, or Dancer on the Stage* (c.1876–77).
Claude Monet	1840–1926	France	A leading figure among the Impressionists. *Waterlily Pond* (1899).
Odilon Redon	1840–1916	France	A leading Symbolist who prefigured Surrealism. *Ophelia Among the Flowers* (c.1905–08).
Auguste Rodin	1840–1917	France	The last great Classical sculptor. *The Kiss* (1901–04).
Pierre-Auguste Renoir	1841–1919	France	Impressionist master of dappled light. *The Parisienne* (1874).
Paul Cézanne	1839–1906	France	Pioneer of modern art. *The Large Bathers* (c.1900–05).
Henri Rousseau	1844–1910	France	Post-Impressionist who came to be recognized as a self-taught genius. *The Dream* (1910).
Paul Gauguin	1848–1903	France	Post-Impressionist inspired by the South Seas. *Woman with a Flower* (1891).
Vincent van Gogh	1853–90	Netherlands	An instinctive genius who imbued inanimate objects with passionate intensity. *Sunflowers* (1888).
Georges Seurat	1859–91	France	Originator of Pointillism and Divisionism. *Sunday Afternoon on the Island of Grande Jatte* (1884–86).
Gustav Klimt	1862–1918	Austria	Leading Viennese painter and founder of the Secession movement. *Danaë* (1907).
Edvard Munch	1863–1944	Norway	Symbolist painter who was an important forerunner of Expressionist art. *The Scream* (1893).
Wassily Kandinsky	1866–1944	Russia	Pioneer of the Modern movement and an early painter of abstract art. *Accent in Pink* (1926).
Henri Matisse	1869–1954	France	Master of colour and a founder of the Modern movement. *Reclining Nude, Back* (1927).
Piet Mondrian	1872–1944	Netherlands	Pioneer of pure abstract art. *Broadway Boogie Woogie* (1942–43).
Paul Klee	1879–1940	Germany	Prolific author of drawings, watercolours, and etchings. *The Golden Fish* (1925–26).

MASTERS OF WESTERN ART (continued)

The French Impressionist Edgar Degas made many studies of ballet dancers, in paintings and in sculpture.

NAME	LIVED	ORIGIN	STYLE/KEY WORK
Pablo Picasso	1881–1973	Spain	Master of the Modern movement. *Guernica* (1937).
Edward Hopper	1882–1967	USA	Painter of American urban landscapes. *Cape Cod Evening* (1939).
Marcel Duchamp	1887–1968	France	Associated with the Dadaists and Surrealism – challenged conventional thought about art. *Fountain* (1917).
Joan Miró	1893–1983	Spain	A leading Surrealist painter and sculptor. *Harlequin's Carnival* (1924).
Henry Moore	1898–1986	Britain	A sculptor best known for his abstract monumental bronze sculptures of the human figure. *Reclining Figure* (1951).
Mark Rothko	1903–70	Latvia/USA	Renowned abstract Expressionist. *White Center (Yellow, Pink, and Lavender on Rose)* (1950).
Barbara Hepworth	1903–75	Britain	Abstract sculptor whose works were inspired by nature. *Two Forms* (1933).
Salvador Dali	1904–89	Spain	Flamboyant Surrealist. *The Persistence of Memory* (1931).
Frida Kahlo	1907–54	Mexico	Mixed indigenous Mexican art with Symbolism. *The Two Fridas* (1939).
Francis Bacon	1909–92	Britain	One of the most significant figurative painters of the post-war period. *Three Figures in a Room* (1965).
Jackson Pollock	1912–56	USA	Pioneering abstract painter of the New York School. *Number 6* (1948).
Andy Warhol	1928–87	USA	Created vivid images from popular culture. *Twenty Marilyns* (1962).
Jasper Johns	1930–	USA	Founder of Pop Art. *Ale Cans* (c.1964).
David Hockney	1937–	Britain	One of the most influential British artists of the 20th century. *A Bigger Splash* (1967).

NOTABLE ARCHITECTS

We are more likely to know the names of those who commissioned the great buildings of antiquity – pharaohs, emperors, and kings – than those of their architects. But over the centuries, architects have become acclaimed as creators of the man-made landscapes that surround us.

ARCHITECT	LIVED	ORIGIN	STYLE/KEY WORKS
Imhotep	*fl. c.*2778 BCE	Ancient Egypt	The first architect to be known by name. Step Pyramid of Djoser, Saqqara (*c.*2778 BCE).
Ictinus and Callicrates	*fl.* mid-5th century BCE	Ancient Greece	Architects of the Parthenon in Athens, temple of the ancient Greek goddess Athena.
Marcus Vipsanius Agrippa	*c.*63–12 BCE	Ancient Rome	Designed the original Pantheon to commemorate the Battle of Actium (31 BCE).
Apollodorus of Damascus	*fl.* 98–123 CE	Ancient Rome	Architect to the Emperor Trajan (98–117 CE). Trajan's Column, Rome (completed 113 CE).
Isidore of Miletus and Anthemios of Tralles	*fl.* 6th century CE	Greece / Byzantium	Engineers and geometers. Church of Hagia Sophia, Constantinople (532–37 CE).
Abbot Suger	1081–1151	France	Abbot of the Abbey of St-Denis; rebuilt its Great Church in pioneering Gothic style (1137–44).
Peter Parler	1330–99	Germany	Master mason. Cathedral of St Vitus (1356–85) and Charles Bridge (1357–1400s), Prague.
Filippo Brunelleschi	1377–1446	Italy	First major architect of the Italian Renaissance. Dome, Florence Cathedral (1419–36).
Michelangelo Buonarroti	1475–1564	Italy	The most original architect of the 16th century. Biblioteca Laurenziana, Florence (1525–34).
Sinan	1489–1588	Ottoman empire	Responsible for the construction or supervision of most major buildings in the empire of his time. Suleiman Mosque, Istanbul (1550–57).
Andrea Palladio	1508–80	Italy	Inventor of the Palladian style, which returned to Classical Roman principles. Palazzo del Capitaniato, Vicenza (1571–2).
Gian Lorenzo Bernini	1598–1680	Italy	Pre-eminent sculptor and architect of 17th-century Rome. Piazza and colonnades, St Peter's Basilica, Rome (1620s–30s).
Sir Christopher Wren	1632–1723	England	The greatest 17th-century English architect. Re-planned London after the Great Fire of 1666. St Paul's Cathedral (1675–1708).
Auguste Pugin	1812–52	Britain	Leader of the Gothic revival in Britain. St Giles's, Cheadle, Cheshire (1840–46).
Gustave Eiffel	1832–1923	France	A renowned engineer who specialized in metallic structures. Eiffel Tower (1887–89).
Henry Hobson Richardson	1838–86	USA	Brought the southern French Romanesque style into US cities. Trinity Church, Boston (1873).

NOTABLE ARCHITECTS (continued)

The distinctive silhouette of the Sydney Opera House, Australia, was designed by Danish architect Jørn Utzon.

ARCHITECT	LIVED	ORIGIN	STYLE/KEY WORKS
Daniel Hudson Burnham	1846–1912	USA	City planner and early builder of skyscrapers. Flatiron Building, New York City (1902).
Antonio Gaudí y Cornet	1852–1926	Spain/ Catalonia	The architectural leader of the Catalan patriotic *Renaizensa* (rebirth). Church of the Sagrada Familia, Barcelona (1883–1926).
Frank Lloyd Wright	1867–1959	USA	One of the most influential 20th-century American architects. Guggenheim Museum, New York (1943–59).
Walter Gropius	1883–1969	Germany	Founder of the Bauhaus Design School. Gropius House, Lincoln, Massachusetts (1937).
Ludwig Mies van der Rohe	1886–1969	Germany/ USA	Created an influential style known as "skin and bones" architecture. Barcelona Pavilion, Spain (1929).
Le Corbusier (Charles-Édouard Jeanneret-Gris)	1887–1965	Switzerland	One of the most influential European architects of the 20th century. Unité d'Habitation, Marseilles (1946–52).
Kenzo Tange	1913–2005	Japan	Combined traditional Japanese styles with Modernism. Tokyo Metropolitan Government Building (1988–91).
Jørn Utzon	1918–2008	Denmark	Winner of the competition to design the Sydney Opera House (1959–73).
Frank O. Gehry	1929–	Canada	Used ordinary materials in extraordinary ways, defying structural logic. Guggenheim Museum, Bilbao (completed 1997).
Lord Richard Rogers	1933–	Britain	Noted for his Modernist and Functionalist designs. Pompidou Centre (completed 1977).
Lord Norman Foster	1935–	Britain	A distinguished practitioner of the High Tech style. Wembley Stadium (2003–07).
Daniel Libeskind	1946–	Poland/ USA	A leading proponent of deconstructivism. Jewish Museum, Berlin (1992–2001).
Zaha Hadid	1950–	Iraq	First female winner of the Pritzker Architecture Prize. Bridge Pavillion, Spain (2008).

GREAT WRITERS

Literature gives us a special insight into the past. Though the plots of novels and plays may be invented, the characters speak and behave in ways that reflect the preoccupations, social mores, and artistic conventions of their time, and in many works, a fictional chain of events plays out against a rich background of verifiable historical happenings.

NAME	LIVED	ORIGIN	GENRE	NOTABLE WORKS
Homer	8th century BCE	Ancient Greece	Poet	*Odyssey* (8th century BCE).
Aeschylus	c.525–456 BCE	Ancient Greece	Playwright	*Seven Against Thebes* (c.467 BCE).
Sophocles	c.496–406 BCE	Ancient Greece	Playwright	*Antigone* (c.442 BCE).
Euripides	c.484–406 BCE	Ancient Greece	Playwright	*Medea* (c.431 BCE).
Aristophanes	c.448–388 BCE	Ancient Greece	Playwright	*The Frogs* (c.405 BCE).
Valmiki	c.400–200 BCE	Ancient India	Poet	*Ramayana* (c.400–200 BCE).
Virgil	70–19 BCE	Roman empire	Poet	*Aeneid* (c.29–19 BCE).
Ovid	43 BCE– c. 17 CE	Roman empire	Poet	*Metamorphoses* (8 CE).
Murasaki Shikibu	c.978–1014	Japan	Novelist	*The Tale of Genji* (c.1001–10).
Dante Alighieri	1265–1321	Italy	Poet	*Divine Comedy* (c.1321).
Petrarch	1304–74	Italy	Poet	*Canzoniere* (1327–68).
Geoffrey Chaucer	1343–1400	England	Poet	*The Canterbury Tales* (1387–1400).
Miguel de Cervantes	1547–1616	Spain	Novelist/ poet/ playwright	*Don Quixote* (1605).
William Shakespeare	1564–1616	England	Playwright/ poet	*Romeo and Juliet* (c.1591–95).
John Milton	1608–74	England	Poet	*Paradise Lost* (1667).
Molière	1622–73	France	Playwright	*Le Misanthrope* (1666).
Jean Racine	1639–99	France	Playwright	*Phèdre* (1677).
Jonathan Swift	1667–1745	Ireland	Novelist/ essayist	*Gulliver's Travels* (1726).
Xueqin Cao	c.1715–63	China	Novelist	*Dream of the Red Chamber* (1791).
Johann Wolfgang von Goethe	1749–1832	Germany	Novelist/ playwright	*Faust* (1808).
William Wordsworth	1770–1850	Britain	Poet	*The Prelude* (1799).
Jane Austen	1775–1817	Britain	Novelist	*Pride and Prejudice* (1813).
John Keats	1795–1821	Britain	Poet	*Endymion* (1818).
Alexander Pushkin	1799–1837	Russia	Poet/ novelist	*Eugene Onegin* (1828).

GREAT WRITERS (continued)

NAME	LIVED	ORIGIN	GENRE	NOTABLE WORKS
Honoré de Balzac	1799–1850	France	Novelist	*La Comédie Humaine* (1827–47).
Alexandre Dumas	1802–70	France	Novelist	*The Three Musketeers* (1844).
Victor Hugo	1802–85	France	Novelist	*Les Misérables* (1862).
Ralph Waldo Emerson	1803–82	USA	Essayist/ poet	*The Conduct of Life* (1860).
Hans Christian Andersen	1805–75	Denmark	Novelist	*Fairy Tales* (1835–37).
Henry Longfellow	1807–82	USA	Poet	*Hiawatha* (1855).
Charles Dickens	1812–70	Britain	Novelist	*Great Expectations* (1860–61).
Ivan Turgenev	1818–83	Russia	Novelist/ playwright	*Fathers and Sons* (1862).
George Eliot	1819–80	Britain	Novelist	*The Mill on the Floss* (1860).
Fyodor Dostoyevsky	1821–81	Russia	Novelist	*Crime and Punishment* (1866).
Walt Whitman	1819–92	USA	Poet	*Leaves of Grass* (1855–89).
Gustave Flaubert	1821–80	France	Novelist	*Madame Bovary* (1857).
Henrik Ibsen	1828–1906	Norway	Playwright	*Peer Gynt* (1867).
Leo Tolstoy	1828–1910	Russia	Novelist	*War and Peace* (1865–69).
Mark Twain	1835–1910	USA	Novelist	*Huckleberry Finn* (1885).
Thomas Hardy	1840–1928	Britain	Novelist	*Tess of the d'Urbervilles* (1891).
Henry James	1843–1916	USA	Novelist	*The Bostonians* (1886).
August Strindberg	1849–1912	Sweden	Playwright	*The Dance of Death* (1901).
George Bernard Shaw	1856–1950	Ireland	Playwright	*Man and Superman* (1903)
Joseph Conrad	1857–1924	Poland	Novelist	*Heart of Darkness* (1902).
Anton Chekhov	1860–1904	Russia	Playwright	*The Cherry Orchard* (1904).

Charles Dickens, the most acclaimed novelist of the Victorian era in Britain, first published his novels in serial form in popular periodicals.

GREAT WRITERS (continued)

NAME	LIVED	ORIGIN	GENRE	NOTABLE WORKS
Rabindranath Tagore	1861–1941	India	Poet/ playwright	*Gitanjali, Song Offerings* (1912)
Edith Wharton	1862–1937	USA	Novelist	*The Age of Innocence* (1920).
William Butler Yeats	1865–1939	Ireland	Poet	*The Wild Swans at Coole* (1917).
Marcel Proust	1871–1922	France	Novelist	*Remembrance of Things Past* (1912–27).
Robert Frost	1874–1963	USA	Poet	*Mountain Interval* (1916).
Thomas Mann	1875–1955	Gemany	Novelist	*Death in Venice* (1913).
Hermann Hesse	1877–1962	Germany	Novelist	*The Glass Bead Game* (1945).
James Joyce	1882–1941	Ireland	Novelist	*Ulysses* (1922).
Virginia Woolf	1882–1941	Britain	Novelist	*Mrs Dalloway* (1925).
Franz Kafka	1883–1924	Czechoslovakia	Novelist	*The Metamorphosis* (1916).
D.H. Lawrence	1885–1930	Britain	Novelist/ poet	*Sons and Lovers* (1913).
Ezra Pound	1885–1972	USA	Poet	*The Cantos* (1915–62).
T. S. Eliot	1888–1965	USA/Britain	Poet/ playwright	*The Waste Land* (1922)
Jorge Luis Borges	1899–1986	Argentina	Novelist	*Labyrinths* (1953).
Karel Čapek	1890–1938	Czechoslovakia	Playwright	*R.U.R.* (1920).
Boris Pasternak	1890–1960	Russia	Novelist	*Doctor Zhivago* (1957).
Mikhail Bulgakov	1891–1940	Russia	Novelist	*The Master and Margarita* (1928).
William Faulkner	1897–1962	USA	Novelist	*The Sound and the Fury* (1929).
Bertolt Brecht	1898–1956	Germany	Playwright	*Mother Courage* (1938).
Federico García Lorca	1898–1936	Spain	Playwright	*The House of Bernarda Alba* (1936).
Ernest Hemingway	1899–1961	USA	Novelist	*The Old Man and the Sea* (1952).
Vladimir Nabokov	1899–1977	Russia/USA	Novelist	*Lolita* (1958).
John Steinbeck	1902–68	USA	Novelist	*The Grapes of Wrath* (1939).
George Orwell	1903–50	Britain	Novelist	*Nineteen Eighty-Four* (1949).
Samuel Beckett	1906–89	Ireland	Playwright/ novelist	*Waiting for Godot* (1954).
W. H. Auden	1907–73	Britain	Poet	*The Sea and the Mirror* (1944).
Naguib Mahfouz	1911–2006	Egypt	Novelist	*The Cairo Trilogy* (1956–57)
Albert Camus	1913–60	France	Novelist	*The Plague* (1947).

GREAT WRITERS (continued)

Death of a Salesman by Arthur Miller, the story of a travelling salesman's road to ruin, has been likened to a modern-day version of Greek tragedy.

NAME	LIVED	ORIGIN	GENRE	NOTABLE WORKS
Saul Bellow	1915–2005	Canada	Novelist	*Humbolt's Gift* (1975).
Arthur Miller	1915–2005	USA	Playwright	*Death of a Salesman* (1946).
Alexander Solzhenitsyn	1918–2008	Russia	Novelist	*One Day in the Life of Ivan Denisovich* (1962).
Iris Murdoch	1919–99	Britain	Novelist	*The Sea, The Sea* (1978).
Yukio Mishima	1925–70	Japan	Novelist	*The Sea of Fertility* (1965–70).
Dario Fo	1926–	Italy	Playwright	*Accidental Death of an Anarchist* (1970).
Gabriel Garcia Marquez	1928–	Colombia	Novelist	*One Hundred Years of Solitude* (1967).
Milan Kundera	1929–	Czechoslovakia	Novelist	*The Unbearable Lightness of Being* (1984).
Harold Pinter	1930–2008	Britain	Playwright	*The Birthday Party* (1958).
Toni Morrison	1931–	USA	Novelist	*Beloved* (1987)
V. S. Naipaul	1932-	Trinidad	Novelist	*A House for Mr. Biswas* (1971).
Philip Roth	1933–	USA	Novelist	*Portnoy's Complaint* (1972).
Wole Soyinka	1934–	Nigeria	Playwright/ poet	*A Dance of the Forests* (1960).
Seamus Heaney	1939–	Ireland	Poet	*Door into the Dark* (1969).
Margaret Atwood	1939–	Canada	Novelist/ poet	*The Handmaid's Tale* (1985)
Peter Carey	1943–	Australia	Novelist	*Oscar and Lucinda* (1988).

WESTERN CLASSICAL COMPOSERS

The great composers have produced the soundtrack to every era since Renaissance times. While it may seem the most intangible of the arts, the skills of musicians and instrument-makers today allow us to hear the music of the past just as it would have sounded at the time.

COMPOSER	LIVED	ORIGIN	MUSICAL ERA/KEY WORKS
Guillaume de Machaut	c.1300–77	France	Early; *De Toutes Flours*.
Thomas Tallis	c.1505–85	England	Early; *Spem in Alium Nunquam Habui*.
Giovanni Pierluigi da Palestrina	c.1525–94	Italy	Early; *Missa Brevis*.
William Byrd	c.1540–1623	England	Early; *Great Service*.
Claudio Monteverdi	c.1567–1643	Italy	Baroque; *L'Orfeo*.
Henry Purcell	c.1659–95	England	Baroque; *Dido and Aeneas*.
Antonio Vivaldi	1678–1741	Italy	Baroque; *The Four Seasons*.
George Frideric Handel	1685–1759	Germany	Baroque; *Messiah*.
Johann Sebastian Bach	1685–1750	Germany	Baroque; *The Well-Tempered Clavier*.
Franz Joseph Haydn	1732–1809	Austria	Classical; String Quartet no. 63, *Sunrise*.
Wolfgang Amadeus Mozart	1756–91	Austria	Classical; *The Magic Flute*; *Eine Kleine Nachtmusik*.
Ludwig van Beethoven	1770–1827	Germany	Classical; Symphony no. 5; Symphony no. 9 (*Ode to Joy*).
Franz Schubert	1797–1828	Austria	Romantic; Piano Quintet, *Die Forelle*.
Hector Berlioz	1803–69	France	Romantic; *The Trojans*.
Felix Mendelssohn	1809–47	Germany	Romantic; *Violin Concerto*.
Frederic Chopin	1810–49	Poland	Romantic; *Funeral March*.
Robert Schumann	1810–56	Germany	Romantic; *Carnaval*.
Franz Liszt	1811–86	Hungary	Romantic; *Sonata in B Minor*.
Anton Bruckner	1824–96	Austria	Romantic; *Te Deum*.
Johannes Brahms	1833–97	Germany	Romantic; *Ein Deutsches Requiem*.

Stringed instruments of unequalled tone were produced by the Stradivari family of Cremona, Italy, in the late 17th and early 18th century; some 700 survive today.

WESTERN CLASSICAL COMPOSERS (continued)

COMPOSER	LIVED	ORIGIN	MUSICAL ERA/KEY WORKS
Pyotr Tchaikovsky	1840–93	Russia	Romantic; *The Nutcracker*; *Swan Lake.*
Gustav Mahler	1860–1911	Austria	Romantic; *Das Lied von der Erde.*
Richard Strauss	1864–1949	Germany	Romantic; *Ein Heldenleben.*
Gioachino Rossini	1792–1868	Italy	Romantic opera; *The Barber of Seville.*
Giuseppe Verdi	1813–1901	Italy	Romantic opera; *La Traviata*; *Requiem.*
Richard Wagner	1813–83	Germany	Romantic opera; *Der Ring des Nibelungen*; *Tristan und Isolde.*
Giacomo Puccini	1858–1924	Italy	Romantic opera; *La Bohème.*
Johann Strauss Jr.	1825–99	Austria	Romantic opera; *Die Fledermaus.*
Camille Saint-Saëns	1835–1921	France	Romantic; *Danse Macabre.*
Antonín Dvořák	1841–1904	Czechoslovakia	Romantic; Symphony no. 9 in E Minor, *From the New World.*
Edvard Grieg	1843–1907	Norway	Romantic; *Holberg Suite.*
Edward Elgar	1857–1934	Britain	Romantic; *Pomp and Circumstance.*
Claude Debussy	1862–1918	France	Romantic/ Modern; *La Mer.*
Jean Sibelius	1865–1957	Finland	Romantic/ Modern; Symphony no. 5.
Maurice Ravel	1875–1937	France	Romantic/ Modern; Piano Concerto in G Major.
Ralph Vaughan Williams	1872–1958	England	Romantic/ Modern; *Sinfonia Antartica.*
Sergei Rachmaninov	1873–1943	Russia	Romantic; Piano Concerto no. 2.
Arnold Schoenberg	1874–1951	Austria	Modern; *Pierrot Lunaire.*
Charles Ives	1874–1954	USA	Modern; *Three Places in New England.*
Béla Bartók	1881–1945	Hungary	Modern; *Concerto for Orchestra.*
Igor Stravinsky	1882–1971	Russia	Modern; *The Rake's Progress*; *The Rite of Spring.*
Sergei Prokofiev	1891–1953	Russia	Modern; *Romeo and Juliet.*
George Gershwin	1898–1937	USA	Modern; *An American in Paris.*
Kurt Weill	1900–50	Germany	Modern; *The Threepenny Opera.*
Aaron Copland	1900–90	USA	Modern; *Appalachian Spring.*
Dmitry Shostakovich	1906–75	Russia	Modern; Symphony no. 5.
Benjamin Britten	1913–76	Britain	Modern; *Death in Venice.*
Leonard Bernstein	1918–90	USA	Modern; *West Side Story*; *Candide.*
Toru Takemitsu	1930-96	Japan	Modern; *November Steps.*
Philip Glass	1937–	USA	Modern; *Einstein on the Beach.*

MAJOR WORLD FAITHS

Originating from almost every corner of the globe, the world's great faiths are as diverse as its cultures. Some have their origin in prehistoric times, yet the 20th century saw the emergence of several new religions that have attracted followers in their millions.

NAME	PLACE/DATE	ADHERENTS	FOUNDER	TEXTS
Chinese traditional religion	Unknown, prehistoric	400 million	Indigenous	n/a
Hinduism	India, prehistoric	900 million	Indigenous	The Vedas, Upanishads, and Sanskrit epics
Shinto	Japan, prehistoric	3–4 million	Indigenous	*Kojiki, Nihon-gi*
Voodoo	West Africa, unknown	8 million	Indigenous	n/a
Zoroastrianism	Iran, 6th century BCE	200,000	Zoroaster	The Avesta
Daoism	China, *c.*550 BCE	20 million	Lao Tzu	*Dao De Jing*
Jainism	India, *c.*550 BCE	4 million	Mahavira	Mahavira's teachings
Buddhism	Northeast India, *c.*520 BCE	375 million	Siddhartha Gautama, the Buddha	Pali canon, Mahayana sutras
Confucianism	China, 6th/5th centuries BCE	5–6 million	Confucius	The Four Books and Five Classics
Judaism	Israel, *c.*1300 BCE	15 million	Abraham; Moses	Hebrew Bible; Talmud
Christianity	Israel, *c.*30 CE	2,000 million	Jesus Christ	The Bible (Old and New Testaments)

Christianity has the most adherents of all the world religions, although Islam is rapidly gaining ground.

MAJOR WORLD FAITHS (continued)

Guru Nanak (centre), founder of Sikhism, was the first of 10 gurus who laid down the tenets of this monotheistic Indian faith.

NAME	PLACE/DATE	ADHERENTS	FOUNDER	TEXTS
Islam	Saudi Arabia, revealed in 7th century	1,500 million	n/a; Muhammad is Prophet	The Qu'ran (scripture); Hadith (tradition)
Sikhism	Punjab, India, c.1500	23 million	Guru Nanak	Adi Granth (Guru Granth Sahib)
Church of Jesus Christ of Latter-Day Saints (Mormons)	New York, 1830	13 million	Joseph Smith	The Bible; *Book of Mormon*
Tenrikyo	Japan, 1838	1 million	Nakayama Miki	*Mikigaurata, Ofudesaki, Osashizu*
Baha'i Faith	Tehran, Iran, 1863	5–7 million	Baha'u'llah	Writings of Baha'u'llah
Church of Christ (Scientist)	New York, USA, 1879	Up to 400,000	Mary Baker Eddy	The Bible; *Science and Health with Key to the Scriptures*
Cao Dai	Vietnam, 1926	8 million	Ngo Van Chieu	Cao Dai Canon
Rastafarianism	Jamaica, 1930s	1 million	Haile Selassie I	*Holy Piby*
Family Federation for World Peace and Unification	South Korea, 1954	3 million (official figure)	Sun Myung Moon	*Sun Myung Moon, the Divine Principle*
Wicca	1950s, but based on ancient beliefs	1–3 million	Gerald Gardner	n/a
Falun Gong	China, 1992	10 million	Li Hongzhi	Writings of master Li, including *Zhuan Falun*

GREAT THINKERS

The earliest enquiries into the nature and meaning of life come from the founders of the great Eastern religions. Since their time, Western philosophers have journeyed to the outer limits of thought and understanding, posing questions that challenge our most fundamental beliefs.

NAME	LIVED	ORIGIN	IDEAS/KEY WORK
Siddhartha Gautama (Buddha)	c.563–483 BCE	India	Founder of Buddhism as a path to achieving *nirvana* (spiritual enlightenment) and thus release from the earthly cycle of reincarnation.
Lao Tzu	*fl.* 6th century BCE	China	Founder of Daoism, concerning an individual's approach to life. *Dao De Jing.*
Confucius	551–479 BCE	China	Founder of Confucianism: social harmony is promoted via social conventions and practices.
Pythagoras	c.550–c.500 BCE	Greece	Polymath interested in esoteric knowledge (that he made available to only a few initiates) and the mystical power of numbers.
Socrates	c.469–399 BCE	Greece	One of the founders of Western philosophy, to whom the quote is attributed: "A life unexamined is not worth living". No surviving writings.
Plato	c.427–347 BCE	Greece	A pupil of Socrates; argued that everything we perceive is a mere shadow of its abstract, ideal Form. *The Republic* (c.360 BCE).
Aristotle	384–322 BCE	Greece	Wide-ranging philosopher with a special interest in logical classification. *Metaphysics* (350 BCE).

Socrates was primarily interested in questions of morality. Falling foul of the Athenian ruling class, he was sentenced to death by taking poison.

GREAT THINKERS (continued)

NAME	LIVED	ORIGIN	IDEAS/KEY WORK
Plotinus	205–270 CE	Greece / Roman empire	Founder of Neo-platonism, a development of Plato's original ideas. *Enneads* (*c.*253–70).
St Augustine of Hippo	354–430 CE	North Africa/ Roman empire	Transmitted Platonism through Christian theology. *The City of God* (413–26).
St Thomas Aquinas	1225–74	Italy	Greatest medieval religious philosopher. *Summa Theologiae* (1259–69).
Niccolò Machiavelli	1469–1527	Italy	Argued that the state should promote the common good, irrespective of any moral evaluation of its acts. *The Prince* (1513).
Francis Bacon	1561–1626	England	Recognized that scientific knowledge could procure power over nature. *Novum Organum* (1620).
Thomas Hobbes	1588–1679	England	Father of English political philosophy, the study of how societies are organized. *Leviathan* (1651).
René Descartes	1596–1650	France	Overturned medieval and Renaissance scholasticism. *Meditations* (1641).
Baruch Spinoza	1632–77	Netherlands	One of the most important 17th-century Rationalists, arguing that knowledge of the world can be gained through reason. *Tractatus Theologico-Politicus* (1670).
John Locke	1632–1704	England	Proponent of empiricism, the view that all knowledge of anything that actually exists must be derived from experience. *Treatises of Government* (1690).
Gottfried Wilhelm Leibniz	1646–1716	Germany	Mathematican and rationalist philosopher. *Monadology* (1714).
George Berkeley	1685–1753	England	Great empiricist who developed an idealist metaphysical system, maintaining that reality ultimately consists of something non-material. *Principles of Human Knowledge* (1710).
David Hume	1711–76	Britain	Leading sceptic of metaphysics, the philosophy concerned with the ultimate nature of what exists. *Treatise of Human Nature* (1734–37).
Jean-Jacques Rousseau	1712–78	Switzerland	Proponent of the sovereignty of the citizen body. *The Social Contract, or Principles of Political Right* (1762)
Immanuel Kant	1724–1804	Germany	Sought to establish the authority of reason by critical examination. *Critique of Pure Reason* (1781).
Thomas Paine	1737–1809	Britain	Governments must respect the natural rights of their citizens. *The Rights of Man* (1791–92).

GREAT THINKERS (continued)

NAME	LIVED	ORIGIN	IDEAS/KEY WORK
G. W. F. Hegel	1770–1831	Germany	Most influential of the German Idealists. *The Phenomenology of Spirit* (1807).
Karl Marx	1818–83	Germany	Radical social theorist and philosopher of Communism. *Das Kapital* (1867).
Arthur Schopenhauer	1788–1860	Germany	Espoused transcendental idealism, the belief that human experience of things consists of how they appear to us. *The World as Will and Representation* (1818).
Søren Kierkegaard	1813–55	Denmark	A forerunner of Existentialism, stressing the individual's unique position as a self-determining agent. *Concluding Unscientific Postscript to Philosophical Fragments* (1846).
Friedrich Nietzsche	1844–1900	Germany	Rejected religious and metaphysical interpretations of the human condition in favour of the principle of the "Superman". *Thus Spake Zarathustra* (1883–85).
Bertrand Russell	1872–1970	Britain	Founder of analytic philosophy, emphasizing clarity and argument. *Principia Mathematica* (1910–13).
Ludwig Wittgenstein	1889–1951	Austria	Most prominent analytical philosopher. *Tractatus Logico-Philosophicus* (1921).
Jean-Paul Sartre	1905–80	France	Leader of the Existentialist movement, which focused on the totality of human freedom. *Being and Nothingness* (1943).

Jean Paul Sartre and Simone de Beauvoir were key figures in Paris's intellectual Left Bank scene.

INDEX

Page numbers in **bold** refer to main references to subject.
Page numbers in *italics* refer to illustrations and captions.

ACKNOWLEDGMENTS

The publisher would like to thank:
Debra Wolter and Sarah Tomley for editorial assistance; Richard Horsford for design assistance; and Dorothy Frame for the index.

Picture credits
The publisher would like to thank the following for their kind permission to reproduce their photographs:

(Key: a-above; b-below/bottom; c-centre; f-far; l-left; r-right; t-top)

1 Getty Images: Sisse Brimberg (t). 2-3 Getty Images: Bruno Morandi. 4 Corbis: India Picture. 5 Getty Images: Travelpix Ltd. 6-7 Getty Images: Tom Bonaventure. 8-9 Getty Images: Jeremy Woodhouse (t). 9 Getty Images: Werner Forman (bc). Getty Images: Check Six (t). 10-25 Corbis: Bettmann (ftl) (ftr). 10-11 Getty Images: Hisham Ibrahim. 12-13 Alamy Images: Porky Pies Photography (t). Getty Images: Fred Mayer (b). 14-413 (Panel image) Getty Images: DEA / G. Cozzi (t) (c). 14 Corbis: Anthony Bannister; Gallo Images (ca). 15 Corbis: Yann Arthus-Bertrand. 16 Corbis: Gianni Dagli Orti (b). 17 Alamy Images: Mary Evans Picture Library (br). Getty Images: Time & Life Pictures (t). 18 Corbis: The Gallery Collection (c). 19 Alamy Images: Keith Heron (b). Ancient Art & Architecture Collection: Uniphoto Press Japan (tl). 20 The Art Archive: Bibliothèque Mazarine Paris (bl). 21 akg-images: akg-images (b). Corbis: Angelo Hornak (tc). 22 Corbis: Leonard de Selva (ca). 22-23 Corbis: William Manning (b). 23 Corbis: Hulton-Deutsch Collection (tr). 24 Corbis: Enzo & Paolo Ragazzini (b). 25 Corbis: The Gallery Collection (t); Reuters (b). 26-27 Getty Images: B. Anthony Stewart (b); Keren Su (t). 28-55 iStockphoto.com: Mustafa Deliormanli (ftl) (ftr). 29 Getty Images: Nico Tondini (b). 30-31 Getty Images: Kenneth Garrett (b). 32 Corbis: Christie's Images (b). 33 Corbis: Stapleton Collection (t). 34-35 Getty Images: Stuart Dee (b). 36 Photolibrary: Imagestate RM (t). 37 Corbis: Araldo de Luca (b). 38 Corbis: Free Agents Limited (b). 41 Corbis: The Gallery Collection (t). 42 Getty Images: DEA / C. Sappa (b). 44 Corbis: Tetra Images (t). 46 Corbis: Werner Forman (b). 48 Corbis: Francis G. Mayer (t). 49 Corbis: Bernard Annebicque (b). 50 Corbis:Bettmann (b). 54 Getty Images: NASA/Handout (t). 55 Corbis: Ron Sachs (tc). 56-57 Getty Images: Joe Cornish (b); Travel Ink (t). 60-79 Corbis: Jonathan Blair (ftl) (ftr); 60 Corbis: Wolfgang Kaehler (t). DK Images: Natural History Museum (t). 61 DK Images: Natural History Museum (br). The Natural History Museum, London: The Natural History Museum, London (ca). 62 Getty Images: The Bridgeman Art Library (cb). 63 DK Images: Natural History Museum (t). Science Photo Library: Javier Trueba/MSF/Science Photo Library (b). 64 Corbis: Jacques Langevin (b); John Van Hasselt (t). 65 DK Images: Natural History Museum (tr). 66 Corbis: The Gallery Collection (cra); Michael Amendolia (br). 66-67 Getty Images: Photolibrary (b). 67 DK Images: American Museum of Natural History (cb). 68 Corbis: Barry Lewis (bl). DK Images: Natural History Museum (b). 69 Corbis: Ali Meyer (cb); Pierre Colombel (tr). 70-71 Corbis: Pierre Vauthey. 72 Corbis: Alfredo Dagli Orti (b). 73 Alamy Images: Ozimages (b). Getty Images: Japanese School (ca). 74 Corbis: Adam Woolfitt (ca). Getty Images: Travel Ink (b). 75 Corbis: Cordaiy Photo Library Ltd (bl). Getty Images: The Bridgeman Art Library (br). 76 Getty Images: The Bridgeman Art Library (b). 77 Corbis: Gianni Dagli Orti (br). Getty Images: Nico Tondini (t). 78 Alamy Images: INTERFOTO (b). Corbis: Charles & Josette Lenars (ca). 79 Corbis: Alfredo Dagli Orti (bl). Getty Images: The Bridgeman Art Library (t). 80-81 Corbis: Bob Krist (b); Kevin Schafer (t). 84-107 Corbis: Ladislav Janicek (ftl) (ftr). 84 Corbis: Bruno Morandi (bl); Nik Wheeler (bl). 85 Corbis: Gianni Dagli Orti (cb). Getty Images: Middle Eastern (cla). 86 Corbis: Gianni Dagli Orti (bl). 87 Corbis: Burstein Collection (ca); The Art Archive (b). 88 Corbis: Gianni Dagli Orti (cra) (bl). 89 Corbis: Jane Sweeney (b). 90 Getty Images: Middle Eastern (ca). 90-91 Corbis: Brooklyn Museum (b). 91 Getty Images: Egyptian (t). 92 Corbis: Brooklyn Museum (bc); Werner Forman (t). 93 Corbis: The Gallery Collection(tc). iStockphoto.com: Jan Rihak (b). 94-95 Getty Images: Ary Diesendruck (c). 96 Corbis: Atlantide Phototravel (b). 97 Corbis: Gianni Dagli Orti (ca). Getty Images: Patrick Landmann (b). 98 Corbis: Neil Beer (bl). 99 Corbis: Fridmar Damm (t); Sandro Vannini (bc). 100 Corbis: Gail Mooney (bl). Getty Images: Guy Vanderelst (t). 101 Corbis: Jean-Pierre Lescourret (cb); Wolfgang Kaehler (cr). 102 Getty Images: Robert Harding (cb). 103 Corbis: Luca Tettoni (bl); Paul Almasy (tr). 104 Alamy Images: Liu Xiaoyang (t). Corbis: Christie's Images (bl). 105 Alamy Images: Liu Xiaoyang (b). Corbis: Asian Art & Archaeology, Inc. (ca). 106 Corbis: Charles & Josette Lenars (bl); Gianni Dagli Orti (t). 107 Corbis: Danny Lehman (br); Gianni Dagli Orti (ca). 108-109 Corbis: Werner Forman (b). Photolibrary: CM Dixon (b). 112ñ157 Getty Images: Image Source (ftl) (ftr). 110 Corbis: Gianni Dagli Orti (t); Paul Almasy (b). 113 Alamy Images: Visual Arts Library (London) (cla). Getty Images: DEA / W. BUSS (b). 114 Corbis: Gianni Dagli Orti (cl) (bl). 115 Corbis: Paul Almasy (b). 116 Corbis: John Heseltine (b). Getty Images: Marco Simoni (br). 117 Alamy Images: Rolf Richardson (b). 118 Corbis: Wolfgang Kaehler (br). 119 Corbis:

Hoberman Collection (ca); José Fuste Raga (b). 120-121 Alamy Images: nagelestock.com. 122 DK Images: Hellenic Maritime Museum (bl). Getty Images: Greek (c). 124 Corbis: Araldo de Luca (tr). DK Images: British Museum (bl). 124-125 Corbis: Araldo de Luca (b). 125 Corbis: Michele Falzone (tr). 126 Corbis: Sandro Vannini (ca). iStockphoto.com: David H. Seymour (b). 127 Corbis: Christophe Boisvieux (b). 128 Corbis: Fred de Noyelle (crb). Getty Images: Glenn Beanland (t). 129 DK Images: British Museum (ca). Getty Images: Panoramic Images (b). 130-131 Getty Images: School of Giulio Romano (b). 131 Corbis: Roger Wood (ca). 132 The Bridgeman Art Library: (b). Corbis: Hoberman Collection (ca). 133 Corbis: Bob Sacha (br). 134 Corbis: Sandro Vannini (bl). 135 Corbis: Barney Burstein (tr); Karl-Heinz Haenel (b). 136 Getty Images: Roman(ca). 136-137 Getty Images: Lee Frost (b). 137 Corbis: image100 (tr). 138 Corbis: Hoberman Collection (ca). 138-139 Corbis: Araldo de Luca (b). 140 akg-images: Tristan Lafranchis (b). 141 Corbis: The Gallery Collection (tr). DK Images: The Board of Trustees of the Armouries (bc). 142 Corbis: Werner Forman (bl). iStockphoto.com: Trudy Karl (t). 143 Corbis: Ary Scheffer (b); Time & Life Pictures (ca). 144 Corbis: Bettmann (t). Getty Images: AXEL SCHMIDT (crb). 145 Alamy Images: Danita Delimont (b). Getty Images: Hulton Archive (ca). 146 Corbis: Adam Woolfitt (t); Lindsay Hebberd (b). 147 Alamy Images: (bl); Sherab (t). 148 Corbis: Philadelphia Museum of Art (ca). 148-149 Getty Images: Panoramic Images (b). 149 Getty Images: Paleo-Christian (tr). 150 Corbis: Asian Art & Archaeology, Inc (br); Frank Lukasseck (c). 151 Corbis: Danny Lehman (b). 152 Corbis: Royal Ontario Museum(ca). 152-153 Getty Images: Tom Bonaventure (b). 153 The Art Archive: British Library (t). 154 Corbis: Danny Lehman (t). Getty Images:Stephen Sharnoff (br). 155 Corbis: Charles & Josette Lenars (ca); Danny Lehman (b). 156 Corbis: Danny Lehman (b). 157 Corbis: Brooklyn Museum (bc); Yann Arthus-Bertrand (tr). 158-159 Corbis: Arthur Thévenart (b). Getty Images: French School (t). 162-213 Corbis: Paul Almasy (ftl) (ftr). 162 Corbis: James Marshall (t). 163 Corbis: Frank Lukasseck (bl). 164 Corbis: Asian Art & Archaeology, Inc (ca); Burstein Collection (b). 165 Corbis: David Sailors (tr). 166-167 Photolibrary: View Stock. 168 Corbis: British Museum (b). 168-169 Corbis: DEA / C. Sappa (b). 169 Alamy Images: The London Art Archive (tr). 170 Corbis: Angelo Hornak (br); Christie's Images (c). 171 Corbis: Asian Art & Archaeology, Inc. (ca); Christie's Images (br). 172-173 Corbis: Christie's Images (b). 174-175 DK Images: The Board of Trustees of the Armouries. 175 The Art Archive: The Art Archive / British Library (tr). 176 Corbis: Fridmar Damm (t). 177 Corbis: Bohemian Nomad Picturemakers (t); Philadelphia Museum of Art (bc). 178 Corbis: Joson (ca). 179 Corbis: Luca Tettoni (ca); Michael Freeman (br). 180 The Trustees of the British Museum: The Trustees of the British Museum (bc). Corbis: Jim Zuckerman (t). 181 Corbis: Roger Wood (b). 182 Corbis: Arthur Thévenart (b). 183 Corbis: The Gallery Collection (br). Getty Images: Bridgeman Art Library (ca). 184 Corbis: (t); Frédéric Soltan (cb). 185 Corbis: Sheldan Collins (b). 186 Corbis: Remi Benali (crb); Staffan Widstrand (t). 187 Corbis: Great Enclosure (b); Paul Almasy (t). 188 Corbis: Alfredo Dagli Orti (b). DK Images: British Museum (bc). 189 Alamy Images: M. J. Mayo (tr). Corbis: Geoffrey Taunton; Cordaiy Photo Library Ltd (ca). 190 Corbis: Gian Berto Vanni (b). 191 Getty Images: The Bridgeman Art Library (tr) (bc). 192 Corbis: Alfredo Dagli Orti(cra). 192-193 Getty Images: Travel Ink (b). Getty Images: Eric Van Den Brulle (tc). 194 Getty Images: David Lomax/Robert Harding (tr). 195 Getty Images: English School (ca); French School (br). 196 Getty Images: Guy Vanderelst (b). 197 Corbis: The Gallery Collection (tr). Getty Images: (bl); Guy Vanderelst (b). 198 Corbis: The Gallery Collection (bl). 199 Corbis: Kevin Fleming (t). 200 Getty Images: French School (tr). 201 Alamy Images: Jeremy Pardoe (b). Getty Images: Hulton Archive (ca). 202 Corbis: Richard T. Nowitz (b); Vanni Archive (t). 203 Corbis: Philip de Bay (ca). 204 Corbis: Keith Dannemiller (t); Paul Almasy (br). 205 Corbis: Bettmann (tc); Charles & Josette Lenars (b). 206 Corbis: Werner Forman (t). DK Images: British Museum (b). 207 Corbis: George H.H. Huey (b); Werner Forman (t). 208 Corbis: (bc). 209 Alamy Images: Deco (br). 210-211 Getty Images: David Madison. 212 Corbis: Macduff Everton (t). DK Images: International Sailing Craft Association, Lowestoft (ca). 213 Corbis: Kevin Schafer (b). Getty Images: The Bridgeman Art Library (ca). 214-215 Corbis: The Gallery Collection (b). Getty Images: The Bridgeman Art Library (t). 218-255 Getty Images: Andreas Cellarius (ftl) (ftr). 218 Corbis: Kimbell Art Museum (t). Getty Images: Keren Su (b). 219 DK Images: British Museum (ca). 220 Corbis: Bettmann (ca). 220-221 Corbis: Brooklyn Museum (b). 221 Corbis: Werner Forman (tc). 222 DK Images: National Museum, New Delhi (bl). Getty Images: Bishn Das (ca). 223 DK Images: National Museum, New Delhi (c). Getty Images: Travel Ink (t). 224-225 Corbis: Steve Allen/Brand X. 226 Corbis: The Gallery Collection (ca). Getty Images: Islamic School (b). 227 Corbis: Francesco Venturi (tr). 228 Corbis: Tilman Billing (b). 229 Corbis: The Gallery Collection (b). Getty Images: Persian School (bc). 230 Getty Images: Neil Fletcher & Matthew Ward (ca). 230-231 Getty Images: (b). 231 Corbis: Gianni Dagli Orti (t). 232 Getty Images: Dioscoro Teofilo de la Puebla Tolin (b); Macduff Everton (t). 233 Getty Images: (ca). 234 Corbis: Danny Lehman (b); Hoberman Collection (bl). 235 Getty Images: Theodore de Bry (tr). 236 Getty Images: Indian School (ca). 236-237 Alamy Images: The London Art Archive (b). 237 Corbis: